Ahsan Academy of Research
Springs, South Africa

Dr Yusuf Bamjee Memorial Series

Tradition of Tafsir
(Qur'ānic Exegesis)
in the Indian Subcontinent

Abdul Kader Choughley

Foreword by Abdur Raheem Kidwai

Tawasul International
Centre for Publishing, Research and Dialogue

ISBN: 978-81-952534-3-2

Ahsan Academy of Research
(Springs, South Africa)
info@ahsanacademy.co.za
www.ahsanacademy.co.za

Tawasul International
Centre for Publishing, Research and Dialogue, Rome, Italy

CONTENTS

Chapter 10 339

Note on Transliteration and Translation

Arabic transliteration in the text and notes is limited to `ayn where indicated, 'hamza in the middle of the word and a where required. Otherwise, Urdu and English words do not always use this transliteration. I have used the term Dar al-`Ulum as standard feature whereas I have written `ulama instead of 'ulama. I have improvised a simple transliteration system for the benefit of non-specialist readers. However, in the footnotes and references the disparity is unavoidable due to the authors' preference. Citation of sources in Urdu and English also reveal a variation in spelling which is retained in the text.

Acknowledgements

No acknowledgement can do justice to the many people who have contributed to the production of this volume. I have to thank Professor Abdur Raheem Kidwai for his unwavering support and guidance in the preparation of this tafsir study which is in line with his vision of promoting the sacred text in academic circles. There are no words to describe my gratitude to Dr Sajjad Akhtar, publisher of Ahsan Academy's books, for his generous spirit. He has been associated with the Qur'anic studies project and his assistance during the preparation of the manuscript is much appreciated.

The support, friendship, and collegiality of friends have sustained me over the years, and I have learned a great deal from them. Sadly, I have to use the past tense for my mentor and friend, Dr Yusuf Bamjee, who had in more ways than one inspired me to work on a number of academic projects. His words of encouragement had given me the strength to continue. My wife, Muniera has shown immense support and dedication in this venture. She has conducted the editing process professionally and caringly, for which I am grateful. My friends who wish to remain anonymous have extended their moral support during the production of this volume and I want to thank them all.

I dedicate this book to my grandchildren Zayd, Rayhaan, Yusuf, Zuhayr, Madeeha, Aadam and Zahreen, with the hope that that the spirit of the sacred text may sustain their future lives.

Finally, our sincere appreciation to our donors and sponsors for making this publication possible.

Abdul Kader Choughley
(Springs, South Africa)

Foreword

In the name of Allah, Most Compassionate, Most Merciful

While the number of translations and tafāsir in major world languages has been impressive, only a few evaluative studies of this exegetical corpus are available. As these tafāsir serve as the only source for the non-Arabic reading public to gain access to the Word of Allah which is in Arabic, these works should be critically scrutinized in terms of their fidelity to the original Arabic Qur'ānic text, their ideological presuppositions, their presentation skills and their strengths and weaknesses. Regrettably, the history of the translation of the Qur'an has been disfigured in a number of works, by the interpolation of extra Qur'ānic, even un-Qur'ānic material. Some of these works are vitiated by Islam-bashing, sectarianism and whimsical notions of their authors. These tafāsir are to be examined also in terms of the translation theory followed in these, their mindset, command over both the target and source languages, reader friendly features, cogent explications of things Qur'ānic, appropriacy, accuracy, fluency, presentation skills and scholarly apparatus. Since their readers may be new to Islam, these works should provide sufficient circumstantial setting of the Qur'ānic text and explain briefly the Qur'ānic allusions to the personalities and places, and explain the salient Qur'ānic concepts and terms. This will enable readers better to grasp the meaning and message of the Qur'an.

It is so gratifying that Dr Abdul Kader Choughley, a distinguished Islamic scholar has undertaken a brilliant assessment of almost all the Urdu *tafāsir* in this valuable work. His study is truly encyclopaedic in its range. The representative tafāsir of all the major schools of thought and *Fiqh* namely, Shah Waliullah school, Deobandi, Barelwi, Nadwi, Jamat-i Islami, Ahl Al-Hadith, Islāhi, Farāhi, and Shi'ah strands of thought have been thoroughly and discerningly analysed. Also he has evaluated some other Urdu tafāsir which do not belong to the above-mentioned categories. His scholarly sweep is both broad and insightful. Not only has he classified scores of Urdu tafāsir under the labels of various schools of thought, he has critically analysed dozens of tafāsir which are representative of these schools.

Dr Choughey's deep and wide familiarity with the domain of *tafsir* comes out sharply in his extensive, more than thirty pages long "Introduction" which covers all that there is to learn about the evolution, function and scope of tafsir. Equally perceptive are his observations on the *nazm* (coherence) theory, problems of translatability, history of the tafsir corpus in the Indian subcontinent and the importance of some works in the field, as for example, *Tafsir-i Mahā'imi.*

His critique on the scores of Urdu tafāsir stands out for its depth, judiciousness and thorough grounding in the norms and principles of tafsir writing. His comments are not limited to providing the bare publication details of each tafsir. He succeeds remarkably in placing each of these tafāsir in the broader perspective of the domain of *tafsir*, its outstanding features and its usefulness or otherwise for today's readers.

Dr Choughley is widely acclaimed for his substantial writings on the intellectual legacy of Islam in South Asia, particularly the accomplishments of Ashrāf Ali Thānawi, Abdul Aleem Siddiqui, Sayyid Abul Hasan Ali Nadwi and Fazlur Rahmān Ansari. The present work underscores his sterling scholarly credentials and his devotion to the cause of *tafsir* and *sirah.*

This book will be read with great benefit by all those interested in Islamic and Qur'ānic studies and Islam in South Asia. It is a commendable work in that it meets many needs, May Allah reward lavishly Dr Choughley for his valuable contribution to the Qur'ānic studies.

Professor Abdur Raheem Kidwai
Director K.A. Nizami Centre for Qur'ānic Studies,
Aligarh Muslim University, Aligarh, India

Preface

A detailed survey of the Urdu tafsirs and Qur'ānic writings in English across the sectarian divide in the Indian subcontinent has been a fairly new attempt in recent years. The present study is a conspectus of the multivolume tafsir project undertaken by the prestigious K.A. Nizami Centre for Qur'ānic Studies (Aligarh Muslim University). This is a pioneering initiative to assemble together the Qur'ānic contributions from different ideological orientations under a single project. Professor Abdur Raheem Kidwai, Director of the Centre, deserves immense credit for publishing this series by capable scholars.

It is a truism that the rich repository of Qur'ānic works has not been comprehensively studied. There are several factors which account for this position. First, tafsirs were initially written in Arabic from the fourteen century for a scholarly audience. A lull followed in the next century with the notable absence of influential Qur'ānic works. However, the sixteenth century witnessed a few tafsirs written during the period of political turmoil and religious upheaval in the subcontinent. The reign of the Mughal Emperor, Jalal al-din Akbar (d.1605) is a case in point. Tafsirs were produced with distinct religious motivations. In contrast, the Waliyullah familial tradition spanning across the 17th and 18th century brought an intellectual reformist revolution in the subcontinent that has had a lasting impact on tafsir studies. Shah Waliyullah wrote a Persian translation which sought to make the universal message of the sacred text accessible to ordinary Muslims. Likewise, Shah 'Abdul Qadir Dehlawi enriched the emerging trends of Urdu literature with his idiomatic translation and concise explanatory notes. Subsequent tafsirs drew upon this work for their exploration of themes, literary styles and teachings of the Qur'an.

Sectarian formulations of the tafsir genre had produced differing positions about core issues relating to the status of the Holy Prophet (SAW), in particular the question of *'ilm al-ghayb* (knowledge beyond the reach of human perception). Essentially, these tafsirs were written with a sectarian slant while upholding the mainstream interpretation of the Qur'an (*Ahl al-Sunnah wa'al Jamā'at*). These trends are examined in the light of their respective ideological leanings. Context and circumstantial settings are important markers of the interpretation of the sacred text.

The plethora of tafsirs and Qur'ānic works in the twentieth century are illustrative of the nurturing of reformist thought against the background of the rapid sociopolitical changes sweeping across the subcontinent. Several tafsirs were written with a particular vision and for a new constituency. Implicit in these tafsirs was the notion of the interpretive reading of the sacred text. Unsurprisingly, these works created a surge of critical response from the traditional exegetes. At the same time, *da'wah*-centred writings added new dimensions to new readings of the sacred text. An overview of these important trends brings to the fore the productive phase of the tafsir writing in the subcontinent.

What are the implications of the tafsir tradition for Muslims for the twenty-first century Muslims? Two points come to mind. Technology has hardwired new frames of reference and created inflection points for a contextual reading of the Qur'an. In a similar vein, the diaspora communities from the subcontinent are faced with challenges of integration in their respective host countries. How do they reshape the Qur'ānic worldview in a changed political setting? These are vexing questions that several Qur'ānic scholars have attempted to address through their writings. In a multiplural and multireligious world like India spirituality is a common denominator. In this regard, the contemporary trends in Qur'ānic studies have shown the ongoing interest in reaching out to faith-based communities through the translation of the Qur'an in regional languages. This aspect is discussed from the prism of religious co-existence.

The study seeks to familiarise English readers with the vast corpus of Qur'ānic literature available in Urdu. Too often it is assumed that the subcontinent has not produced works of any substantive merit. However, the unbroken link of Islamic authenticity in the subcontinent with other parts of the world, particularly the Arabic countries, is a reassuring sign of its equally significant contributions to the tafsir tradition. Irrespective of the differing sectarian positions, the mainstream interpretation of the sacred text in this region is firmly grounded.

Salient features of the study:

- Arabic words /are retained throughout the text for the purpose of clarity of meanings.
- Titles of lengthy tafsirs are shortened as these are cumbersome for English readers who are generally unacquainted with their peculiar style. Where necessary, the complete title is provided in the footnotes.
- The Urdu volumes contain biographical details which, however, are briefly mentioned in the study.
- Extensive citations of Qur'ānic verses (*āyāt*) and their explanatory notes are not included; instead, the gist of these discussions is given.
- An exegetical timeline is not consistently followed as several volumes have also highlighted particular tafsirs or works on Qur'ānic themes or aspects.
- The selection of exegetical works is intended to bring into broad relief the significant contributions of these *maslaks* (schools of thought). Occasionally, there is notable mention of other exegetical works which are omitted in these volumes.
- The overlapping entries of exegetical works in several volumes have allowed for flexibility in the study.

It has been a daunting task to present, albeit briefly, the rich history of the Urdu tafsir genre and Qur'ānic works in English. Two different languages with divergent linguistic and cultural temperaments reflect the challenges that come with a work of this nature. However, the redeeming factor is the hope that the study will encourage future research on the varied aspects of Qur'ānic studies with a special focus on the tafsir tradition in the subcontinent.

Introduction

The Tafsir Tradition in the Indian Subcontinent
Evolution of Tafsir

The first written tafsir attributed to the Companion of the Holy Prophet (SAW), 'Abdullāh ibn 'Abbas is a seminal contribution[1] to the study of this genre. It represents the formalised structure of tafsir developed within specific frameworks. Ibn 'Abbās's stature as a *mufassir*[2] was recognised during the lifetime of the Holy Prophet (SAW): the honorific title of *Bahr al-'ulum* (ocean of knowledge)[3] is a testimony to his profound grasp of the Qur'ānic text. His work is considered an authoritative source of understanding the historical and eschatological issues as discussed in the sacred text. Furthermore, early tafsirs built their interpretations around *Tanwir al-Miqyās* which established its credentials as an indispensable guide to the evolving genre.[4] Interestingly, it continues to serve as a point of reference[5] for tafsirs articulating the traditional approach around which the vast corpus of hadith literature features prominently.

It is a truism that the growth and development of tafsir studies

---

[1] The tafsir attributed to 'Abdullāh ibn 'Abbās bears the title *Tanwir al-Miqyās i Tafsir ibn 'Abbās.* According to Muhammad Taqi Usmani, it is an erroneous assumption to ascribe this tafsir to Ibn 'Abbas. For a detailed discussion, see Muhammad Taqi Usmani, *An Approach to the Qur'ānic Sciences* (New Delhi, 2006), 405 -10.

[2] The terms *mufassir,* exegete and commentator are interchangeably used in the study.

[3] Ibid., 466. He is also remembered by the title *Tarjumān al -Qur'ān* (Interpreter of the Qur'ān).

[4] Muhammad Ruhullah Naqshbandi explains that the tafsir is a posthumous compilation and its copies were deposited in several libraries in the twentieth century. Additionally, it has been published in Cairo and the subcontinent. See Muhammad Naqshbandi, *Ahd i-Risālat ke Mufassirin i-Kirām* (Karachi, 2010), 117 -8.

[5] Ibn 'Abbas's students belonged to the Makkan school which formulated a coherent presentation of *'ilm al-tafsir* (science of Qur'ān ic exegesis). A detailed discussion appears in Thameem Ushama, *Methodologies of the Qur'ānic Exegesis* (Kuala Lumpur, 1995), 70 -5.

was initiated by Ibn 'Abbās. At the same time, there were other eminent exegetes who enriched this nascent tradition by their scholarly insights. 'Abdullāh ibn Mas'ud[6] stands out as a distinguished *mufassir* who by virtue of his exceptional expertise and remarkable learning in the Qur'ānic field developed a nuanced analysis of verses (*āyāt*) that had multilayered meanings. In sum, there were visible signs of exegetical activities under the guidance of the Holy Prophet (SAW).

The formative period of tafsir[7] saw the emergence of voluminous works like Tabari's *Tafsir al-Tabari*. Essentially, it is a comprehensive work which is structured along the hadith and history lines.[8] His other multivolume encyclopaedia explores the history of the ancient nations, rise of Islam and history of the Islamic world down to the year 915. This work has its imprints on Tabari's formulation of tafsir by including Isra'ilite material[9] to adduce particular Qur'ānic accounts. Likewise, under the taxonomy of tafsir the work is generally classified as *tafsir al-ma'thur*;[10] in other words, exegesis based on sound traditions. This distinction with *tafsir bi'al-ra'yi*[11] (exegesis of arbitrary opinions)

---

[6] The fourth Caliph, 'Ali lauded 'Abdullāh ibn Mas'ud scholarship and depth of Qur'ān ic knowledge. See Abdur Rahman Doi, *'Ulum al- Qur'ān: A Study in Methodology and Approach* (Pretoria, 1997), 222 - 3.

[7] Ibid., 270 - 89. Doi gives an overview of the historical development of tafsir writing.

[8] For a critical analysis on the tafsir, see Rashid Ahmad Jullundhry, *Qur'ānic Exegesis in Classical Literature* (Kuala Lumpur, n.d.), 26 -9. "Nevertheless, this collection represents a valuable contribution. It is an encyclopaedia of traditional commentary in which weak and trustworthy views, rigid and flexible opinions about religion, and traditional and intellectual concepts of those days can be seen side by side."

[9] The centuries-long debates about the validity of the Isra'ilite traditions have captured the imagination of exegetes. The consensus (*ijmā'*) makes pointed reference to adopting a cautious approach which does not contradict the tenor of the Qur'ān ic historical accounts. Usmani provides the gist of the Isra'ilite traditions in his *Qur'ānic Sciences*. Cf. Doi, *The Sciences of the Qur'ān*, 226 - 39.

[10] This classification encompasses the sayings of the Holy Prophet (SAW), his Companions, and their Successors as proper sources for the understanding of the Qur'ān . See Jullundhri, *Qur'ānic Exegesis*, 22. This view is supported by Ibn Taimiyyah who considers Tabari's tafsir as representative of the *salaf* tradition. See Ushama, *Methodologies of the Qur'ānic Exegesis*, 87 - 8.

[11] The classification of *tafsir bi'al ra'yi* as an arbitrary explanation undermines its intrinsic merit in comparison to other disciplines of Islamic learning. This

broadened the scope of the genre as a discursive tradition. In fact, the formation of the tafsir tradition expanded the notion of *'ulum al-Qur'ān* by incorporating other Islamic disciplines which gave it a systematic form and structure.[12] For example, *Fiqh* (jurisprudence), linguistics and *kalām* (theology) informed the activity of the exegetes and expanded the production of knowledge in its holistic dimension. To the earlier works belong tafsirs like *Qurtubi*[13] *and Kashshāf* with their respective ideological orientations. This genealogical tradition[14] was based on the self-conception of the exegete. Typically, it is involved a polyvalent reading of the text with variant interpretations against the backdrop of sectarian preference. This approach accommodated a rationalistic-oriented tafsir like *Kashshāf* whose author was condemned for his Mu'tazilite views and his deviation from the mainstream tafsir tradition.[15] Sadly, this mindset vitiates the dynamic character of tafsir which over the centuries has drawn

---

mindset presupposes the independent, judgmental overemphasis of rational thought. In contrast, several widely-acclaimed tafsirs bear the unmissable characteristics of this form of tafsir.

[12] According to Mahmood Ahmad Ghazi, there exists an integral link between knowledge and the Qur'ān . This domain is not time- specific but encompasses the broad spectrum of knowledge which Muslims had articulated in the Qur'ān ic perspective. See Ghazi, *Muhādarāt i-Qur'ān* (New Delhi, 2011), 284.

[13] It is A thirty-volume tafsir, which has carved a niche in the field of linguistics and *ahkām* (legal injunctions). Its author 'Abdullāh Ansari Qurtubi (d. 1273) was among the illustrious galaxy of exegetes who developed new trends in Qur'ān ic studies. For a review of the English translation of volumes 1 -3 by Ayesha Bewley, see Abdur Raheem Kidwai, "Tafsir Al-Qurtubi", in *The Muslim World Book Review*, 40:3, 2020, 18 - 21.

[14] According to Walid Saeh, the genealogical tradition takes into account the intellectual endeavours for compiling the existing tradition by making conscious selections, identifying motives and mechanisms to the tafsirs. See Andreas Gorke and Johanna Pink, *Tafsir and Islamic Intellectual History: Exploring the Boundaries of a Genre* (London, 2014), 5 -6.

[15] The common assumption by the *Salafis* that the non-conformist tafsirs are an aberration has inevitably narrowed down the intellectual dynamism that characterised the tafsir tradition. Unsurprisingly, this mindset has engendered a culture of polemics in recent tafsirs which rigidly adhere to the *salaf* era. However, a balanced account of their literary merits is discussed in Muhammad Husayn Dhahabi, *Al-Tafsir wa'l Mufassirun*, vol.1. (Beirut, 1986), 428 -86. Also, the author gives a conspectus of the Mu'tazilite creed and its critique by classical scholars.

upon the rich repository of diverse and divergent interpretations. Obviously, the focal point is the earliest generation source (*salaf*) which also offered difference of opinions, textual variations and most importantly, invaluable perspectives. In the history of the tafsir tradition, there is no evidence to suggest a rupture between the exegetical production of the earliest generations and the twentieth-century scholarly contributions.

This point is important to understand the uninterrupted, robust exegetical activity in the Muslim world. Moreover, the timeline approach demonstrates the contestation of scholarly ideas and productive exchange of views that shaped the genre. The analytical tools employed by the exegetes invariably produced different outcomes.[16] Self- conception determined the trajectory of the scholarly production. In this process a variety of interpretations came to the fore. The *tasawwuf*-centred tafsirs were another facet of the traditional tafsirs. The Qur'ānic hermeneutics by sufi scholars is a case in point.[17] The *Latā'if al-Ishārat*[18] by Abul Qāsim al-Qushayri (d.1072) represents a key source to the classical understanding of the mystical thought and teachings of important and influential sufis. This tafsir offers useful insights into the moral universe of *tasawwuf* in relation to the ethical dimensions of religious life. Additionally, it makes particular reference to hadith literature and anecdotes of sufis

---

[16] For example, *Tafsir al-Kabir* by Fakhruddin Razi (d. 1210). The *mufassir* has focused primarily on grammar, *ahkām*, refutation of deviant sects and the *nazm* aspects in the Qur'ān . In many instances, Razi expressed independent views that were in direct conflict with the mainstream interpretation. For an overview of Razi's singular contributions, see Usmani, *Qur'ānic Sciences*, 516 -8.

[17] Jullundhri maintains that the Qur'ān ic hermeneutics advocated by *suis* were based largely on the spiritual significance of the Qur'ān ic teachings. It implied a hierarchy of spiritual values that underscored the explicit meanings of the Qur'ān . Jullundhri, *Qur'ānic Exegesis*, 60 -2.

[18] Ibid., 130 -47. For example, the *Latā'if* had a significant impact on Muhammad Gezudarazi's tafsir bearing the title *Al-Multaqat*. An influential figure of the Chishtiyah order in the subcontinent, Gesudaraz (d.1422) was a prolific author and poet. He was responsible for implanting the spiritual order in the Deccan region, South India. For a comprehensive account of his life and thought, see Khusro Hussaini, *Sayyid Muhammad al-Husayni Gisudarāz on Sufism* (Delhi, 1983).

to press home the eternal message of the sacred text. By all accounts, the esoteric interpretation has a qualified endorsement among exegetes who have strong inclinations to *tasawwuf*. These commentaries are contextualised in order to promote the ethical aspects of the Qur'ān. The moral tenor is emphasised by referring to the anecdotal accounts culled from these tafsirs.

This form of tafsir is commonly termed as *tafsir bi'l ishāri* (mystical explanation) and has elicited conflicting responses from contemporary scholars. For example, Adnan Zarzour deplores its esoteric interpretation that had crept into the multilayered interpretations advanced by sufis. His critique stems from the interpretation of textual meanings that borders in many instances on pantheism. The theories developed by a cohort of *suis* transgressed the limits of *'aqidah* (belief system).[19] However, from the sufi viewpoint, the Qur'ān ic meaning and message are encoded in the language of truth. It has its religious and inner expressions, and, therefore, allows for personal interpretation based on freedom and subjectivity. Obviously, this approach has been vehemently criticised by the traditional exegetes for its *ta'wil* and is considered a deviation from the received norms of traditional scholarship. We may cite *Ruh al-Ma'āni* by Mahmud al-Alusi (d. 1854).[20] This monumental work encompasses much of the previous explanations of the Qur'ān including *tasawwuf*. According to Taqi Usmani, it enjoys an unrivalled status on account of its multifaceted features and most importantly, synthesis of traditional and *tasawwuf* thought. Implicit in Usmani's laudatory comments are the Deobandi 'ulama's endorsements[21] of this celebrated work. In sum, the variation and divergence have enhanced the tafsir tradition over the centuries. The claim that

---

[19] Adnan Zarzour, *The Qur'ān and its Study: An In-Depth Exploration of Islamic Sacred Scripture* (Leicester, 2018).

[20] This celebrated work running into thirty volumes has attracted scholarly interest since its publication. Alusi's theological credentials have given rise to multiple assumptions about his *Sufi-Salafi* credentials. It must be remembered that he lived during the political ferment of the Ottoman Caliphate.

[21] Usmani, *Qur'ānic Sciences*, 519 – 21. It finds resonance in Mufti Shafi's multivolume *Ma'āriful Qur'ān*.

these productions are repetitive, divisive and recycled versions of the earlier tafsir sources are tendentious in view of the recent academic studies that have provided an articulate picture about the genre's growth and development.

The Function of Tafsir

Tafsir has always been at the centre of the Islamic intellectual history and the Qur'ān being understood through the language of this genre. It functioned at two levels: collective and individual endeavours. As a tradition it was guided by the element of continuity (*tasalsul*) through which the Muslim world understood and interpreted the Qur'ānic teachings, truth and wisdom. This collective endeavour ensured that the primacy of the Qur'ān supported by the hadith literature and the legacy (*turāth*) of the earliest generation of Muslims (*salaf-al-sālih*) were preserved and exemplified for the *ummah.* Across the spectrum of individual endeavours, exegetes (*mufassirs*) were at liberty to write independent tafsirs. This implied, in a particular sense, the freedom to explicate their viewpoints without institutional sanction. These parallel developments defined the religious outlook of the *ummah* over the centuries. In fact, tafsir has been one of the most active fields in the Islamic intellectual history and owes its popularity to the vast expanse of the Qur'ānic horizons that offers new meanings and dimensions for exegetes willing to undertake the journey of self-enrichment.

Classical tafsirs, by and large, have influenced the intellectual tradition and are invaluable guides to an interpretive reading of the sacred text. Their global influence can be gauged by the robust translation project in the West. These works with different ideological orientations are avidly studied in academia. More importantly, they are easily accessible and rank among the major contributions to the tafsir tradition. Jalalal al-din Suyuti's *Jalālayn* which has been into English[22] is illustrative of this trend. Another

---

[22] 'Abdur Rahmān al-Suyuti (d. 1505) was a prolific author in the annals of Islamic history. Seven hundred and twenty-three works covering a range of Islamic disciplines are attributed to him.

work dealing with the *ahkām* of Qur'ānic verses is the three-volume translation of *Tafsir al-Qurtubi*.[23] According to Abdur Raheem Kidwai, Aisha Bewley "deserves credit for having taken up this massive scholarly project and provided English speaking students of Qur'ān ic and Islamic studies with an easy access to this major classical tafsir."[24] For our study purpose, the multiple translations and marginal notes (*hawāshiyah*) of classical tafsirs are an indication of their embedded presence in the Indian subcontinent. Likewise, subsequent works written from the eighteenth century onwards drew upon their source of authorities from these celebrated tafsirs. In this way, the authenticity (*asālah*) is perpetuated in a Qur'ānic perspective.

Scholarly interest in the tafsir genre in the West has recently seen a spate of original works devoted to the historical and sociopolitical dimensions of Qur'ānic commentaries. However, contemporary studies extended the scope of hermeneutics which is derived from a Biblical angle. In some instances, the liberation theology discourse has taken centre stage by developing new interpretations that are at odds with the meaning and message of the sacred text. These assumptions are based along ideological lines that obfuscate an objective assessment of the contemporary trends in tafsir writing. Apart from the tafsirs of modernity, the rise of militant interpretational works in the Sunni regions has exacerbated the dynamism of the Islamic intellectual tradition. In the same vein, the *Salafi* trend is most vociferous in projecting an idealised Islamic past by elevating tafsirs like *Ibn Kathir* for their ideological interests. Meanwhile, the 'richness and complexity of mainstream classical tafsirs'[25] are now relegated to the margins of secondary sources of Islamic authenticity. Again, state support through *Salafi-* aligned institutions serves as a catalyst for the widespread dissemination of selective tafsirs. As a result, critical

---

[23] Abu 'Abdullāh Muhammad al-Qurtubi (d. 1273) was one of the greatest classical commentators of the Holy Qur'ān who focused largely on its legal aspects.

[24] Review of *Tafsir al-Qurtubi* by Abdur Raheem Kidwai in *The Muslim World Book Review* (40: 3), 21.

[25] Seyyed Hossein Nasr, *The Study Qur'ān and Commentary: A New Translation* (New York, 2015), 1658.

readership is compromised for public consumption.

For our study purpose, three key aspects are examined in relation to the evolution of the tafsir genre in the subcontinent. These are an overview of the literary features that characterise the approach, methodology and structure of the translation/tafsir production since the fourteenth century. The aspects that are common to the tafsirs are briefly discussed in the study.

I'jāz of the Qur'ān

Our discussion of *i'jāz* of the Qur'ān will focus on its aesthetic and literary appeal. Indeed, the genius of its language, eloquence, rhythm, its weaving of styles and techniques of expression make the sacred text a work of eternal perfection. Classical authorities have written prolifically on the *i'jāz* element from different dimensions (*ib'ād*). Bassam Saeh in his groundbreaking study evaluates the miraculous language of the Qur'ān to explain its divine origin. For him the 'filters of self-appraisal'[26] are interlinked to the linguistic perfection of the Qur'ān that sets out its moral ethos at the same time. In other words, the language of the Qur'ān is not time or culture specific nor is its richness constrained by the peculiarities of human language.

According to Saeh, the semantic phenomenon is influenced by the Qur'ān which introduced the linguistic framework of the Arabic language. In his incisive analysis of language formation, Saeh makes a perceptive comment that has a direct bearing on the translations and commentaries of the Qur'ān:

> The discerning researcher should never lose sight of the fact that no matter whatever forms or approaches it takes, any human interpretation or linguistic analysis of the Qur'ān and any disclosure of its miraculousness, be it in the realm of rhetoric, language or science, is a process of

---

[26] Bassam Saeh, *The Miraculous Language of the Qur'ān: Evidence of Divine Origin* (London, 2015), viii.

> weighing probabilities that necessarily remains
> subject to the possibilities of human error.[27]

Like translations in other languages, Urdu, too, offers a reflection of the 'infinite, the divine and the miraculous' expressions of linguistic perfection.

In his brief survey of Arabic literature, Saeh brings out a less studied aspect of the language of the Qur'ān: its newness. This form determined the "[linguistic] vision of the Arabic language. Behind every Qur'ānic verse and word lies a miracle that lends charm, beauty and vigour to its expressional aspects."[28] In essence, the Qur'ānic language is perennial: no dissonance is evident after a lapse of more than fourteen hundred years. Therefore, by its 'newness' we can reconstruct the language that was contemporary for the Arabs of the Qur'ān ic milieu. Furthermore, its *i'jāz* consists "[in] its having constructed a new language on the very foundations of the old language."[29] Thus Qur'ānic Arabic is the lodestar that has authoritatively accorded a status to pre-Islamic Arabic in its various forms and features.

Our understanding of *i'jāz* is that it has distinguishing features that are embedded in the surahs. In fact, the literary templates introduced by the Qur'ān opened up vistas beyond human imagination. One historical example reinforces this assertion. The Qur'ān inaugurated the most widespread scientific revolution the world has ever known and unprecedented over a short period of time. It continues to influence the scientific terrain with its unique presentation of the intellectual discourse.[30]

In the context of Qur'ānic discourse, the 'newness of construction and expression' is critically examined in Surah Al-Mudatthir (74: 1-56). This surah has a unique linguistic personality in terms of its "[language] that bears no connection to our everyday human experience despite the fact that is based on the

---

[27] Ibid., 5.

[28] Ibid., 12. Abul Hasan Ali Nadwi shares a similar observation in his *Qur'āni Ifādāt* (Rae Bareli, 2013), 305-6.

[29] Ibid., 18.

[30] Ibid., 27.

same rules."[31] Indeed, it was the Qur'ān which invested new meanings that could be understood on the linguistic and rhetorical levels.

In sum, Saeh raises an important point about the *i'jāz* of the Qur'ān in its linguistic perspective:

> The Qur'ān surprised the Arabs of the Prophet's day with a new type of language possessed of many facets that were in complete harmony with each other. The flexible divine language had the capacity to remain alive down the ages in such a way that people could discover within its meanings that their forebears had not discerned because the realities of their particular era or generation or the limited knowledge available to them had prevented them from seeing them.[32]

Belonging to the same strain of the Qur'ān 's literary excellence, 'Abdullāh Draz states that the sacred text "[invests] the minimum possible wording to generate the broadest possible meaning."[33] It is a common feature of the Qur'ānic style that it dexterously employs words that require a paraphrase for explanation or clarification. Every single word unlocks a necessary and intrinsic meaning. In the realm of translations, the Qur'ān ic *i'jāz* requires a mastery over Arabic literature and Islamic disciplines (*'ulum*) to unravel its elegance and linguistic perfection. Its illustrative vocabulary removed inherited images from the existing expressional stockpile and gave it fresh enduring images. Its choice of words defined the trajectory of a standardised Arabic and invested it with expansive meanings. More importantly, the Qur'ānic vocabulary shaped the discourse of Islamic learning up to the present day. The Dar al-'Ulums and other Islamic

---

[31] Ibid., 41. An alternative reading of this surah with socioeconomic overtones is offered by Ubaidullah Sindhi in *Majmu'ah Tafāsir i- Sindhi*, 412-50.

[32] Ibid., 77.

[33] Muhammad Abdullah Draz, *The Qur'ān: An Eternal Challenge* (Leicester, 2001), 109.

institutions have preserved over the centuries the reservoir of Qur'ānic vocabulary. The subcontinent, too, is illustrative of this trend.

Equivalence and Non – Equivalence

Since no two languages are identical in the meanings given or to the corresponding symbols as arranged in a phrase or statement, there can be no exact translations. Even the total impact of rendering a translation close to the original will not yield an identical text (in translation). This equivalence is also not attainable in Urdu in respect of a Qur'ānic translation. For a number of historical and religious reasons, the original words and terms have been lost in the translation process. Furthermore, the original Arabic meanings have been diluted in the Urdu language.

According to Hussein Abdul Raof, "[equivalence], still an important principle in translation studies, is dramatically underachieved and, in some cases, not achieved at all in Qur'ān ic translations."[34] Urdu is no exception to this principle. Its cultural hybridity offers an array of meanings that in many instances is remotely connected to the Qur'ān ic terms. Additionally, language barriers are unavoidable, further alienating a semblance of commonality between languages. Urdu, for example, has an Indo-Aryan base whereas Arabic belongs the Semitic languages. Despite being loaded with Arabic loan words, its syntactic structure is radically different from the morphological construction and literary genius of the former which is shaped by grammatical rules of the Qur'ān. Muhammad Saliem Adam has critically examined the problems related to the translation of the Qur'ān. While his target language is English, there are shared characteristics with Urdu. The nuanced meanings and multilayered interpretations framed from explicit and implicit angles make the translation more challenging.

---

[34] This point shows the distinction between a particular translation and a transparent representation. See Gowhar Quadir Wani (ed.), *Waleed al- Amri's The Luminous Qur'ān: Critical Views* (Aligarh, 2019), 35.

Overall, the exact-meaning translation of the Qur'ān is not possible.[35] Consider the sociocultural milieu of the Qur'ānic revelation. Classical Arabic was at its apogee with no rival in rhetoric and eloquence (*balāghah*). The Qur'ānic phenomenon set new precedents for literary composition and surpassed existing masterpieces on content and style.[36] Thus the sacred text remains unrivalled after a lapse of more than fourteen hundred years.

Nazm theory

In our analysis of *i'jāz* of the Qur'ān, the *nazm* is a distinguishing facet pertaining to divine origin of the sacred text. A close study, albeit briefly, will show how revelation (*wahy*) manifested in circumstantial settings provides a distinct *nazm* format. Verses, clusters of verses or complete surahs possess an internal logic or order that give a structural flow to the meaning and message of the Qur'ān.

Exegetes from the early years of the Islamic intellectual tradition have analysed the *nazm* encoded in the surahs. Later centuries saw the emergence of methodological approaches or critical analyses that defined the constituents of *nazm*. 'Abdul Qahir Jurjani (d. 1082) was among the pioneers who made significant contributions to the theory of structural flow.[37] His *Dalā'il al-I'jāz* is representative of this trend. *Nazm*, according to Jurjani, has nuanced interpretations for which linguistic and literary appreciation is essential. Classical exegetes examined the interlinking (*rabt*) verses in order to develop a better understanding of the *nazm* theory. Thus order, structure and linkages are the pearls on a thread to make a necklace. Successive generation of scholars added new insights into the theory of *nazm*.[38]

---

[35] Cited in *Aligarh Journal of Qur'ānic Studies*, Volume 2, Issue 2, October 2019, 101-25.

[36] Cf. Draz, *The Qur'ān: An Eternal Challenge*, 87-92.

[37] For a critical examination of Jurjani's literary contributions, see Zarzour, *The Qur'ān and its Study*, 390 - 413.

[38] Ibid., 382 -90.

For readers not familiar with the literary approaches to the Qur'ān, the *nazm* in many ways elucidated its coherence and structural flow. For example, how do unrelated verses or disconnected clusters of verses provide a unifying theme? This is amplified in surah 'Alaq (96).[39] Likewise, the circumstances for revelation (*asbāb al-nuzul*) are integral to a clear understanding of the import of particular verses or surahs. Jalal al - Din Suyuti has made an invaluable study about this phenomenon in his celebrated work *Al-Itqān i 'ulum al-Qur'ān*.[40] It is a conspectus of the circumstantial settings and contextual relevance concerning revelation. Chronology is emphasised although it is not religiously followed in view of verses/surahs revealed in Makkah and Madinah respectively. To borrow Suyuti's phrase, successive segments and whole surahs revealed over a period of twenty three years were placed in a particular order under divine guidance. Hence the distinct Makkan and Madinan settings were not a criterion on its written compilation.[41]

The progressive theories of *nazm* down the ages received greater attention from the early nineteenth century onward. Formulations were conceived in respect of its theories by leading exegetes in the subcontinent.[42] The focus was now more pronounced on broadening the scope of *i'jāz*. To this end, the reception theory was vigorously debated and the outcomes saw the emergence of the Qur'ān ic schools of thought exploring the concept of *nazm* in different *i'jāz* perspectives. The study seeks to highlight the rationale employed by exegetes in their critical examination of the *nazm* theory.[43]

A brief survey of the traditional interpretation of the *nazm* theory reveals its direct bearing on the *i'jāz* of the Qur'ān. As

---

[39] The divine arrangement of the verses was done by the Holy Prophet (SAW). The first five verses are the first in their order of the revelation history (chronology) but appear in surah 96. Cf. Doi, *The Sciences of the Qur'ān*, 43.

[40] The work (vol. 1) was translated into English by Hamid Algar (Reading, 2011).

[41] Ibid., 79 -80. Cf. Muhammad Mustafa Azami, *The History of the Qur'ānic Text: From Revelation to Compilation* (Kuala Lumpur, 2011), 43 - 58.

[42] See Nazeer Ahmad Ab. Majeed (ed.), *Qur'ān Interpretation in Urdu: A Critical Study* (New Delhi, 2019), 167 - 216.

[43] See Ghazi, *Muhādarāt i - Qur'ān*, 315 -44.

such Muslim scholars developed a fully- fledged study of this aspect in relation to *nazm*. A review of ideas connected to traditional scholarship brings out the importance of the word-meaning relationship. Khattabi (d. 998), for example, explains the interconnection of words, meanings and *nazm* that deal with *balāghah*. For him words are arranged in a particular order for the purpose of structure, coherence and integration. Moreover, *nazm* represents a key aspect of *i'jāz*. Al-Baqillani (d.1013) uses this term in so many ways that it becomes difficult to assign a definite meaning to it. For him the literary term *badi'* is used to express the communicative richness of the Qur'ān ic text. This is borne out by his presentation of *nazm* as "[the] unique relationship that the Qur'ān establishes between word and meaning."[44]

Elsewhere in the chapter reference is made to the seminal works on interconnectivity (*munāsibat*) by the classical scholars of the Qur'ān . Their commendable efforts at unraveling the *i'jāz* element are built around its unique features, structural design, textual relation that reinforce the divine origin of the sacred text. In contrast, the twentieth century tafsirs made a definite break with the traditional interpretations. The theme of unity and its subsidiary disciplines form the discourse of tafsir. A number of exegetes have vindicated the received arrangement of the verses in the surahs. The geographical spread of tafsirs bears testimony to the self- contained unity-coherence matrix of the surahs. More remarkably is the analytical-schematic approach adopted by these exegetes to present the organic dimension of the surahs as a unified concept. Muntasir Mir has correctly observed that this conceptual framework 'is indigenous to the Muslim intellectual world.' In other words, it is not a recent phenomenon as some scholars would argue nor is it an Orientalist construct as articulated in Qur'ānic academia.

A problematic area in respect of the surah as a unity theme is the function of the extra-Qur'ānic sources. A verse-by-verse approach therefore challenges the notion of the rich tradition that

---

[44] Muntasir Mir, *Coherence in the Qur'ān: A Study of Islāhi's Concept of Nazm in Tadabbur-i Qur'ān* (Indianapolis, 1986), 10-3.

informs the *i'jāz* of the Qur'ān. For example, the concept of *asbāb al-nuzul* gives context to sections and segments of surahs. However, the hermeneutical tools adopted by some exegetes limit the scope of the surah- as-a-unity thesis. It would mean that a greater degree is attached to the Qur'ān ic context. Indeed, a scrupulous and rigorous analysis of the *nazm* theory presupposes a radical break from the traditional interpretation of the sacred text.

In addition, a new method entails generating techniques to establish plausible links between verses and passages as well as meanings that are otherwise challenging.

Muhammad Asad details two fundamental rules of interpretation as pointed references to the timeless message of the Qur'ān. He observes:

> Firstly, the Qur'ān must not be viewed as a compilation of individual injunctions and exhortations but as *one integrated whole:* that is, an exposition of an ethical doctrine in which every verse and sentence has an intimate bearing on other verses and sentences, all of them clarifying and amplifying one another. Consequently, its real meaning can be grasped only if we correlate every one of its statements with what has been stated elsewhere in the pages, and try to explain its ideas by means of cross-references, always subordinating the particular to the general and the incidental to the intrinsic. When this rule is faithfully followed, we realise the Qur'ān is, in the words of Muhammad Abduh - "its own best commentary".
>
> Secondly, no part of the Qur'ān should be viewed from a purely *historical* point of view: that is to say, all its references to historical circumstances and events - both at the time of the Prophet and in earlier times, must be regarded as illustrations of the *human condition* and not as

ends in themselves. Hence, the consideration of the historical occasion on which a particular verse was revealed -a pursuit so dear, and legitimately so, to the hearts of the classical commentators- must never be allowed to obscure the underlying *purport* of that verse and its inner relevance to the ethical teaching which the Qur'ān, taken as a whole, propounds.[45]

Tafsir in the Indian subcontinent

The study is intended to demonstrate the unbroken link of tafsir tradition in the subcontinent, which was remotely connected to the metropolis sites in the Muslim world. However, Muslim conquests and the establishment of sultanates had consolidated the Islamic presence[46] in the far-flung regions of the subcontinent. The ebb and flow of medieval Muslim history[47] coincided with the major political events in the Muslim world. For example, the Mongol invasion[48] in the thirteenth century caused a wave of mass exodus of scholars who found asylum in the subcontinent. Over the course of time, these scholars/'ulama produced original works in the diverse fields of Islamic learning. In a particular sense, disciplines like *Fiqh,* hadith and *kalām* were vigorously pursued by these scholars. Likewise, these works were written in Arabic[49] for a readership beyond the subcontinental borders. In fact, the porous borders that existed between the subcontinent and Central Asia were indistinct following the ambitious conquests and invasions by the foreign military rulers. As a result, the acculturation of literary works[50] on the Indian soil assumed an indigenous character. The tafsir works written largely in Arabic mirrored the genealogical tradition. No different were

---

[45] Muhammad Asad, *The Message of the Qur'ān* (Gibraltar, 1980), vii.

[46] The consolidation of Islam in the subcontinent straddling several centuries is examined in Mohammad Mujeeb, *The Indian Muslims* (Lahore, 1982).

[47] See Abul Hasan Ali Nadwi, *Muslims in India* (Lucknow, 1976), 36 - 49.

[48] Ibid., 37 - 8.

[49] Ibid., 23 - 9.

[50] Ibid.

some of these tafsirs from the methodology adopted by the widely acclaimed exegetes in the Muslim world. Tafsirs like *Qurtubi* had a significant influence on the Indian exegetes as early as the thirteenth century.

In more ways than one, the parallel development of tafsir writing also saw the emergence of original works in the subcontinent. Like their contemporaries and predecessors, these tafsirs, too, covered a terrain of divergent interpretations. Their Qur'ānic explanations were informed by geopolitical developments in their respective regions. Also, the presence of the Hindu majority had a decisive influence on their alternative readings of widely-held or consensual interpretations. It must be remembered that geographical distance did not, however, create a culture of insularity; rather, it connected these exegetes to the transnational networks that were gradually strengthened by several historical factors.[51]

Our thrust area of surveying the tafsir tradition predates the Shah Waliyullah era. Additionally, the selection of tafsirs for the study is representative of the growing interest in this genre. These tafsirs cover a specific timeline and are illustrative of the different interpretations largely influenced by local factors, temperaments and scholarly outputs. Interestingly, these works were written in Arabic, which are a testimony to their impressive scholarship in the field of tafsir writing.

Tafsir al -Maha'imi

Born to a Nawa'it family[52] who claimed their lineage to the Quraysh tribe, Makhdum 'Ali Maha'imi (d.1431) was a prolific scholar in *kalām*, *Fiqh* and *tasawwuf*. He was assiduously devoted to the study of the Qur'ān and produced a tafsir of exceptional merit

---

[51] Muhammad 'Ali Shawkani (d.1834), a distinguished Yemeni scholar, served as a nexus between the Indian 'ulama and the Arab world.

[52] The contribution of the Nawa'its to Islamic learning, particularly in South India is meticulously documented in Sayyid Muhammad Ibrahim, *Qāzi 'Ubaidullah: Life and Works* (Ajmer, n.d), 38 - 50. Cf. Nawab 'Aziz Yar Jangh, *Tārikh al- Nawā'it* (Hyderabad, 1904).

in Arabic. No detailed study[53] has been done about his multidimensional contributions, particularly his *tajdidi* (reformist) efforts. Maha'imi is venerated as a saint by Muslims and non-Muslims alike attracting thousands of devotees from different religious backgrounds to his shrine in Mumbai.

Tafsir al-Mahā'imi was published in Egypt in 1878. Subsequent editions were brought out in Lahore and Hyderabad. According to Sayyid 'Abdul Hayy, author of the encyclopaedic work *Nuzhat al-Khawātir,* Maha'imi's tafsir even surpasses several notable classical works belonging to this genre on two counts: i) its original and structured approach to the Qur'ān as a contemplative, literary masterpiece and ii) the profundity of Maha'imi's grasp of *kalām* and *tasawwuf.*[54]

Salient features of *Tafsir al-Mahā'imi*

The interlinking connectors of Qur'ān ic verses (*āyāt*) feature prominently in his methodology. Interestingly, his *nazm* and *tartib* (sequence) approach is a precursor to the detailed appraisal by subcontinental exegetes. Furthermore, his *nazm* analysis takes into account the Qur'ānic wisdom which is accompanied by a brief presentation of mystical thought relevant to particular verses. This blending is inspired by the classical works of erudite sufis like Muhiyuddin ibn 'Arabi. Maha'imi's mystical leanings are discernible in his tafsir. Methodology serves as an analytical tool to his worldview. Accordingly, he adeptly incorporates concise comments within brackets to give textual fluency. In other words, he avoids annotation, which, in his view, mars the original intent of the text.[55]

A noteworthy feature of this work are the introductory comments to the surahs. Historical accounts are also presented as

---

[53] According to Muhammad 'Arif 'Azami, several sketchy biographies have been written in the twentieth century about this illustrious exegete. See Muhammad 'Arif 'Azami, *Tadhkirah Mufassirin i-Hind* (Azamgarh, 2006), 29 - 30.

[54] Azami, 36. Cf, 'Abdul Hayy Hasani, *Yād i-Ayyām* (Aligarh, 1919), 59.

[55] Ibid., 46 - 7.

additional titles linked to the surahs under discussion. By way of example, the *basmala* prefixed to each surah (except Surah Tawbah) is explored in a contextual setting. This approach is reflective of his meticulous study of the Qur'ān in relation to its key themes. In a similar vein, Maha'imi identifies the rationale for the disjointed letters (*huruf al-muqatta'āt*) in the surahs. His approach is twofold: first, to show that the *huruf* in its inchoate form was not unfamiliar to the educated class of the *Jāhiliyyah* period. Second, these letters are encoded to articulate a distinctive aspect which is not clearly elaborated in the surah. This conceptual framework augments its usage and unfolds layers of multiple meanings.[56]

Maha'imi brings to the fore his perceptive insights into the *nazm* theme of the sacred text. In Surah Sad (38), the letter *sād* relates to the oath that Allah takes to reaffirm the praiseworthy qualities of the Holy Prophet (SAW). He was trustworthy (*sādiq*) in his dealings, his veracity as a Messenger is highlighted and his sublime position is established. Maha'imi's interpretation does in no way suggest that it is a definitive conclusion. Rather, he draws upon these insights from his extensive study of Qur'ān ic themes and his strong inclination to *tasawwuf*. A more telling example about his thorough familiarity with the Islamic disciplines (*'ulum*) is his linguistic competence. He deploys his deep understanding of Arabic grammar and literature to elucidate the various shades of meanings in the context of legal rulings (*ahkām*).[57]

In sum, *Tafsir al-Mahā'imi* has enjoyed immense popularity on account of its distinctive features and has been widely consulted over the centuries. Shaykh 'Abdul Haq Dehlawi (d.1642), an illustrious hadith scholar, made appreciative comments about the prominent aspects of the tafsir.[58] Likewise, the twentieth

---

[56] The salient features of the tafsir are critically examined in Muhammad Zubayr, "Tafsir i-Maha'imi ka Tahqiqi wa Tajziyati Mutala", in *Islamic Culture*, 2019: 41, 103 - 18.

[57] 'Azami's critical examination of the tafsir illustrate Maha'imi's versatility in the field of tafsir studies. *Tadhkirah Mufassirin*, 44 - 53.

[58] Khaliq Ahmad Nizami, *Hayāt i-Shaykh 'Abdul Haq Muhaddith Dehlawi* (Aligarh, 2015). The erudite scholar wrote important works on Qur'ānic studies apart from his

century exegete, 'Abdullāh Yusuf Ali has also referred to this classical work. Interestingly, the *nazm* theme as outlined by Maha'imi is further developed in the tafsirs of Ashrāf 'Ali Thānawi and Amin Ahsan Islāhi, which are examined elsewhere in the study.

Divergent Tafsirs: An Assessment

No study of the tafsir tradition is complete without examining the historical circumstances that gave rise to divergent interpretations over time. In some instances, these works were at odds with the mainstream understanding of the sacred text. The Mughal Empire is illustrative of the trends of tafsirs outside the framework of authoritative sources.

Two trends of scholarship defined the areas of contestations during the Mughal emperor Akbar's reign. The second half of the fifteenth century was marked by a period of political ascendancy for the Mughal rule. By extension, it implied a firmer foothold for Islam as a state religion in the subcontinent. However, the historical accounts of Jalaluddin Akbar's religious policies are generally described as the greatest tumult of the tenth century *hijri*[59]. There were several factors that crystallised his *Dini Ilāhi* movement as a reaction to mainstream Islam. Akbar's reign coincided with the emergence of the Mahdawi movement. Founded by Sayyid Muhammad Jawnpuri (d. 1505), the movement stressed on moral purity and the regeneration of the ailing Muslim society beset with corruption, political disarray, and religious degeneration. Jawnpuri's charismatic personality and puritanical outlook produced two conflicting strands of religious thought. First, his followers invested him with an almost infallible stature - a promised Mahdi who would restore the Islamic order amid the political and religious anarchy that threatened the supremacy of Islam in the subcontinent. Second, the Mahdawi's

---

contributions to the hadith literature.

[59] For a detailed account of Akbar's rule, see Khaliq Ahmad Nizami, *Akbar and Religion* (Delhi, 1989).

relations with Akbar were ambivalent. Akbar was initially sympathetic towards the movement and so were the state 'ulama. However, the movement was unequivocal in its condemnation of Akbar's religious excesses prompting him to take decisive action against its growing presence.[60]

Religious ferment during Akbar's reign contributed greatly to his promulgation of his new religion. The *Dini Ilāhi* was a brazen attempt at amalgamating an eclectic mix of religious beliefs, rituals and practices. In the process, the universality of Islam was undermined. Outside influences in the form of the Batinite movement and the pervasive Shi'ite impact from the emergent Safavid Empire of Iran entrenched their presence in the royal court.[61] As a result, the culture of patronage network weakened the role of Islam as a unifying force in the Mughal Empire.

The three phases of Akbar's religious thought were marked by his conflicting personality. In the first phase, his overzealous orthodoxy and predisposition to shrine veneration (*mazār*) were identifiable markers of his shari'ah-compliant mindset. Later his disillusionment with the traditional 'ulama brought him to the margins of heterodoxy.[62] Furthermore, some state 'ulama endorsed his formulation of the syncretic creed that delinked him from mainstream Islam. Intriguingly, they promoted the *mazhar* (Hall of Worship) and elevated Akbar as a Just Ruler (*sultān al-'ādil*) bearing infallible credentials. Implicit in these titular claims was an open rejection of the shari'ah. The hotchpotch of beliefs and religious practices derived from many faiths were brewed in the cauldron of syncretism. In other words, *Dini Ilāhi* was emblematic of a progressive, vision-inspired pluralistic movement embedded in the culture of religious tolerance.[63] It was obvious that deviance

---

[60] Ibid., 42 - 51.

[61] Another important factor that strengthened Akbar's universal religion was his marriage to Rajput women of royal descent. They, too, had a decisive influence on his religious policy. See Annemarie Schimmel, *Islam in the Indian Subcontinent* (Leiden, 1980), 83.

[62] Ibid. Schimmel describes this phase as a heterodoxy personality cult.

[63] The history of *Dini Ilāhi* is graphically recounted in Nizami, *Akbar and Religion*, 163 - 236. Cf. Abul Hasan Ali Nadwi, *Saviours of Islamic Spirit,* vol. 3 (Lucknow, 1983), 88 - 102.

was the common denominator of this 'religion'.

An appraisal of the millennium theory makes interesting reading. Religious freedom was conflated with *ijtihād* (independent legal reasoning); charisma was equated with spiritual illumination. Akbar, too, began his journey of faith through the traditional understanding of Islam. Over time, he underwent a religious transformation that showed distinct signs of alienation. Finally, his misguided movement and vaulting ambitions spurred him to announce a universal creed[64] nurtured on the Indian soil. This errant decree sought to accommodate the diverse, conflicting belief systems of Hinduism, Zoroastrianism, Buddhism and Christianity alongside the selective teachings and message of Islam. Worse was the mindless endorsement by religious functionaries *('ulama i-su')* who sought through the corridors of power to entrench their own credentials. In fact, their gratuitous endorsement of Akbar's infallible status was equated with divine dispensation.

Against these bleak circumstances of religious upheaval, there were activist 'ulama who stood up against these nefarious designs that permeated the intellectual ambience in the royal court. In the *tajdidi* strain, the un-wavering efforts of restoring the primacy of the Qur'ān and sunnah against the perversion initiated by Akbar were undertaken by Shaykh Ahmad Sirhindi (d. 1624). The Mujaddid, as he was eponymously remembered, inaugurated the renewal paradigm that had far-reaching consequences on the collective identity of the Muslims in the subcontinent. The crux of his *tajdidi* efforts was his critique of religious pluralism which was gradually gaining rootage as a result of state patronage. He is credited for restating Islamic authenticity amid the religious anarchy spawned by Akbar's *Dini Ilāhi* movement.[65]

Three tafsirs belonging to different historical periods of the Muslim rule in the subcontinent are illustrative of the wide-ranging and often contesting perspectives on the Qur'ānic genre.

---

[64] Ibid., 190 - 213. The *Sulh i-Kul* (peace with all) policy had political implications for Akbar's expansionist designs. Largely on account of religious tolerance, his 'matrix of religious thought' was successfully implemented.

[65] Nadwi, *Saviours of Islamic Spirit*, vol.3, 252 - 91.

Their respective approaches were influenced by these factors: intellectual thought, royal patronage and *tasawwuf* leanings. For several reasons, these strands were woven into the Qur'ān ic hermeneutics and created space for divergent expressions of the rich tafsir tradition. However, this is not to suggest that these original works were templates for other tafsirs. Rather, these contributions pointed out to the distinctive features of the sacred text which transcended human expression.'

We now focus on two tafsirs written in the background of religious ferment during Akbar's reign.

The Axis of Heterodoxy

Shaykh Mubarak Naguri (d.1593) and his sons, Faizi and Abul Fazl played an immense role to the propagation of Akbar's *Dini Ilāhi*.[66] Their rise to fame in the royal court can be attributed to their personal ambitions and political maneuvering. Moreover, their elevation as Akbar's confidantes and advisers saw them as influencers of the syncretic religious discourse. Thereafter, it was a meteoric rise to authority, wielding their pen and mind to create an aura of divinity over Akbar's rule[67].

Common traits of the family disposition bring to the fore their respective ambitious designs. As a result, Islam was relegated to one of the faiths discussed, debated and ironically distorted in the *mazhar.* Shaykh Mubarak was a reputed scholar who mastered the Islamic disciplines of the day. However, his complex personality[68] was a barrier to his academic accomplishments. Egotism and his self- serving interests goaded him to ingratiate himself with the royal court. His religious inclinations were inconsistent with mainstream Islam and thus he was easily swayed by heterodox tendencies.

---

[66] Ibid., 73 -8.

[67] Ibid., 79 - 80. "Abul Fazl wielded considerable influence over Akbar's religious leanings. When Akbar built his *'Ibādat Khāna,* which was a hall of debate and discussion for religious matters, Abul Fazl made it a point to attend these discussions and support Akbar's views."

[68] Ibid., 74 - 5.

Faizi, in contrast, was a versatile genius. His poetic compositions were unrivalled; his mastery over Arabic and Persian was peerless. He served as Akbar's envoy to several Indian royal courts and also worked for some time on the Sanskrit translation project.[69] As a close ally of Akbar, Faizi's insidious activities brought him into conflict with the conscientious 'ulama who condemned his un-Islamic postures. No different was Abul Fazl, a brilliant historian whose literary masterpiece[70] are a treasure trove of historical documentation. He took the lead in the translation of the Hindu religious text *Mahābhārata*. Moreover, his exaggerated elevation of Akbar as an infallible ruler[71] also drew the ire of the 'ulama who were alarmed by the sweep of events against Islam.

In sum, the family's conspiratorial role was an existential threat to Islam's universal teachings. In a religious context, their status as nominal Muslims has elicited divergent responses. From censure to outright condemnation - these conflicting opinions have blurred out an objective assessment of their affiliation to mainstream Islam. For example, Abul Fazl is reported to have recanted his heterodox views and expressed his remorse for his active complicity in the *Dini Ilāhi* fitnah.[72] Nonetheless, our focus is on their respective Qur'ānic contributions.

Manbi'al 'Uyun[73]

Salim Kidwai has made a detailed study of Shaykh Mubarak's multivolume tafsir[74]. Historical accounts suggest that his blindness in the latter years of his productive life did not deter him from dictating the tafsir to his students. By way of example, volume 1

---

[69] Schimmel, *Islam in the Indian Subcontinent*, 85.

[70] The *A'in i-Akbari* is an instance in point.

[71] Nizami, *Akbar and Religion*, 131 - 2. Abul Fazl's exaggerated claims about Akbar's divine status stem from his sycophancy - a psychological trait of Shaykh Mubarak and his sons. According to Qureshi, "[the] father and his two sons were cast in the same mould." Ishtiaq Husain Qureshi, *Ulema in Politics* (Karachi, 1972), 46.

[72] Nadwi, *Saviours of Islamic Spirit*, vol.3, 82.

[73] The complete title is shortened in the text for brevity purpose. This method applies to other tafsirs cited in the study.

[74] Salim Kidwai, *Hindustāni Mufassirin awr unki 'Arabi Tafsire*, (Lahore, 1993).

is prefaced by a personal account of his education, teachers as well the methodology he adopts in his tafsir. The reasons for writing the tafsir are elucidated in the Introduction.[75] It is clear that the sources consulted for the tafsir are classical works which include *Kashshāf*, acclaimed for its literary and rationalist approach. These comments prepare the readers for an 'orthodox' explanation of the sacred text which is in sharp contrast to his heterodox views propounded in the royal court. Noteworthy features of his tafsir include his elaboration of the term 'Arab' in a broader setting.[76] Following Maha'imi's tafsir style, Shaykh Mubarak gives a detailed explanation of *'ulum al-Qur'ān*. It also reveals his deep reflections on the verses that have a mystical significance.[77]

A comprehensive work covering multifaceted aspects of tafsir, Shaykh Mubarak offers fresh insights into the coherence theory.[78] The affinity of verses and surahs is a recurrent theme as demonstrated in Surah Al-Layl (92) and Surah Al-Duha (93) both of which have a circumstantial setting. According to Shaykh Mubarak, the first surah relates to the praises of the first Caliph, AbuBakr Siddiq while the latter surah is a lucid veneration of the Holy Prophet (SAW).[79] Overall, the format and structure of these surahs require familiarity with *asbāb al-nuzul*, grammatical proficiency and most importantly, a proper understanding about the meaning and message of the Qur'ān. Shaykh Mubarak successfully delivers on the broad framework as outlined in the tafsir's Introduction.

It is a paradox that two strands of Shaykh Mubarak's complex personality provide conflicting portraits of his Qur'ān ic contributions. Perhaps the tafsir was an act of redemption for his disingenuous attempts to dislodge the primacy of the Qur'ān and sunnah against the fraught backdrop of Akbar's reign.

---

[75] Ibid., 54 - 6.

[76] Ibid., 55. Shaykh Mubarak examines the historical significance   of the generic term 'Arab' with specific reference to Qur'ānic hermeneutics.

[77] Ibid., 59.

[78] 'Azami, *Tadhkirah Mufassirin*, 82 - 3. Shaykh Mubarak makes reference to earlier tafsirs to support his *nazm* explanation, which is a core element in the tafsir studies.

[79] Salim Kidwai, *Hindustāni Mufassirin*, 59.

Sawāti' al – Ilham

The undotted commentary is an unprecedented attempt in the tafsir genre by Faizi, the poet laureate of Akbar's royal court. Faizi employed a peculiar Arabic figure of speech[80] to write this tafsir. The title *Sawāti'* refers to flashes through which he dexterously maintains this style in the text. The enigmatic elements[81] are embedded in abstruse ways making the text inaccessible and incomprehensible at times for specialist readers. To illustrate this point: Faizi adopts this style to describe his family background, information about his life in Agra and eulogies to Akbar. As much as it is a formidable task for him to avoid dotted letters, the overstrained approach is definitely pedantic.[82] The noted historian of Akbar's era, 'Abdul Qadir Badayuni is acerbic in his comments about the *Sawāti'*: "He could set up the skeleton of the verse well, but the bones had no marrows in them."[83]

A literary critic like Shibli Nu'mani (d.1914) criticised Faizi for his liberal outlook while expressing a guarded response to the tafsir.[84] Viewed from the prism of authenticity, the tafsir does not reflect Faizi's heterodox ideas. In contrast, concise explanations are given in historical settings while the reasons for the revelation of particular verses and proofs of Prophethood are briefly mentioned. In a broader context, it is problematic to speculate on the reasons for the undotted tafsir. One view suggests that Faizi intended to demonstrate the unique nature of *i'jāz* of the Qur'ān.[85] Interestingly, there has been no critique on the tafsir's contents

---

[80] Arabic literary tools were employed by classical scholars in the subcontinent along the pattern of Persian works. The pedantic style is very much evident in these writings.

[81] Zunaid Ahmad has critically analysed the stylistic feature of *Sawati'* in *The Contribution of Indo - Pakistan to Arabic Literature* (Lahore, 1968), 24 - 6.

[82] Ahmad argues that the tafsir "[has] no value. the self- imposed restriction has made the brief comments that he offers more difficult than the text itself." Ibid., 27. This assessment is at variance with Salim Kidwai's views. See *Hindustāni Mufassirin*, 68 - 9.

[83] Schimmel, *Islam in the Indian Subcontinent*, 85.

[84] Nadwi, *Saviours of Islamic Spirit*, vol. 3, 76.

[85] Salim Kidwai, *Hindustāni Mufassirin*, 70.

which perhaps is a validation of his scholarly credentials among his contemporaries. Even so, there still exists a divided opinion about his literary contributions. Abul Hasan Ali Nadwi is of the view that a contemporaneous tafsir far surpassed Faizi's work in content and literary style. The Syrian scholar Muhammad Badr al-Din (d. 1550) composed a poetical commentary consisting of 180 thousand verses along with a summary which was strictly in conformity with the mainstream tafsir.[86] In sum, the contestation of ideas has not resolved Faizi's standing among scholars. However, Manazir Ahsan Gilani maintains that Faizi was a unique individual whose composition is peerless and a landmark contribution to the tafsir genre.[87]

It is worthwhile to make a brief comment about the religious policies after Akbar's demise in 1605. His successor Jahangir under the influence of the Mujaddid made concerted efforts to stem the tide of religious apostasy (*irtidād*) embodied in the *Dini Ilāhi* doctrines. Parallel to this development was the consolidation of the Naqshbandiyyah order in the subcontinent. Its role was twofold: i) to restore the primacy of Islam and ii) to reach out to royalty through the corridors of power. Guided by this pragmatic approach, the Mujaddid advocated interaction with the influential figures in the royal court to realise his vision of returning Islam to its rightful position. His sons also wielded a considerable influence over the Mughal royalty.[88]

Awrangzeb Alamgir (d.1707) represented the Islamic ideal in terms of his conviction and commitment to establishing shari'ah as the rule of law. His prolonged expansionist rule did not deter him from fostering an ambience of Islamic learning. In this instance the *Fatāwā Alamgiri*[89], a Hanafi reference work on *Fiqh*, is his lasting collaborative contribution.

During Awrangzeb's reign, the production of classical Islamic works was on the rise. To this end, the *Tafsir i-Ahmadi* is

---

[86] Nadwi, *Saviours of Islamic Spirit*, vol.3, 77.
[87] Salim Kidwai, *Hindustāni Mufassirin*, 72 - 3. Differing perspectives, a euphemism for professional jealousy, also accounted for the harsh criticism of Faizi's tafsir.
[88] Nadwi, *Saviours of Islamic Spirit*, vol.3, 103 - 53.
[89] Ibid., 57 - 8.

representative of this literary output. The *mufassir*, Ahmad Abu Sa'id commonly known as Mullah Jiwan (d.1717) was an outstanding scholar and a tutor in the royal court of Awrangzeb. His *hajj* travels broadened the scope of his literary endeavours, judging by the number of works in the field of *Fiqh*, tafsir and *tasawwuf*. In his teenage years his written works in Arabic showed promising signs of an adept scholar. A noteworthy contribution to *usul al-Fiqh* is Mullah Jiwan's *Anwār al-Mashāriq*. Likewise, he penned in his autobiographical account his spiritual affiliation to the Qadiriyyah order. Overall, he articulated the amalgam of shari'ah and *tariqah*.

Tafsir i-Ahmadi is not in a conventional sense a complete tafsir as it largely covers a broad spectrum of legal injunctions (*ahkām*). The work identifies verses that have a bearing on *Fiqh* issues. Unlike other exegetes, work on this tafsir project took seventeen years to complete. Written in fluent Arabic, Mullah Jiwan offers a systematic presentation of linguistic analysis, theological perspectives and most importantly, the elucidation of Hanafi juristic views (*maslak*).[90]

Two points emerge from an overview of Mullah Jiwan's significant work. First, his thorough familiarity with classical tafsirs like Razi's *Tafsir al-Kabir* and Abu Bakr al- Jassas's *Ahkām al-Qur'ān* which has a strong Hanafi bias[91]. Second, the proliferation of Fiqh works took precedence over the systematic study of the hadith literature. During this period under discussion, the evolution of *Fiqh* under the patronage of rulers became a catalyst for promoting the Hanafi school of thought as the officially recognised *madhab* in the subcontinent. In contrast, the Shafi' *Fiqh* maintained its predominant presence in many regions of South India. There were other factors which contributed to the growth of Hanafi *Fiqh*. Mullah Jiwan by virtue of his vast learning was not *taqlid*-bound; his independent views were at odds with widely

---

[90] 'Azami, *Tadhkirah Mufassirin*, 126 -7.

[91] The codification of Qur'ānic *ahkām* along *Fiqhi* lines developed into a sub-genre of tafsir. Ashraf 'Ali Thanawi (d. 1943) supervised a Hanafi compendium bearing the same title of al-Jassas's tafsir, *Ahkām al-Qur'ān*.

accepted juristic opinions. In this regard, he argued that the Qur'ānic injunction of marriage to disbelieving women is accorded the same status for women belonging to the *Ahl al-Kitāb*.[92]

The hadith studies assumed greater importance following the transnational networks established in the sixteenth century. Indian hadith scholars like 'Ali Muttaqi (d. 1567) studied under distinguished 'ulama in Makkah and restarted a comprehensive study of hadith in the subcontinent. The prevailing course of study was limited to a few hadith works with a major work like *Bukhāri* receiving negligible attention. It is also to the credit of Shaykh 'Abdul Haq Dehlawi that a well-structured study of hadith works was popularised in the subcontinent. Dehlawi's extensive study of hadith works under the tutelage of Shaykh 'Abdul Wahhab Muttaqi was a productive phase in his academic career. Qureshi's thoughtful comments about Dehlawi's reformist contribution are instructive:

> [Dehlawi] was a prolific writer and was the author of books and treatises on the exegesis of the Qur'ān, the principles of reciting it correctly, hadith, *Fiqh*, *tasawwuf*, ethics, philosophy, logic, history, biographies and grammar. His books were widely read and his contribution in hadith was so important that he earned the title of *muhaddith*, an authority on hadith. Such voluminous literature, so varied in its scope, of such high quality and produced over such a long period could not fail to produce significant results.[93]

A few decades later, the Waliyullah family inaugurated a well-

---

[92] Mullah Jiwan refers to the following verse in support of his view: "Do not marry disbelieving women until they bring faith." (2: 21). Cf. 'Azami, *Tadhkirah Mufassirin*, 132.

[93] Qureshi, *Ulema in Politics*, 83. Cf. Nizami, *Hayāt i-'Abdul Haq*, 183 -4. Dehlawi's critique of *Tafsir al-Baydāwi* is indicative of his approach to the tafsir studies.

developed, comprehensive study of hadith whose imprints are visible in the subcontinent and beyond.[94] A significant development in the tafsir genre was the growing number of incomplete/partial commentaries. Likewise, surah-related tafsirs rose in importance. Both Ahmad and Salim Kidwai have provided a conspectus of this trend to illustrate the productive tafsir activity in the pre-Waliyullah period. However, these works lacked originality and were in many respects the recycled versions of earlier commentaries.

A sub-genre of tafsir, the *hāshiyah* was a markedly distinctive feature that underscored the growing interest in important classical works. Walid Saleh, in his comprehensive study of tafsir tradition, makes the following comments about the *hawāshiyah* (super-glosses):

> Like much of the scholastic tradition in Islam, the tafsir tradition had an active sub-genre of super-commentaries that were primarily written on two Qur'ānic commentaries used in the teaching of tafsir, the *Kashshāf* and *Anwār al-Tanzil*, and to a lesser extent on a third commentary, *Tafsir al-Jalālayn*.
>
> In the thirteenth *hijri*/nineteenth and early fourteenth *hijri*/twentieth centuries, before the Romantic notions of a medieval Islamic decline and decadence penetrated the traditional Muslim establishments, publishing houses in the Islamic world were busy issuing many of the voluminous 'medieval' glosses on tafsir works. They were an essential part of the madrasah curriculum and were considered part and parcel of the exegetical tradition, not medieval corruptions of a once classical tradition.[95]

---

[94] See Mahmood Ahmad Ghazi, *Islamic Renaissance in South Asia, 1707-1867: The Role of Shah Wali Allah and his Successors* (Islamabad, 2002), 189-262.

[95] Seyyed Hosein Nasr, et.al, *The Study Qur'ān: A New Translation and Commentary* (New York, 2015), 1648.

In a similar vein, Ahmad has shared a similar observation about the *hāshiyah* activity in the subcontinent.[96] No different is this trend more pronounced than in West Africa as discussed in Andrea Brigaglia's meticulous study on the intellectual history of tafsir in the Islamic region.[97] A celebrated work like *Jalālayn* is an indispensable source of reference on which several glosses have been written. Significantly, these tafsirs are intersection points to connect the Islamic institutions with a diverse geographical spread. A telling example of their popularity is *Jalālayn* that serves "as a symbol of the continuity of the African exegetical tradition."[98]

We may also refer to *Kashshāf* which enjoys much popularity notwithstanding its Mu'tazilite leanings. A number of *hawāshiyah* have been written over the centuries on it. Of course, the considerable controversies around its non-Sunni viewpoints have drawn hostile receptions from the exegetes of different ideological backgrounds.

According to Walid Saeh, the reception history of *Kashshāf* reveals the conflicting perceptions through the *hāshiyah* tradition. Many of these works were written to stem the tide of Mu'tazilite thought. Equally irksome for them was its popularity as a textbook in the madrasah curriculum. The spate of anti-*Kashshāf* polemical writings through the *hāshiyah* was thus understandable. There were, however, exceptions to the work's perceived threat to mainstream Sunni doctrines. Suyuti's critique is a case in point. In his critique, he identifies *Kashshāf's* main drawback: the sparing use of hadith sources which by all accounts could have classified it as *tafsir al-ma'thur*. Despite this shortcoming, Suyuti attributes its historical reception to an important literary aspect: the prominence of *bayān* and *ma'āni* (rhetoric). Unsurprisingly, *Kashshāf* was selectively consulted by the Deobandi 'ulama for its linguistic contribution. For example, *Ma'āriful Qur'ān* by Mufti

---

[96] Ahmad, *The Contribution of Indo-Pakistan*, 16. To illustrate this point, Shaykh Muhammad Ahmad (d. 1547) who composed *Al-Tafsir al-Muhammadi* also wrote glosses on *Tafsir al-Baydāwi*. Cf. Salim Kidwai, *Hindustāni Mufassirin*, 197 - 250.

[97] Cited in Andreas Gorke and Johanna Pink (eds.), *Tafsir and Islamic Intellectual History: Exploring the Boundaries of a Genre* (Oxford, 2015), 379 - 415.

[98] Ibid., 391.

Muhammad Shafi illustrates the intellectual history of *hāshiyah* as a sub-genre of Arabic literature.

Conclusion

The robust tafsir activity during this formative period in the subcontinent has historical antecedents. Muslim conquests brought in an influx of scholars from Central Asia. Also, *da'wah* was a decisive factor for families from the Arab world who settled in various regions of the subcontinent. They worked tirelessly to foster a culture of the Islamic intellectual tradition. Their contributions have been exemplary judging by their writings which continue to shape the Islamic intellectual discourse. The continuity of this tradition is best represented by the Waliyullah family and their pioneering contributions to the tafsir genre.

Chapter 1

The Waliyullah Family Tafsir Contributions

A structured, nuanced interpretation of the tafsir tradition in the subcontinent became prominent in the seventeenth century through the sterling efforts of the Waliyullah family. Their reformist vision was anchored on the study of the foundational sources of Islam. Given the peculiar circumstances and the deviant religious tendencies of Muslims in the subcontinent, the urgency of re- establishing links with the Qur'ān was of pivotal importance. The chapter examines the far-reaching influence of Shah Waliyullah and his descendants to the dissemination of the Qur'ānic message and teachings.

Shah Waliyullah: An Intellectual Icon

The Waliyullah tradition had a powerful impact in shaping the Islamic intellectual patterns in South Asia. Essentially, the true greatness of Shah Waliyullah (d.1762) lies in his academic works which were assiduously studied beyond the borders of the subcontinent. The key theme in Waliyullah's reformist vision (*tajdid*) was directed at evolving a common tradition that "could be adopted with ease by the Muslim philosopher, sufi, *mutakallim* (theologian) and jurist."[1] This vision was feasible if intuition, intellect, and revelation were reconciled (*tatbiq*) so that a holistic Islamic outlook could emerge.[2] To this end, the major writings of Waliyullah reflect these bold attempts at reconciliation.

The timeline of Waliyullah's literary output gives an indication about the background for writing these celebrated works. Nevertheless, they are a synopsis of his varied and immense contributions to the intellectual renewal project. These important writings are contextualised within the Qur'ānic framework. Take for example, his magnum opus *Hujjat Allah al-Bālighah* (The

---

[1] Mahmood Ahmad Ghazi, *Islamic Renaissance in South Asia: 1707- 1867*, 157.
[2] Ibid.

Conclusive Proof of God),[3] which was widely read in the eighteenth century with several translations expanding its global reach. In more ways than one, its chief merit lies in Waliyullah's reformulation of the ideals of the shari'ah in its traditional sense. His theorisation of *irtāqāt*,[4] a central concept in the work, delineates the matrix of ethics rooted in specific contexts. According to Waliyullah, the hierarchy of values which is intrinsic to man's quest for moral and spiritual excellence is positioned in a cosmic order. These values represent a blending of identities that are in harmony with the moral universe. Additionally, the relationship reinforces the progressive ideals (*irtāqāt*) that are in consonance with human nature. Conversely, any disruption is likely to cause a crisis in the environment. By way of example, it may create a capitalist economy with identifiable streaks of a consumerist society, shorn of morality and ethical considerations.

The well-structured analysis of society by Waliyullah is reflective of his scholarly acumen on the themes contained in the Qur'ān. Thus his *Hujjat* and other significant works encapsulate an integrated approach to his interpretive reading of the sacred text.

Before we attempt to examine the salient features of his Persian tafsir *Fath al-Rahmān*, the historical circumstances prevailing in the subcontinent offer refreshing insights into Muslims' response to the Qur'ān. Three factors account for this mindset. First, India, Iran and Afghanistan formed a landmass of Persian-oriented cultural influences. The wave of migration patterns to the subcontinent included scholars who were generally inclined to *Fiqh*. As a result, the Hanafi *Fiqh* dominated the religious discourse. Second, the un-Islamic practices or cultural appropriation among Muslim communities diluted the unambiguous teachings of the Qur'ān, which had gained ground on the Indian soil. Third, Muslim scholars and 'ulama discouraged the study of the Qur'ān through

---

[3] For a detailed of these themes contained in the *Hujjat*, see Muhammad Al-Ghazali, *The Sociopolitical Thought of Shah Wali Allah* (Islamabad, 2001). A translation of the *Hujjat*, vol.1 was completed by Marcia Hermansen, *The Conclusive Argument from God* (Islamabad, 2003).

[4] Al- Ghazali presents a brilliant elucidation on the theory and principles of *irtāqāt* in *The Sociopolitical Thought*, 136, 175-6.

translation on the assumption that ordinary Muslims would misinterpret the sacred text. Implicit in this mindset was the potential loss of authority which scholars had exercised over the centuries as the purveyors of Islamic knowledge.[5]

Keeping in mind the above reasons, Waliyullah's tafsir was a bold attempt to restore the primacy of the Qur'ān by making it accessible to and reader-friendly for the educated class and ordinary people. By the same token, concise explanatory notes (*shuruhāt*) restated the essential message of the Qur'ān. Moreover, *Fath al-Rahmān* was among the few Persian translations catering for the burgeoning Muslim population.[6]

History of *Fath al-Rahmān*

The Introduction (*muqaddimah*) of Waliyullah's pioneering work details the reasons for attempting a work of this stature. With his immense intellectual prowess, his reconstruction of the Islamic sciences (*'ulum*) was well conceived. Furthermore, his Qur'ānic scholarship was enhanced in the company of his revered father, 'Abdur Rahim, who was renowned for his mastery over Islamic *'ulum.* In this way the nurturing and maturing process equipped Waliyullah to undertake a robust study of the Qur'ānic genre that was not tethered to exegetical blemishes in Arabic and Persian.[7]

Ghazi provides the following account of Waliyullah's focus on the translation project:

> I had several occasions to study the Holy Qur'ān
> at the feet of my father with deep reflections on
> its meanings, explanation of the occasions on
> which relevant verses and surahs were revealed,
> and with research in the exegeses and

---

[5] Ghazi offers a historical assessment about the factors that shaped Waliyullah's intellectual consciousness. See *Islamic Renaissance in South Asia*, 61-72.

[6] According to Hamidullah Marazi, several Persian tafsirs predated Waliyullah's *Fath al-Rahmān* in the subcontinent. See Muhammad Mubeen Saleem Nadwi Azhari, *Hindustān me Mutāla'a Qur'ān: Mu'āsir Manzar Nāma* (Aligarh, 2020), 1-3.

[7] See Abul Hasan Ali Nadwi, *Saviours of Islamic Spirit*, vol. 4, (Lucknow, 1993), 102.

commentaries. With the help of this study, a great portal of knowledge and comprehension of the truth was opened for me.[8]

Truth, for Waliyullah, meant opening new gateways to the authentic expression of the sacred text. He deplored the laborious approach adopted by the earlier *mufassirs* to highlight the Qur'ān's simple, direct and forceful message. As a result, the power of idiom and language had lost its charm on account of juristic jingoism and scholastic sophistry.[9] His sensitive soul had witnessed these trivial pursuits that vitiated the dynamism of the perennial source of Islam. To remedy this anomalous situation, Waliyullah developed a conceptual framework: the Qur'ān represented a fundamental shift away from the myriad of conflicting mindsets that ruptured the South Asian Muslim identity.

In his quest for Islamic authenticity, Waliyullah's sojourn in the Hijaz was a turning point to his intellectual endeavours. His study of hadith and ancillary Islamic subjects under reputed scholars, many of whom had settled in the Hijaz, exposed him to the cross-currents of Islamic authenticity. At the same time, he became acutely aware and perhaps disillusioned about the low standing of the sacred text among his compatriots. His renewed motivation to undertake a systematic study of the Qur'ān was carefully planned. Again, his versatile genius is to the fore in respect of his renewal (*tajdidi*) project.[10]

After five years of his return from Hijaz, the impulse to resume his Persian translation gained momentum. His pre-Hijaz sojourn saw the translation of Surah Al-Baqarah and Surah Al-Nisa. In the words of Waliyullah:

> A few years after that (Hijaz sojourn), a student started studying under me which revived my earlier resolve. I decided to pen down the

---

[8] Ghazi, *Islamic Renaissance in South Asia*, 159.
[9] Nadwi, *Saviours of Islamic Spirit*, vol. 4, 102.
[10] Ibid., 75-9.

translation. Additionally, I taught tafsir every day and in this way one third of the translation was completed. Then the student had to undertake a journey which again suspended the work. After a prolonged period the desire to complete the translation was re-awakened resulting in the completion of two thirds of the work.[11]

Finally, the manuscript was completed in 1738 and released in its book form in 1743. In the preparation of the tafsir, Waliyullah also wrote *Al-Fawz al-Kabir*[12] outlining the principles and methods he adopted. It is a concise but extremely valuable treatise of Qur'ānic exegesis. Originally written in Persian, it has been translated into Arabic, Urdu, Turkish and English. Another seminal work *Al-Fath al- Kabir* (Arabic)[13] deals with the difficult words described as *gharā'ib* in the Qur'ān. These are unfamiliar terms in common Arabic diction. Both these works are representative of Waliyullah's outstanding grasp of the *ʿulum* embodied in the tafsir genre.

According to Ghazi, these books paved the way "to acquaint the common man with the Holy Book, the main source of all Islamic teachings. Direct acquaintance with the Qur'ān and the sunnah has the potential to divert attention from trivial theological and doctrinal issues to the fundamentals of religion."[14] In this way, Waliyullah succeeded in breaking Muslims' perfunctory attachment to the Qur'ān.

The popularity of *Al-Fawz al-Kabir* can be gleaned from its several translations in English. The recent translation titled *The Great Victory on Qur'ānic Hermeneutics* is an annotated edition dealing with the five fundamental sciences of the Qur'ān. These

---

[11] Ibid., 102.

[12] A recent translation, *Al-Fawz al-Kabir: The Great Victory on Qur'ānic Hermeneutics* by Tahir Mahmood Kiani (London, 2014) is an annotated work containing detailed references. Kiani's Introduction enhances the merit of this invaluable translation.

[13] Waliyullah, *Al-Fath al-Kabir* (Lucknow, 1314H). It deals with the explanation of difficult words used in the Qur'ān.

[14] Ghazi, *Islamic Renaissance in South Asia*, 159.

are elaborated by Waliyullah to enable readers to delve into the subtleties of tafsir. The following comment by Waliyullah reveals the importance of this work:

> It is hoped that with the Grace of Allah students would find in it a way so clear from grasping the meanings of the Qur'ān even after spending a lifetime accessing commentaries and writings of exegetes.[15]

The work navigates key themes of the Qur'ān, which underscore Waliyullah's impressive command over the literary aspects of Arabic. His critical assessment of *i'jāz* (miraculous nature of the Qur'ān) and the *nāsikh* (abrogating) and the *mansukh* (abrogated) verses brings in full his varied contributions and independent thinking. In a historical context, Waliyullah showed remarkable traces of a visionary with strong leanings towards *ijtihād*. His endorsement of Ibn Taimiyyah's reformist works has implications for his own reformulation of the Islamic sciences. Although a time gap of almost four hundred years existed between them, Ibn Taimiyyah's enduring legacy gave fresh impetus to creative thinkers like Waliyullah to review, redefine and refine Islamic thought in circumstantial settings.[16] The synergy of reformist thought may also be found in their principal works on Qur'ānic hermeneutics. Ibn Taimiyyah wrote an introduction to the principles (*usul*) of tafsir[17] in which he elucidated the methodology adopted by the *salaf* (pious predecessors). However, in terms of comprehensiveness, *Al-Fawz al-Kabir* surpasses Ibn Taimiyyah's work for its rational and analytical approach.

We now focus on the prominent features of *Fath al- Rahmān*:

---

[15] Nadwi, *Saviours of Islamic Spirit*, vol. 4, 106.

[16] Ibid., 114-7. Waliyullah's admiration of Ibn Taimiyyah can be gleaned from the following excerpt: "Nothing in the writings of Ibn Taimiyyah is unsupported by textual authority from the scripture and the sunnah or the practice of the earliest Muslims. He was a scholar of exceptional abilities. Is there anybody who can be compared with him either in speech or writing?"

[17] Ibn Taimiyyah, *An Introduction to the Principles of Tafseer* (Birmingham, 1993).

- o Brevity presupposes a nuanced interpretation of the text. In other words, preference is given to words which for accurately conveying syntactic structure and contextual relevance. Waliyullah keeps in mind his target audience: educated and ordinary Muslims seeking to access the meaning and message of the Qur'ān.
- o Unlike other exegetes, Waliyullah makes concise comments on legal matters (*ahkām*) without resorting to minutiae. This approach facilitates direct contact with the essential teachings of the sacred text. Additionally, the text becomes relevant and relatable. Waliyullah dexterously blurs out the distinction between *ahkām* and ethics to allow readers to be in conversation with the Qur'ānic worldview.
- o Accounts relating to the Messengers and historical events are limited to minimal details. Waliyullah's purpose is meant to reinforce the timeless teachings of the sacred text. The notes are precise, accurate and lucid.[18] Unlike other exegetes who rely on embellished Isra'ilite traditions[19] that sometimes border on the bizarre, Waliyullah is selective in this regard.

It is worthwhile to examine two major writings that have a direct bearing on Waliyullah's tafsir writing.

The *Hujjat* is primarily derived from his deep reflection, analytical study and intuitive grasp of the Qur'ān. The convincing proof or conclusive argument as the title suggests, according to Waliyullah, "refers to the inner meanings of religious obligation and requital and the inner dimensions of the divine laws revealed

---

[18] These points are summarised from 'Azami's *Tadhkirah Mufassirin*, 157-8.

[19] Dhahabi devotes an exhaustive chapter regarding the impact of Isra'ilite traditions on exegetical works. See *Al-Tafsir wa'al Mufassirun* (Cairo, 2000).

for mercy and guidance."[20] Essentially, the Qur'ān provides a framework to develop the hierarchy of *wahy* - inspired values for the benefit of mankind. In this respect, the coordination of the Islamic disciplines has the potential to create the *khilāfah* (custodianship) as enshrined in the Qur'ān.

Ta'wil al-Hadith[21] is a unique presentation that explores the evolution of the human mind. It traces important events in the lives of the Messengers, including miracles and their natural causes. Waliyullah employs technical terms that in some instances are interlinked with his exposition in the *Hujjat*. For example, the *irtāqāt* term is a recurrent theme in his study on the lives and contributions of the Messengers. These thought processes and logic are largely derived from his perceptive understanding of the linkages between verses and surahs that underpin his intellectual acumen.

Waliyullah conceives human activity under the rubric of *tadhkir*. This term is employed to reinforce mankind's multifaceted role and obligations in the world. The categories or subdivisions are drawn from the Qur'ānic concepts to present a clear, well-developed understanding about the purpose of creation. In a broader sense, the dynamic thrust of these activities encapsulates the Qur'ānic vision of *khilāfah*, transparency and accountability. Furthermore, these complementary activities spur man to actualise his objectives in the world.

From the realms of *ahkām* to civilisation, Waliyullah pointedly references the sense of equilibrium dominating man's life. There are no structural flaws or negative factors that impede man's progress to fulfil the Divine plan of creation. In fact, man has to unearth the natural resources and use them productively. In the evolution of his religious consciousness or experience, man's understanding of the Creator and the cosmos has undergone a metamorphosis. The simple message of *tawhid* presented by the Messengers was distorted in the process of deification (*shirk*) over time. Myriads of idols sculpted for the purpose of worship distorted the simplicity of *tawhid*. As Islam is *da'wah*-oriented,

---

[20] Marcia Hermansen, *The Conclusive Argument from God* (Islamabad, 2003), xv.
[21] Waliyullah, *Ta'wil al-Hadith*. Translated by G.N. Jalbani (Lahore, 1977).

Muslims are urged to use *mukhāsama* for the Abrahamic religions, Judaism and Christianity in order to identify their deviance from the unerring path of *tawhid*, guidance and salvation. Again, Muslims are reminded to follow the path of decorum rather than polemical posturing in their engagement with these faith groups. Obviously, in Waliyullah's view, the tenor of the Qur'ānic style aims to highlight the history or anecdotal accounts of previous nations who had rejected *da'wah* or the call to *tawhid* and righteous life by the Messengers. Thus the divine punishment that befell these transgressive nations were a consequence of their defiant conduct.

Waliyullah also includes the polytheists (*mushriks*) and hypocrites (*munāiqs*) within the ambit of *mukhāsama*. The Qur'ān again does not discriminate their excesses in comparison to the People of the Book (*Ahl al-Kitāb*). In a specific sense, it condemns the hypocrites of Madinah for their twisted agendas, hostile policies and aggressive ploys to undermine the growth of the nascent Muslim community. For Waliyullah the timely warnings in the Qur'ān have relevance for all times.

The seismic shift from Waliyullah's era to our fast- paced society has a time gap of approximately 250 years. The advancement of technology has dramatically altered our lives. Data captures information containing huge, bulky volumes within seconds. Likewise, the unprecedented and pervasive presence of technology also defines our religious outlook. It is designed in such a way to offer us options or choices. This is no different from the Qur'ān's integrated presentation of its universal message. It takes into account civilisational diversity that is derived from the unitary experience of mankind. Sayyid Abul A'la Mawdudi (d.1979) gives a synoptic assessment of Waliyullah's multidimensional contributions:

> The Shah's works show how deeply he had pondered over the social conditions of the Muslims of his day. Such a critique necessarily creates an anxiety for reform. and to draw a distinction between the wholesome and harmful custom usages. The urge for

reform and regeneration is to chart out a well-defined programme for the reconstruction of society for giving it a correct direction. This is what we find the Shah doing with complete precision according to a comprehensive plan present in his critique of the Muslim society.[22]

Two points emerge from Waliyullah's *tajdidi* endeavours: the reconstruction of the Muslim society and the demonstration of the foundational sources of Islam within the intellectual framework.

Tafsir Fath al-'Aziz

The scion of the Waliyullah family, Shah 'Abdul 'Aziz (d.1824) contributed greatly to Islamic learning. Like his father, the Shah gathered around him a vast network of students as the nucleus of his movement in the intellectual domain. He concentrated mainly on formulating a reformist framework in line with the Waliyullah tradition of Islamic renaissance. His sermons on the Qur'ān helped him to build a base of public opinion.[23]

Shah 'Abdul 'Aziz was an eloquent orator; his speeches reflected his depth of scholarship and missionary zeal. Equally impressive were his literary masterpieces in the field of hadith studies. His *fatāwā* compendium also revealed the profundity of his intellectual prowess. In the realm of Qur'ānic studies his incomplete commentary is a testament to its "rational and scholarly handling of problems, its vast canvas, and its elegant language and style (which) gives it a place of prominence among the best works of tafsir produced by Muslim scholarship."[24]

There are divergent opinions about *Fath al-'Aziz*. It is generally held that the Shah wrote his commentary only up to the 184th verse of Surah Al-Baqarah as well as the last two *ajzā* (parts) of the

---

[22] Cited in Abdul Kader Choughley, *How to Study the Qur'ān: Sayyid Abul Hasan Ali Nadwi's Approach* (Aligarh, 2018), 72.

[23] Ghazi, *Islamic Renaissance in South Asia*, 166.

[24] Ibid., 170.

Qur'ān. According to bigrophical accounts, the Shah was a chronic patient, compelling him to dictate the complete tafsir to a team of students. In his *Fatāwā 'Azizia* there are several references to his tafsir that support the view of a complete work. It is probable that the first draft of the manuscript was completed which was not revised or edited.[25] These allusions or suggestive clues, however, are not definitive conclusions about the existence of a detailed commentary.

Another plausible explanation is the dictation method adopted by the Shah. His busy schedule in teaching the Qur'ān was his primary focus. Like Waliyullah, he advocated a direct access to the sacred text through Persian. Implicit in this approach was a critique of the conventional tafsir-based understanding that was limiting and stifling, to say the least. The common line of his reformist thought was clear: the unmediated role of the Qur'ān as was revealed, understood and practised during the Prophetic era. In other words, the Shah argued that the meaning and message of the Qur'ān can also be understood through a reader- friendly translation.[26]

Context is a defining feature of *Fath al-'Aziz*. By way of example, the opening verse in Surah Al-Mutaffifin (83) condemns the defrauders. In the light of the *sui* interpretation, the Arabic word is expanded to include social vices that impinge on the moral fabric of society. For the Shah, the erosion of ethical values is akin to treachery and 'proves the wickedness of one's inner-self.'[27] This trenchant critique of the Indian Muslim society is a pointed reference to the universal teachings of the Qur'ān.

The power of language, according to the Shah, has a transformative potential. In the Qur'ānic parlance, words/ terms denoting the power and sovereignty of Allah may be explained by analogies. An instance in point is the descriptive phrase *wa huwal ʿaziz* (He is the Mighty). The Shah presses home the point of Allah's divine power. Human beings have been given the *khilāfah*

---

[25] Ibid., 258. Cf. 'Azami, *Tadhkirah Mufassirin*, 170-6.

[26] Nadwi, *Saviours of Islamic Spirit*, vol. 4, 158.

[27] Saiyid Athar Abbas Rizvi, *Shah 'Abd al-'Aziz: Puritanism, Sectarian Polemics and Jihād* (Canberra, 1982), 129.

to act freely but in the event of their transgression Allah has no difficulty in reproving or punishing them.[28] Thus man's finite understanding of Allah's attributes is explained through the medium of analogy.

This remarkable Persian tafsir, albeit an incomplete one, is widely used among the 'ulama. Like the hadith and *Fiqh* works of the Shah, it is a substantive contribution to the Islamic renewal project.

In the political sphere, British colonialism gained a firm foothold in the subcontinent. Through the policy of divide and rule the political fortunes of the Mughal Empire were rapidly reaching its lowest ebb. Dynastic rules created factional identities, which surrendered to the rising British Empire. It is a historical fact that colonialism possessed the military arsenal to subjugate the Indian nation. Likewise, missionary activities played a significant role in challenging Islam on the intellectual terrain. Gradually, the arena of ideological battles was fought in the name of religion[29]. Mercenary ambition and missionary fervour worked in collusion to dislodge the supremacy of Islam in the subcontinent. A lesser known activity appeared surreptitiously by English scholars/theologians: the Qur'ān translation project. Abdur Raheem Kidwai has surveyed the growth of English translations of the Qur'ān framed around the question of political landscapes[30]. Our focus is on colonialism and its ramifications for Muslims. The British were adept in fomenting hostility between Muslims and the Hindu majority who had co-existed in harmony straddling many centuries. In fact, the Indo-Islamic culture was a confluence of the cultural and religious traits that strengthened the Ibrahimi creed. Regardless of the syncretic elements or the hybrid process that percolated into mainstream Islam, the spirit of tolerance was

---

[28] Ibid., 128.

[29] Qureshi, *The Ulema in Politics*, 138-9.

[30] As early as 1734 the English translation by George Sale showed polemical streaks and an obvious overdose of Islamophobia. According to Kidwai, "Sale appears as a Christian missionary, polemicist and Orientalist in the light of his pronouncements on Islam, the Prophet and the Qur'ān." Abdur Raheem Kidwai, *Translating the Untranslatable: A Critical Guide to 60 English Translations of the Qur'ān* (New Delhi, 2011), 244.

a marked feature of Muslim rule during these turbulent times. In contrast, British rule had a clear agenda: to dismantle Islam from the portals of power.[31]

In a revivalist perspective, the Waliyullah family stood out for their deep-rooted attachment to the Qur'ān. They expanded the reconstruction of the Muslim society paradigm to an intellectual level. These intersection points defined the collective Islamic identity (*tashakkhus*) of the subcontinental Muslims. At the heart of Islamic revivalism was the impact of print in South Asia. Francis Robinson has identified the following factors that contributed to the adoption of print by the Muslim scholars:

> [Muslims] were coming to realise the extent to which, after six hundred years of domination on the subcontinent, they had lost power: they were coming to understand the severity of their competition with the European civilisation who had ruled over them, and the Hindu world which rivalled them. They were undergoing an intense period of religious revival in which there was a strong pressure to renew Islam both inside and outside South Asia... Indeed, they were faced with the problem of how they could still be good Muslims and at the same time enable their community to survive under foreign Christian power.[32]

In the light of these historical developments, Shah 'Abdul 'Aziz Dehlawi, his family and spiritual descendants played a major role in the dissemination of Islamic knowledge through print. In a similar vein, two of the earliest books printed were those of Sayyid Ahmad Shahid (d. 1831).[33] These works had a wider public consumption embedded within the reformist vision. Also, these

---

[31] See Nadwi, *Muslims in India,* 244.

[32] Francis Robinson, *Islam and Muslim History in South Asia* (New Delhi, 2001), 75.

[33] A two-volume work details the life and times of Sayyid Ahmad Shahid by Abul Hasan Ali Nadwi, *Tārikh Da'wat wa 'Azimat* (Karachi, 1992).

seminal writings were a critique of the deviant practices observed in the name of Islam. Therefore, the mass production of these works was a vigorous attempt by the 'ulama to preserve the authentic expressions of Islamic knowledge. In this way, it broadened the 'ulama's vision to connect with the rest of the Muslim world.

Arabic as a national language displaced local languages through the Muslim conquests. The Arab countries and Muslim Spain are representative of the unprecedented sweep of the Arabic influence. Persia with its vast swathes of territories fell under Muslim sway following the early conquests by the Arab armies. "Arabic now became the dominant written word for several centuries until Persian was reintroduced as the official language under the Safavids."[34]

The Persian language was heavily influenced by Qur'ānic terminology. Interestingly, Persian played a significant role to the promotion of Arabic grammar, and authoritative texts covering almost every Islamic discipline were written by Persian scholars who infused the language with a broad range of Qur'ānic terms. Another literary dimension of the Persian language was its prosody: it possessed distinct characteristics of the Qur'ānic structure. In this way, South Asia was a beneficiary of the changing dynamics of the Persian language. And it was mostly through Persian that Arabic words, more specifically Qur'ānic terms and expressions penetrated into the languages of South Asia such as Sindhi, Punjabi and Urdu. Although belonging to the Indo-Aryan family, the evolution of Urdu had far-reaching influence in the religio-political domain. More importantly, the displacement of Persian as the official court language saw the emergence of an indigenous language nurtured in an Islamic environment.

The choice of Urdu was a response to the decline of Persian among the Muslim masses. The common people in particular employed Urdu in their daily conversation amid their waning interest and semblance of attachment to Persian. Even the

---

[34] Seyyed Hossein Nasr (ed.), *The Study Qur'ān: A New Translation and Commentary*, 1639.

educated class saw the intrinsic merit of writing in Urdu. In this perspective, the emergence of Urdu as a literary language also contributed richly to Islamic works. Belonging to this genre was the prodigious Qur'ānic translation project which drew readers closer to its meanings and message.

It is a historical fact that Urdu has had its Islamic rootage following the gradual decline of Persian as the official language of Muslim India. The diverse populations representing regional language identities hindered possibilities of Persian assuming a much bigger role. Unlike other Muslim countries in which Arabic became their mother tongue, the subcontinent was exposed to a wave of Muslim conquests from several nations. This resulted in the assimilation of hybrid cultures - a synthesis that gave shape to the composite Indo-Islamic identity.

Political developments and language formations also influenced Islam's response to the markers of religious identity. In other words, Muslim communities across the subcontinent needed a cohesive voice to articulate their link to the foundational sources of Islam. To this end, Arabic was taught for the purpose of recitation (*tilāwat*) and ritual- based practices. Of course, the 'ulama's efforts over the centuries to provide religious guidance were noteworthy. These were discernible in their writings in vernacular languages for a particular audience. However, there was no mass movement to sustain these efforts on account of the historical circumstances that gave rise to peculiar Islamic orientations on matters relating to *'aqidah* (Islamic belief). By way of illustration, shrine-based versions of Islam were given preference over the unalloyed Islamic teachings and practices. These were unmistakable signs that an almost parallel religion was established in the name of popular Islam. Nowhere was this alarming development more palpable than in North India. Against the background of rising tensions and conflicts by various dynastic rulers, among whom was the mighty Mughal Empire, the role of the 'ulama underscored their reformist endeavours. Of particular importance was the seventeenth century, which was rightly described as the cauldron of political ferment. Apart from the political decline which had weakened Muslim rule, the emergence of Shah Waliyullah as a multidimensional reformer established new trends of Islamic intellectual thought. His primary focus was on making the sacred text accessible to the educated class and ordinary people. Written in elegant Persian it was a shift away from the strictures of formalism and passive reception that were associated with the Qur'ānic translations in the subcontinent.

Shah Waliyullah's sons did not lag behind in the translation project of the Qur'ān. In fact, both Persian and Urdu translations were produced in view of the changing political climate in the country. It was glaringly evident that Persian no longer enjoyed its unrivalled status among Muslims. Thus the crucible of change was inevitable. Instead, Urdu was the preferred medium to communicate the truth and wisdom of the Qur'ān. In a particular sense, there existed a tenuous link between Persian and the vast corpus of Islamic learning.

Before we attempt to examine the rise of Urdu translations of the Qur'ān, a brief comment is useful to assess its growing importance. By the early twentieth century, Urdu was promoted as a conduit of Islamic literacy through whose writings the reformist slant was produced. It was no fortuitous circumstances that the *tajdidi* movement of Sayyid Ahmad Shahid launched a systematic campaign through the medium of Urdu to disseminate the pristine teachings of Islam. Implicit in the writings of these reformers was a return to the ideal past of the *salaf al- sālih*, a marked reference to the Islamic legacy. Employing simple, chaste and forceful language the reformist message had a widespread impact. Another salient component was the construction of authenticity (*asāla*) in the Islamic discourse. Urdu was not exposed to the modernist elements that otherwise would have given it a syncretic identity shorn of the Islamic norms and values. In the course of its multifaceted history, Urdu has vigorously retained, in its overwhelming form and shape, Islamic characteristics that it can rightly be called a Muslim language after Arabic and Persian.

Mudih al-Qur'ān

We now focus on the tafsir of 'Abdul Qadir Dehlawi (d. 1815) bearing the title *Mudih al-Qur'ān*. A scion of the Waliyullah family, Dehlawi's academic pedigree has established his status as the most influential figure in the Urdu tafsir tradition. His pioneering work by all accounts has shaped the attitudes of translators/ exegetes across the spectrum of ideological and sectarian persuasions. Furthermore, his *Mudih al-Qur'ān* is a conspectus of the authoritative tafsirs that are widely accepted in the Muslim world. It has also had a huge impact on a cross section of Urdu readers for its lucidity, readability and relatability.

Dehlawi was noted for his mastery over Arabic and Islamic '*ulum* which were recognised by his peers. He had strong *tasawwuf* leanings; his unassuming lifestyle endeared him to both the common people and educated class. Biographical accounts refer to his prolonged years of teaching at the Akbarabadi mosque. It was here that he authored his monumental tafsir work.[35] In his Foreword Dehlawi introduces his tafsir as follows:

> The language of the Qur'ān is Arabic and an Indian cannot comprehend it as such. Therefore, as my father Shah Waliyullah has translated the Qur'ān into Persian, I thought to render it into comprehensible, simple and easy Indian language. By the Grace of Almighty Allah, I completed it in 1205H. Some points should be kept in mind before reading the translation: The first one is that it is not a word- to - word translation because Urdu and Arabic are two different languages in their approach of grammar and usage. The second point is that the language of the translation is not rhetorical but simple and commonly used so that everyone can comprehend it. The title of the work is *Mudih al-*

---

[35] 'Azami, *Tadhkirah Mufassirin*, 199.

> *Qur'ān.* This title is introductory and the year of
> its completion is 1205H.[36]

It is important to locate the tafsir in a circumstantial setting. Generally, Indian Muslims' link with the Qur'ān often bordered on storytelling and ritualistic practices that had no bearing on its life-enriching message. The myth factor was a distinguishing trait largely drawn from their centuries-old exposure to Hinduism. It vitiated the simple presentation of *tawhid* and the clear teachings of the Qur'ān. In response to these deviant beliefs, Dehlawi's translation offered renewed hope for Muslims to connect with the authentic expression of Islam through its foundational sources.

Raziul Islam Nadvi has made some thoughtful comments about Dehlawi's linguistic competence. For him, the choice of words used by Dehlawi is accurate, precise and purposeful. By the same token, the translation steers away from the pedantic expressions and embellished stylistic usage. Not surprisingly, therefore, context is given preference over the literal meanings which otherwise tend to mar the aesthetic beauty, and more importantly, the literary charm contained in the sacred text. This approach, however, does not suggest an arbitrary translation adopted by Dehlawi. On the contrary, he is sensitive to semantic structures and cautiously presents a translation that is faithful in form and meaning of the sacred text.[37]

A word-to-word translation requires further explanation. More often than not a literal translation fails to capture the essence of the divine text. This point is pressed home by Abdur Raheem Kidwai that translators (in this case, Urdu translators) "do not adequately prepare readers mentally to approach the Qur'ān." Likewise, grammatical and syntactic structures do not often correspond with the source language (Arabic) and target language (Urdu). As a result, the Qur'ānic terminology and allusions may be compromised for a rigidly literal translation. Another inadequacy by translators is the lack of naturalness of expression. Safi Kaskas

---

[36] Cited in Nazeer Ahmad Ab. Majeed (ed.), *Qur'ān Interpretation: A Critical Study* (Aligarh, 2019), 3.
[37] Ibid.

echoes a similar view: "They (exegetes) ignore the fact that translated material sound natural and are readily understood by readers. These include word order, sentence length, idiomatic phrases and figurative expressions. Added to these positive features is the use of common words that has a direct appeal to readers. Therefore, outdated modes of expressions add an extra strain to fluency of the text."[38]

Keeping in mind the period when *Mudih al-Qur'ān* was written, the laudatory comments by later translators are a testimony to its linguistic richness. For example, Shaykh al-Hind Mahmud al-Hasan (d.1920) made the following remarks about the translation:

> Shah Sahib's usage of colloquial language is considered unparalleled with regard to the very few changes and alterations (in the sequence of words according to the sequence of the Qur'ān.

Obviously, modes of expression change according to the needs of the time. In sum, the translation considered to reflect streaks of divine inspiration is an easy-to-comprehend work.[39] In terms of supplementary notes, Dehlawi provides insightful comments in context of the Qur'ānic verses. He does not take recourse to academic sophistry to support his viewpoint, which in many instances characterises the Qur'ānic contributions of renowned scholars who were his contemporaries. Instead, his incisive analysis bears the hallmarks of the Waliyullah tradition based on a deep study of early tafsirs.[40] Translations are human endeavours influenced by environmental factors, individual predispositions and intellectual insights. It is erroneous to assume that a definitive, error-free translation/tafsir is available for readers throughout the centuries. Sectarian prejudice is a contributing factor to this assumption. In a similar vein, *Mudih*

---

[38] Safi Kaskas and David Hungerford, *The Qur'ān with Reference to the Bible* (Fairfax, 2016), xxxiii-xxxix.

[39] Mahmud-al-Hasan's Urdu translation is discussed in *Tafsir-e- Uthmāni*, vol. 1 (Azaadville, 1999), 17-42.

[40] Ghazi, *Islamic Renaissance in South Asia*, 180-1.

al-Qur'ān suffers from several blemishes. The critical reappraisal of this translation/tafsir points out to Dehlawi's choice of archaic and unfamiliar words, ostensibly to reach out to the Hindu community for understanding the Qur'ān. Whatever the plausible explanation, this blemish has not diminished interest in the translation. The influence of Isra'ilite traditions is also found in this tafsir. Reliance on far-fetched historical accounts to explain the Qur'ānic events is problematic on two counts. First, the Qur'ān is primarily focused on moral lessons drawn from these events. Second, its universal message transcends these embellished accounts from a source that is contentious as well as hagiographical.[41]

Raziul Islam Nadvi draws the readers' attention to the positive impressions by eminent scholars. Their lavish praise for *Mudih al-Qur'ān* is illustrative of its distinctive features: linguistic finesse, rhetorical beauty and literary excellence. According to Sayyid Abul Hasan Ali Nadwi, the translation "excels many giant scholars such as Raghib Isfahani and Zamakhshari."[42]

The timeline associated with the tafsir brings to the fore its widespread popularity over two centuries across the sectarian line. Consider the number of editions after Dehlawi's demise in 1815. In 1829 the first edition was published in Kolkata. The city was the hub of religious and cultural activities during British colonial rule. More interesting is the popularity of the tafsir in the far-flung regions like West Bengal in relation to Delhi, the metropolis of the Mughal rule which was already in the throes of terminal decline. Another motivation for the several editions of the tafsir is the missionary factor. In 1876, this edition was published with a Preface by Thomas P. Hughes, author of *Dictionary of Islam*. A priest by profession his contributions to Islamic studies had an evangelical thrust. In other words, the missionaries played a pivotal role in the Orientalist project under the patronage of British imperialism.

The tafsir has seen several editions in its revised forms. Taj

---

[41] Majeed, *Qur'ān Interpretation*, 12-3.
[42] Ibid, 5.

Company was instrumental in bringing out several editions with improved formats over the last decades. Likewise, the translation of the tafsir has appeared in several regional languages including Pushto.[43]

Belonging to the Waliyullah tradition, Shah Rafi'uddin's Urdu translation is recognised for its lucid style in terms of brevity of expression and idiomatic usage. Several scholars have preferred his translation over 'Abdul Qadir's tafsir. However, it has not gained popularity or built a scholarly base other than being consulted for sectarian purpose.

In the domain of the surah perspective, Rafi'uddin has made commendable contributions. His stylistic charm and linguistic finesse have enriched his commentary, particularly Surah Al-Nur. Shah 'Abdul 'Aziz was greatly impressed by his younger brother's deep study of the Qur'ān and his exposition of themes contained in the surah.

In Surah Al-Baqarah, Rafi'uddin categorises its contents along thematic lines. For example, *tawhid* is given prominence and is linked to the historical events mentioned in the surah. Also the theory of abrogation is extensively dealt with under the rubric of juristic rulings. Like other exegetes, Rafi'uddin examines the *muqatta'āt* in relation to the subject matter of the surah. His thoughtful comments are suggestive of his consummate ability to blend the classical interpretations with his independent reflections. In contrast, other exegetes have ventured to extrapolate the significance of the *muqatta'āt* in this context with no desirable results.[44]

Many scholars and Islamic movements trace their intellectual lineage to the Waliyullah tradition. This distinctive feature is closely examined in the volume. The contours that shaped the subcontinental attitudes to Islamic authenticity are best represented in the tafsir genre. Regardless of their ideological affiliations, the tafsirs reflect in more ways than one the underpinnings of *Mudih al-Qur'ān*. These works are examined

---

[43] Ibid., 3-4.
[44] See Shah Rafi'uddin, *Al-Qur'ān al-Karim* (Lahore, 2000).

through the prism of affinity to the Waliyullah movement. For example, Sayyid Ahmad Khan, founder of Aligarh Muslim University sought to advance a rational interpretation of the Qur'ān which drew the ire of traditional scholars. However, the Deoband school of thought paralleled their Qur'ānic contributions to the reformist vision of Waliyullah and his illustrious family. The Barelwi movement articulated their *tasawwuf*-oriented exploration of the Qur'ānic message through popular practices. In contrast, the Ahl i-Hadith were vociferous in their censure of *taqlid* which they considered a deviance from the *salaf* path. Again, the reformist vision of Waliyullah and by extension the tafsir contribution of Dehlawi was invoked to formulate their respective ideological orientations. In a similar strain, the political activist exegetes like Ubaidullah Sindhi (d. 1944) and Abul Kalam Azad (d.1958) drew their inspiration from these scholarly works. Overall, the decisive influence of the Waliyullah movement continues to map out the scholarly tradition in the subcontinent.

Contemporaneous Qur'ānic Contributions

The Waliyullah family dominated the tafsir landscape for almost a hundred years. Their academic pedigree was constructed on two levels: i) reconstruction of the Muslim society and ii) reaching out to the masses through their respective tafsir efforts. The widespread influence of the Waliyullah tradition also produced commentators of eminence. These celebrated figures included Qadi Thana'ullah Pānipati (d. 1820). A student of Waliyullah he positioned himself as an amalgam of scholarship and *tasawwuf.*

The multivolume *Tafsir i-Mazhari* written in chaste Arabic is dedicated to his spiritual guide, Mirza Jan i- Janan,[45] a notable Naqshbandi shaykh. This work was written in the fraught backdrop of Sunni-Shi'ah polemics in the Awadh principality. Additionally, the Shi'ite influence[46] under the patronage of the

---

[45] Wael Hallaq and Donald Little (eds.), *Islamic Studies: Presented to Charles C. Adams* (Leiden, 1991), 14-20.
[46] Ibid., 15.

Nawabs posed a great challenge to the established status of the mainstream Islamic thought in this region.

Before discussing Pānipati's works it will be helpful to determine his readership and the purpose of his writing in Persian and Arabic. His tafsir was produced in Arabic for the 'ulama whereas his Persian works were presumably written for the general readership.[47] Pānipati maintained a rigorously scholarly approach by drawing extensively from the contributions of previous exegetes to support his independent views. Yet he was undaunted in questioning the authoritative positions on various theological issues and in giving free expression to his own views. In a specific sense, he established a superior position for the 'ulama within the Muslim community by citing particular verses that ostensibly referred to their religious authority.[48] This collective obligation by the Muslim community was an explicit endorsement on the role of the 'ulama.

For Pānipati, the reconstruction of Muslim society through the renewal and revival paradigm (*tajdid*) was imperative as envisioned by the Mujaddid and Waliyullah. However, the sociopolitical setting in his times distinctly pointed out to the almost disintegration of Muslim authority. The collective will of the Muslim community had reached its lowest ebb with Islamic learning plummeting to levels of mediocrity. Under these bleak circumstances, the urgency of exercising *ijtihād* according to Pānipati was non-negotiable. His monumental tafsir in twelve volumes brought into sharp relief new methodological approaches that underpinned the timeless message of the sacred text. In this respect, Waliyullah's *Al-Fawz al-Kabir* had a decisive influence on his formulation of Qur'ānic perspectives. According to Alvi, Pānipati "[tried] to maintain a balance between tradition (*riwāyat*) and understanding (*dirāyat*) of the Qur'ānic text and between exegesis (*tafsir*) and interpretation (*ta'wil*). His Qur'ānic hermeneutics was embedded in authoritative sources and

---

[47] Ibid., 21.
[48] Ibid., 18.

principles of *ijtihād*."[49]

Prominent Features of *Tafsir i-Mazhari*

Pānipati's extensive study of the classical commentaries is incorporated in his work.[50] Therefore, the citation of relevant sources allows for a critical assessment of his views. Interestingly, he references a variety of Islamic disciplines that include *Fiqh, kalām*, linguistics and *sui* texts.[51] Through these sources readers have a clearer idea about his varying positions on subsidiary issues (*furuhāt*). As a Hanafi scholar, Pānipati presents legal arguments to support the school's *Fiqh* position on particular Qur'ānic issues. In this process, several verses yield variant meanings and interpretations; therefore, *ikhtilāf* is unavoidable. Yet there are instances when his independent views are at variance with the established Hanafi position, which is a strong indication of his inclination to the Waliyullah *i'tidāl* (balanced) line of thought.[52]

Pānipati also holds differing positions on abrogated verses. For him, the verse "There is no compulsion in religion" has a circumstantial context. The phrase 'no compulsion' is only applicable when unrest and turmoil cease to exist. As a corollary, fighting or armed resistance (*qitāl*) and *jihād* are essential to consolidate the corporate identity of Islam. This approach is indicative of his mastery over the *sirah* sources.

Like other exegetes, Pānipati's contribution to the *nazm* theory is illuminating. He cites the Bani Isra'il accounts to establish several linkages. First, Allah mentions his favours to mankind in general. As a Madinan revelation, it addresses the Jewish communities who were an educated class and were familiar with the previous scriptural text (Torah). The relevance of these verses thus have a direct bearing on them on two counts: i) they should acknowledge Allah's favours in general, and ii) their

---

[49] Ibid., 23.

[50] A comparative analysis of *Tafsir i-Mazhari* is elucidated in Mahmud al-Hasan 'Arif, *Tadhkirah Qādi Muhammad Thanā'Allah Pānipati* (Lahore, 1995), 259-83.

[51] Ibid., 347-60.

[52] 'Azami, *Tadhkirah Mufassirin*, 205, 209.

unconditional acceptance of the divine message revealed to the Prophet would have a positive impact on the Arab tribes who were not acquainted with the Jewish trials and tribulations which they had faced during the Messengership of Prophet Musa (peace be upon him).[53]

Mention has been made of Pānipati's spiritual affiliation to the Naqshbandi order. It is, therefore, not surprising when he explores particular Qur'ānic verses in a *tasawwuf* perspective. In this light, the term *taqwā* is explained as follows:

> Purification of the heart in *sui* terminology in turn invests an individual aspiring the path of *suluk* with *wilāyat* (close proximity). Essentially, he has to be physically pure, abstain from doubtful things and also shun all forms of prohibitions. This is *taqwā*.[54]

In sum, Pānipati's significant contributions continue to shape the intellectual horizons in the subcontinent.

Among the descendants of Waliyullah who left indelible imprints on the tafsir tradition is Muhammad Ishaq, grandson of 'Abdul 'Aziz Dehlawi. His specialisation areas were tafsir and hadith which he taught uninterruptedly for sixty years in Delhi and Makkah. His circle of students included scholars who would later systematise the hadith studies along ideological lines.[55]

Nawab Qutbuddin Khan Dehlawi was a notable student of Shah Ishaq.[56] He acquired proficiency in the sciences of *iqh* and hadith from the 'ulama of *haramayn* (Makkah and Madinah). He wrote a number of books of which *Mazāhir i-Haq* is considered a notable commentary of the widely recognised hadith collection *Mishkāt al-Masābih*.

---

53 Ibid., 216.

54 Ibid., 217.

55 Ghazi, *Islamic Renaissance in South Asia*, 245.

56 Shah Muhammad Ishaq's illustrious career in hadith studies was further advanced by notable scholars who made their mark in the *tajdidi* tradition. See Nadwi, *Saviours of Islamic Spirit*, vol. 4, 260-1.

In the field of tafsir Qutbuddin Dehlawi authored *Jāmi'al-Tafāsir*. According to 'Azami, only one volume was available which gives a sketchy detail about his methodology.[57] Nevertheless, the distinguishing features of the tafsir, to a large extent, are similar to the *ma'thur* genre. In regard to *nazm*, there is no evidence of the linear connection between preceding and succeeding surahs (eg. surahs Yasin and Al-Fatir). Dehlawi makes passing references with no particular formulation in mind. However, two redeeming aspects make the tafsir a useful contribution. Dehlawi discusses the stylistic approach of the Qur'ānic in terms of repetition (*takrār*) to reinforce the Qur'ānic presentation of the cosmos. He presses home the fact that the natural phenomena are indisputable proof of a Creator, which cannot be denied by any rational being.[58] These repetitive verses illustrate the inexorable patterns of divine authority.

Exhortation (*maw'izat*) has a special place in Dehlawi's Qur'ānic perspectives. His critique of the prevalent rites and practices deemed as *bid'ah* in shari'ah terminology is an accurate indicator of the Muslim community's deviance from pristine Islam. In a similar vein, he castigates the 'molvis' - a generic term for the 'ulama who were steeped in the malpractice of distorted interpretation (*ta'wil i-bātila*) of the sacred text.[59] Overall, his sensitive soul balked at the growing rise of the anti-shari'ah tendencies.

Dehlawi' tafsir is largely based on Hanafi *Fiqh*. This is quite understandable if we have to consider his line of thought in his commentary of *Mishkāt*. A noteworthy feature of his tafsir is the copious citation of views from the Waliyullah family's tafsirs.[60] In sum, the academic pedigree of the Waliyullah tradition is discernible for the last 250 years among almost all tafsirs produced in the subcontinent.

---

[57] 'Azami, *Tadhkirah Mufassirin*, 231-2.
[58] Ibid., 234-5.
[59] Ibid., 235.
[60] Ibid., 237.

Transnational Scholarship

To speak of Muslim scholarship in relation to a specific region is somewhat misleading as it seems to suggest the existence of a regionally-defined entity. According to Peter Hartung, the mobility among Muslim scholars was a connector for transmitting and acquiring knowledge. The *rihlah*[61] (travel) factor, to a large extent, developed the transnational character of scholarship over the centuries. Another circumstance which consolidated translocality was the affiliation of scholars to *sui* orders.

The subcontinental connection of Qur'ānic scholarship was preceded by the proliferation of hadith studies in the Hijaz. It was Waliyullah, however, who drew upon the sources of hadith literature during his sojourn in Hijaz. Scholars from the Muslim world who settled there also transmitted the knowledge of Qur'ānic *'ulum*. Waliyullah was not immune to these influences and his interpretive reading had a widespread influence in the subcontinent. Likewise, transnational scholarship connected the works of the Yemeni exegete, Muhammad 'Ali Shawkani (d. 1834) through the literary efforts of Nawab Siddiq Hasan Khan (d. 1890).[62] By this time, the rise of Salafiyyah[63] had made its mark in the Arab world. In the subcontinent, a parallel development shaped the formation of the Ahl i-Hadith movement. In this way, the exchange of ideological ideas and the production of writings with a *Salai* slant was vigorously introduced in the subcontinent. Apart from the polemics that struck root in the sectarian discourse, the writings of Yemeni scholars in particular were positively received. It must be borne in mind that the works under study were contemporaneous with *Mudih al-Qur'ān*. Methodological approaches varied considerably and so did the

---

[61] On the *rihlah* literature, see Muhammad Zubayr Siddiqui, *Hadith Literature: Its Origins, Development and Special Features* (Cambridge, 1993), 40-2.

[62] A brief overview of Siddiq Khan's literary contributions appears in Andreas Gorke, *Tafsir and Islamic Intellectual History*, 355.

[63] For a critical evaluation of the Salafiyyah in the twentieth century, see Abdul Kader Choughley, *Islamic Resurgence: Sayyid Abul Hasan Ali Nadwi and his Contemporaries* (New Delhi, 2011), 62-75.

interpretations. These variant readings were influenced by sociopolitical and ideological factors. However, common to these commentaries was the articulation of Islamic authenticity derived from *'ulum al-Qur'ān*. Shawkani's *Fath al-Qadir*[64] is emblematic of this trend.

The study of Shawkani's major work is framed from the spectrum of ideological interpretation. Dhahabi treats it as a Zaydi commentary[65] on account of the predominance of the sect in Yemen. Additionally, Saudi Arabia has promoted this work presumably for its Wahhabi leanings. Another view suggesting its pre-modern character is the rejection of *taqlid*. A closer study of the tafsir certainly contradicts these impressions.

Fath al-Qadir by all accounts is a traditional commentary[66] structured along well-defined hermeneutical lines. Shawkani embraces the polyvalent readings to support his viewpoints. He cites a whole range of opinions of exegetical authorities to critically engage readers with the function and scope of *ikhtilāf*. Occasionally when he deems an issue important does he bolster his arguments. Furthermore, two other aspects reveal his hermeneutical method. His non- conformist approach (*ghayr taqlid*) does on occasion border on polemics, which is a response to the prevalent *shirk*-laden practices in Yemen.[67] In the main, he avoids partisanship with a particular school of thought if the *salaf* authority is not invoked.

Semantic structure is another hermeneutical tool Shawkani employs to strengthen his viewpoint. Although he upholds the principle of literal meaning (*dhāhir al-ma'na*) as opposed to allegorical interpretation, the semantic dimensions suggest an inclusive position. The following verse is illustrative of the semantic meaning he employs:

---

[64] Gorke, *Tafsir and Islamic Intellectual History*, 326.

[65] Ibid.

[66] Ibid., 329.

[67] Ibid., 330. *Shirk*-laden practices were more prevalent in the subcontinent on account of the exaggerated veneration of saints (*awliyā*). Waliyullah, too, condemned these syncretic practices in his major writings.

> *Be kind to parents, and the near kinsmen, and to*
> *orphans, and to the needy, and to the neighbour who is*
> *a stranger, and to the companion at your side (al-sāhib*
> *al-junb).*
>
> (4:36).

Shawkani explains:

> It is not unlikely that all of these opinions are
> included in the meaning of the verse, and several
> more. It can mean anyone who can aptly be
> described as being a companion at your side, such
> as someone who is at your side in the acquisition
> of knowledge, or when learning a craft or
> engaging in trade, and so forth.[68]

Hadith studies, without doubt, is also Shawkani's forte. He contextualises the *ahādith* that have a direct correlation to historical accounts. For example, the verses relating to the campaign of Tabuk is built around the hadith narrative.[69] Shawkani scrutinises the *asbāb* in order to present an alternative reading of the incident. In the light of the conflicting opinions, he takes recourse to the *sirah* sources. In his discussion of the verses, the multiple meanings are meant to determine their intent and rationale. All in all, Shawkani displays his linguistic competence within the broader framework of the hadith literature.

Shawkani's commentary has elicited positive responses from reformists like Rashid Rida whose pioneering tafsir has been enthusiastically received in the *salai* circles. It is a moot point to debate the term 'salai' in respect of Shawkani's academic credentials. His tafsir in a specific sense is non-traditional because it does not always accept the *salaf* viewpoint as authoritative. Likewise, his non-madhab stance indirectly challenges the

---

[68] Ibid., 337.

[69] For a detailed account on the Tabuk expedition, see Abul Hasan Ali Nadwi, *Muhammad Rasulullah* (Lucknow, 1979), 345-64. Cf. Adil Salahi, *Muhammad: Man and Prophet* (Leicester, 2002), 696-712.

notion of Salafiyyah. In different perspectives, the intellectual history of the tafsir has attracted scholarly interest from 'ulama of the subcontinent.[70] Joanna Pink's perceptive comments about the commentary as a production of modernity is revealing:

> *Fath al-Qadir* is neither a 'modern' commentary on the Qur'ān, nor is it part of the pre- modern tradition of the tafsir. The question of it modernity does not make sense. Clear- cut categorisation and periodisation might have a certain analytical value in the study of tafsirs, but they do have their limits, and Shawkani's tafsir is a case in point.[71]

Tafsir tradition in West Africa

The intellectual tradition of tafsir in West Africa centres on two spheres: oral transmission and the written word. More often than not the prominence of oral transmission in the public space served as an outreach programme to familiarise the masses with the essential teachings of the Qur'ān. To this end, the *majālis* featured conspicuously among the 'ulama class. The amirs of the various empires patronised the *majālis* and over time it became an elite tradition.[72]

Our focus is on the *tajdidi* contribution by Usman dan Fodio (d. 1817). His *jihād* efforts were primarily aimed at the establishment of an Islamic caliphate for the promulgation of the shari'ah. Common to other *mujaddids* in the far-flung countries of the Muslim world, was dan Fodio's tireless *da'wah* to promote Islam in its pristine form. In effect, these reforms posed a threat to the syncretic practices among West African tribes and clans. However, the founding of a caliphate in North Nigeria with Sokoto as its capital[73] eclipsed the authority of the amirs who

---

[70] Gorke, *Tafsir and Islamic Intellectual History*, 355.
[71] Ibid., 356.
[72] Ibid., 382-4.
[73] The *tajdidi* efforts of Dan Fodio are examined in Abdur Rahman Doi, *'Uthmān Dan*

maintained the status quo regarding the prevalent cultural rituals among Muslim communities.

Dan Fodio's intellectual contributions advanced the cause of Islamic revival. His brother, 'Abdullahi played a collaborative role in shaping the religious environment of the Sokoto caliphate. A brilliant scholar and strategist, 'Abdullahi wrote his famous tafsir *Diyā al-Ta'wil* in 1815-6. Among his prolific writings the tafsir "[contains] remarks on rhetoric and grammar, an examination of the positions of the various Sunni schools on most legal issues and short outlines of the theological implications of some Qur'ānic verses."[74]

The composition of the tafsir has a contextual significance. It attempts to "[revive] and synthesise the multidisciplinary corpus of tafsir studies transmitted by classical exegetes and also trace the doctrines of the mainstream Sunni schools (*madhabs*) to the foundational source, the Qur'ān. Equally important, it aims to strengthen the relevance and influence of the 'ulama in a local context."[75]

A brief survey of the sources cited by 'Abdullahi suggests his proficiency in the Qur'ānic genre. There are definite traces of the Maliki scholars' exegetical works which were widely used in the Maliki region. Although there is no evidence to suggest that the *Diyii* is an original work, 'Abdullahi's tafsir had a precise agenda: "to re-elaborate in one single work three authoritative syntheses of traditional exegetical knowledge, each related to the principal domains of tafsir: philology and linguistics, dialectic theology and law."[76]

It is generally held that Suyuti's *Jalālayn* and its *hawāshiyah* (annotations) were the main sources of authority in West Africa. This assumption is incorrect if we have to examine the sources cited in *Diyā*. These works cover the principal domains of tafsir consulted by the 'ulama - a reaffirmation of their scholarly credentials. Moreover, the *rihlah* aspect was synonymous with

---

Fodio, The Grand Mujaddid of Africa (Pretoria, 1998), 113-4.
[74] Gorke, *Tafsir and Islamic Intellectual History*, 399.
[75] Ibid.
[76] Ibid., 401.

transnational scholarship and contributed to the popularisation of tafsir.[77]

Conclusion

The Waliyullah family's contribution to the tafsir studies had far-reaching implications for scholars and Islamic institutions sharing a similar vision. Three 'offshoots' were intellectually connected to the family's mission statement: Dar al-'Ulum Deoband, Nadwat al-'Ulama and Aligarh Muslim University. Despite their different ideological orientations, their singular contributions to Qur'ānic studies have opened up new pathways to interpret and assimilate the essence, wisdom and teachings of the sacred text. The following chapters explore these strands of Qur'ānic thought within the ambit of ideological/sectarian affiliations.

---

[77] Ibid., 389-92.

Chapter 2

Deobandi Contributions to Qur'ānic Studies

The history of Dar al-'Ulum Deoband[1] (hereafter Deoband) is inseparable from its Qur'ānic contributions since its establishment in 1866. Co-founded by Imam Muhammad Qasim Nanautwi (d.1880),[2] its thrust areas were primarily the restoration of the Islamic *'ulum* patterned in a structured form. The erudite scholar himself benefitted considerably from Delhi College and was thus familiar with emergent methodologies of learning and instruction. Therefore, his mission statement of providing quality-oriented Islamic education must be understood in the context of continuity (*tasalsul*) and change (*taghayyur*). The vast corpus of material relating to Deoband reveals the missionary spirit of Qasim Nanautwi: a well-developed syllabus based on the modified *Dars i-Nizāmi,* which was rooted in an *islāhi* ethos.[3]

The scholarly profile of the institution is a testament to its remarkable achievements in the diverse fields of Islamic learning. Since its establishment Deoband has produced 'ulama of international renown and reformist movements like the Tabligh Jama'at[4] whose global footprint is unprecedented in modern history. In the field of political activism, Mahmud al-Hasan (d. 1920) popularly known as Shaykh al-Hind[5] represents another dimension of Deoband's tireless struggle for the freedom of the country against British rule. In Shaykh al-Hind's charismatic personality the 'alim-activist amalgam comes to the fore.

In sum the reformist mission Deoband is succinctly expressed by Metcalf:

---

[1] Sayyid Mahbub Rizwi, *Tiirikh Dār al-'Ulum Deoband,* 2 vols. (Deoband, 1992.

[2] Manazir Ahsan Gilani, *Sawāni Qāsimi,* 2 vols. (Multan, 1427H).

[3] Ibid. A comprehensive coverage of the *Dars i-Nizāmi* appears in the earlier writings of Deobandi scholars.

[4] See Abul Hasan Ali Nadwi, *Life and Mission of Mawlana Muhammad Ilyas: Founder of Tabligh Jamā'at* (Lucknow, 1980).

[5] Syed Muhammad Mian, *The Prisoners of Malta: Asirān i-Malta* (New Delhi, 2005), 1-84.

The Deobandis epitomised the pattern of many religious movements in the nineteenth century that rejected the customary style of religious practice in favour of emulating the practice of an authentic text or an idealised historical period. All such movements fostered a sense of cultural pride and self- esteem. The Deobandi emphasis was on the centrality of the religious law, an emphasis that seemed a particularly effective response to the implicit or explicit challenge of the alien culture. Based on revelation and cherished over the centuries, the Law was deemed the most fundamental guide to the faith. It was, moreover, susceptible to generalisation by carefully defined rules, a characteristic that made it analogous to the British legal system. Muslim culture was thus understood to be the equivalent of British culture in its ability to generate a coherent and inclusive system and superior to that culture in divine sanction and scope.[6]

The Deobandi contribution to Qur'ānic studies by Muhammad Mushtaq Tijarwi illustrates the institution's global presence in the Islamic resurgence discourse. Tijarwi has succinctly discussed the visionary spirit of Deoband against the backdrop of British colonialism. Its founder, Muhammad Qasim Nanautwi had envisioned an institution of higher Islamic learning which was committed to the preservation of the Islamic legacy under changed political circumstances.

Tijarwi has explored the multifaceted dimensions, albeit briefly, of Deoband's scope and function. It was not   a replication of an

---

[6] Barbara Metcalf, *Islamic Revival in British India: Deoband, 1860-1900* (Karachi, 1982), 253. This comment does not suggest that Deoband replicated the British system of education. Rather, it crafted its own methodology while cognisant of the prevalent educational systems.

existing madrasah that was reliant on the patronage of royalty. Nor was it a seminary which was synonymous with the existing theological sites of learning. Rather, Deoband maintained a distinctive presence as an institution promoting a revolutionary system of education rooted in a particular ethos. In contrast, British colonialism in line with its policy of divide and rule had ruptured the prevalent educational system in which holistic knowledge was offered. To counter its Eurocentric agenda, Deoband devised an educational system that also accommodated non-Muslim students. It was not uncommon for these students to learn the Islamic disciplines *('ulum)* alongside secular subjects on the campus. A noteworthy feature of the nascent institution was its sense of financial independence. It promoted the concept of donation from businessmen and ordinary people. The founder strongly believed that an institution unencumbered by budgetary constraints had the choice to design its own syllabus. The independent and democratic spirit of the institution was embodied in the eight principles which formed its constitution. For Nanautwi, public participation or *shurā* lent greater weight to its mass contact appeal.[7] For this reason he encouraged donation from ordinary people in a show of solidarity and acknowledgement of their supportive role to the madrasah.

Tijarwi has made some important points about the global profile of Deoband. Of interest to us is its Qur'ānic contributions. In its early years plans were already conceived for the promotion of Qur'ān studies. These academies were established for the purpose of disseminating the message and teachings of the Qur'ān. They also reflected the institution's broad spectrum of Qur'ān-based activities. In this perspective, the syllabus incorporated classical tafsirs like *Baydāwi* and *Jalālayn* (which are discussed elsewhere in the Tijarwi's volume). Interestingly, there was no fixed notion of teaching a particular tafsir; instead, curriculum changes entailed a review of tafsirs as prescribed texts. In more ways than one, Deoband attempted to steer clear from polemical literature as it

---

[7] Ziya-al-Hasan Faruqi, *The Deoband School and the Demand for Pakistan* (Lahore, 1976), 26-7.

would undermine its primary role as a facilitator of higher Islamic learning.

One of the remarkable features of the Deoband is the production of Qur'ānic literature. No other Islamic institution has to its credit a plethora of tafsirs and works of Qur'ānic relevance. In the subcontinent, its Qur'ānic contribution is more pronounced. It has been an unenviable task for Tijarwi to provide details of prominent works dating back to the early 1900s. His work, however, is a laudable contribution to the growing interest of Qur'ānic studies in the subcontinent. [8]

Mahmud al-Hasan (Shaykh al-Hind)

A brilliant exponent of Qur'ānic and hadith studies, Shaykh al-Hind produced an Urdu translation of the sacred text for a Muslim readership of the early twentieth century. No doubt, *Mudih al-Qur'ān* was a pioneering work in the Waliyullah tradition which has had an enduring influence on major tafsir works. However, the need for a simplified, easy-to-understand translation was synonymous with the evolution of Urdu as a vehicle of Islamic reformist thought. Modes of expression undergo significant changes and *Mudih al-Qur'ān* was no exception. Its colloquial style in the early twentieth century became outdated and in many instances incomprehensible. The task of reconstructing its language for a different target audience was daunting challenge. To this end, Shaykh al-Hind produced his *Mudih al-Furqān*[9] which retained the essence of *Mudih al-Qur'ān*. Likewise, the concise marginal notes (*hawāshi*) were simplified.

Mudih al-Furqān was expanded by Shabbir Ahmad Usmani (d. 1953),[10] an accomplished scholar and student of Shaykh al-Hind. Its popularity (*Tafsir i-'Uthmāni*) can be gauged from its

---

[8] Muhammad Mushtaq Tijarwi, *Fuzalā i-Deoband ki Qur'āni Khidmāt* (Aligarh, 2020), 13-20. Cf. Mubeen Saleem Nadwi Azhari, *Model Syllabus for Teaching Qur'ān in the Madrasahs* (Aligarh, 2019), 168-208.

[9] See Shabbir Ahmad Uthmani, *Tafsir i-'Uthmāni*, vol.1 (Azaadville, 1999), 4.

[10] Ibid., 14-6.

widespread distribution by the Saudi Arabia government at the recommendation of Shaykh Nadwi on account of its brevity of expression and concise marginal notes.

Muhammad Wali Razi (d. 2019) who was responsible for the improved version of *Tafsir i-'Uthmāni,* incorporated explanatory headings and restructured the explanatory notes in accordance with the norms of modern style of publication. His elucidation of the salient features of the tafsir is reproduced hereunder:

- Despite it being concise, it is so comprehensive in conveying the import and meaning of the Qur'ān that in most places it makes voluminous books of *tafsir* dispensable or redundant to the student of the Qur'ān.

- The interrelation of the verses of the Qur'ān is so clear that the person who reads the translation continuously does not even perceive any gap in this interrelation.

- Whenever there is an apparent ambiguity between the verses of the Qur'ān, they are verified and the ambiguity removed in a very simple manner.

- An unequivocal answer has been given to the objections and misgivings of the contemporary era. In most of these places he has provided logical proof in his impressive style.

- Wherever there are several explanatory opinions, he has chosen the preferred opinion and given the reasons for this preference.

- In most places he has made such intricate intellectual references for the 'ulama, whereby he has provided a solution to the expected difficulties.

- He has paid so much attention to simplicity in language and conformity to modern modes of expression that despite sixty years having elapsed since the completion of this task, it is as though this *tafsir* was written today.[11]

Two English translations of this important tafsir have relevance for South Asian Muslims.

Shaykh al-Hind was an eminent Deobandi scholar and an activist committed to the freedom of India from the British rule. Also known as the prisoner of Malta he was instrumental in the establishment of Jami'a Millia Islamia in New Delhi. Shabbir Ahmad Usmani (d. 1949) was a renowned hadith scholar of Deoband. He participated actively in the establishment of Pakistan. His pioneering contribution to Qur'ānic studies is his enduring legacy. The Urdu translation was completed by Shaykh al-Hind and its accompanying commentary by Usmani.

'Translation of the translations' is a sub-genre of Qur'ānic studies. Common to all these versions is the advancement of divergent schools of thought *(maslaks).* Kidwai offers an overview of the subcontinental production of translation that focus on or rather vindicate the "supremacy of the particular school *Fiqh* which they represent." These productions are time-bound attempts in their circumstantial settings. However, their wide-ranging popularity in the West and countries like South Africa is an indicator of the presence of the fragmented Muslim communities along sectarian lines. Kidwai explains:

> The English translator, Ashfaq Ahmad does not provide any background information about its Urdu version. In fact, his lack-lustre translation compounded by his unfamiliarity with idiomatic English baffles rather than enlightens readers in their study of the Qur'ān.
>
> Worse, is Ahmad's unintelligible translation of tafsir comments as outlined by the Urdu translators. Verbosity, pedantic embellishments are self-explanatory. In sum, *The Noble Qur'ān* is mired by the translator's interpolation of his

---

[11] Ibid., 6.

whimsical views in a posthumous publication.

The revised editions of *The Noble Qur'ān* were subsequently undertaken to redeem its poor translation. In 1997 Kidwai translated the Urdu afresh in a partial translation published by Islamic Academy (UK). The Dar al- 'Ulum Azaadville (South Africa) produced a multivolume revised and expanded version of the translation. Source material from Arabic *tafāsir* was incorporated, making it an independent translation of the existing work.[12]

Another institution, Jami'ah Islamia established in Dabhel (Surat), enlisted the teaching expertise of eminent scholars like Anwar Shah Kashmiri, 'Allamah Shabbir Ahmad Usmani, thus enhancing its image as a satellite madrasah of Deoband. Saharanpur and Dabhel in certain respects were epicentres of the Qāsimi tradition.[13] The regional spread of Nanautwi's vision has thus come to have important significance.

Akhlaq Husayn Qāsimi

Mudih al-Qur'ān has made its mark in the last two centuries as a unique composition of tafsir in Urdu. It has served as a source of reference (*marja'*) for successive tafsirs in the subcontinent and the diaspora communities of the United Kingdom and United States of America. It is to the credit of Akhlaq Husayn Qāsimi that a revised version has added to its merit as an enduring piece of work.

Akhlaq Husayn's academic profile is remarkable in terms of Qur'ānic studies. His collaborative efforts with reputed scholars like Sa'eed Ahmad Dehlawi[14] who authored *Kashfur Rahmān* and insightful articles on other mufassirs' have earned him the coveted title of an exegete par excellence.

A well-documented exploration of *Mudih al-Qur'ān* illustrates its

---

[12] Choughley, *The Contributions of Abdur Raheem Kidwai*, 75-6.

[13] Abdul Qayyum Rajkoti, *Nuqush i-Buzurgān*, 2 vols. (Simlak, 2003). Cf. Muhammad Anzar Shah, *Naqsh i-Dawām: Hayāt i-Muhaddith Kashmiri* (Multan, 2006), 50-4.

[14] Ahmad Sa'eed Dehlawi was a noted scholar and political activist whose novel on Christianity, *Isabella* won recognition in comparative religious studies.

singular contribution to Qur'ānic studies. Akhlaq Husayn has detailed the timeline of the tafsir's production, linguistic features and comparative analysis with other contemporary tafsirs. Essentially, his *Mahāsin Mudih al-Qur'ān* is a supplementary volume to the revised translation. It represents an authoritative version of the scholarly efforts of Shah 'Abdul Qadir. All the previous grammatical errors and archaic words have been expunged to give it a more comprehensible form. Explanatory notes for archaic Urdu/Hindi words in the text provide clarity of meaning. The Shah's concise points listed as *fawā'id* are adequately discussed. Likewise, his independent (*ijtihādi*) views are contextualised around *ikhtilāfi* matters. It is a truism that an original work like *Mudih al-Qur'ān* contains original ideas which in several instances are at variance with the Waliyullah's Qur'ānic elucidation. Nevertheless, Akhlaq Husayn explores these *ikhtilāfi* dimensions within the Qur'ānic framework. In Chapter 1, mention is made of the Shah's inclination to incorporate some Isra'ilite traditions to support Qur'ānic anecdotes or accounts. By and large, these traditions have been critically examined by other exegetes. Akhlaq Husayn introduces a broad range of exegetical views in this regard thus enriching the function and scope of Isra'ilite traditions in the Qur'ānic discourse. Another contentious issue are the somewhat polemical overtones employed by several Qur'ānic scholars. The erudite mufassir has critiqued the sweeping generalisations made by a cohort of scholars whose avowed aim is to discredit the intrinsic merits of this great work which has survived the vagaries of time.[15] Its popularity extends to English translations with a strong Deobandi bias. Kidwai has offered perceptive comments on an English translation by the well-known scholar, Mufti Afzal Hoosen (d. 2018).

Essentially, this work is in the English version of Mahmudul Hasan and Shabbir Ahmad Usmani's *Tafsir-i Usmani* in Urdu, and hence a representative Deobandi interpretation of the

---

[15] See Tijarwi, *Fuzalā i-Deoband*, 27.

Qur'ān. It is worth adding that the *Tafsir-i Usmani* itself is actually an updated and expanded version of Shah Abdul Qadir's *Mudih al- Qur'ān*. Shah Abdul Qadir was an illustrious son of the renowned Islamic revivalist, Shah Waliullah, thus the pedigree of this work is impeccably sound, rooted deep into the mainstream Qur'ānic scholarship of the Indian subcontinent. This work has been published from Pakistan, underscoring as it does the depth and the geographical spread of the Deoband school.

More importantly, this work is characterised by several reader-friendly features which facilitate an easy access to the meaning and message of the Qur'ān to even those readers who possess no or little background knowledge of the Qur'ān. The translator's insertion of helpful authentic material within parentheses has made the study of the Qur'ān easy. In doing so, he has shed sufficient light on circumstantial setting and contextual information which resolves occasionally ambiguity arising out of pronominal shifts and ellipsis, explained most of the Qur'ānic allusions, metaphors, parables and also figurative expressions.[16]

Akhlaq Husayn has drawn upon the subject index from *Mudih al-Qur'ān* to outline the Shah's *ijtihādi* approach. Based on this revised edition, 202 topics are listed and cover themes such as *tawhid, shurā*, tabligh, spirituality, eschatology, creation of the universe, etc. The surahs and particular verses delineate the thrust of his Qur'ānic presentation.

According to Akhlaq Husayn, the Hasani family (reference to Shaykh Nadwi) had the honour of studying this pioneering tafsir

---

[16] Kidwai, *God's Word, Man's Interpretations*, 116-9.

at the time of the great reformer, Sayyid Ahmad Shahid (d. 1831).[17]

Mudih al-Qur'ān: An Assessment

It is an indisputable fact that the Qur'ānic studies/ tafsir output by Deobandi 'ulama has broadened the scope of interpreting the Word of Allah (*Kalām Allah*) in contextual settings. For the overwhelming majority of the Urdu tafsirs, the unbroken link is *Mudih al-Qur'ān*. Even the commentaries (*shuruhāt*) on classical tafsirs written by Deobandi 'ulama are identifiable markers of the Waliyullah tradition. Qur'ānic studies by contemporary scholars have also not deviated from the normative framework of *Mudih al-Qur'ān*. It will, therefore, be not incorrect to assume that the inspired (*ilhāmi*) nature of this outstanding tafsir is a reflection of the pioneering role of the Waliyullah family to the promotion of the sacred text.

Ubaidullah Sindhi

The normative articulation of mainstream tafsir (in this instance, *Mudih al-Qur'ān*) has not always been rigidly followed. Our focus is on a brilliant student of Shaykh al- Hind, Ubaidullah Sindhi (d. 1944)[18] who is considered a liberal religious figure, a political thinker and a revolutionary of the twentieth century. Though he was trained as an 'alim at Deoband he was able to break away from conventional religious thought which in many ways were shaped by his teacher and mentor Shaykh al-Hind, a political activist whose contribution to the freedom struggle of India against the British rule is documented in detail.[19] It was at his behest that Sindhi went into exile to Afghanistan to establish a

---

[17] Reference is made to Shaykh Nadwi's maternal great grandmother, Sayyidah Humayrah. See Akhalq Husayn Qāsimi, *'Ulama Deoband ki Tafsiri Khidmāt* (Deoband, n.d.), 53.

[18] For a biographical account on Sindhi, see Muhammad Hajjan Shaikh, *Mawlana Ubaid Allah Sindhi: A Revolutionary Scholar* (Islamabad, 1986).

[19] Ibid., 8-11. Cf. Farhat Tabassum, *Deoband Ulema's Movement for the Freedom of India* (New Delhi, 2006), 98-135.

semi-government with other leading political leaders. Interestingly, the government in exile was not established along confessional lines[20] and the varied responses to Islam's adaptability in public space dominated the political landscape during this turbulent period.

Crucial to our understanding of Sindhi's Qur'ānic hermeneutics is his sojourn in Russia, Turkey and Hijaz. In Russia, his short stay exposed him to the currents of Socialism and Communism[21] which he adapted to his vision of Islamic socialism, a counter response to Capitalism. In a similar vein, his four years stay abroad coincided with the dissolution of the Ottoman Caliphate and the rise of secularism rooted in democratic settings. Sindhi's admiration for the emerging political dispensation in a Muslim country[22] opened up new vistas of understanding a redesigned Islamic caliphate built around democratic principles. Previously his self-imposed exile in Afghanistan was a liberating experience from the shackles of traditionalism generally associated with the 'ulama world. In a specific sense, Afghanistan was on the cusp of modernism[23] and embraced radical social mores which were lauded by Sindhi. Finally, his political activities in the Hijaz were restrained as he was monitored by British intelligence. Political activism was curtailed; instead, he devoted his later years to teaching the Qur'ān and the writings of Waliyullah.[24]

Sindhi's return to India in 1939 was characterised by his less strident voice of political activism. His revolutionary ideas were received with mixed reaction. A small cadre of scholars,

---

[20] Shaikh, *Mawlana Ubaid Allah Sindhi*, 30-118.

[21] Curiously enough, Sindhi saw Communism as close to Islam, an anomaly that drew the condemnation of 'ulama. See Aziz Ahmad, *Islamic Modernism in India and Pakistan, 1857-1964* (London, 1967). Cf. Fazlur Rahman Ansari, *Communist Challenge to Islam* (Karachi, 2018). The author's critique of Communism is in stark contrast to Sindhi's endorsement of the ideological system.

[22] Sindhi advocated Turkey's embrace of secularism against the fraught backdrop of the dissolution of the Ottoman Caliphate. See Abul Hasan Ali Nadwi, *Western Civilisation Islam and Muslims* (Lucknow, 1974), 33-59.

[23] Ibid., 18-23. The account by Sindhi's associates offers revealing insights into the rise of modernism in a country like Afghanistan which paradoxically was steeped in economic backwardness.

[24] Shaikh, *Mawlana Ubaid Allah Sindhi,* 225-7.

intellectuals appreciated his interpretive reading of Waliyullah's sociopolitical thought while the majority of his co-religionists dismissed his eccentric views. Paradoxically, his alma mater branded him a deviant for his radical Qur'ānic views. All in all, Sindhi remains a controversial figure who represented a strand of multiple modernism in South Asia.

SherAli Tareen critically examines the revolutionary hermeneutics embedded in Sindhi's commentary of the Qur'ān in Urdu titled *Qur'ān i-Shu'ur i-Inqilāb* (The Qur'ān's Conscience of Revolution).[25] Apart from this translation, Sindhi authored a Sindhi translation and dictated an Arabic commentary to Musa Jar Allah, a Tartar emigrant in Hijaz. Other slim volumes containing Qur'ānic themes were written with a revolutionary thrust.[26]

Keeping in mind the historical context, political ferment and social construct that had a direct bearing on the Muslim collective identity, Sindhi's exploration of Qur'ānic themes within the orbit of modernity[27] is revealing. In fact, a radical departure from the conventional reading of the Qur'ān informs his hermeneutics. At the core of his commentary is extrapolating Waliyullah's intellectual tradition to key issues that are generally associated with class struggle, reminiscent of the proletariat in Communist Russia.[28] The deepening crisis engendered by capitalism is deplored by Sindhi. To counter these conflicting ideological systems, he approaches the study of the Qur'ān as a manifesto for revolution. To this end, several surahs revealed in Makkah, are examined by Sindhi as "they offer entirely new paradigms of

---

[25] Tareen offers an excellent exploration of Sindhi's Qur'ānic hermeneutics from the prism of historical circumstances and ideological factors that underpinned his unconventional approach to the sacred text. SherAli Tareen, "Revolutionary Hermeneutics: Translating the Qur'ān as a Manifesto for Revolution", in *Journal of Religious and Political Practice*, 3: 1-2.

[26] According to Shaikh, the Arabic translation has distinct traces of Waliyullah's progressive thoughts. Shaikh, *Mawlana Ubaid Allah Sindhi*, 186-8.

[27] Ibid., 188. The noted exegete of Egypt, 'Allamah Tantawi Jawhari wrote a scientific commentary of the Qur'ān. He consulted with Sindhi concerning several verses during his visit to the Hijaz.

[28] Ansari's brilliant analysis of the proletariat underscores the propaganda ploys of the Communist regime. Ansari, *Communist Challenge to Islam*, 134-7.

interpretation. through a hermeneutical engine propelled by an intense longing for revolution."[29]

Consider Surah Al-Muzammil (73) which has a particular circumstantial relevance. The *sirah* sources explain clearly the heightened spiritual consciousness of the Holy Prophet (SAW) and the spiritual devotion and discipline for all Muslims to emulate. By contrast, Sindhi offers a novel interpretation to the word *Muzammil* with strong political overtones. For him, *Muzzamil* is a cognate term for 'comrades'[30] that fits neatly into his hermeneutics. Subsequent verses in the surah are explicit about its devotional discipline: the *tahajjud* (extra-nightly) prayer. However, Sindhi stretches its meaning with a 'call for action' rhetoric.[31] Intriguingly, he argues that the Qur'ān's call for a revolutionary programme is a reflection of its general manifesto as explained in the surah. Sindhi's unconventional commentary has resonance in parts of surah Al- Mudathhir (74). For him, the concept of surplus value is established in the following verse: "*And do not through giving seek yourself to gain.*" (74:6). To borrow a term, political economy is invested with a peculiar interpretation of clear-cut meanings. Sindhi emphatically declares: "The foundational principle of a just revolution is to protect humanity from hardship and injustice by establishing institutions of public welfare instead of opening avenues of exploitation for self-benefit."[32]

Tareen has correctly observed that Sindhi's hermeneutical imaginary was time and history specific. As much as he expounded on the divine sovereignty[33] in relation to socioeconomic justice as envisaged by Waliyullah, its impact was less significant. This is borne out by the opposition he faced from

---

[29] Tareen, "Revolutionary Hermeneutics", 12.

[30] Ibid.

[31] Ibid., 13. Despite the fact that these verses under discussion have unambiguous meanings, Sindhi's preoccupation with political profiling of the sacred text is absurd, to say the least.

[32] Ibid.21.

[33] For Sindhi, capitalism or capital worship is largely theological in nature. It must not be forgotten that the battle lines between divine sovereignty and colonial incursion were a grim reality.

the contemporary 'ulama. His progressive thinking reflected in his commentary was essentially "revealing and rediscovering the Prophetic past to changing geopolitical developments." Sindhi was not alone in calling for a rereading of the Qur'ānic text. Inayatullah Khan Mashriqi (d. 1963)[34] was another political activist who attempted to offer a scientific commentary of the sacred text.

Mashriqi's academic background at Oxford University honed his skills to an activist interpretive reading of the Qur'ān which reflected the challenges of the day. In a broader framework, Mashriqi represented the growing generation of Islamic modernists who relegated hadith to the margins.[35] A point of difference, however, is that Sindhi was an 'alim who acquired Islamic disciplines (*'ulum*) from Deoband under notable scholars like Shaykh al-Hind. Among his non-conformist views about the Qur'ān, Sindhi is of the view that it "represents the basic unalterable ideology of the whole humanity, of all world religions and philosophies" which he calls *Fitrat Allah* (the nature of God) or the human conscience.[36] His inclusive definition of a Muslim stems from his belief that other faith groups are followers of the *din i-hanif* (religions that promotes 'upright' beliefs and actions). Not unsurprisingly, the storm of controversy among the 'ulama led to *kufr*-bashing *fatwās* (apostasy) against him. Likewise, his analysis of the chronological order of the surahs suggest that "it will help understand the objectives and goals of the revelation itself, and ultimately establish a revolutionary state and society."[37] In sum, Sindhi's Qur'ānic interpretation encapsulated revelation and

---

[34] Under Mashriqi's leadership, the Khaksar movement took on a distinct religious symbolism to bring into sharp focus its 'infallible and divine sociology.' In other words, it was a striking departure from the traditional interpretation of the sacred text. Cited in Schimmel, *Islam in the Subcontinent*, 240.

[35] Muhammad Mazheruddin Siddiqui, *Modern Reformist Thought in the Muslim World* (Islamabad, 1982). The book deals with the intellectual, political and social views of modern Muslim thinkers who argued that that the traditional interpretation of Islam was an obstacle for the Muslim elite.

[36] Tanvir Anjum, "Bridging Tradition and Modernism: An Analysis of Ubaid-Allah Sindhi's Religious Thought", in *Journal of the Pakistan Historical Society (Historicus)*. Vol. lxi, No. 3, July-September, 2013, 7.

[37] Ibid., 8.

revolution. This binary term perhaps embodied his complex personality and sensibility to the rapid developments taking place across the world in which Islam was on the anvil of significant change.

Ashrāf 'Ali Thānawi

Ashrāf 'Ali Thānawi (d. 1943), a prolific author and spiritual guide for thousands of Muslims was an extraordinary exponent of reform. His base at Thana Bhawan was the hub of his diverse Islamic activities which included writing voluminously, teaching, correspondence and counselling for visitors and aspirants (*murids*) seeking guidance and spiritual solace. In sum, his passion for reform, his integrity and his spirituality epitomised his remarkable reformist contributions. His famous works include *Bahesthi Zewar* (Heavenly Oranaments) written specifically for Muslim women,[38] *Tarbiyat i-Sālik* - a comprehensive guideline in *tasawwuf*[39] and his multivolume *Fatāwā* compilation. A specialist in hadith studies, his writings have a strong sunnah tenor.

The motivation for writing his tafsir *Bayān al- Qur'ān* stemmed from the deviant interpretations by several translators who were in many instances influenced by pre- modernity taking roots in a colonial milieu of the British India. By the beginning of the twentieth century his tafsir work appeared with a distinct mission statement: to make the sacred text accessible to academia. Bearing in mind Thānawi's intellectual temperament, *Bayān al-Qur'ān* was a bold attempt to synthesise different strands of Qur'ānic 'ulum with a strong *tasawwuf* bias. It was a marked departure from the traditional tafsirs predating *Mudih al-Qur'ān*.

Of course, Shah 'Abdul Qadir's work was a template for successive tafsirs; however, the volatile political situation under British dominance compelled 'ulama to restore the primacy of the Qur'ānic teachings for the Muslim community burdened by

---

[38] Barbara Metcalf, *Perfecting Women: Mawlana Ashraf Ali Thānawi's Bihishti Zewar* (Oxford, 1992), 4-5.

[39] Ashraf 'Ali Thānawi, *Tashil Tarbiyat al-Sālik*, 4 vols. (Karachi, 2009).

syncretic versions of Islam.

The reformist mission was undertaken by Thānawi with great fervour. A comprehensive multivolume tafsir encompassing a broad range of Islamic subjects, the stylistic features of *Bayān al-Qur'ān* have a direct bearing on Thānawi's scholarly erudition. Muhammad Mubeen Saleem has identified the following stylistic features of the tafsir:

a. Interlinear translation: this format was in vogue up to the middle of the twentieth century.

b. Coherence (*nazm*): Based on the subject matter, the

c. *nazm* of verses or surahs is concisely explained.

d. Explanatory translation: It generally follows after the interlinear translation.

e. Brief commentary: the symbol **f** signifies *fawā'id*

f. which gives a brief description of the related verses.

g. Subject headings: theme-based subjects and narratives are classified accordingly.

h. *Ihsān* and *Suluk*: these terms elucidated in a separate volume are inserted as footnotes to highlight its relevance to particular verses.

i. Qur'ānic lexicon: *Lughāt* is assigned a separate section to explicate meanings.

j. Syntax: syntactic structures of verses are discussed.

k. Rhetoric: the literary significance of verses are contextualised in relation to the Qur'ānic *i'jāz*.

l. Differences of *Qirā'at*: An accomplished *Qāri*, Thānawi elaborates its different forms to derive shades of meaning.

m. *Kalām*: the theological content is discussed from the

n. *Ahl al-Sunnah* viewpoint.

o. Hadith narration: the *riwāyāt* (transmissions of hadith reports) augment the interpretation of different Qur'ānic verses.

p. Justification of translation: In accordance with grammatical construction, Thānawi substantiates his translation approach.

q. Refutation of objections: the *radd* (refutation) is integral to his marginal notes.

r. Modes of recitation: the seven modes *(huruf)* are generally of an academic nature and written in Arabic.

s. Monographs: Several monographs are included in the tafsir for a particular purpose, eg. The benefits of the sky.

t. Indices: Two indices form part of the tafsir. These cover the subject matter of the Qur'ān and tafsir respectively.[40]

Thānawi is of the opinion that an idiomatic translation of the Qur'ān has limitations as it may not be fully understood in all regions of the subcontinent where Urdu is widely spoken. Therefore, he has adopted an academic translation that retains its textual beauty and rhetorical charms. In a similar strain, his explanatory translation is intended to convey a rational approach in keeping with its textual spirit and wisdom. Likewise, a comprehensive summary is provided with titles, underscoring its thematic contents. While adhering to standard works of hadith literature, Thānawi discerningly employs particular hadiths that allow for flexibility of interpretation. Thus preference is given for authenticated hadiths or supported by Arabic literary sources. For Thānawi, the correlation of verses has a sequential significance and is therefore conciliatory *(tawfiqi)* in scope and function.[41]

The impact *of Bayān al-Qur'ān* on subsequent Urdu translations has been substantial. Several tafsirs have simplified the translation and marginal notes to make it comprehensible for ordinary readers. Ghulam Yahya Anjum's citation illustrates its widespread popularity:

---

[40] Majeed, *Qur'ān Interpretation in Urdu*, 51-2.
[41] Ibid., 53-5.

Thānawi's translation of the Qur'ān is more literary and understandable as well as more explanatory and interpretative than other translations. His style of translation and interpretation of the Qur'ān was adopted and further developed by many subsequent scholars of the Qur'ān such as Abul Kalam Azad. This modified style of interpretation was firstly called as *Mafhoom i-Qur'ān* (Understanding of the Qur'ān).[42]

An understudied aspect of *Bayān al-Qur'ān* is Abdul Majid Daryabadi's appreciable contribution. While it is generally assumed that Daryabadi's *Tafsir i-Mājidi* is an almost replication of *Bayān al-Qur'ān*, the *Nuqush wa Ta'thurāt* documents in varying degrees the Qur'ānic correspondence between Thānawi and Daryabadi. The recommendations or changes proposed by Daryabadi were later incorporated by 'Abdus Shakur Tirmidhi to the updated *Bayān al-Qur'ān*. Thānawi accepted in a qualified way Daryabadi's views and differing positions, which dispelled the misperception about the former's rigid conformity in respect of his tafsir.

There is no plausible explanation to Muhammad Taqi's Usmani's reservations about Daryabadi's viewpoints on particular verses that have a historical context. It must be borne in mind that Usmani is considered a *tarjumān* (articulator) of Thānawi's prolific writings; hence his defensive posture. The differing positions between Thānawi and Daryabadi relate to their perspectives of Biblical and Jewish sources. On this count, Daryabadi surpasses his contemporaries in the field of comparative religions. Another point of contention is Darayabadi's selective citation of Rashid Rida's *Tafsir al-Minār*, which in Usmani's estimation is a deviation from the mainstream tafsirs. His aversion to *Tafsir al-Minār* stems from its *Salafi* mindset, and to a lesser extent to its reformist

---

[42] Ghulam Yahya Anjum, *Qur'ān i-Karim ke Hindustani Tarājim wa Tafsir ka Ijmāli Jā'iza* (New Delhi, 2017), 266.

tendencies, which are clearly evident in his book review.[43]

There have been three approaches to make *Bayān al-Qur'ān* accessible to ordinary readers. The *talkhis* (summary) was opted by Mufti Shafi in his *Ma'āriful al-Qur'ān*. It is an easy-read version that presents Thānawi's explanation to a modern readership. Another initiative, the *tashil* series was aimed at simplifying the tafsir without tampering with the broad spectrum of the Qur'ānic styles (*uslub*) adopted by Thānawi. Another distinctive feature is the collection of Thānawi's elucidation of Qur'ānic topics and themes culled from his encyclopaedic *maw'āiz* (talks) delivered at his *khānqah* (spiritual lodge). These are explored in a multivolume work entitled *Ashrāf al-Tafāsir* which is edited by Muhammad Iqbal Quraishi.

Mufti Muhammad Shafi Usmani

A pre-eminent scholar, jurist and exegete, Mufti Muhammad Shafi' Usmani (1976) was a graduate of Dar al-'ulum Deoband. A professor at the same institution, his brilliant exposition of hadith and *Fiqh* was well recognised in the 'ulama institutions. After his resignation from Deoband in 1943 he was involved in political activities and championed the cause for the establishment of Pakistan. His dedication to imparting Islamic *'ulum* saw the establishment of his Dar al-'Ulum in Karachi which is considered among the leading institutions of learning in the country. His *fatāwā* compilation and voluminous works on *Fiqh* have rightly earned him the honorific title of *Mufti 'Azam* (The Grand Mufti) of Pakistan.[44]

In the field of tafsir, Mufti Shafi's multivolume *Ma'āriful Qur'ān* has carved out his niche as a leading exponent of the sacred text in the twentieth century. The history of this celebrated work has been translated as an eight-volume tafsir in English bearing the same Urdu title. A Summary of its background is given by Mufti Muhammad Taqi Usmani:

---

[43] See Muhammad Taqi Usmani, *Tabsirah* (Karachi, 2008), 122-4.
[44] Muhammad Rafi Usmani, *Hayāt i-Mufti i-'Azam* (Karachi, 2005).

The origin of *Ma'āriful Qur'ān* goes back to the third of Shawwal 1373 A.H. (corresponding to the 2nd of July 1954) when the author was invited to give weekly lectures on Radio Pakistan to explain selected verses of the Holy Qur'ān to the general audience. This invitation was accepted by the author on the condition that he would not accept any remuneration for this service and that his lectures would be broadcast without any interference by the editing authorities. The permanent title of this weekly programme was *Ma'āriful Qur'ān* (the Wisdom of the Holy Qur'ān) and it was broadcast every Friday morning on the network of Radio Pakistan. This series of lectures continued for ten years up to the month of June 1964 whereby the new authorities stopped the programme for reasons best known to them. This series of lectures contained a detailed commentary on selected verses from the beginning of the Holy Qur'ān up to the Surah Ibrahim (14).

This weekly programme of Radio Pakistan was warmly welcomed by the Muslims throughout the globe and was listened to by thousands of Muslims, not only in Pakistan and India but also in Western and African countries. After the programme was discontinued, there was a flood of requests from all over the world to transfer this series in a book-form and to complete the remaining part of the Holy Qur'ān in the shape of a regular commentary.

These requests persuaded the esteemed author to revise these lectures and to add those verses which were not included in the original lectures. He started this project in 1383 AH (1964) and completed the commentary of Surah Al-

Fatihah in its revised form and started the revision of Surah Al-Baqarah. However, due to his numerous involvements he had to discontinue this task, and it remained unattended during the next five years.

In Shawwal 1388 (1969) the esteemed author suffered from a number of diseases which made him restricted to his bed. It was during this ailment that he restarted this work while in bed and completed Surah Al-Baqarah in the same condition. Since then he devoted himself to the *Ma'āriful Qur'ān*. Despite a large number of obstacles in his way, not only from the political atmosphere of the country and the difficult responsibilities he had on his shoulders in different capacities, but also from his health and physical condition, he never surrendered to any of them and continued his work with a miraculous speed until he accomplished the work in eight volumes (comprising about seven thousand pages) within five years only.

After appearing in a regular book form, *Ma'āriful Qur'ān* was highly appreciated and widely admired by the Urdu-speaking Muslims throughout the world. Thousands of copies of the book are still circulated every year and the demand for the book has been increasing.[45]

Stylistic features of the Tafsir

Ma'āriful Qur'ān combines two translations, *Bayān al-Qur'ān* and *Mudih al-Furqān*, which underscores Mufti Shafi's mastery over these textual sources. It is actually a simplified version and labelled as *Khulāsat i-Tafsir* (summary). Additional information 'Insights and Issues' demonstrate his in-depth knowledge and

---

[45] Mufti Muhammad Shafi, *Ma'āriful Qur'ān*, vol.1 (Karachi, 1996), xv-xvi.

familiarity with current issues. However, in the English commentary, some important points which have not appeared in the summary have been merged into the main commentary to facilitate a better understanding for English readers.[46]

A detailed commentary of Surah Al-Fatihah is analysed from several perspectives. The merits of *Bismillah* are examined from *Fiqh* and *fadhā'il* viewpoints. An overview of Surah Al-Fatihah is given in relation to Allah-servant relationship *('ubudiyyah)*. Additionally, the cumulative view of guidance is contextualised in the backdrop of the dilemmas facing mankind. For example, in Mufti Shafi's estimation, "the scope of the third degree of guidance is limitless, and its levels indefinite."[47] Progress is equated with virtuous deeds which brings an increase in divine guidance. Even the greatest of Prophets and men of Allah strove tirelessly for this purpose. Two reviews of *Ma'āriful Qur'ān* are a conspectus of its methodology. Shahid Ali remarks about Muhammad Shafi's tafsir in these words:

> *Ma'āriful Qur'ān* is purely an academic commentary of the Qur'ān which throws light upon everyday issues of people. Shafi has followed the pattern of his mentor, Ashraf 'Ali Thānawi and modified the latter's commentary into a new version. It discusses the Islamic belief system, modern technology, principles of shari'ah and the Islamic system of economics, etc. in detail there by testifying to his authorial expertise.[48]

---

[46] Ibid., xxi.

[47] Ibid., 74.

[48] Majeed, *Qur'ān Interpretation in Urdu*, 137.

Ghulam Yahya Anjum writes:

> The most striking feature of this commentary is that it explains the Qur'ānic verses on *ahkhām* (practical commandments) minutely and discusses the issues and challenges under the title 'Insights and Issues' which makes it more significant. Under the title 'Insights and Issues' the author elaborates many academic and literary topics and discusses the issues and challenges in detail. The author has assembled many exemplary accounts and narratives which are fascinating and captivating besides being educative, informative and enlightening. In short, this commentary is exceptionally remarkable among the contributions of Dar al-'Ulum Deoband to the Qur'ānic studies.[49]

The multivolume work of Mufti Shafi has attracted interest from a cross section of readers in both Urdu and English. The points under discussion are meant to highlight the distinguishing features of the tafsir. A brief background is given to illustrate its importance in a Deobandi tradition perspective. The *Bayān al-Qur'ān* is referenced for the purpose of connecting Mufti Shafi's tafsir in the light of readers seeking an authentic interpretation of the sacred text. In fact, *Ma'āriful Qur'ān* is in many respects a simplified version of *Bayān al-Qur'ān*.

Mubeen Saleem Nadwi has given an overview of the tafsir. At the same time he dilates on the *Fiqh* aspects that are in keeping with Mufti Shafi's calibre. Belonging to this genre is his contribution to the *Ahkām al-Qur'ān*, authored by a team of scholars under the supervision of Thānawi. This is a Hanafi work for which the *ahkām* (legal injunctions) of the Qur'ān are extracted. 'Abdus Shukur Tirmidhi's work has been relied on to elucidate the salient features of the tafsir. Essentially, *Ma'āriful Qur'ān* encompasses the

---

[49] Ibid., 137-8.

scholarly analysis of classical *mufassirs* with a *tasawwuf* slant. At the same time, Mufti Shafi has attempted to provide a detailed explanation of Qur'ānic verses that have a direct bearing on Islam as a way of life (*din*).[50]

For Mufti Shafi, the sacred text is a lived experience shorn of technicalities. In this context, he has added new dimensions to approach the Qur'ān with a sense of reverence, open mind and soulful reading.

It is interesting to note that there were three translators of the *Ma'āriful Qur'ān* in English. Professor Muhammad Askari, a well-known English litterateur undertook this translation of volume 1. Sadly, his untimely demise in 1977 only saw the translation of 156 verses of Surah Al- Baqarah. Professor Muhammad Shamim offered to resume the translation in 1989 after a delay of 12 years. The seven volumes were then translated by Muhammad Shamim (d. 2002), Shamshad Siddiqi and Professor Ahmad Khalil Aziz of South Africa. The latter translated volume 8 (Surah Muhammad to Surah Al-Nas).[51]

Tafsir, hadith, *Fiqh* and Islamic economics are some of the specialised areas of study of the international scholar, Mufti Muhammad Taqi Usmani (b. 1943). His Urdu translation rendered into English as *The Meaning of the Noble Qur'ān* is a revised translation that originally appeared in *Ma'āriful Qur'ān* (English). According to Muhammad Taqi, "it is a totally new translation of the meanings of the Holy Qur'ān and a brief introduction to every surah and many explanatory notes to formulate understanding of the text for the common reader."[52]

---

[50] Majeed, *Qur'ān Interpretation in Urdu*, 135-7.
[51] The details are gleaned from the multivolume tafsir.
[52] Muhammad Taqi Usmani, *The Meanings of the Noble Qur'ān with Explanatory Notes* (Karachi, 2010).

Muhammad Idris Kandhelwi

A tafsir bearing the same title as Mufti Shafi's *Ma'āriful Qur'ān* was composed by Muhammad Idris Kandhelwi   (d. 1974). A noted hadith scholar who taught at Deoband and later emigrated to Pakistan. Kandhelwi also wrote a multivolume *Sirat i-Mustafā* which is a significant contribution to the genre. His association with Jami'ah Ashrafia (Lahore) was a productive phase of his teaching career.

Ma'āriful Qur'ān was written over a period of 34 years. However, Kandhelwi completed the tafsir only up to surah Al-Saff (61). It was his son, 'Abdul Malik who completed the remaining parts of the tafsir. A cursory survey of the tafsir points out to three tafsirs that Kandhelwi relied on: *Mudih al-Qur'ān*, *Bayān al-Qur'ān* and *Tafsir i-Haqqāni*. At the heart of the tafsir are issues pertaining to structural flow (*rabt*), discussion of complex issues, refutation of atheism and deviant figures/movements, and approaches to contemporary issues. In terms of primary sources, Kandhelwi has cited extensively from tafsirs, which in Tijarwi's estimation diminishes the scholarly profile of a *muhaddith* like Kandhelwi, judging by his celebrated works in this field.[53]

Qadi Muhammad Zahid al-Husaini

A brief comment on *Tadhkirat al-Mufassirin* by Qadi Zahid al-Husaini reveals his mastery over the tafsir genre. It is a synopsis of the well-established exegetes over the centuries who have enriched the tafsir tradition by their respective contributions. Al-Husaini avoids the trodden path of presenting mainstream tafsirs in the light of sectarian bias.[54] Another noteworthy contribution is his *Ma'āriful Qur'ān* which takes into account the levels of understanding by ordinary readers. He touches on topics like *wahy*, Qur'ānic style and approaches and blind spots of arbitrary interpretation. Al-Husayni's overall aim is also to reach out to the

---

[53] Tijarwi, *Fuzalā i-Deoband*, 35-6.
[54] Usmani, *Tabsirah*, 163.

educated class who are inclined to adopt a liberal approach to the sacred text.[55] In response to these growing concerns, the *Ma'āriful Qur'ān* is one of the few works written in the 1980s to meet the needs of modern readership.

Al-Husayni has had an interesting career. A student of erudite divines like Shaykh Husain Ahmad Madani (d. 1957) his fame as a versatile scholar was established in Qur'ānic studies. He devoted his teaching career at government schools in Campbellpur (Pakistan) which served as his base for his major writings. He also published a popular magazine *'Arafāt* which attracted contributors like Muhammad Asad, translator of *The Message of the Qur'ān*.[56]

In the strain of the *Durus* genre, Al-Husaini produced a 25 volume tafsir which was transcribed from audio recordings. According to the renowned scholar Muhammad Yusuf Ludhianwi (d. 2000), the *Durus al-Qur'ān* was teaching-based and contained instructive lessons of *tadhkir* (reminder). Written in comprehensible Urdu, it avoids technical details and instead reinforces the central teaching of the *Qur'ān* through the repetition of key ideas. This overlapping method is intended to consolidate the message, wisdom and teachings for the educated class grappling with new challenges and realities in their environment. Al-Husaini is acutely aware of the changing religious settings and makes concerted efforts to compose a tafsir that reaches the heart of the matter.[57]

Dars i-Qur'ān: A Synoptic Overview

The *Durus al-Qur'ān* features prominently among Deobandi 'ulama. Abdul Hamid Khan Sawati (d. 2008) brought out a 20 volume tafsir *Ma'ālim al-'Irfān* on the pattern of Al-Husaini's tafsir. Tijari has given an overview of this multivolume work. To assess

---

[55] Ibid., 448-9.

[56] In fact, Asad produced his own magazine in English bearing the same title Arafat (Lahore, 1946-8). See Ikram Chaghatai, *Muhammad Asad: Islam's Gift to Europe* (Lahore, 2006), 73-7.

[57] Tijarwi, *Fuzalā i-Deoband*, 105-6.

its relevance, we may refer to volume 18. Key themes cover *tawhid*, Prophethood, Hereafter, anecdotal accounts of several influential Prophets in the light of their tabligh mission, etc. Across the spectrum of *ahkām*, topics like virtues of loans (*qard al-hasanah*), *jihād* are emphasised. Likewise, the traits of hypocrites (*munāfiqun*) are contrasted with those of the martyrs (*shuhadā*).[58] For an average reader, *Mā'ālim al-Irfān* has a wide-ranging appeal for its simplicity, readability and connectivity. The introductory comments contained in volume 1 are useful guidelines to understand Sawati's methodology to producing this comprehensive tafsir. One point stands out in the tafsir: the *salaf* tradition is emphasised as a frame of reference to interpret the essential teachings of the sacred text.[59]

As an eminent scholar/activist, Sarfaraz Khan Safdar (2009) was the elder brother of Abdul Hamid Khan. His tafsir work bears the hallmark of the Deobandi tradition: reformist thought and outreach initiatives across all sections of society. His 21 volume *Dhakhirat al-Jinān* is aimed precisely for readers wishing to connect with its authentic message. In vol. 1 reference is made to Mahmud al-Hasan's perceptive remarks about 'the *ummah's* disconnect from the Qur'ān.' Khan, too, focused on the vision of Mahmud al-Hasan and worked tirelessly at societal and political platforms to alleviate the plight of the Indian Muslims.[60] His institution *Nusrat al-Islam* (Gujranwala, Pakistan) served as the hub of Qur'ānic activities. For him the sacred text should be of primary importance rather than liturgical books (very much in vogue in the subcontinent) that promises exponential rewards for the recitation of specific surahs. His censure was directed at men and women who built a fixation around these surahs by disregarding the complete recitation of the Qur'ān. To this end, Khan structured classes for ordinary people through the medium of Punjabi. For graduates of his madrasah, a two-year course was offered. Also his

---

[58] Ibid., 131-7.
[59] Abdul Hamid Khan Sawati, *Ma'ālim al-'Irfān Durus al-Qur'ān*, vol. 1 (Lahore, 2008), 9-18.
[60] Ibid., 17-8.

post- graduate Qur'ānic classes during the months of Sha'ban and Ramadan attracted students from across the subcontinent.[61] This approach was reminiscent of Shaykh Ahmad Ali Lahori whose fame rests on his preoccupation with teaching the sacred text for several decades.[62]

Ghulamullah Khan (d. 1980) compiled *Tafsir Jawāhir al-Qur'ān* at the behest of Shaykh Husain Ali. The genealogical tradition of tafsir can be traced back to the Waliyullah family, linking this work to the reformist vision of Deoband. *Tawhid* is strongly embedded in Husain Ali's *durus.* Likewise, Ghulamullah Khan compiled the tafsir for the purpose of reinforcing *tawhid* in its pristine form. The accretion of cultural norms derived largely from Hinduism was at odds with the unambiguous teachings of the Qur'ān. The *ifādāt* (explanatory notes) serve as a nexus of Islamic reformist thought. Ghulamullah Khan's meticulous compilation in the form of the tafsir assumes greater significance in the backdrop of ritualistic Islam. Furthermore, the work is supplemented by classical tafsirs to give it a systematic and well-developed form.

A detailed Introduction covers three sections: philosophical concepts, Qur'ānic terms and *tawhid.* Needless to add, *tawhid* is discussed under various subheadings. First, the concept of deity (*ilāh*) is critically examined in relation to its universal significance. The Qur'ānic concept of *tawhid* is cogently expressed to repudiate the multiplicity of deities (*shirk*) formulation. In a specific setting, new-fangled doctrines like *nadhr* (offering), *tawassul* (intercession) and attribution of divine status to *awliyā* are critically examined in this section. Moreover, the *piri-muridi* syndrome is censured for its anti-*tawhid* rhetoric. A salient feature of the tafsir is the overview which Ghulamullah Khan provides to facilitate a better understanding of the surahs. The comments are concise and lucid.[63]

The *durus* sub-genre has a two-fold purpose: i) to make the Qur'ānic teachings accessible to a growing readership, and ii) to counter ritual practices (*bid'āt*) that have been entrenched for

---

[61] Tijarwi, *Fuzalā i-Deoband*, 78-9.
[62] Ibid.
[63] Ghulamullah Khan, *Jawāhir al-Qur'ān* (Rawalpindi, 1984).

different reasons among a large segment of the *ummah* and has thus eroded the pristine form of Islam.

The antecedents of the *tawhid* discourse are articulated in Shah Isma'il Shahid's *Taqwiyat al-Imān*.[64] A scion of the Waliyullah family, the Shah (d. 1831) critiqued *shirk-* laden rituals and practices in the subcontinent. His work was warmly received by reformist 'ulama and institutions for its condemnation of *bid'āt* (innovations) and *khurāfāt* (distortions) that had crept into the social fabric of Muslim life.[65] At the opposite end of the spectrum, the Shah was equally condemned for what was deemed *takiri* (kufr- laden) beliefs. This cleavage continues to dominate the religious controversies in the subcontinent and the diaspora Muslim communities in Europe and United States. *Taqwiyat al-Imān* was widely acclaimed in the Arab world on account of its Arabic translation by Shaykh Nadwi.[66]

Mufti Muhammad Zafiruddin Miftāhi

A renowned 'alim, Muhammad Zafiruddin Miftāhi (d. 2011) earned accolades for his *Fiqh* output. His compilation of *Fatāwā Dār al-'Ulum* (12 volumes) and indexing the manuscripts deposited in the institution's library are his singular accomplishments. His biographical work on Sayyid Manazir Ahsan Gilani (d. 1956), author of *Sawānih Qāsimi*,[67] co-founder of Deoband is illustrative of his literary flair.

Tafsir Dars i-Qur'ān is one of his major contributions in Qur'ānic studies. This six- volume work which initially appeared in thirty instalments was a welcome addition to the tafsirs brought out by the Deobandi 'ulama. The tafsir is not classified as a lesson-based explanation in the conventional sense nor was it transcribed from audio recordings. Essentially, it covers a distinct format consisting of clusters of verses with brief, explanatory

---

[64] See Muhammad Ismail Shahid, *Taqwiyat al-Imān* (Lahore, 1990).
[65] See SherAli Tareen, *Defending Muhammad in Modernity* (Notre Dame, 2020).
[66] It was translated into Arabic entitled *Risālat al-Tawhid* by Abul Hasan Ali Nadwi.
[67] This is a two-volume comprehensive work on the life and times of Muhammad Qasim Nanautwi.

notes. It is aimed at meeting the needs of college students and professionals who owing to their busy schedules can only devote limited time to read a tafsir. First, the meaning of particular words is given as background information for the readers. Second, Thānawi's idiomatic translation is given which prepares the readers for an overview of the Qur'ānic teachings and message. Third, the words/terms listed are concisely explained. Brevity is preferred over technicality. Fourth, the comments are linked organically to the themes under discussion. Miftahi has adopted a didactic approach with enable to readers of different backgrounds to internalise in their lives the perennial guidance from the Qur'ān. In the words of the publisher, there should be collective effort to understand the Word (*kalām*) of Allah. It is hoped that every home becomes a Qur'ānic school. To realise this ambitious goal, a page of the tafsir should be regularly read for five minutes. One should read it and encourage others to read it as well.[68]

An important point that emerges from this invaluable tafsir is its impact on a cross-section of readers. Miftahi consulted several tafsir works and drew upon his interpretive reading to maintain the link of authenticity. In this way, readers can locate his tafsir sources for augmenting their interest in this field.

Mufti Sa`eed Ahmad Palanpuri

Versatility in Islamic disciplines (*'ulum*) has been a characteristic feature of Deobandi scholars since its establishment in 1866. Mufti Sa'eed Ahmad Palanpuri (d. 2020) was an embodiment of his predecessors in the field of hadith studies and *Fiqh*. His scholarly temperament is best represented in his multivolume commentaries of *Bukhāri* and *Tirmidhi*. Similarly, his proficiency in *Fiqh* may be gleaned from his *fatāwā* compilation and the excellent annotated Urdu translation of Waliyullah's magnum opus *Hujjat Allah al-Bāligha*. In sum, his prolific writings underscore his brilliant approach to these disciplines which have defined

---

[68] Tijarwi, *Fudhal i-Deoband*, 125-6.

Deoband's fame as a site of higher Islamic learning and culture.[69] Palanpuri's works stand out from the plethora of writings that are characterised by mediocrity. Indeed, Palanpuri is a scholar of international repute who has enriched the scholarly engagement of classical texts through his incisive commentaries. It is, therefore, not surprising when his mufti profile obscures his tafsir credentials.[70]

The eight-volume *Tafsir Hidāyat al-Qur'ān* has placed Palanpuri among the distinguished exegetes in the subcontinent. Initially, nine parts were completed by Mawlana 'Uthman Kashfi over a prolonged period which diminished a sustained interest in the tafsir. The tempo of completing the work by Palanpuri was hampered by his other literary commitments. Finally, the tafsir saw the light of the day in 2017, after a hiatus of many years. For Palanpuri the immediate challenge was to reconcile Kashfi's simple translation with his technical explanations into a single work. The transitioning process was a formidable task which he executed with clarity of purpose and efficiency.[71] Palanpuri's methodology shows clear instances of his hadith and *Fiqh* predisposition. Keeping in mind that the earlier volumes were written almost 25 years before he undertook this onerous task, variation in style is unavoidable. Palanpuri's expertise is pressed home on two counts: i) his analysis of the text (*nass*) through the lens of *iqh* technical terms, and ii) the critical engagement of tafsir views in the light of hadith literature. This explains his presentation of technical details for an advanced readership. Consider his rigorous appraisal of *rabt*. He states that there are two views that determine the exegetes' respective interpretation of it. One view presupposes a well-structured divine arrangement that leaves no room for arbitrary interpretation. The other view argues that the text seeks to connect the readers with its overall

---

[69] Obituary: Mufti Saeed Palanpuri. www.islamicportal.co.uk. Accessed on 17 August 2020.

[70] See Afzal Hoosen, *Knowlegeable Discourses of 'Allāmah Mufti Sa'eed Ahmad Palanpuri* (Karachi, 2014).

[71] Tijarwi, *Fuzalā i-Deoband*, 90-3.

message of guidance which is meant for all times and all ages.[72]

An overview of Surah Al-Fatihah reveals Palanpuri's multifaceted approach to tafsir. He proffers a cogent presentation relating to the multiple titles of the surah. Likewise, the virtues of the surah are concisely explained, a testament to his mastery over the hadith corpus. Where necessary he makes references to Mahmud al-Hasan's brief comments on the surah to support his viewpoint. An interesting feature is the simple translation of Arabic words in Urdu. Readers are thus able to build appropriate vocabulary and get a 'feel' of the subject matter contained in Surah Al-Fatihah. The grammatical explanation is neither technical nor abstruse; only relevant details are provided to allow for the seamless understanding of the text. The *Fiqh* aspect is thoroughly discussed from the *madhab* viewpoint.

Based on his decades-long teaching experience at Dar al-'Ulum Deoband, the Hanafi position is given preference. While not departing from mainstream explanations of terms like *maghdub* (misguided) and *dāllin* (led astray), Palanpuri maintains that they have relevance for Muslims who indulge in deviant customs.[73]

In line with Deoband's vision of inclusive knowledge, Khalid Saifullah Rahmani is a trailblazer in the field of *Fiqh*. His association with the Islamic Fiqh Academy, local and international, has earned him immense popularity on his contributions to current issues. His balanced approach combined with his thorough familiarity with contemporary socioeconomic trends is his major strength.[74] As an executive member of All India Muslim Personal Law Board[75] his proactive role has been recognised during the volatile political upsurge against Muslim interests. In the field of Qur'ānic studies[76] societal concerns are

---

[72] Sa'eed Palanpuri, *Hidāyat al-Qur'ān*, vol.1 (Deoband, 2017), 25-38.

[73] Ibid., 34.

[74] For example, Khalid Saifullah Rahmani, *Modern Problems: Islamic Perspectives* (Hyderabad, 2010).

[75] See Khalid Saifullah Rahmani, *Muslim Personal Law awr Badh Ghalat Fehmiya* (Hyderabad, 2017).

[76] For a simplified version of the principles of tafsir, see Khalid Saifullah Rahmani, *Asān Usul i-Tafsir* (Hyderabad, 2014).

expanded with greater clarity by Rahmani. Therefore, his *Asān Tarjuma* is written for this purpose. As discussed in the Introduction, the benchmark of his translation is centred around the emergent trends in the Indian Muslim society. The standard and style is written in idiomatic Urdu. Keeping in mind the linguistic and cultural temperament of Arabic and Urdu, Rahmani attempts to frame his translation within the norms of morphology and contextual relevance. He deftly assigns meanings to words for which denotation is inadequate. In other words, expanded meanings clarify Qur'ānic terms that may otherwise be misconstrued. To this end, Rahmani relies on authoritative Urdu tafsirs like *Bayiān al-Qur'ān* to elucidate these Qur'ānic terms.

The tendency to interpolate meanings is a dangerous precedent for liberal and errant interpretations. Rahmani in this respect unequivocally calls out recent attempts by liberal scholars who divest Qur'ānic meanings from its established tradition. For him the perils of religious anarchy are a grim reality.[77] *Da'wah* - focused themes are also at the heart of his explanatory notes. These are concisely crafted and lucidly expressed. Unlike other commentaries Rahmani advocates a 'relevance' theory: providing appropriate explanatory notes for particular verses. Otherwise, the Qur'ān should speak for itself. According to him, the barriers to understanding, appreciating and contextualising the spirit of the sacred text are like thorns strewn along the path. To clear these hurdles *da'wah* must be tempered with love and affection to win over the hearts of hard-hearted people.[78] Tijarwi expresses his admiration of Rahmani's elegant style to bring out the principal themes of the Qur'ān. A positive feature of the tafsir is the absence of polemics. Although Rahmani opts for the Hanafi viewpoint on *ahkām*, these do not detract him from articulating the overarching vision and mission statement of the shari'ah. This approach defines his *Fiqh* expertise for which he has received wide acclaim in the scholarly domain. Essentially, his tafsir is an authoritative expression of the sublime message contained in the

---

[77] Tijarwi, *Fuzalā i-Deoband*, 71-2.
[78] Ibid., 74.

sacred text.[79]

Mufti Jasimuddin Qāsimi

New trends in Qur'ānic scholarship have impacted on a cohort of young Deobandi graduates in the twenty-first century. Jasimuddin Qāsimi holds an enviable record of academic distinction: *iftā* in Saharanpur and MA in English/ Communication at Mawlana Azad University (Hyderabad). He is currently based in Mumbai contributing significantly to *Eastern Crescent*, an international monthly magazine published in Mumbai since 2006, which identifies itself as *Alternative Media, People's Choice*. The prestigious magazine brings out well-researched articles from 'ulama and intellectuals. It has also a column for day-to-day religious problems besides analytical articles on current issues and world politics.[80]

Qāsimi is well-recognised for his *Qur'ān ka Paighām*. Written over a short period of time, the tafsir has a two fold aim: i) to disseminate the message and guidance of the Qur'ān, and ii) to make the sacred text accessible through the social media platforms. For Qāsimi technology and its paraphernalia has established its pervasive presence in Muslim society; therefore, it serves as a communicative tool for spreading God's word.

Brevity defines Qāsimi's tafsir: concise notes are succinctly presented without compromising the timeless teachings of the Qur'ān. For this purpose the technicality overload which is characteristic of the comprehensive tafsirs is avoided. Likewise, repetition of anecdotal accounts particularly of the Prophets are condensed under a single rubric. In other words, where repetition of these accounts appear, Qāsimi instead makes pointed reference to its underlying wisdom. Likewise, he relies on three authoritative commentators for his tafsir: Shabbir Ahmad Usmani, Muhammad Taqi Usmani and Khalid Saifullah Rahmani. Context is given prominence to facilitate a proper connection with

---

[79] Ibid.

[80] See *Eastern Crescent*, an organ of Markaz al-Ma'arif (Mumbai), a proactive organisation dedicated to the educational upliftment of the Muslim community.

the sacred text. To meet the growing needs of a different generation, Qāsimi's Ramadan classes have been enthusiastically received.[81] Time management and focused explanation are his personal attributes.

We reproduce an excerpt from the Eastern Crescent regarding Qāsimi's approach to tafsir:

> Surah Al-Fatihah is also described as *Umm al-Kitāb* in hadith which means 'Mother of the Qur'ān'. This surah is also known as the summary of the Qur'ān. It is compulsory to recite this surah in every *salāh*. The Holy Prophet (SAW) described it as the greatest surah of the Glorious Qur'ān (*Bukhāri*). It starts with the praise of Almighty Allah, Lord of the universe. Seeking help from Allah is then mentioned which is termed as the most fruitful supplication.[82]

A positive development of the Deobandi alumni contributions is their familiarity with current issues. In the spirit of reaching out to the diverse readership, their Qur'ānic writings are reflective of their *ummatic* concerns. In sum, the centrality of the Qur'ān lies at the heart of their reformist endeavours.

The Hindi translations of the Qur'ān have been vigorously undertaken by Jama'at i-Islami to advance their *da'wah* mission. These are, of course, original works written in chaste Hindi for both Muslim and non-Muslim readership. The Deobandi alumni have not lagged behind in presenting the Hindi translations of popular tafsirs that have been widely received in the subcontinent and abroad. Many of these tafsirs have been translated into English.

Muhammad 'Imran Qāsimi (b. 1967) is representative of this trend. His Hindi translation output is remarkable judging by the choice of his voluminous tafsirs. Two tafsirs, *Tafsir Ibn Kathir* and *Ma'āriful Qur'ān* which run into several volumes have been

---

[81] Tijarwi, *Fuzalā i-Deoband*, 68-70.
[82] *Eastern Crescent*, November 2019, 5.

meticulously translated by him. To this end, he offers a variety of scholarly works which have made their mark in the tafsir tradition. 'Imran Qāsimi's proficiency in Arabic and Hindi, as well as being a post-graduate student of Aligarh Muslim University has enhanced his contributions in this important field of study.[83]

Mufti Fuzail al-Rahmān Hilāl Usmani

Mufti Hilāl Usmani (d. 2019) was the former Grand Mufti of Punjab, patron of Dar al-'Ulum (Waqf) Deoband, and member of the AIMPLB. "He was an expert jurist, outstanding scholar of Islam, proficient writer, gifted orator, fine academic, visionary intellectual of a kind."[84]

Hilāl Usmani's extensive teaching career in Deoband and Malerkotla (Punjab) was an embodiment of his intellectual acumen.[85] His two-year study in Madinah developed his skills in reaching out to Muslims of different sectarian backgrounds. He was instrumental in preparing a structured course in Persian and also offering classes in other Islamic subjects on sound educational patterns. It was in Punjab that his reformatory endeavours were successfully implemented. The Jami'a Dar al-Salam established in 1986 was the nexus of his multifaceted activities. It offered holistic education and was accredited by tertiary institutions in the country. Hilāl Usmani advocated the uncomplicated transition to the *iqrā* paradigm which he vigorously supported. More importantly, he worked tirelessly for societal reform among the Muslim communities who were mired in religious ignorance (*jahālat*) and misguided beliefs.[86]

Hilāl Usmani authored more than seventy books covering a wide range of subjects. His *Mi'mār i-Insāniyat* addresses the importance of fostering mutual tolerance, harmony and respect

---

[83] Ibid., 154.
[84] On Usmani's life and works, see 'Arif Qāsimi, *Voice of Darul Uloom*, vol.3:9. Jan-March, 2020, 13.
[85] For a historical account of Malerkotla and its religio-cultural background, see Anna Bigelow, *Sharing the Sacred: Practicing Pluralism in Muslim North India* (Oxford, 2010).
[86] *Voice of Darul Uloom*, vol.3: 9, 14-5.

in a plural society. This vision is also echoed in the *Payām i-Insāniyat* movement[87] established by Shaykh Nadwi.

An eminent scholar, Hilāl Usmani broadens the scope of *ahkām* by addressing current issues within the context of classical works. In the field of Qur'ānic writings his *Nur al-Qur'ān* is a testament to his visionary acumen. The tafsir is aimed at spreading the Qur'ānic guidance for modern man. His methodology is straightforward: *Fiqhi* matters are relegated to the margins to allow an unfiltered understanding of the sacred text. Implicit in this multivolume tafsir is the counter response to objections raised by rationalists on particular Qur'ānic issues. His cogent refutation of the Qadiani menace effectively restored the primacy of the Qur'ān in the lives of Punjabi Muslims who were exposed to this movement.[88]

Initially, *Nur al-Qur'ān* was titled *Ruh al-Qur'ān* as it incorporated the translation of *Jalālayn*. However, a fresh translation was brought out by Hilāl Usmani making it an original piece of work. Written in chaste, simple Urdu, grammatical rules are economically used to explain the meaning of Qur'ānic terms. Under the rubric of titles and themes, explanatory notes are given for the purpose of clarity. Another positive feature of the tafsir is the segment analysis of verses through the *hāshiyah* method. In this way Hilāl Usmani strongly maintains that his tafsir will have a direct appeal to madrasah students as well as modern readers.[89]

Incomplete Tafsirs

Incomplete tafsirs and commentaries of classical works are closely examined in Tijarwi's volume. For our study a random selection is done to give the gist of the Deobandi contributions in these areas. Only the distinctive aspects of their Qur'ānic writings are briefly mentioned.

---

[87] Ibid., 15.
[88] Tijarwi, *Fuzalā i-Deoband*, 162-3.
[89] Ibid.

Mufti Ahmad Khanpuri

A renowned scholar of Gujarat, Mufti Ahmad Khanpur (b.1946) was closely associated with Mufti Mahmud al- Hasan Gangohi (d.1996). Under his tutelage he gained expertise in hadith and *iftā*. The *Mahmud series* is dedicated to his mentor. Like the *dars* trends his *Asān Qur'ān* (4 volumes) has developed out of his lectures (*mawā'iz*). For example, Surah Al-Fatihah (vol. 1) deals with *nuzul* and peripheral issues like black magic, etc. Keeping in mind its style, the tafsir has much value for ordinary people seeking to learn and practise the teachings of the Qur'ān.[90]

A brilliant exponent of the Islamic `ulum, *Anwar Shah Kashmiri* (d. 1933) was an influential figure in the Qāsimi tradition.[91] A *muhaddith* par excellence, his discourses and writings range from hadith studies to Qur'ānic interpretation. As the title suggests, *Mushkilāt al-Qur'ān* is an elaboration of 190 verses in Arabic and Persian. Yunoos Osman has made some thoughtful comments about this meritorious work:

> The main objective of undertaking to write this work was to interpret only those verses of the Holy Qur'ān which are generally considered to be difficult to understand. Thus, while analysing these verses, Shah Sahib began first by discussing the opinions of some of the notable *mufassirun* (exegetes) and thereafter he gives his personal view. Shah Sahib believed that a proper commentary of the Holy Qur'ān could best be done in the light of *asbāb al- nuzul*. Knowing the causes for the revelation would assist the exegete to be in a position to relate Qur'ānic verses to contemporary times. A special feature of this particular work is that the author has, in

---

90 Tijarwi, *Fuzalā i-Deoband*, 211-2.

91 See Shah Mas'udi, *Naqsh i-Dawām: Hayāt i-Muhaddith* Anwar Kashmiri (Multan, 2006).

addition, set aside 190 verses which, in his opinion, required further discussion and repeated consideration. *Mushkilāt al-Qur'ān* was published after Shah Sahib's demise by Majlis i-'Ilmi in Dabhel. Mawlana Ahmad Bijnori edited the manuscript and included in the footnotes a list of all the sources that Shah Sahib had cited in it. However, the inclusion of the footnotes has inevitably enhanced the value of this work. The 228-page book was later republished by one of Shah Sahib's renowned students, Mawlana Muhammad Yusuf Binuri with a 38 page introduction.[92]

This scholarly pedigree is best represented by the Shah's son, Anzar Shah Kashmiri (d.2008). An orator and enlightened 'alim, he has to his credit Urdu translations of classical works like Ibn Kathir's multivolume tafsir. His Urdu translation is based on *Bayān al-Qur'ān* while the explanatory notes are the condensed version which in many instances are aligned to the Hanafi *Fiqh*. The gist of *Bayān al-Qur'ān* (*talkhis*) is incorporated as well. Overall, Anzar Shah's approach is an eclectic choice of classical and early twentieth century tafsirs.[93] In a different perspective, 'Allamah Tantawi's tafsir *Al-Jawāhir i Tafsir al-Qur'ān* (Arabic) has been critically examined by scholars like Anzar Shah as well as other exegetes in the subcontinent. Sadly, two or three parts (*ajzā*) were completed but have not been published to date. Otherwise, it would have been a significant work to the Urdu tafsir genre.[94]

A scion of the Qāsimi family, Qari Muhammad Tayyab (d. 1983)[95] was a leading figure of Deoband. His multidisciplinary

---

contributions and activist career during his decades-long tenure as Rector of the institution has earned him immortal fame. Among his literary productions, Qur'ānic studies are a testament to his deep reflections on the sacred text. Under his illustrious leadership, Deoband expanded its footprints in various parts of the world as a premier site of higher Islamic learning. His illuminating discourses on Surah Al-Mulk which were initially recorded on audio tapes were later published in a book form. His brilliant exposition of the themes contained in the surah underscores his mastery over the tafsir literature.[96] An equally noteworthy work of his on *da'wah* delineates the Qur'ānic paradigm in a circumstantial context. Qari Tayyab by virtue of his deep learning is able to reach out to an academic readership. In this regard, AMU recognised his vast learning when he delivered the *Islam and Science* lectures at the university.

Belonging to the *maqālat* (lectures) series is the thought-provoking work by Jamil Ahmad Thānawi (d.1994). These lectures delivered at several institutions in Pakistan contain a wealth of information related to the varied aspects of Qur'ānic guidance and wisdom. Of particular note is Thānawi's reappraisal of external issues like correct pronunciation (*tajwid*) in order to develop reverence of the sacred text. Likewise, he does not lose sight of the importance of acquiring knowledge of the Qur'ān from authoritative sources i.e the 'ulama. For him, the arbitrary interpretations of the sacred text are indisputable streaks of egoism and liberal thought.[97] In sum, these lectures are intended to enlighten readers about their commitment to the Qur'ānic teachings.

Tafsir on selected surahs is a marked feature of the Deoband tradition. Shabbir Ahmad Azhar Meeruti was a famous tafsir and hadith specialist whose expertise was recognised among the 'ulama fraternity. His *Miftāh al-Qur'ān* series covering several surahs illustrates his independent approach to the study of the Qur'ān. In several instances he has deviated from the mainstream

---

[96] Muhammad Tayyab, *Tafsir Surah Al-Mulk* (Karachi, n.d.).
[97] Jamil Ahmad Thānawi, *Maqālat al-Qur'ān* (Lahore, 2001), 143-5, 200-15.

translation by adducing grammatical and morphological arguments in support of his viewpoints. A distinguished hadith specialist, Meeruti was more disposed to adopt the intra-Qur'ānic methodology which in his estimation was more in accord with the *salaf* tradition.[98] Regarding the structural flow (*rabt*) aspect, there are clear signs of his conformity with traditional Qur'ānic thought. However, he has framed his interpretation around a hierarchy of Qur'ānic principles that allow him to critically examine core *masā'il* which are generally upheld by mainstream exegetes.[99] Perhaps for this reason his tafsir has not gained popularity in the subcontinent.

Muhammad Manzur Nu'mani

A versatile scholar and accomplished *dā'i*, Muhamad Manzur Nu'mani (d. 1997) epitomised the amalgam of higher Islamic learning and reformist thought. His prolific writings set new pathways to approaching the fundamental issues affecting the Muslim corporate identity in India.[100]

There are interesting strands related to his reformist thought. As a brilliant student of the eminent *muhaddith* Anwar Shah Kashmiri, Nu'mani imbibed a deeper understanding about the relevance of hadith for the modern mind. His *Ma'ārif al-Hadith*[101] lent knowledge to his mastery of this primary source. Likewise, his early association with Mawdudi provided him with consummate skills to critically examine reformist organisations like Jama'at i-Islami advocating the establishment of Islam as a way of life (*iqāmat i-din*).[102] A sensitive soul, Nu'mani deplored the proliferation of *bid'ah* among Muslim communities, which

---

[98] Tijarwi, *Fuzalā i-Deoband*, 234.

[99] Ibid., 235. For example, Meeruti contends that the *Ahl al-Bayt* does not include the wives of the Prophet.

[100] For Nu'mani's detailed autobiographical account, see Muhammad Nu'mani, *Tahdith i-Ni'mat* (Lahore, n.d.).

[101] Translated into English by Mohammad Asif Kidwai as *Meaning and Message of Traditions*.

[102] Hs critique of Jama'at i-Islami was prompted by the cultic status around Mawdudi's personality and his 'deviant' readings of mainstream Islamic concepts.

regrettably blurred out the true essence of Islamic faith and practice. His debates (*munāzarāt*) with the Barelwi school of thought were primarily aimed at critiquing their popular shrine-based practices and defending the reformist position of the maligned figures like Shah Isma'il Shahid (d. 1831) for his *Taqwiyat al-Imān*.[103]

Among his Qur'ānic contributions, two books are representative of Nu'mani's profound learning in tafsir. The first work, *Qur'ān and You* has been widely acclaimed for his simplicity and directness of style and the universality of his approach.'[104] Nu'mani has attempted to cover the entire range of Qur'ānic teachings for both Muslim and non-Muslim readers. The clarity and conciseness are his outstanding traits that characterise his literary style. The translation is intended to facilitate a better understanding for his readers without delving into the nuanced features of tafsir writings. More importantly, the book offers a direct and forceful approach to Qur'ānic teachings in the light of modern needs.[105]

We reproduce two extracts that are illustrative of Nu'mani's insightful approach to the Qur'ānic teachings:

> *O you who believe! If you keep your duty to Allah, He will give you discrimination (between right and wrong) and will rid you of your evil thoughts and deeds, and will forgive you. Allah is of Infinite Bounty.*

> (8: 29)

> The word, *Furqān* in the above verse, which literally means the *Criterion*, commands a wide range of significance. The English translators of the Qur'ān have generally, used phrases like 'power of discrimination,' and 'quality of

---

[103] A slim volume *'Ilm al-Ghayb* is representative of Nu'mani's polemical literature. In a similar vein, his *Iranian Revolution* (2001) is a trenchant criticism of Shi'asm.

[104] Manzur Nu'mani, *Qur'ān and You* (Lucknow, 1978), 5.

[105] His *Dars i-Qur'ān* has been warmly received among the educated class.

distinction', to explain its meaning. However, it covers the instinctive perception of good and evil and the ability to draw a line between what is allowed and what is not. It encapsulates the extraordinary grace and dignity which characterises the personality of the devout servants of the Lord and evokes love and reverence for them in the hearts of others and the very special help of Allah which enables them to be miraculously successful in their endeavours. All these are covered by it. The Lord Creator has promised these matchless rewards to His virtuous slaves in this life in addition to forgiveness in the Hereafter.[106]

Like generosity, contentment, also, is one of the nobler qualities of man. The two, in fact, are intimately connected with one another. By contentment it is meant that a person should be satisfied with what he earns through his toil and industry and from legitimate means. He should consider it to be his just share, and refrain from casting a covetous glance at the riches of others or stretching his palm before them. From the Qur'ānic standpoint, everyone is a servant of the Lord and He, alone, is Kind and Compassionate, Nourisher and Sustainer. It is, therefore, not fitting and proper for him to look to anyone else for the fulfilment of his needs. There is no dearth or scarcity in the treasures of Allah and His Mercy is sufficient for one and all. Says the Qur'ān:

Is Allah not sufficient unto His slave? (Then why should he stretch his hand before anyone else?)

(39: 36)[107]

---

[106] Nu'mani, *Qur'ān and You*, 130.
[107] Ibid, 183.

Through the pages of the magazine *Al-Furqān*, Nu'mani held Qur'ānic *dars* at the Tablighi markaz (New Delhi) which was widely received in different circles. The published work of *Dars i-Qur'ān* may be appreciated from two angles: first, it is an engaging discussion of Qur'ānic themes and aspects that had a direct relevance to readers. Second, it stimulated a strong interest in approaching the Qur'ān with an open mind as a living text that embodies the lived experience of its readers.

Ziauddin Falahi has analysed the core themes in *Dars i-Qur'ān.*[108] For example, in Surah Al-An'am the following aspects are covered by Nu'mani: the nature of resurrection, the position of Nabi 'Isa (peace be upon him) in relation to the deviant claims of the Christians, the unalloyed *tawhid* of Nabi Ibrahim (peace be upon him) in contrast to the pervasive influence of *shirk* in belief and practice by the disbelievers.[109]

It must be noted that *Dars i-Qur'ān* spanning over thirty years is the cumulative presentation of Nu'mani's breadth of Qur'ānic knowledge. Although an incomplete tafsir, it does not follow conventional formats as Nu'mani envisaged a robust engagement with the sacred text. This approach is summarised to develop a meaningful, intimate relationship with its message, wisdom and teachings.

- o Create a right frame of mind for the purpose of individual reform.
- o Reiterate the integral components of *tawhid*, Hereafter which have been given secondary importance.
- o Restore the original message of the Qur'ān which over the centuries was exposed to the intrusive influence of Greek philosophy and literature.
- o A common thread that binds the verses (*āyāt*) as an organic unity.
- o The contextualisation of the *asbāb al-nuzul* (reasons

---

[108] See Ziauddin Falahi, *Hind-wa-Pak ke Mashā'ikh ki Qur'āni Khidmāt* (Aligarh, 2020). The book *Dars i-Quran* is examined in this volume.
[109] Ibid., 134.

for revelation) or background information as an expression of the sacred text's timeless and universal significance.

o The application of the Prophetic style and methodology to reconnect mankind with the Qur'ānic legacy for which a mature and positive approach is essential.[110]

Falahi has raised two important issues that have a direct bearing on Nu'mani's approach to the Qur'ān. First, the *rabt* (sequential order) is elucidated to highlight the Qur'ān's logical structure. Second, the tafsir sources consulted are realigned to a modern setting.

We may refer to the thoughtful comments by Nu'mani on the following verse:

> *(O Messenger): If you are among the believers and rise (in a state of war) to lead the Prayer for them, let a party of them stand with you to worship, keeping their arms.*

> (4:102)

This injunction regarding Prayer in the state of either fear or insecurity, refers to the condition when an enemy attack is anticipated as was the case in several wars fought by the Holy Prophet (SAW). Nu'mani reminds readers about the meaning of *tawakkul* (reliance) which generally has been distorted by the Muslim masses. In a war situation, the strategies offered by the Qur'ān are realistic and effective. While it does not exempt the soldiers from performing prayers (*salāh*), the method is emphasised. For Nu'mani, the Qur'ānic wisdom is embedded in a military engagement that requires the Muslim army to present a formidable presence rather than retreat in a vulnerable position. Flexibility is determined by circumstances thus ruling out

---

[110] Falahi, *Hind-wa-Pak*, 146-8.

rigidity. By way of trenchant criticism, Nu'mani extends the relevance of the Qur'ānic dispensation to other scenarios against which Muslims either show indifference or an uncompromising posture.[111]

The lecture on Surah Al-Tawbah, delivered in 1971,[112] is a concise explanation of its significance to Muslim collective life. Nu'mani presents a comprehensive account about the varied aspects of the surah to enable readers to draw upon life-changing lessons. Segments of verses have a historical narrative while other segments are a clear reference to the spirit of sacrifice under trying circumstances. For instance, the Battle of Tabuk was a major challenge for the Muslim army to face the mighty force of the Roman army whose numbers exceeded 200 000 against 3 000 Muslim soldiers. Under these dire circumstances, every able-bodied Muslim was recruited to mobilise against the Roman forces. It was a real test of faith for Muslims on account of the unprecedented strategic policy adopted by the Holy Prophet (SAW). Nu'mani redirects the lessons derived from the surah to the Indian Muslims in respect of their commitment to the spirit of sacrifice and altruism. He laments their obsession for material gains and their indifference to the shari'ah.

For example, many leading businessmen are embroiled in litigation with no regard to social upliftment initiatives. Overall, their attitude militates against the Qur'ānic directives of commitment and sacrifice.[113]

Needless to add, the prolific writings of Nu'mani continue to inspire generations of Muslims seeking an authentic interpretation of the sacred text.

Aspects of Tafsir

The history of the Qur'ān is a sub-genre of tafsir. It is a wide terrain that requires specialist knowledge on a range of historical

---

[111] Ibid.,145-6.

[112] Ibid., 135.

[113] Atiqur Rahman Sambhali, *Hadhrat Mawlana Muhammad Manzur Nu'māni: Special Issue* (Lucknow), April-August 1998, 399-413.

issues, in particular the compilation of the Qur'ān. On several counts, the Orientalist project over the last two centuries has focused on the divine origin of the Qur'ān. Leading scholars like Kidwai, Maher Ali[114] have countered the dubious researches by Orientalists whose nefarious agenda is to tarnish the image of the Holy Prophet (SAW). The Deobandi 'ulama, too, have written books pertaining to the history of the Qur'ān. For example, Abdus Samad Sarim has provided a detailed discussion about the chronology of revelation, the compilation history and the status of the *mushafs* within a timeline framework. The work has been developed out of the notes by the author.[115]

Professor Muhammad Mustafa 'Azami (d. 2017) was a contemporary Indian scholar of hadith best known for his critical investigation and scrutiny of some Orientalist writings on the hadith literature.[116] His well-researched work *The History of the Qur'ānic Text* provides unique insights into the holy text's immaculate preservation, as well as countering many of the accusations levelled against it. By way of comparison, the author investigates the history of the Old and New Testaments, relying entirely on Judeo-Christian sources and uncovers a startling range of alterations in the Scriptures."[117] 'Azami's appraisal of the Orientalist research[118] debunks the distortions of Western writers whose prejudices are entrenched in their dubious works.

The Deobandi alumni also held important positions at several universities. Manazir Ahsan Gilani (d. 1956) belonged to that cohort of 'ulama who rose to prominence on account of their extensive studies in the diverse fields of Islamic learning. His brilliance was recognised by Osmania University (Hyderabad) which offered him the coveted post of Professor of Theology.[119]

Gilani was an educationist who advocated curriculum reform in

---

[114] See Choughley, *The Contributions of Abdur Raheem Kidwai*, 9-21.

[115] Tijarwi, *Fuzalā i-Deoband*, 258.

[116] Muhammad Mustafa 'Azami, *Studies in Early Hadith Literature* (Indianapolis, 1978).

[117] 'Azami, *The History of the Qur'ānic Text: From Revelation to Compilation*. See blurb of the book.

[118] Ibid., 335-72.

[119] See Miftahi, *Hayāt i-Gilāni*. Cf. Nadwi, *Purān i-Charāgh*, vol.1 (Karachi, 1984), 63-95.

madrasahs. According to Ebrahim Moosa, Gilani's proposed reforms of the madrasah curriculum were intended to "preserve Muslim identity in a multireligious and multicultural post-independent India with a Hindu majority via education. Only a select a number madrasahs, he argued, should be preserved and dedicated to serious and advanced theological education."[120]

In Qur'ānic Studies, the articles (*maqālat*) composed in a book form saw the publication of Surah Al-Kahf. Gilani's exploration of the themes are aimed at the modern mind.[121] His *Tadwin al-Qur'ān* details the process of the compilation of the sacred text. Additionally, his perceptive comments on the Qur'ān's divine preservation is a refutation of the Orientalist penchant to undermine its divine origin. Although Gilani did not write tafsirs, his diffuse writings bear the hallmark of excellent scholarship.[122]

No different is the scholarly profile of the renowned scholar, Saeed Ahmad Akbarabadi (d. 1984).[123] He served as a dean of Sunni Theology at AMU and was a visiting professor at Harvard University (US). Two books have earned him an important place in Qur'ānic studies. The Qur'ānic revelation (*Wahy Ilāhi*)[124] focuses on the phenomenon of revelation, eschatology and the Qur'ānic revelation, and the role the archangel Jibril in the communication of the divine message. Akbarabadi's familiarity with the Western trends of hermeneutics is cogently expressed in his critique of their anti-Qur'ān rhetoric.[125] A comparative study of its literary compilation also sheds light on the marked difference between pre-Islamic poetry and the sacred text's inimitable rhetorical style. Akbarabadi dispels the myth around the Qur'ān's borrowing from foreign sources in the light of authentic classical sources. In recent decades the emergence of the Ahl i-Qur'ān movement has raised serious doubts about the relationship between the Qur'ān and hadith. Ghulam Ahmad Parwez (d. 1985) advocated the

---

[120] Moosa, *What is a Madrasa*, 138.
[121] Cf. Abul Hasan Ali Nadwi, *Faith versus Materialism* (Kuala Lumpur, 2005), 5-6.
[122] Tijarwi, *Fuzalā i-Deoband*, 383-4.
[123] A national seminar was hosted on Akbarabadi's life and works by the Department of Sunni Theology (AMU).
[124] Akbarabadi, *Wahi Ilāhi* (Karachi, n.d.).
[125] Ibid., 189-92.

primacy of the Qur'ān[126] by undermining the hadith literature as the indispensable source for the proper understanding of sacred text. The *Fahm al-Qur'ān* as the title suggests, provides a well-structured response to these deviant tendencies. It gives a historical appraisal of the early years of Islam as irrefutable proof to the established importance of hadith for the correct understanding of the sacred text.[127]

A bibliophile, researcher, Qur'ān and hadith scholar - these are the academic credentials of 'Abdul Haleem Chishti (d. 2020). Belonging to a scholarly family who have made their mark in historiography and hadith literature, Chishti was the amalgam of classical and contemporary excellence. A remarkable achievement of Chishti is his specialisation in Library Science - a subject that has not received any attention among the 'ulama. His groundbreaking study on Islamic libraries is a mine of information about its growth and development. In the realm of Qur'ānic studies his examination of Suyuti's contribution to the tafsir genre is perhaps an original piece of work in Urdu. His Introduction (*muqaddimah*) to *Bayān al-Qur'ān* covers 18 topics/aspects in twelve chapters. These aspects include:

- o Revelation of verses/surahs during night and day, summer and winter. These are suggestive clues about the revealed verses according to seasons.
- o Conditions of revelation.
- o Repetition of verses (an overview)
- o Final verses of revelation.[128]

Chishti is regarded as an eminent scholar who has made a significant impact on the new approaches to tafsir writing, bearing in mind the prescribed classical tafsirs in the Deoband curriculum.

The academic credentials of Professor Saud Alam Qāsimi is an

---

[126] Ghulam Ahmad Parwez, *What is Islam: The Qur'ānic Perspective* (Lahore, 2000).
[127] Akbarabadi, *Fahm al-Qur'ān* (Karachi, n.d.).
[128] Tijarwi, *Fuzalā i-Deoband*, 349-55.

impressive record of his scholarly contributions.[129] His published works include several well-researched books on Qur'ānic studies. As a distinguished scholar in the Sunni Theology Department (AMU) his thrust areas are wide and varied. A welcome addition to the study of Waliyullah's Qur'ānic contribution is his critical examination of the latter's approach to the translation project in the subcontinent. A pre-eminent figure in Islamic reformist thought, Waliyullah initiated the translation project which has had an enduring impact on successive tafsirs. Simplicity and brevity characterise his Persian translation of the Qur'ān.

Methodology defines a translator's ideological temperament. Likewise, Saud Alam has made a comparative study of selected Urdu exegetes in the light of Waliyullah's Qur'ānic paradigm. The *i'jāz* theme is framed from the lens of Waliyullah and Farahi's intellectual contribution. A recurrent theme of the Waliyullah Qur'ānic discourse is explored in this thought-provoking work.[130] From a different angle, the Qur'ānic contributions by Shibli Nu'mani (d. 1914) are critically examined. Saud Alam's mastery over the Qur'ānic *'ulum* is embodied in this work.

Presently Saud Alam serves as the editor of the *Tahzib al-Akhlāq* of AMU.

Conclusion

The epic journey navigated by this prestigious institution in Qur'ānic studies over 150 years is a reaffirmation of the centrality of the sacred text in Deoband's mission statement. Muhammadullah Qāsimi has documented the Deobandi contributions to the diverse fields of Qur'ānic studies. Translations, *dars*, lectures, *qirā'at* (recitation) are some of the aspects that define Deoband's remarkable contributions to disseminating the message and teachings of the Qur'ān in the subcontinent and beyond. The satellite *madāris* /Dar al-'Ulums in the UK, US and South Africa have expanded Deoband's footprints and

---

[129] See Saud Alam's curriculum vitae: www.amu.ac.in.
[130] Tijarwi, *Fuzalā i- Deoband*, 335-7.

strengthened its reformist contributions. Likewise, the translation of popular tafsirs into regional languages and English have made the sacred text accessible to readers seeking a simplified understanding of its teachings.

Deoband has not lagged behind in presenting the varied facets of the Qur'ānic themes in modern idiom. Although its output in this respect is limited, there are positive signs that a number of Deobandi alumni are adopting technology to reach out to educated Muslims seeking a better understanding of the eternal message of the Qur'ān. This trend augurs well for the illustrious institution which has preserved the corporate Islamic identity in the subcontinent. Through its *tajdidi* efforts, Deoband has perpetuated the Waliyullah tradition in the field of Qur'ānic studies. By the same token, the establishment of Shaykh al-Hind Academy augurs well for Qur'ānic studies within the environs of the pioneering institution of Islamic learning.

Chapter 3

Barelwi Contributions to the Tafsir Tradition

No tafsir study is complete without closely examining the evolution of the Barelwi reformist thought in the subcontinent. Eponymous founder of the Barelwi *maslak*, Mawlana Ahmad Raza Khan (d. 1921) articulated an Islamic vision in which particular doctrinal issues were given greater importance.[1] In other words, veneration of the Prophet, knowledge of the unseen (*'ilm al-ghayb*), intercessory status of saints (*awliyā*) were associated with popular Islam.[2] The Barelwi/Deobandi divide is largely based on these controversial issues. However, the rise of sectarianism was preceded by polemical works like *Taqwiyat al-Imān*,[3] which was a critique of customary practices deemed un-Islamic by the reformist zeal of Shah Isma'l Shahid (d. 1831). Over time raging debates (*munāzarāt*) followed in rapid uccession causing widening cleavage along sectarian lines. Furthermore, the establishment of these *madāris* exacerbated the phenomenon of *kufr*-bashing *fatwās*. Tragically, *ikhtilāf* was buried under the debris of religious intolerance and bigotry.

The Barelwi school of thought or Sunnis as they are widely known contributed substantially to the Qur'ānic studies tradition. Notwithstanding their unwavering position on certain doctrinal matters which separate them from other *maslaks*, they are considered frontline activists in defending the status and dignity of the Prophet (*Nāmus i-Risālat*), and in Pakistan they have been largely responsible for vociferously advocating the blasphemy

---

[1] Many books have been written on the life and times of 'Allamah Ahmad Raza Khan. See Usha Sanyal, *Devotional Islam and Politics in British India: Imam Ahmad Riza Khan Barelwi and his Movement, 1870- 1920* (New York, 1996). Cf. Ishtiaq Husain Qureshi, *Ulema in Politics* (Karachi, 1974), 224. Cf. Yasin Akhtar Misbahi, *Imām Ahmad Raza awr Jadid Afkār wa Tahrikāt* (New Delhi, n.d.).

[2] See Yasin Akhtar Misbahi, *Ta'āruf i-Ahl i-Sunnat* (New Delhi, 2019).

[3] The politics of *takir* has been a salience around Isma'il Shahid's controversial work *Taqwiyat al-Imān*.

laws despite dissenting voices from secular organisations and political parties. Overall, their markers of religiosity are clearly identifiable. For them, veneration is extended to the religious figures belonging to the Holy Prophet's family (*sādāt*) and the spiritual grace (*fayzān*) of the *awliyā*.[4]

An extraordinary Islamic personality, Ahmad Raza was a polymath; in fact, his writings cover an exceptional range of subjects that attest to his brilliance. Hadith and *iqh*[5] are his areas of specialisation; his published works without doubt have a global reach. In *tasawwuf*, too, Ahmad Raza integrated *tariqah* and shari'ah which informed his strict adherence to the sunnah.

In the field of Qur'ānic translation, Ahmad Raza's *Kanz al-Imān* is considered a pioneering work, reflecting strong Sunni expression. His mastery over Arabic is to the fore with his novel interpretation of particular verses that relate to the exalted status of the Holy Prophet (SAW). Surah Al-Duha (93: 1-11) is illustrative of this approach.[6] It is interesting to note that five English translations of the tafsir have been produced to date, a telling evidence of its popularity in the West. Likewise, it has been translated into Dutch and Turkish that indicates the growing interest about the life, thought and mission of the illustrious scholar.

According to Muhammad Aiyyoob Akram (hereafter Akram), a research associate and contributor to the multivolume tafsir series, there have been multiple annotations (*hawāshi*) on *Kanz al-Imān* since the beginning of the twentieth century. To this series belongs *Khazā'in al-'Irfān*[7] by Sayyid Na'imuddin Muradabadi (d. 1948). A noted jurist, *mufti* and outstanding teacher of philosophy and logic (*kalām*), Muradabadi's explanatory notes have enhanced the popularity of the *Kanz* within the Sunni framework. His *hāshiyah* (annotation) contains a wealth of Islamic 'ulum. There are also distinct traces of the *tasawwuf* elements for garnering a

---

[4] See Ahmad Raza Khan, *Thesis of Imam Raza Khan* (Durban, 2012). Cf. Diedrich Reetz, *Islam in the Public Sphere: Religious Groups in India: 1900-1947* (Oxford, 2006), 82-171.

[5] Khan's *Fatāwā Rizwiyyah*, a multivolume work on *Fiqh*, is representative of his mastery over the Islamic disciplines ('ulum).

[6] See Kidwai, *Translating the Untranslatable*, 186-7.

[7] Na'imuddin Muradabadi, *Khazā'in al-'Irfān* (Lahore, 2012). There is no preface or introductory comments to the tafsir.

mystical approach to the sacred text. The title itself suggests a treasure trove of gnostic knowledge - an allusion to works and theorisation by *sui* masters. Thus *tasawwuf* is pivotal to the translation works of Sunni writers.

Ahmad Yar Khan (d. 1971) is a distinguished *mufassir* who has condensed the *Khazā'in* of Muradabadi for his *hāshiyah, Nur al-'Irfān*.[8] He has developed a sub-genre of tafsir by incorporating his 'tafsir' in the Kanz. In this perspective it stands out as an independent work with distinctive features. The linkages between verses and surahs are clearly explained while keeping in mind the *nuzul* factor. In addition, the translation is followed by essential points of discussion and *tasawwuf* perspectives within a particular framework. Also *Fiqh* literature from a Hanafi position is copiously utilised in the tafsir.[9]

As discussed elsewhere in the chapter, Sunni scholars advocated the primacy of doctrines (*'aqā'id*) pertaining to *'ilm al-ghayb*, veneration of the Holy Prophet (SAW), etc. In counter response, the rhetoric of polemics is built around these core formulations from the Deobandi and Ahl i-Hadith interpretations.[10] In reality, the polemical discourse is an integral aspect of this tafsir genre within these *maslaks.* Khan has adopted a two-tier translation system for his tafsir: literal and idiomatic translations are intended to reinforce the textual interpretations of the Qur'ān.

The above summation of the annotation element is a pointed reference to Ahmad Raza's authoritative translation (*marja`*). The difference between his translation and *Mudih al-Qur'ān* is about modification; the latter has been revised in the twentieth century to facilitate an easy-to-comprehend version. In terms of the linguistic features of the *Kanz*, Akram has outlined its pertinent style. Ahmad Raza's idiomatic expressions in many instances depart from the traditional interpretations of the verses under discussion. For him, the verses in context should reflect the sense

---

[8] An English translation also known as *Nur al-'Irfān* was brought out by Dar al-'Ulum Pretoria (2006).

[9] Mohamed Aiyyoob Akram, *Barelwi Fuzalā ki Qur'āni Khidmāt* (Aligarh, 2020), 42-3.

[10] For a comprehensive account and engaging work about the contentious Barelwi/Deobandi divide, see SherAli Tareen, *Defending Muhammad in Modernity*.

of reverence *('azmat)* in line with the Sunni viewpoints. Simply put, Ahmad Raza explores alternative meanings in support of his interpretations. This approach has given him the unique distinction among Urdu exegetes. To this end, Akram has made a comparative analysis of tafsirs belonging to different sectarian groups *(maslaks)* to highlight Ahmad Raza's eminent translation.[11]

Khawājah Hasan Nizāmi

The life and thought of Khawājah Hasan Nizāmi (d. 1955) offers interesting insights into the changing attitudes towards the contested discourses among Muslims in the twentieth century. Belonging to the spiritual lineage of the Chishtiyah order,[12] Nizami's chequered life mirrors the internal critique that shaped Muslim response to issues affecting their collective identity. The nexus of modern education, women's rights and *tasawwuf* was addressed by scholars like Nizami who advocated a reformed Muslim society shorn of religious accretions that had come to be associated with the Indian version of Islam.

Nizāmi lived in a colonial milieu and several of his writings reflect the tension between continuity and change. According to Daryabadi, Nizāmi was self-made as an influential figure of the Muslim community. However, his controversial views evoked hostile responses from reformist movements like Deoband.[13] Interestingly, in a sufi tradition he did not settle with a custodial role; rather through the network of scholarly initiatives he attempted to reform the prevalent customary rites by articulating an amalgam of the shari'ah and *tariqah* practices. In the same strain, his novels had a reformist thrust for Muslim women who were cloistered in their traditional upbringing with no access to modern education. *The Education of the Wife* is an

---

[11] Akram, *Barelwi Fuzalā*, 34-9.

[12] The Chisthi order had a decisive influence in the formulation of a distinct worldview by Barelwi 'ulama. See, Khaliq Ahmad Nizami, *Tārikh Mashā'ikh Chisht* (Allahabad, 1980).

[13] See Abdul Majid Daryabadi, *Mu'āsirin* (Kolkata, 1979), 95-6. Daryabadi, too, criticised Nizami for his devotional acts in the *mazārs* (shrines) which had no sanction in the shari'ah.

instance in point.[14]

Nizāmi was given the honorific title of *musawwir i-Fitrat,* the depicter of nature[15] probably because of his talent for bringing out human nature and writing in a more natural and accessible style. Likewise, his ardent support of secular education for both girls and boys highlighted 'his appeal to secular virtues of the colonial realm' in the backdrop of the anti-British campaign in the country. Nonetheless, Nizāmi 's religious views in the form of his prolific writings and publishing output exemplified the spirit of his age.[16]

Akram has listed three important Qur'ānic translations (trilogy) undertaken by Nizāmi. These are representative of Nizāmi's sincere attempts to make the Qur'ānic truth and wisdom accessible to ordinary Muslims who for various reasons were disconnected with had a teachings of the sacred text. Moreover, the overwhelming dominance of popular Islam had a tenuous link with Islamic authenticity, which Nizāmi too deplored. The choice of his Qur'ānic titles are indicative of his reformist mission. As a *muballigh* (preacher), Nizāmi adopted a fluent style for his translation that appealed to ordinary readers. In fact, the tafsir was concise, precise in expression and focused primarily on the objectives and legal rulings (*ahkām*) pertaining to their everyday life.[17]

As a novel approach to the translation tradition, Nizāmi provided an annotation to the work of Shah Rafi'uddin, the noted son of Shah Waliyullah. Wherever necessary, he inserted additional notes in brackets for clarity to the text. In view of his *tasawwuf* background, Nizāmi added new meanings and forms to the tafsir tradition by incorporating *adhkār* and related practices ostensibly to reconnect readers with a *tasawwuf* predisposition.[18]

The decline of Urdu as a literary language among Muslims coincided with the rapidly changing political situation in colonial

---

[14] Carl Ernst and Bruce Lawrence, *Sufi Martyrs of Love* (New York, 2002), 114.

[15] Ibid., 116.

[16] Ibid., 115.

[17] Akram, *Barelwi Fuzalā,* 73.

[18] Ibid., 70. Shah Rafi'uddin Dehlawi was an erudite translator of the Qur'ān in Urdu.

India. The patronage of Hindi was on the rise with political ramifications.[19] Nizāmi was sensitive to these official policies and in response produced a Hindi tafsir for Muslims who were familiar with Hindi. The seven- year work was completed in 1929. A discernible feature is the inclusion of Sayyid Nadhir Ahmad's translation in the Hindi (Devanagiri) script together with his simple translation and tafsir. Nizami secured the assistance of Hindi specialists in the preparation of this work.

Another translation in simple Urdu contains novel features. It is a combination of literal and idiomatic expressions to enable readers to develop a sense of familiarity with the text. Additionally, the transcription system is employed for Urdu, an unconventional style, to facilitate a proper understanding of the text.[20]

Overall, these translations bear a distinctive style consistent with Nizami's *da'wah* outreach programme.

Dr. Syed Hamid Hasan Bilgrāmi (2001)

Dr. Syed Hamid Hasan Bilgrāmi (d. 2001) was a well- known educationist and scholar of Islamic studies. He delivered lectures on Iqbal at several universities in England. He is best remembered for his translation of the Qur'ān in Urdu, *Fuyudh al-Qur'ān* which gained appreciation from both 'ulama and intellectuals in Pakistan. At the recommendation of the government he was instrumental in establishing the Islamic University of Bahawalpur in 1963 along the pattern of Al-Azhar University. Dr. Bilgrāmi was closely associated with Dr. Fazlur Rahmān Ansari at the Quetta University and his willingness to accept the post of Director of the Aleemiyah Institute was a testament to the intellectual affinity he shared with the latter. It was the Institute's fortune to have an educationist of the calibre of Dr. Bilgrāmi who guided it to achieve its stated goals as envisioned by Ansari. Among other publications, his *Islamic System of Education* examines the

---

[19] Abul Hasan Ali Nadwi, *Muslims in India* (Lucknow, 1976), 131-40.
[20] Akram, *Barelwi Fuzalā*, 75-6.

significance and role of Islam within an ideological framework. He together with Syed Ali Ashrāf laid out the blueprints of an Islamic university.[21]

The multivolume *Fuyudh al-Qur'ān*[22] has an interesting history as described by Bilgrāmi in the introductory pages of volume 1. Technical production was a serious challenge which delayed its publication. The first edition in 1965 was marred by poor quality printing and did not meet the standards befitting a work of tafsir. However, after much perseverance and the supportive role from his colleagues at Bahawalpur University, *Fuyudh al-Qur'ān* was brought out in 1973.

An unusual feature of this Urdu translation/tafsir is the compilation of an exhaustive Index by the noted scholar and litterateur, Professor Abul Khayr Naqshbandi. It reflected new approaches to making the sacred text reader- friendly. The endorsements by scholars from different schools of thought (*maslaks*)[23] also enhanced the merit of this valuable work. For Bilgrāmi, the title implied layers of spiritual grace (*fuyudh*) derived from the innumerable blessings of the Prophet (SAW). Interestingly, the three- volume work was finished in Madinah al-Munawwarah.[24] The endorsement by Pir Muhammad Karam Shah Azhari stands out for its brief comments about the methodology adopted by Bilgrāmi. In fact, the learned commentator also refers to Azhari's *Diyā al-Qur'ān* (vol. 1) which he consulted extensively in the preparation of his tafsir. Likewise, the erudite Deobandi scholar, Shamsul Haq Afghani (d. 1983),[25] who was a professor of tafsir at Bahawalpur University, highlighted four distinctive aspects of *Fuyudh al-Qur'ān*. Bilgrāmi adhered strictly to the *salaf al-*

---

[21] Cited in Abdul Kader Choughley, *Fazlur Rahman Ansari: Life and Thought* (Springs, 2012), 124. Cf. H.H. Bilgrāmi, *Islamic System of Education: Search for a Solution* (Karachi, 1992).

[22] Bilgrami, *Fuyudh al-Qur'ān*, vol. 1 (Karachi, 1973), 3-4.

[23] For example, Mufti Shafi, author of *Ma'āriful Qur'ān*.

[24] Allamah Muhammad Yusuf Binori (d.1977), wrote the following comments in appreciation of Bilgrāmi's tafsir: "*Dedicated to Allah in the blessed precincts of Masjid al-Nabi (SAW).*" See Bilgrāmi, *Fuyudh al-Qur'ān*, vol. 1, 13.

[25] A prolific scholar of Qur'ānic studies, Afghani held the position of *Shaykh al-Tafsir* in Bhawalpur University (Pakistan).

sālih interpretation of the sacred text. According to him, the text of the Qur'ān was a rallying point for the educated class who, by and large, were inclined to search for variant opinions compatible with their secular mindset. By virtue of his vast experience in the educational and academic fields, Bilgrāmi successfully presented a rational style that had a direct appeal to the rising generation of Muslims who sadly pursued secular studies as a priority. The authoritative sources were widely consulted to explicate the logical structure *(rabt)* of the sacred text.[26]

The introductory pages (vol.1) states Bilgrāmi 's motivation for authoring *Fuyudh al-Qur'ān*. He maintains that the pressing need for modern society is the forceful presentation of the Qur'ānic message without streaks of apologia. It should focus on its essential teachings, coherent structure and inimitable style.[27] Most importantly, the true meaning of the Qur'ān should be interlinked with its message of guidance so that modern man may assimilate its spiritual blessings. According to Akram, the translation is couched in an elegant and graceful style that reflects the linguistic charm and beauty of the Qur'ān. In Azhari's estimation, Bilgrāmi has brought out the spiritual contents to reconnect readers with the intrinsic truths embodied in the text of the Qur'ān.[28]

Pir Muhammad Karam Shah Azhari

A pre-eminent figure in the Islamic revivalist movement, Pir Muhammad Karam Shah Azhari (d. 1998) was a remarkable scholar in the Pakistan religious landscape. A distinguished 'alim, jurist, educationist and spiritual guide, Azhari was an institution builder whose contributions have resonance in Pakistan and abroad. Azhari completed his

M.A. in Islamic law (shari'ah) at Al-Azhar university which developed his expertise to serve as a judge in the Shari'ah court of

---

[26] Bilgrāmi, *Fuyudh al-Qur'ān*, vol.1, 17.
[27] Ibid., 6.
[28] Akram, *Barelwi Fuzalā*, 56.

Pakistan.[29] Azhari's cutting-edge scholarship and social activism earned him many prestigious awards, a recognition of his outstanding achievements in the various Islamic disciplines.

Keeping in mind his Chishtiyah lineage, Azhari used the *khānqah* in Bherah (Sargodha) to develop his vision of an inclusive site of learning and spiritual culture. In this strain, his prolific writings encompass a range of subjects that have value-oriented ideals. Among his major contributions is his seven-volume *Diyā al-Nabi*,[30] considered to be a masterpiece in the *sirah* genre. The title *Diyā* is illustrative of his deep-seated reverence for the personality of the Holy Prophet (SAW). Following a similar approach is his celebrated tafsir *Diyā al-Qur'ān*. A 'love of labour' spanning 14 years of comprehensive study and revision (1965 - 79),[31] the five-volume tafsir has attracted a wider readership for its scholarly erudition. At the heart of the tafsir, is Azhari's summative assessment of the Qur'ān's impact on sincere readers and its potential transformative character.

As an introduction, Azhar offers perceptive comments on the ways to grasp the essence of the Qur'ān. In his perspective, the Qur'ān's timeless truth and wisdom are embedded in its miraculous style. It is an inexhaustible repository of knowledge that transcends the intellectual discourse. By its very inimitable style, it changed the course of history and created a civilisation that had, in unprecedented ways, influenced science, philosophy and other related disciplines. From the valleys of *Fārān* (Makkah and its environs), the Arabian Peninsula impacted greatly on world civilisation. However, Azhari laments Muslim apathy to appreciate the beauty and teachings of the sacred text. Instead, vices like self-love, pride and corruption have vitiated positive and productive ideals that are embodied in the Islamic moral code. In the spirit of reform (*islāh*), Azhari reminds the Muslim community in the subcontintent that they have disregarded the Qur'ān as the source of guidance. In a spirit of counsel *(nasihah)*, Azhari

---

[29] Majeed, *Qur'ān Interpretation in Urdu*, 119-20.
[30] Karam Shah Azhari, *Diyā al-Qur'ān*, vol.1 (Lahore, 1978), 5-6.
[31] Ibid., 7-9.

reiterates that hearts can only be illumined by the Qur'ān which transformed the *Jāhiliyyah* Arab nation into saviours of mankind and torch bearers of civilisation and culture.[32]

Azhari criticises the different segments of Muslim society for their indifference to the eternal message of the sacred text. His evocative descriptions of their failings stem from their disconnect mindset. In essence, the Qur'ān has provided a complete code of life (*dābita hayāt*)[33] through which Muslims can restore their role as custodians/stewards of Allah (*khalifah*). However, the spectre of factionalism and sectarianism has taken on alarming proportions. As a result, the distorted version of *ihktilāf*[34] has eroded the *adab* (culture) of scholarly disagreement which defined the proud Islamic intellectual tradition. Particularly in the subcontinent, groupism or the *maslak* mindset has its deep roots in religious bigotry. Azhari deplores this ugly trend which has fragmented the unity of the *ummah*. The above point is pertinent to understand Azhari's reverential approach to the Qur'ān. His Sunni interpretation is based on primary sources which avoids contentious issues and steers away from the bane of rigidity and laxity (*ifrāt wa tafrit*).[35] Overall, the tafsir advocates a sectarian-free approach by stimulating readers' interest to the Qur'ān's brilliant exposition (*tibyān*) and unsurpassed style (*uslub*). In this way, Azhari reaffirms the eloquence of the Qur'ānic Arabic to press home the importance of mastering the language.

Stylistic features of *Diya al-Qur'ān*

One distinguishing feature of his translation is that it incorporates both literal and idiomatic styles. For Azhari, fluency and context define the intent of the Qur'ānic verses. To this end, the translation is free from embellishment and interpolation of

---

[32] Ibid., 10.

[33] Ibid.

[34] Ibid., 11.

[35] Muhammad Sultan Shah, *Diyā al-Qur'ān: A Unique Qur'ānic Commentary and the Commentator* (Lahore, n.d.), 8.

the sacred text. His focus is on authenticity rather than projecting a sectarian viewpoint that is characteristic of several translations.[36]

A meticulous exegete, Azhari employed calligraphers to give the text an aesthetic appeal. Likewise, exegetical notes are written below the translation of the Arabic text, a marked departure from the interlinear translations. A praiseworthy feature of the tafsir is the subject index which helps readers to locate a particular verse. These subject indexes are useful tools for linguistic purposes, historical sources and eschatological issues. Maps are also included to provide a sense of history to places mentioned in the Qur'ān. Essentially, these maps have a historical connotation and allow readers to examine the Qur'ānic narratives of previous civilisations, the evolution of human progress, etc.[37] Also the timeline is used as a framework to reconnect these nations or civilisations with matters relating to the concept of Prophethood. In other words, how did these nations respond to their respective Prophets who brought the message of *tawhid*, Afterlife, etc.?

Methodology of *Diyā al-Qur'ān*

In the strain of early commentators, Azhari elucidates the importance of literary Arabic. His tafsir reflects the vast corpus of Arabic literature gleaned from classical sources. By the same token, Azhari gives a holistic presentation of *asbāb al-nuzul* (occasions of revelation) by pinpointing their relevance to political or historical incidents described in the Qur'ān. His erudition is to fore in his explication of *ahkām* (shar'i injunctions). For example, with regard to the eight sub-headings of charity, Azhari is of the opinion that *zakāh* can be disbursed to the administrative personnel in the light of the Qur'ānic verse. As a judge (*qādi*), he argues that the government is responsible for collecting and distributing *zakāh* as an institutional obligation.

Azhari adopts a sense of balance (*i'tidāl*) in his presentation of

---

[36] Majeed, *Qur'ān Interpretation in Urdu*, 124.
[37] Ibid., 124.

different viewpoints for which there exists disagreement among exegetes. In the matter of Isra'ilite traditions he adopts a cautious approach: traditions which contradict the spirit of the Qur'ānic text are rejected.[38] Similarly, he is circumspect about supporting or countering incidents mentioned in the Qur'ān for which no clarity exists. The divergence of opinions about *mi'rāj* is a case in point. Azhari produces a detailed account without pronouncing his judgement on the matter. This approach is in keeping with his cosmopolitan outlook and mastery over the Qur'ānic literature.

A literary critic, Azhari "has also drawn extensively on poetry for a better understanding of the meaning of the verses of the Qur'ān. Also, he has pointed to the poetry inspired by the Qur'ān, thus depicting [its] influence. In his tafsir, he has quoted from Arabic, Persian and Urdu."[39]

An outstanding Qur'ānic scholar, Azhari was very much familiar with the emerging trends of non-traditional tafsirs. Ghulam Ahmad Parwez,[40] ideologue of the Ahl al-Qur'ān movement is representative of this trend in the subcontinent. Azhari's critique of his works draws a parallel between the Jewish predilection to reject parts of the Torah and the anti-hadith mentality advocated by Parwez. Another dimension of his scholarly reputation relates to the distorted historical accounts of the Orientalists.[41] Azhari's well-developed counter response is a testament to his excellent grasp of the *sirah* genre. In fact, his multivolume *Diya al-Nabi* supplements his brief historical comments in the tafsir.

As a spiritual guide (*sufi*), the elements of *tasawwuf* are embedded in his tafsir. Azhari quotes Alusi's *Ruh al-Ma'āni* and other classical *tasawwuf* sources to demonstrate the organic link between the shari'ah and *tariqah*.[42]

---

[38] Ibid., 125.

[39] Juneefa Bilal, "Muhammad Karam Shahal-Azhari's Contribution to Qur'ānic Studies: A Study of his *Diyā al-Qur'ān*", in *Aligarh Journal of Qur'ānic Studies*. Volume 3, Issue 2. October 2020, 22.

[40] Ghulam Parwez authored *Mafhum al-Qur'ān* and *Lughāt al-Qur'ān*, both works reflect his anti-hadith position.

[41] Azhari, *Diyā al-Qur'ān*, vol.1, 5-6.

[42] Ibid., 9.

The eulogy of the Holy Prophet (SAW) is summed up in Surah Al- Sharah (94) as an expression of his unconditional reverence for the personality of Holy Prophet (SAW).[43]

Diyā al-Qur'ān enjoys a significant place in contemporary Urdu tafsirs and is considered an authoritative text in the Sunni academic tradition.

Muhammad Tāhir al-Qādri

A twenty-first century Islamic intellectual, Tāhir al-Qādri (b. 1951) has established his international fame in the various fields of Islamic learning. His literary output epitomises his academic pursuits. A constitutional law professor (Punjab University), hadith expert, *Fiqh* specialist and *tasawwuf*-oriented guide, Qādri has contributed significantly to the Islamic renewal project. His writings and lectures encompass a wide range of subjects that appeal to the modern mind.

A visionary, Qadri founded the Al-Minhaj Foundation International as his *da'wah* outreach initiative. The establishment of organisations and tertiary institutions around the world bears out his inclusive approach to reconfiguring Islamic activism. Through the print media he has developed a network of disseminating the teachings of the Qur'ān within specific contexts.[44] Currently he resides in Canada.

In the field of Qur'ānic studies Qādri's contribution is remarkable. Take for example, the Qur'ānic encyclopedia (2019) which contains a wealth of information pertaining to the vast corpus of Qur'ānic literature. Additionally, separate volumes have been written on particular aspects of the Qur'ān. By virtue of his specialised Qur'ānic knowledge and expertise, Qādri explores the dimensions of the word 'Qur'ān' as used in the sacred text. He is able to weave a thread of common themes that have relevance for readers interested in understanding the multidimensional facets of the Qur'ān. For Qādri, the Qur'ānic worldview is

---

⁴³ Ibid.

⁴⁴ www.minhaj.org/. Accessed on 12 July 2020.

quintessentially modern and relatable to the educated class who are in search of true happiness. His sufi leanings and analytical study of Islamic disciplines (*'ulum*) are best represented in these Qur'ānic series.[45] The plight of modern man is a recurrent theme in his other writings.

Qādri's translation *'Irfān al-Qur'ān,* is a comprehensive explanatory translation of the sacred text. Key themes include Qadri's elaboration of hermeneutics and strict adherence to linguistic accuracy and parenthetical explanations supported by translated sentence structures. This method allows for a number of multiple interpretations without sacrificing textual authenticity, clarity and precision of expression.[46] Other notable aspects include Qādri 's elaboration of scientific knowledge and the elucidation of the inner spiritual dimensions of many verses (*āyāt*). Kidwai's review of the English translation titled *The Glorious Qur'ān* (2011) is instructive:

> Qadri, as a representative of the Barelwi school, has a strong predilection for *tasawwuf* (Islamic mysticism). At places, the same surfaces in his Qur'ān translation. For example, the Prophet's mandate as teacher, conferred upon him by the Qur'ān, is spelled out in the following terms of reverence laden with mysticism. "[The Prophet (SAW)] teaches you the Book and inculcates in you logic and wisdom and enlightens you (on the mysteries of spiritual gnosis and divine truth) which you did not know". (Al-Baqarah 2: 151, p. 25). Also, the Index identifies scores of Qur'ānic verses which, according to him, focus on "gnosis" and "spiritual excellence" (pp. 1070 and 1094). Likewise, Khidr in Surah Al-Kahf is introduced as an 'elite servant who possessed the inspired knowledge of secrets and gnostics.' (p. 490)[47]

---

[45] Ibid.

[46] Akram, *Barelwi Fuzalā,* 97.

[47] Kidwai, *God's Word, Man's Interpretations,* 78.

Although his (Qādri) notes are not many, he has compensated this with his usually helpful parenthetical comments in the body of the translation. His paraphrase-like translation goes a long a long way in conveying fully the message and meaning of the Qur'ān to readers. Qādri's intelligent and perceptive grappling with the Word of God in order to derive divine guidance regarding current issues and challenges is evident from his Index, signifying his attempt to relate several Qur'ānic verses with such concerns of *Jihād* in order to 'eliminate terrorism, militancy, human resources, dignity of women, etc.' Appended to the work is a useful note on the excellent etiquette and virtues of the recitation of the Qur'ān. This note is based on authentic *ahādith* and bears out Qadri's thorough grounding in the primary Islamic sources.[48]

Akram has commented on Qādri 's comprehensive tafsir *Minhāj al-Qur'ān* (14 volumes) published in 2000 of which volume 1 deserves brief mention. It is an excellent tafsir bearing the following hallmarks. First, it is couched in modern idiom allowing for a flow of ideas which focuses on current issues to make the Qur'ānic text relatable to the modern mind. The synthesis of literal and idiomatic styles signifies a reader-friendly approach. Furthermore, parenthetical explanations are given to clarify meanings where applicable. Several allusions to *tazkiyah* (spiritual purification) are given prominence in the tafsir. In sum, Qādri does not delve into grammatical and semantic structures as his tafsir has a specific readership. According to Akram, the tafsir is unique in its presentation and is representative of modern trends of Qur'ānic scholarship.

---

[48] Ibid., 81-2.

'Allāmah Ghulam Rasool Sa'eedi

A vociferous spokesman (*tarjumān*) for the Sunni/Barelwi interpretation of contested doctrines, Ghulam Rasool Sa'eedi (d. 2016) has come to represent the intellectual voice of 'traditional' Islam. His impressive achievements in hadith, *Fiqh* and Qur'ānic studies are emblematic of serious scholarship that is taking shape in the madrasah sector.[49] On an optimistic note, the academic standard has improved significantly considering the prodigious output of writings, particularly in the hadith genre.

A versatile figure in Islamic `ulum, Sa'eedi held key positions in the Federal Shari'ah Court (Pakistan) and his vast *Fiqh* expertise has been recognised in Islamic legal circles. Likewise, his thorough grounding in hadith sciences (*'ulum al-hadith*) nurtured over decades of study and teachings has seen a notable contribution in this field by his monumental multivolume *Ni'mat al-Bāri*. Similarly, the primacy of hadith studies has also seen a surge of hadith compilations in Pakistan. In many instances these works have been developed over the years from the *durus* (lessons) system, which is a peculiarity of these Dar al-'Ulums. Among Sa'eedi's contemporaries was Shaykh Saleem'ullah Khan, a prolific scholar of hadith who had authored *Kashf al- Bāri*.[50]

Sa'eedi had enlisted a number of students, many of whom made their mark in Qur'ānic and hadith studies. Mention may be made of Dr. Sarfaraz Naeemi, an influential figure and president of Jami'a Naeemia. Ebrahim Moosa makes the following observations about Naeemi's Islamic learning and social activism:

> Naeemi led public protests against the Danish cartoons that were deemed to dishonor the Prophet Muhammad (SAW) and outraged Muslim sentiment globally. He also petitioned the government of Pakistan to pioneer an effort at the United Nations to create an international

---

[49] Akram, *Barelwi Fuzalā*, 102-3.
[50] For a detailed account of Sa'eedi's literary contributions, see Shagufta Jabi, *'Allāmah Ghulam Rasul Sa'eedi: Hayāt wa Khidmāt* (Lahore, 2012).

protocol that would protect Prophets and sacred figures of all religions from blasphemous and denigrating representations. Public disturbances associated with Naeemi's protests and petition resulted in his arrest.[51]

Veneration of the Holy Prophet (SAW), sacred figures and relics associated with venerable saints (*awliyā*) is central to Sa'eedi's formulation of an authentic expression of Islam. These form 'landscapes of piety' and have dominated Sunni/Barelwi traditional thought. This is best illustrated in Sa'eedi's popular tafsir *Tibyān al-Qur'ān*. Volume 1 is a summary of his tafsir approach that delineates his excellent grasp of hadith and *Fiqh* literature. Sa'eedi makes a clear distinction about his work from the classical commentators. His translation conforms to traditional sources; however, this is a qualified statement about his elucidation of *taqlid*. This point is explained as follows: If a single narration (*hadith*) by Suyuti is transmitted through different chains of authorities that does not imply that the multiple *ahādith* of this narration can be uncritically endorsed. The same rule applies to *Fiqh* issues which are derived and supported by a single narration. According to Sa'eedi, this approach smacks of deception (*talbis*)[52] in the technical sense as it hinders possibilities of critical appraisal. In contrast, he advocates a nuanced interpretation of Qur'ānic verses that have a *Fiqh* import. Again, Sa'eedi reiterates an important point: disagreement (*ikhtilāf*) is a corollary of *ijtihād* and evolves according to changing circumstances. Therefore, it is an on-going process that requires deep knowledge and insight. Sa'eedi sets outs his framework to approaching *āyāt* that have multiple layers of interpretation. In this process the culture of equilibrium (*i'tidāl*) is emphasised.[53]

---

[51] Moosa, *What is a Madrasa*, 165-6.

[52] Ghulam Rasul Sa'eedi, *Tibyān al-Qur'ān*, vol. 1 (Lahore, 2000), 37.

[53] Ibid., 37. Cf. Omar Husain, *Gateway to the Qur'ānic Sciences* (London, 2017), 19. The author highlights Suyuti's lenient transmission of weak and fabricated in several of his writings.

As a renowned 'alim, Sa'eedi seeks to demonstrate the continuity of the tafsir tradition. While relying on several classical works, Sa'eedi has also consulted contemporary tafsirs like Qutb's *Fi Zilāl al-Qur'ān* to amplify his viewpoints on current issues. The blending of reformist thought with traditional interpretation is a hallmark of *Tibyān al-Qur'ān* which seeks to unravel the intent of Allah's revelation.

In his *Introduction,* Sa'eedi elucidates the important aspects related to tafsir as a genre. His rigorous analysis bears out his familiarity with the vast corpus of Qur'ānic studies and hadith literature. The evolution of tafsir receives a detailed account. In the light of his profound study of 'ulum al-Qur'ān, Sa'eedi presents irrefutable arguments about the status of *naskh* (abrogation) of Qur'ānic verses. In the same strain, he critiques Ghulam Parwez's anti-hadith rhetoric. His objective analysis about the theory of *inhirāf* (distortions) of the Qur'ān is indicative of his extensive reading of Shi'ah sources. Likewise, a synoptic assessment of the growth and development of the tafsir tradition is illuminating. His intelligent and perceptive comments about contemporary tafsirs in the light of their respective *maslak* orientations come a long way to the sectarian-free scholarly trends.[54]

A cursory examination of the table of contents reveals the breadth of Sa'eedi's knowledge, familiarity with core issues in Surah Al-Baqarah. Among the characteristic features of *Tibyān al-Qur'ān* is the refutation (*radd*) of scholarly positions held by scholars like Ibn Taimiyyah on the permissibility of *wasilah* (mediated prayers), etc. These controversial doctrines are framed in a Sunni/Barelwi perspective.

In sum, *Tibyān al-Qur'ān* is a significant contribution to the tafsir genre on two counts: first, it is an authoritative work synthesising classical and contemporary interpretation of the sacred text. Second, it is representative of the new trends in the Urdu tafsir tradition.

---

[54] Ibid., 41-131. Core issues are given in the *Introduction* of the tafsir.

Sayyid Muhammad Madani Ashrafi

A scion of the Ashrafi Jilani family, Sayyid Muhammad Madani (b. 1938) acquired his Islamic education in Mubarakpur, bastion of the Barelwi institutions in India. He received his formal training from his father who was popularly known as the *Muhaddith i-'Azam*, in recognition of his prolific works in the hadith field.

Ashrafi's global reach is visible in the institutions he had established for the purpose of disseminating the Islamic teachings, in particular *tasawwuf*-oriented counsels. His Qur'ānic contributions were initially inspired by his father whose incomplete *Ma'ārif al-Qur'ān* was incorporated into his *Tafsir i-Ashrafi*. A ten-volume work, Ashrafi has adopted a simple, direct translation to enable readers to grasp the meaning and spirit of the sacred text. Accessibility and readability are his primary focus and these are embodied in his presentation of an authoritative version of the Qur'ān.

Two dominant features inform his style of translation. First, syntax (choice of words) is crafted in such a way to ensure that the exalted status of the Holy Prophet (SAW) remains intact. In general, sensitivity and veneration define the Barelwi interpretation of verses relating to the Holy Prophet (SAW), a trend set by *Kanz al-Imān*. Second, the *ahkām* (legal injunctions) are simplified for ordinary readers of the modern age.

The publisher of the voluminous work has provided statistical details about the number of words, sentences, paragraphs which appear in volume 2. Included in the tafsir is the exegete's referencing of *sufi* lives as a form of building life-enriching experiences - a trait that has found salience in Sunni tafsirs. In the same spirit, it contains refutations of objections raised by dissenting voices (sectarian difference) and generally by rationalists and deviant groups. The core content of the tafsir is the salvation for mankind.[55]

---

[55] Adapted from Akram, *Barelwi Fuzalā*, 199-201.

Faiz Ahmad Uwaisi

An outstanding academic pedigree, Faiz Ahmad Uwaisi (d. 2010) represented the amalgam of Qur'ānic and *Fiqh* studies. His competence in Arabic may be gleaned from his writings and translations of major works in the Qur'ānic field. It is to his credit that several Qur'ānic works have been translated into Sindhi. This contribution has enriched the tafsir tradition in Pakistan.

Uwaisi's spiritual affiliation is embedded in his Qur'ānic studies as well. Indeed, he has lent knowledge to the vast corpus of Islamic *'ulum* that reaffirms his scholarly credentials. In relation to his *Fiqh* contributions, his works on the Pakistani blasphemy laws are instructive. Likewise, he has vociferously supported initiatives in respect of the *Khatm al-Nabuwwat* (Finality of Prophethood) discourse.

Apart from the tafsirs which are germane to Qur'ānic methodology and principles (*usul*), his translation of classical works are a laudable contribution. Take for instance, his *sharah* (annotation) of Suyuti's *Jalālayn*, which is a must-read for students at Dar'al-'Ulums. Also the theories of *naskh* (abrogation) and *nazm* (coherence) are examined in separate volumes.

A thirty- volume tafsir *Fuyudh al-Rahmān* is the Urdu translation of the celebrated Turkish exegetical work of Isma'il Haqqi Busrawi (d. 1725), *Ruh al-Bayān* which has been widely read and appreciated by scholars across the sectarian divide. The *tasawwuf* trajectory is comprehensively covered in the tafsir. In a similar vein, the mystical doctrines of Ibn 'Arabi and other leading *suis* make up the core formulation of *tasawwuf* in a tafsir perspective. Uwaisi has ably constructed a well-developed framework about the inner dimensions (spirituality) embedded in the surahs. Of course, veneration of the Holy Prophet (SAW) receives a detailed discussion against the Sunni background. Overall, Uwaisi's commendable translation is a landmark contribution to the expanding horizon of the tafsir tradition.[56]

---

[56] Ibid., 153-62. This is a summative assessment of Uwaisi's wide-ranging Qur'ānic contributions. Akram has been able to document, albeit briefly, the distinguished scholar's thorough grounding in Islamic *'ulum.*

Shahid `Ali Misbāhi

Jami'ah Ashrafiyah (Mubarakpur)[57] is the epicentre of the Sunni traditionalist thought and has produced several thousand graduates, many of whom have excelled in Qur'ānic, *Fiqh* and hadith studies. Shahid 'Ali Misbahi (b. 1973) may be counted as one of its distinguished alumni, who has been widely recognised for his excellent annotation (*sharah*) of *Tafsir Jalālayn*. Written in elegant Urdu, *Kanz al- Dārayn* covers the terrain of linguistic structures. Misbahi has offered detailed grammatical explanations about the origin of words like angels (*malā'ikah*) and their Qur'ānic connotations. His translation bears the imprint of *Kanz al-Imān* and thus his views subscribe to Sunni/Barelwi discourse. Interestingly, an innovative approach, the *sharah* has *'irāb* (Arabic declensions) to facilitate an uncomplicated reading of the text. Also, the *ahkām* constitutes another merit- worthy feature of this important work.[58]

Ghulam Anjum Yahya

A noted professor of Arabic and Islamic studies at Jamia Hamdard, Ghulam Yahya Anjum (b. 1958) is best known for his biographical writings on Mawlana Ahmad Raza Khan, *sufi* shaykhs and Egyptian historians. His research papers and articles are a treasure house of the spiritual genealogy of leading *tariqahs* in the subcontinent. He has to his credit a versified version of Surah Al-Fatihah.[59]

Kidwai has written an excellent review of Anjum's brief survey of Qur'ānic translations in Urdu.[60] A tafsir enterprise is a daunting task keeping in mind the vast array of interpretations that have

---

[57] See Mubarak Husain Misbahi, *Al-Jamiatul Ashraia* (Mubarakpur, n.d.).
[58] Akram has noted that sketchy details are available for several tafsirs listed in his *Barelwi Fuzalā*, making it daunting task to assess their respective merits. In view of the paucity of information available, the gist of tafsirs like *Kanz al-Dārayn* is given.
[59] Ibid., 144-7.
[60] Abdur Raheem Kidwai, "Qur'ān Kareem ke Hindustani Tarajim wa Tafasir", in *Tahqiqāt i-Islami Aligarh*. July-September 2020.

given it shape and form. Needless to say, intellectual disposition and sectarian temperament are variables that inform the exegete's worldview which in many instances is a pale reflection of the true essence, guidance and wisdom of the sacred text. Anjum's creditable efforts to bring into broad relief the translations/tafsirs of the subcontinent written over several centuries, however, have some drawbacks. Kidwai has correctly observed that his work does not accurately represent a historical overview of the rich tafsir tradition that is deeply rooted on the indigenous soil. Additionally, the paucity of information diminishes the merits of several tafsirs, classical and contemporary, discouraging readers to appreciate the exegetes' scholarly acumen. Kidwai stands out as an authority of Qur'ānic reviews in the subcontinent and abroad and his works are widely recognised in the academic world. Therefore, his critical review of Anjum's work is intended to flesh out areas that need to be improved. For example, Anjum's predilection for Barelwi-oriented tafsirs is a serious shortcoming as it blurs out an open-ended reading of Allah's revelation.[61] Likewise, his cursory reference to important tafsirs does not help readers to form a proper assessment about their singular contributions.

In 2020 a number of tafsir works have appeared on the market that give an idea about the proactive initiatives among Barelwi scholars. For example, *Tafsir Gowhar al-Bayān* and *Tanwir al-Imān*[62] are located within the framework of *Kanz al-Imān* and very much infused with *tasawwuf* concepts. These work augur well for a critical appraisal of Barelwi tafsirs.

---

[61] Ibid., 288-9.

[62] I am indebted to Ahmad Tarazi of Karachi (Pakistan) who has provided me the relevant details to these tafsirs.

Chapter 4

Nadwi Contributions to Qur'ānic Studies

The history of Nadwat al-'Ulama, Lucknow[1] (hereafter Nadwah) is generally associated with the reinterpretation of the *Dars i-Nizāmī*[2] in the backdrop of the sweeping geopolitical developments in the subcontinent. Since its establishment, Nadwah's focus was influenced by two distinct impulses: challenges and changes.[3] Its main emphasis was on Qur'ānic studies (*tafsir*), Arabic literature and Islamic history. Nadwah's mission statement embodied a synthesis of classical Islamic education and the modern sciences. This meant the integration between the eternal fundamentals of the faith and the ever- changing values of human life.[4]

According to Muhammad Tariq Ayubi,[5] early efforts to introduce an analytical study of tafsir were undertaken by Shibli Nu'mani (d. 1914).[6] Classical texts like Baqilani's *I'jāz al-Qur'ān* formed the basis for a direct access to the vast corpus of tafsir literature. However, the tafsir did not develop into a systematic science like hadith and *iqh*, which were avidly pursued in the traditional *madāris*. Ayubi has correctly observed that specialisation in tafsir did not attract widespread interest among students on account of the *madāris's* lack of visionary input to the foundational sources of Islam. Even Nadwah did not produce a cadre of Qur'ānic scholars whose contributions could be

---

[1] Shams Tabrez Khan, *Tārikh Nadwat al-'Ulama*, 2 vols. (Lucknow, 1984).

[2] See Francis Robinson, *The 'Ulama of Farangi Mahal and Islamic Culture in South Asia* (Lucknow, 2001).

[3] Cited in Abdul Kader Choughley, *Sayyid Abul Hasan Ali Nadwi: Life and Works* (New Delhi, 2012), 34.

[4] Ibid., 35.

[5] An erudite scholar, Muhammad Tariq Ayubi Nadwi has authored several books on Nadwah and Shaykh Nadwi in Arabic and Urdu. He has contributed a volume to the tafsir series co-ordinated by the K. A. Nizami Centre for Qur'ānic Studies (AMU). See Muhammad Tariq Ayubi Nadwi Ayubi, *Nadwat al-'Ulama ki Fikri wa Milli Shu'ur* (Aligarh, 2015).

[6] For a comprehensive study of Shibli Nu'mani's multifaceted contributions, see Sulayman Nadwi, *Hayāt i-Shibli* (Azamgarh, 2014).

justifiably acknowledged.[7] There are several factors that point out to Nadwah's limited role in the tafsir tradition. First, Arabic literature was assigned prominence in its curriculum. Its global reach to the Arabic-speaking world was impressive both in its scope and content. Second, Nadwah focused vigorously on the 'adaptation' process: production of comprehensible texts for hadith and *Fiqh.* In some ways, it diminished the prospects for a focused-based study of tafsir. Third, locating the institution in a modern setting meant a reconfiguration of its vision. In other words, Nadwah invested its energies to the production of effective literature that would meet the challenges of the day.[8]

Another candid assessment by Ayubi is the scholarly tenor of the Nadwi contributions to the tafsir tradition. There have been several exceptional pieces of writings that discuss tafsir in a modern idiom. We may cite Sayyid Sulaymān Nadwi (d. 1953) and Sayyid Abul Hasan Ali Nadwi (d. 1999) for their scholarly treatment of specific topics related to Qur'ānic studies.[9] However, by and large, in recent years the trend has been limited to the compilation series by Nadwi scholars. Topics of contemporary relevance or *islāhi* contents are written for a modern readership. In view of their exposure to the Arab world, both Urdu and Arabic are employed to disseminate their views on Qur'ānic themes. Again a comprehensive tafsir does not feature in their scholarly contributions.

There is however, a redeeming factor that may be attributed to Nadwah's cosmopolitan character: ideological overlapping. Several scholars belonging to Jama'at i-Islami and the Ahl i-Hadith movement are graduates from Nadwah. Their tafsir contributions find entries in their respective ideological affiliations. A case in point is the tafsir of Mawlana Muhammad Haneef Nadwi,[10] which is examined in chapter 5.

Ayubi provides a conspectus of selected scholars in the domain

---

[7] Ayubi, *Nadwi Fuzalā ki Qur'āni Khidmāt* (Aligarh, 2019), 10-11.

[8] Ibid., 11.

[9] Ibid.

[10] See Rafiq Ahmad *Salai, Ahl i-Hadith Fuzalā ki Qur'āni Khidmāt* (Aligarh, 2019), 119-28.

of Qur'ānic studies. His survey varies from detailed examination to brief comments of the scholars under review. A multivolume like this project has its own limitations: concise discussion sometimes supplemented by brief comments and also a paucity of information on several scholars do not allow for full justice to provide a well-constructed presentation. Notwithstanding these academic challenges, Ayubi's work is an important contribution to Qur'ānic studies.

Sayyid Sulaymān Nadwi: Peerless Qur'ānic scholar

Several strands of Islamic thought reflect the multidimensional personality of Sayyid Sulaymān Nadwi. His versatility and brilliant exposition of Qur'ānic themes epitomise the standards of excellence of Nadwah's graduates. It was his illustrious teacher Shibli Nu'mani who developed his skills in Arabic literature and the *sirah* genre. A cursory survey of the *Sirah al-Nabi*, initiated by Nu'mani and completed in seven volumes by Nadwi is a testament to the latter's literary acumen and unrivalled mastery over the *sirah* sources, classical and contemporary.[11] Sulaymān Nadwi's other creditable accomplishment is the establishment of Dar al-Musannifin (Azamgarh), an academic institution of high renown, and the promotion of Arabic at Nadwah. His varied literary pursuits in various Islamic institutions point out to his profound knowledge of Qur'ānic and hadith studies, Arabic and history.

The niche area of Sulaymān Nadwi's Qur'ānic sciences *('ulum)* has only recently been critically examined. Shaykh Nadwi offers insightful comments about Sayyid Sulaymān's Qur'ānic scholarship.

> I also had the privilege of discussing the meaning of some Qur'ānic verses with Mawlana Sayyid Sulaymān Nadwi. I listened to some of his talks on the Qur'ān as well. To my mind Mawlana

---

[11] Ibid.

Nadwi was not equaled by anyone in his deep understanding of the Qur'ān. This may come as a revelation to some, for the Mawlana's fame rests mainly on his singular contribution to history, theology and philosophy. However, in my opinion, he was one of the leading scholars of the Qur'ān in the whole of the Indo-Pak subcontinent in terms of the depth and range of his study. What accounted in the main for this was this thorough familiarity with the Arabic language and its literature, as also rhetoric and Qur'ānic studies. His companionship with Mawlana Hamid al-Din Farahi had further sharpened his insights into the Qur'ān. I recall his perceptive exposition of Surah Al-Jumu'ah when I was at Dar al-Musannifin, Azamgarh. I have yet to hear such a scholarly, articulate talk on the Qur'ān. I wish it could have been recorded for posterity.[12]

We now focus on the key elements of Sulaymān Nadwi's Qur'ānic contributions. As mentioned elsewhere in the chapter, there has not been a single translation of tafsir by Nadwi scholars. However, works of Qur'ānic import have seen a steady growth in Arabic and Urdu. Sulaymān Nadwi's writings are perhaps a summative assessment of Nu'mani's influence on a select group of energetic Nadwi scholars. Keeping in mind the meritorious efforts of *Al-Nadwah* journal, his contributions mark out his scholarly temper. The timeline is 1906 – 1911.

Distinctive features of Sulaymān Nadwi's articles:

- Qur'ān and modern philosophy: a critique
- The Qur'ānic view of Darwin's evolutionary theory

- Eschatological issues
- Literary contents: repetition (*takrār*) in the Qur'ān[13].

Sayyid Sulaymān's remarkable contributions in the field of Qur'ān studies are indisputable. Likewise, he contributed a series of articles to Abul Kalam Azad's *Al- Hilāl* (of which he served as editor for a brief period) and the *Ma'ārif* journal as early as 1916.[14] In sum, there were three reputed journals edited by Sayyid Sulaymān which in many ways grew in importance and popularity on account of his substantive contributions. The progressive trends set out by him were, in the main, the exposition of the universality of the Qur'ānic message and teachings.

Among Sayyid Sulaymān's early works on Qur'ānic studies, his geographical history of the Qur'ān is an original contribution. Citing both classical Islamic and Western scholarship, Shaykh Sulaymān traces historical and geographical sites[15] alluded to particular surahs of the Qur'ān. Two important points emerge from this brilliant study. First, the authenticity of historical and geographical sites in the Qur'ān are expanded by accessing the vast corpus of Islamic history. Second, the entrenched Orientalist prejudice is Islamophobic in both scope and content. Their nefarious designs to cast doubts about the veracity of the Qur'ānic sources are countered by the scholarly and objective treatment in Sayyid Sulaymān's brilliant piece of work.[16]

Another important work *Maqālat i-Sulaymān*[17] is a collection of articles on different Qur'ānic topics. Its compiler, Mu'inuddin Ahmad Nadwi has given a theme-based chapterisation of articles contained in different journals. The

---

[13] Ayubi, *Nadwi Fudhāla*, 23.

[14] Ibid., 24.

[15] For an updated translation of *Ard al-Qur'ān*, see Syed Muzaffar- ud-Din Nadvi, *A Geographical History of the Qur'ān* (Lahore, 1981). The learned author has assimilated the contents of *Ard al-Qur'ān* and supplemented them by other contemporary sources. In this respect it may be considered to be an original work.

[16] Ibid., 1-19.

[17] Mu'inuddin Ahmad Nadwi, *Maqālāt i-Sulaymāni*, vol.3 (Azamgarh, 1971). For an obituary of Mu'inuddin Nadwi, see Nadwi, *Purān i- Charāgh*, vol. 3, 446-64.

range and depth of topics examined by the erudite compiler is emblematic of the emergent trends in Qur'ān studies.[18] Keeping in mind the period under review, Sayyid Sulaymān's works were original contributions to the tafsir genre.

According to Professor Syed Salman Nadvi, his father used to highlight important points during his recitation of the Qur'ān. His reflections on Surah Al-Fatihah[19] were gleaned from the notes that he developed over the years as a Qur'ānic scholar of exceptional merit. Sayyid Sulaymān's competence in English has drawn considerable interest in academic circles. Apart from consulting English sources for his *Ard al-Qur'ān* as listed in the bibliography, Sayyid Sulaymān was the first traditional 'alim to comment favourably on Yusuf Ali's commentary of the Qur'ān. He says: "The Muslim scholars have with unanimity spoken very highly of the beauty, eloquence and grandeur of the translation."[20]

Closely linked to the common interest in unraveling the literary gems of the Qur'ān is an interesting work by his contemporary, 'Abdul Bari Nadwi (d. 1967). A philosophy professor[21] at Osmania University (Hyderabad), he produced works on *islāh* (reform) largely on account of his spiritual affiliation to the pre-eminent figure, Ashrāf 'Ali Thānawi (d. 1943).[22] His commentary of Surah Al-'Asr (103:1-3) merits an objective study in terms of its reformist content. However, Ayubi maintains that it diverges from the technical definition of tafsir because its contents are too discourse-centred.[23]

---

[18] Ayubi, *Nadwi Fuzalā*, 25-6.

[19] Ibid., 26.

[20] Cited in Choughley, *The Contributions of Abdur Raheem Kidwai*, 44.

[21] Abdul Bari Nadwi's Urdu translation of philosophical works include David Hume's *A Treatise of Human Nature*. It must be remembered that he was not a graduate in Western philosophy. By dint of his extraordinary intelligence, he was appointed as professor in the Philosophy Department. See Nadwi, *Purān i-Charāgh*, vol. 1, 119.

[22] His *Jāmi' al-Mujaddidin* is representative of the *islāh* books inspired by Thānawi.

[23] Ayubi, *Nadwi Fuzalā*, 29.

'Abdus Salām Kidwai

A proficient scholar, 'Abdus Salām Kidwai (d. 1979) rose to prominence in two fields: academic pursuits and Qur'ānic contributions. He taught history and economics in Nadwah and was also appointed a lecturer at the Jamia Millia University (New Delhi). An 'alim with impeccable academic credentials, Kidwai influenced a generation of Nadwi graduates whose contributions in the diverse fields of Islamic learning represented new trends in Islamic scholarship.

Qur'ānic studies was Kidwai's forte. He assiduously strove to make the sacred text accessible to the educated class who were largely overwhelmed by Western civilisation. Together with Shaykh Nadwi, Kidwai established the Idārah Ta'limāt i-Islam. Its primary purpose was to impart Qur'ānic classes to government officials and ordinary people with an interest in Islamic studies. Many students excelled in their studies and through the Idārah were enrolled for the pre-graduate course in Nadwah.[24]

The resource material were designed by Kidwai to facilitate an easy-to- understand approach to the Qur'ānic text. The collection of Qur'ānic lessons was published as *Ruh al-Qur'ān* (The Spirit of the Qur'ān). As the title suggests, Kidwai presented the Qur'ānic worldview to students to enable them to access its life-enriching message directly.[25] Interestingly, the informal course which was extended to three years was a brilliant effort to develop the students' proficiency in Arabic and other Islamic disciplines.

We may mention two notable graduates from the Idārah who have enriched the Qur'ānic studies tradition. Professor Sayyid Rizwan Ali Nadwi (d. 2016) was a distinguished academician whose prolonged teaching career in the Arab world earned him worldwide renown. Of particular importance is his critical edition of classical works pertaining to Qur'ānic themes. In this strain, two important works deserve mention. 'Izzat-din 'Abdus Salām (d. 1262) authored a work[26] along tafsir lines that dealt with the

---

[24] Choughley, *How to Study the Qur'ān*, 13.

[25] Ayubi, *Nadwi Fuzalā,* 37-8.

[26] Sulami, *Al-Fawā'id i Mushkil al-Qur'ān* (Cairo, 1968). The edition contains critical

linguistic, literary and theological aspects of particular *āyāt* (verses). Rizwan Ali's critical editing illustrates his rigorous evaluation of textual sources contained in this work.

Written in Urdu is a compilation of articles[27] that formed the basis of his Qur'ānic lessons. Rizwan Ali steps out of the domain of the traditional interpretation of Qur'ānic verses by contextualising their relevance for a modern readership. Its referential framework points out to his mastery over English and Arabic sources. This perhaps explains his choice of English words for a concise explanation of Qur'ānic terms.[28] Rizwan Ali is a literary critic and boldly engages in the critical reading of traditional interpretations that appear to be at variance with the Qur'ānic vision.

Professor Muhamad Salim Kidwai who was tutored by his revered father, Abdus Salām Kidwai, has to his credit several books dealing with Qur'ānic studies. His groundbreaking survey of the tafsir genre[29] in the subcontinent encapsulates his excellent grasp of tafsirs, classical and contemporary, with a primary focus on their distinctive features.

Hasani-Husayni Qur'ānic contributions[30]

Not following strictly the chronology of Qur'ānic contributions by Nadwi scholars as outlined by Ayubi, a different approach is adopted for Shaykh Nadwi and his family. In a nuanced way, their respective contributions represent almost a century of scholarly writings that have been widely acclaimed in the Arab and Urdu

---

comments appended by Rizwan Ali. Furthermore, the introduction and annotation have enhanced the merit of this tafsir work. Cf. Syed Rizwan Ali, *Izzadin al-Sulami: His life and Works* (Islamabad, 1978).

[27] Syed Rizwan Ali, *Qur'ān ki Roshni me* (Karachi, 2005).

[28] Ayubi, *Nadwi Fuzalā*, 69.

[29] Muhammad Salim Kidwai, *Hindustāni Mufassirin awr unki 'Arabi Tafsire* (Lahore, 1993). I have benefited immensely from this work on Arabic tafsirs in the subcontinent.

[30] For details of Shaykh Nadwi's lineage, see Muhammad Thani Hasani, *Khānwade 'Alam al-lāhi* (Rae Bareli, 1992), 12-4.

speaking world. In a similar vein, Shaykh Nadwi's works, translated into English, bear the hallmarks of his extensive study of the sacred text. Therefore, it may not be out of place to state that like the Waliyullah tradition, the Hasani-Husayni family enjoyed an academic pedigree which was marked by an enviable record of scholarly excellence.

Shaykh Nadwi's celebrated writings contain historical events/anecdotes that are infused with the Qur'ānic spirit. Before we attempt to explore the contours of his Qur'ānic- based writings, a booklet entitled *Islam in the West: The Qur'ānic Paradigm*[31] reaffirms the nexus of the Qur'ān and history. Shaykh Nadwi cites 14: 24-5[32] to articulate his vision of *da'wah* for a Western society. He references a particular historical account from the Mongol dynasty to show Islam's penetrative influence among this notorious nation which struck a fatal blow to the Islamic caliphate of the day.

Shaykh Nadwi's intellectual contributions to Islamic reformist thought are wide and varied. Additionally, his elaboration of Qur'ān topics forms an appreciable output to his literary works.

Our focus is on his major writings which provide an overview of his Qur'ānic erudition. *Studying which Glorious Qur'ān*[33] is an immensely readable book which allows readers to understand and appreciate the Qur'ān as the source of divine guidance. It covers, albeit briefly, the principles and methodology that reinforce the sacred text's eternal message. Key themes are framed from the lens of connectivity: a personal engagement with the Qur'ānic text for the purpose of guidance and drawing life-enriching experiences from it. In a similar vein, *The Islamic Concept of Prophethood,*[34] which is a collection of lectures delivered in Madinah University

---

[31] Abul Hasan Ali Nadwi, *Da'wah in the West: The Qur'ānic Paradigm* (Leicester, 1992), 12-4.

[32] *Do you not see how Allah has given the example of a good word? It is like a good tree, whose root is firmly fixed, and whose branches reach the sky, ever yielding its fruit in every season with the leave of its Lord. Allah gives examples for mankind that they may take heed. (14: 24-5)*

[33] Abul Hasan Ali Nadwi, *Studying the Glorious Qur'ān: Principles and Methodology* (Leicester, 2003).

[34] Abul Hasan Ali Nadwi, *The Islamic Concept of Prophethood* (Lucknow, 1976).

highlights the universal significance of Prophethood.

For Shaykh Nadwi, the Qur'ānic presentation brings under its purview a detailed discussion of central issues that are relatable to modern life. The incursion of Western civilisation in Muslim societies is an instance in point. In this regard, his *Faith Versus Materialism*[35] is a brilliant exposition of the key themes of Surah Al-Kahf. The surah is "the story of an unending struggle between two ideologies or concepts which are diametrically opposed to each other. One is materialism. and the other asserts the existence of realities which lie beyond the range of human perception (Afterlife)."[36] Belonging to a similar approach is Shaykh Nadwi's tafsir of Surah Al- Shu'ara[37]. The major Prophets' tabligh mission is discussed in greater detail to develop a holistic presentation of the Qur'ānic ideals. For Shaykh Nadwi their common linkages of *tawhid*, Afterlife, etc. underpin the Qur'ān's forceful message to mankind for all times. A supplement to this important work is *Inviting to the Way of Allah.*[38] Muhammad Rabey Nadwi's comments are instructive:

> The Glorious Qur'ān provided answers to all these questions in such a novel and forceful manner that nobody can think of better ways. It reproduces dialogues of the Prophets with their contemporaries and shows how they silenced these quibblers, the way they conveyed the glad tidings to the obedient and the mode they adopted in warning the disobedient and how they invited people to the 'Way of Allah'.[39]

In a broader context, *Guidance from the Qur'ān*[40] is a two-volume

---

[35] Abul Hasan Ali Nadwi, *Faith versus Materialism: The Meaning of Surah Al-Kahf* (Kuala Lumpur, 2005).

[36] Ibid., 18.

[37] Ayubi, *Nadwi Fuzalā*, 50.

[38] Abul Hasan Ali Nadwi, *Inviting to the Way of Allah* (Leicester, 1996).

[39] Ibid., 6.

[40] Risaluddin Nadwi compiled a two-volume work, *Qur'āni Ifādah*. Cf. Nadwi, *Guidance from the Holy Qur'ān* (Leicester, 2005).

collection of writings and speeches culled from Shaykh Nadwi's elaboration of Qur'ānic themes. These pieces give a better understanding of the Qur'ān. "Being thoroughly grounded in the immensely rich field of Islamic scholarship, and displaying a native like command over Arabic, Shaykh Nadwi brings home valuable points which are aimed at preaching the meaning and message of the Qur'ān."[41] According to Ayubi, Shaykh Nadwi brings to the fore the linguistic and literary elegance that indisputably reaffirms the *i'jāz* of the Qur'ān. For Shaykh Nadwi, the sacred text is built around words and phrases hat have a temperature and texture enabling readers to connect spontaneously with its revolutionary message.[42]

In sum, the writings of Shaykh Nadwi, in particular on Qur'ānic topics, are infused with an inimitable literary style.

Sayyid Muhammad Rabey Hasani

A scion of the Hasan family, Sayyid Rabey Nadwi's tenure as Rector of Nadwah is a glowing tribute to his visionary leadership. His decades-long teaching career at the institution brings into sharp focus his competence in Arabic literature and geography - thrust areas which have seen his several publications in Arabic and Urdu. A close associate of his maternal uncle, Sayyid Rabey replicated the latter's *islāhi* project. Common to their literary contributions is *da'wah* to the Arab world.[43]

In the field of Qur'ānic studies, Sayyid Rabey has authored several books that bring out his deep study of the sacred text. According to Professor Yasin Mazhar Siddiqui, a leading figure of the *sirah* genre, Sayyid Rabey's abiding interest is in tafsir. This explains his cogent explanation of particular surahs in the light of his extensive study of Qur'ānic sources.[44]

---

[41] Ibid., xi.

[42] Muhammad Tariq Ayubi Nadwi, *Nadwi Fuzalā*, 54. Cf. Muhammad Tariq Ayubi, *Mawlana Sayyid Abul Hasan Ali Mia ki Qur'āni Fehmi* (Aligarh, 2020).

[43] For a biographical account of Rabey Nadwi, see 'Abdul Hannan Nadwi, *Hadhrat Mawlana Sayyid Muhammad Rabey Hasani Nadwi: Shakhsiyyat awr Khidmāt* (Lucknow, 2012).

[44] Ayubi, *Nadwi Fuzalā*, 71.

Before we attempt to comment briefly on his important writings, two prominent points emerge from his Qur'ānic approach. First, his literary background accounts in the main for his brilliant exposition of Qur'ānic topics. Second, his range and depth of Islamic scholarship is lucidly expressed in his intra-Qur'ānic verse approach. Brevity and simplicity are characteristic features of his literary style.[45]

A cursory review of this work (*Qur'ān Majeed*)[46] makes interesting reading. Originally, a collection of Sayyid Rabey's articles, it covers an array of topics with central themes. The nexus of the Qur'ān and man, interrelationship between man and nature encompass the Qur'ānic dimensions of *khilāfat* (vicegerency). Likewise, Sayyid Rabey provides a holistic interpretation about the eternal message and teachings of the sacred text. In a literary perspective, the *i'jāz* features prominently in this work. Overall, Sayyid Rabey attempts to contextualise the importance of ethical duties in a contemporary setting.[47]

Apart from the articles written by Sayyid Rabey, the lessons (*durus*) recorded at various places have been transcribed and edited by adept Nadwi scholars.[48] Three books have been compiled on particular surahs. The themes deal with societal responsibilities, guidelines to develop the spirit of *taqwā* (Allah-consciousness) and Prophetic ideals as a catalyst for moral and spiritual transformation.[49] These works delineate Sayyid Rabey's thorough grounding in tafsir. Moreover, he avoids technicalities that are likely to mar the proper understanding of the sacred text.

A prolific writer and eloquent orator, Sayyid Salman Husayni (b. 1954) belongs to that generation of Nadwi scholars who have carved a niche in Islamic reformist thought. His literary output is impressive judging by the range of topics he covers. A hadith

---

[45] Muhammad Rabey Nadwi, *Qur'ān Majeed Insān i-Zindagi ka Rehbar i- Kāmil* (Lucknow, 2013).

[46] Ibid., 214-21.

[47] For example, *Islāmi Mu'āsharāt Surah Hujarāt ki Roshni me* (Lucknow, 2011).

[48] Ayubi, *Nadwi Fuzalā*, 73-4.

[49] Ibid., 74.

scholar by specialisation, Sayyid Salman has made substantive contributions to Qur'ānic studies. By way of illustration, he makes copious references to the Qur'ān for his critical evaluation of the hadith genre. Hence the touchstone of his writings bears clear traces of the tafsir tradition.

Sayyid Salman is credited with a brilliant translation of Waliyullah's *Al-Fawz al-Kabir*[50] (discussed in Chapter 2). In Ayubi's estimation, this work is representative of Sayyid Salman's fame as a brilliant Arabic scholar. Essentially, it is an improved version of previous translations, which otherwise are mediocre efforts to a brilliant work of Waliyullah's calibre. Other noteworthy writings also reflect his in-depth study of the Qur'ānic sciences. Ayubi has rightly remarked that Sayyid Salman possesses the consummate skills to demonstrate the linguistic, literary and circumstantial nuances of the Qur'ānic subject matter. Linguistic and cultural shifts in meaning or equivalence are integral to a context-based reading of the Qur'ānic intent for particular verses. Sayyid Salman employs phrases which are inserted in brackets for the purpose of clarity. Even if Arabic words of Qur'ānic origin have been assimilated in Urdu they are, to say the least, diluted meanings.[51] Additionally, there is no correlative or mutual relationship between Arabic and Indo-European languages. As such, the limitations of a successful translation project are glaringly evident.

We may assess Sayyid Salman's explanation of the 'hierarchy of meanings' for particular Qur'ānic verses in his works. For example, the word *ittaqu* has different shades of meaning which gives a sense of clarity of the Qur'ān's intent. Generally, the loose paraphrase of 'fear of Allah' associated with *taqwā* by commentators yields unintended consequences. Actually it mitigates against the Qur'ānic spirit and message. According to Ayubi, several meanings may suffice to underpin Sayyid Salman's

---

[50] Ibid., 114-5.

[51] The foreignisation of Qur'ānic terms has resonance in Urdu translations. See Gowhar Quadir Wani (ed.), *Waleed al-Amri's The Luminous Qur'an: Critical Views* (Aligarh, 2019), 70-1.

linguistic mastery. Consider verse 2: 189: in the Qur'ānic parlance it is taken to mean precaution or to take a serious account of Allah's law for *taqwā*.[52]

Following an unconventional approach, Sayyid Salman identifies interlinking ideas for his translation of the Qur'ānic text. For example, Surah Al-Fatihah explores the particular attributes of Allah and their relationship to man and the universe. Likewise, the standard of guidance is explored against the backdrop of Allah's scale of justice.[53]

Another noteworthy contribution by Sayyid Salman to the Qur'ānic sciences is the history of revelation. In this field, Suyuti ranks among the pioneers who have critically examined the *Asbāb al-nuzul* to illustrate the historical factors that shaped the compilation of the Qur'ān, i.e. the (codex) as received during the caliphate of AbuBakr. It must be remembered that this work highlights previous efforts of classical and contemporary exegetes. One of its distinctive features is the *da'wah* thrust adopted by Sayyid Salman.[54] In a similar vein, he has adapted earlier works related to Qur'ānic studies.

Sayyid Bilāl Abdul Hayy Hasani (b. 1969) is an illustrious member of the Hasani family whose contributions are widely recognised in India. Two levels of his Islamic activities have leveraged his pro-active role to the *islāhi* tradition. Sayyid Bilāl has continued with the *Payām i-Insāniyat* (Message of Humanity) movement[55] initiated in the 1970s by Shaykh Nadwi. It is an interfaith initiative anchored on the ideals of morality, social justice and ethical integrity. The distinguished scholar-activist has brought into sharp focus the urgency of social work through the forum of the *Payām* movement.

Alongside Sayyid Bilāl 's social welfare activities is his literary output. The establishment of the Abul Hasan Ali Centre[56] is a

---

[52] Ayubi, *Nadwi Fuzalā*, 114-5.

[53] Ibid., 118.

[54] Ibid., 122.

[55] For an overview of the *Payām* movement, see Abdul Kader Choughley, *Towards Salvaging Humanity* (Aligarh, 2019).

[56] www.abulhasanalinadwi.org.

testament to his visionary leadership. The plethora of Shaykh Nadwi's works published by the Centre has made his writings accessible online for scholarly pursuits. Two books from Sayyid Bilāl 's prolific writings represent his *da'wah*-centred approach. Social reform in the light of Surah Al-Hujurat[57] brings to the fore the Qur'ānic guidelines for an ideal Muslim society. Vices like backbiting, naming and shaming are frowned upon in keeping with the Qur'ānic presentation of a moral code. Sayyid Bilāl has provided a concise Qur'ānic guideline which are essential teachings for Muslims' success.

It is to the credit of Sayyid Bilāl that the family has produced the first Qur'ānic translation in Urdu.[58] As the title of the work suggests, it is an easy, comprehensible translation for both the educated and common man seeking to gain guidance from the sacred text. At the same time, Sayyid Bilāl makes no claims about its academic credentials. In his view, the translation enjoys three distinctions: close meaning to the original text, easy-to-read approach and fluency. In this perspective, Sayyid Bilāl attempts an integrated method in his translation by highlighting the overall message of the Qur'ān as well as citation from the hadith literature about the virtues of surahs under discussion. All in all, the translation steers away from technicalities, a common feature of the general trend in Urdu, and focuses on its meaning, teachings and message.

Muhammad Uwais Nigrāmi

A distinguished graduate from Nadwah, Muhammad Uwais Nigrāmi (d. 1976) built an enviable reputation of scholarship in the field of Qur'ānic studies. According to Shaykh Nadwi, Nigrāmi stood out for his extensive reading of the *salaf* writings, in particular Hafidh ibn Taimiyyah and his worthy successor, Ibn Qayyim.[59] His erudite presentation of tafsir framed around the *tajdid* (renewal) discourse was acknowledged by the 'ulama

---

[57] Ayubi, *Nadwi Fuzalā*, 139-40.

[58] Bilal Abdul Hayy Hasani, *Asān Ma'āni Qur'ān* (Rae Bareli, 2015). The English translation by Abdur Raheem Kidwai has yet to be published.

[59] Nadwi, *Purān i-Charāgh*, vol. 2, 252.

fraternity. Likewise, his close association with Sayyid Sulaymān at Azamgarh deepened his understanding of the Qur'ānic hermeneutics. Nigrāmi 's preoccupation with tafsir study extended to contemporary Arabic work[60] - a testament to his catholicity of views in an Indian milieu which was marked by rigidity and prejudice. In truth, few scholars could overcome their bias to tafsirs expressing independent scholarly views.

There are several layers that mark out Qur'ānic contributions. Among these is his detailed commentary of Waliyullah's *Al-Fawzal-Kabir*[61] a testament to his wide learning and extensive examination of the latter's methodological approach. Likewise, Nigrāmi made a concerted effort to reach out to professionals, government officials by offering Qur'ānic classes at a private home. These lessons were life-enriching, informative and inspiring. In fact, after the demise of his patron who offered his home as a 'Qur'ānic centre' Nigrāmi continued with his classes.[62] The thrust of his lessons was understanding the meaning and message of the sacred text.

Nigrāmi is among the first Qur'ānic scholars to have had the distinction of compiling a volume entitled *Al-Tafsir al-Qayyim*.[63] It was an assiduous task to collate Ibn Qayyim's explanatory notes of verses from his various writings. On a positive note, the Arab publishing houses were largely responsible for its popularity as the number of editions to this date suggest.

Trends in contemporary Qur'ānic scholarship are discernible in the second half of the twentieth century. These works are representative of linguistic and scientific approaches to the study of the sacred text, which several Nadwi graduates have pursued as doctoral courses in the field of Arabic studies. In this respect, 'Abdullāh 'Abbās Nadwi (d. 2006)[64] is among the leading intellectual figures who has devoted his academic career to promoting the Arabic language and literature in a Qur'ānic

---

[60] Ibid., 253-5.

[61] Ibid., 256-7.

[62] Ibid., 257.

[63] Ayubi, *Nadwi Fuzalā*, 64-5.

[64] For 'Abbās Nadwi's obituary, see *Ta'meer i-Hayāt* (Lucknow, 2006), January, 18-20.

perspective. A graduate of Edinburgh University (Scotland), 'Abbas Nadwi spent many years at the renowned universities in Saudi Arabia overseeing postgraduate programmes in Arabic.[65] By virtue of his extensive reading of literary Qur'ānic theories, classical and contemporary, he authored an outstanding book[66] on this genre in Urdu. It is a comprehensive account about *i'jāz* of the Qur'ān. Ayubi examines in detail the linguistic elements in particular verses of the Qur'ān.

Brevity informs its literary approach. Likewise, rational arguments contained in terse descriptions are a trajectory of the Qur'ānic worldview.[67] Overall, this work remains unsurpassed in Urdu.

Two important works *Vocabulary of the Qur'ān* and *Learn the Language of the Qur'ān*[68] are an elaboration of the structured features of Qur'ānic Arabic. 'Abbas Nadwi has adopted a didactic and methodological approach to unfold the linguistic beauty of the sacred text. An equally influential work for non-Arabic readers, it also counters the deviant contributions by Orientalists who made their forays in the late nineteenth century. Mention may be made of John Penrice's *A Dictionary and Glossary of the Koran* (1873),[69] which by all accounts is not an authoritative contribution to Qur'ānic grammar, was consulted as a reference work.

Qur'ānic reviews of English translations have seen uneven developments in terms of their critical and scholarly treatment. In many instances, random articles appeared in journals which received little recognition. However, it developed into a genre in the early 1980s and established a watermark place in peer-reviewed journals. Abdur Raheem Kidwai, an illustrious scholar in Qur'ānic studies is considered a pioneer in this important field of study. A collaborative initiative with *The Muslim World Book Review*

---

[65] 'Abbas Nadwi also held the position of Director: Education in Nadwah. His close association with Shaykh Nadwi is lucidly covered in *Mir Kārwān* (New Delhi, 1999).

[66] 'Abdullah 'Abbas Nadwi, *Qur'ān i-Karim: Tārikh i-Insāniyat ka sabse Barā Mo'jizah* (New Delhi, n.d.).

[67] Ayubi, *Nadwi Fuzalā*, 93, 95.

[68] These works originally published by Iqra International (Chicago), have seen several editions due to its popularity as part of an Arabic series.

[69] Cf. Choughley, *The Contributions of Abdur Raheem Kidwai*, 32-3.

(Islamic Foundation, Leicester), Kidwai has penned prolific reviews of English translations dating as far back as 1649.[70] 'Abbas Nadwi's critical examination of selected Qur'ānic translations (Arabic/Urdu) may best be understood from the perceptive comments about the translation project by Kidwai:

> The present work, a critical study of sixty complete English translations of the Qur'ān seeks to guide readers in selecting a suitable translation for their study out of the many available in bookshops and libraries. For this collection of analytical reviews on each translation, carried out from 1649 to 2009, attempts to identify the ideological and sectarian affiliation, mindset, features and strengths and weaknesses of every translator. Unsuspecting English-speaking readers stand in need of this important information. For their only access to the meaning and message of the Word of God is through a translation. Even millions of Muslims today, being unfamiliar with Arabic, rely on these translations for their study of the Qur'ān.
>
> Regrettably, many unscrupulous English translators have unabashedly foisted their ideological presuppositions, sectarian notions and personal whims on the Qur'ānic text in their renderings, which is bound to mislead na'ive readers. In this consists the rationale and genesis of the present work.[71]

'Abbās Nadwi has attempted to outline the linguistic challenges faced by translators regardless of their sectarian orientation. In keeping with his academic credentials, 'Abbas Nadwi explores the syntactic structure of English translation in relation to the

---

[70] Ibid., 98-9.
[71] Kidwai, *Translating the Untranslatable*, xvii-xviii.

Qur'ānic Arabic.[72] It is an indisputable fact that linguistic and cultural equivalence have a direct impact on accuracy and authenticity. Thus divergent translations, in many instances at odds with the original text, are a formidable undertaking. Notwithstanding these hurdles, translations in the main are a sincere attempt to project the meaning of the sacred text. 'Abbas Nadwi has reviewed four important translations which are included in Kidwai's work. Merits and demerits follow a similar pattern. However, unlike Kidwai's articulate presentation, 'Abbas Nadwi highlights the inaccuracies, shortcomings, and to a lesser extent, the blemishes of these translations.[73] A comparative review of Daryabadi's *The Glorious Qur'ān* brings to the fore their respective Qur'ānic perspectives.

According to 'Abbas Nadwi, Daryabadi's monumental work contains a few blemishes: elaborate discussion of particular issues supported by an exhaustive reference which perhaps mars the merit of the work. Additionally, it employs Biblical English that presumably is not appealing to English readers. By contrast, Yusuf Ali's translation possesses charm and elegance and is considered a literary masterpiece. It must be borne in mind that 'Abbas Nadwi's linguistic background has influenced him to assess a popular English tafsir like Daryabadi within a specific framework. *Tafsir i-Mājidi* in Urdu, a landmark contribution in the first half of the twentieth century, is without doubt an unsurpassed piece of work that regrettably was a casualty to the 'ulama's prejudice on account of its perceived non-traditional interpretation. Curiously enough, the interweaving of two tafsirs, *Bayān al-Qur'ān* and *Tafsir ul Qur'ān* is an implicit endorsement of Daryabadi's competence in the tafsir field.

Kidwai makes a pertinent point about the posthumous, revised edition of *The Glorious Qur'ān* and its far-reaching impact it has had on intellectuals, professionals and seekers after truth.

It is gratifying that Mawlana Abdul Majid's

---

[72] Ayubi, *Nadwi Fuzalā*, 98-9.
[73] Ibid., 101-2.

revised translation of the Qur'ān has been brought out at the behest of Sayyid Abul Hasan Ali Nadwi, especially because his earlier translation The Holy Qur'ān (Taj Company, Lahore, 1957) was marred by numerous typographical errors, an irksome page setting and the use of archaic Biblical expressions. For Daryabadi's outstanding contribution to the Qur'ānic studies has remained largely unacknowledged. He is the first Muslim scholar to have contributed a commentary in English, which is in total accord with the consensus view of the *ummah*. Moreover, far from being a loose or lax paraphrase, his translation is faithful to the original.

Another distinction of Daryabadi's work is the abundance of material on comparative religion gleaned painstakingly from mostly primary sources. Thirdly, in sharp contrast to other leading Muslim exegetes like Abdullah Yusuf Ali and Muhammad Asad, Daryabadi's comments on certain Qur'ānic teachings like eschatology, polygamy or slavery, do not smack of any apologia. In fact, his cogent notes on such issues, along with references to the Bible and other sources of modern scholarship not only bring to the fore and reinforce the eternal message and force of the Qur'ān, but also help allay the doubts agitating, in particular, the minds of Muslims exposed to the currents of Western intellectuality.[74]

Another controversial translation, *Al-Qur'ān: A Contemporary Translation* (1984) By Ahmed Ali underpins their respective Qur'ānic perspectives. Common to the reviews of 'Abbas Nadwi

---

[74] Ibid., 102. For a comprehensive study of Daryabadi's Qur'ānic contributions, see Gowhar Quadir Wani and Abdul Kader Choughley (editors), *Abdul Majid Daryabadi's Tafsir-ul- Qur'ān: A Critical Study* (Aligarh, 2021).

and Kidwai is the primary importance of norms to be scrupulously followed for the purpose of translation. While highlighting the shortcomings of this work, 'Abbas Nadwi believes it is a futile exercise to undermine its intrinsic merits. However, Kidwai strongly argues that the work is 'brazenly apologetic and an erroneous foray into the field (Qur'ānic translation).'[75] In sum, 'Abbas Nadwi is an eminent scholar steeped in classical and contemporary Islamic traditions. He is widely recognised for his diverse contributions to Islamic culture and civilisation - an intellectually engaging legacy.

The productive output of Arabic writings by Nadwah is indeed remarkable judging by the rising number of Nadwi alumni pursuing postgraduate studies at prominent universities in India. Their works are also widely recognised in the Arab world. These progressive trends developed over time augur well for Nadwah's profile as a leading representative of Islamic authenticity in the subcontinent. For example, mention may be made of *Rābita Adab*[76] which has made appreciable strides in presenting the Islamic perspective on Arabic literature.

A general survey of Nadwah's response to science and technology is ambivalent. While embracing the importance of these disciplines, there has been no meaningful efforts to develop the *iqrā* paradigm by Nadwah. Although Shaykh Nadwi articulated this vision in his celebrated works,[77] which is reflective of his progressive outlook, by and large, the *iqrā* model remains a utopian ideal.

In our study of the Nadwi Qur'ānic contributions, Muhammad Shihābuddin Nadwi (d. 2002) is considered a forerunner to the Qur'ān and science discourse. His autobiography gives poignant details about his preoccupation with scientific theories and discoveries in the backdrop of the Qur'ānic presentation in this

---

[75] Kidwai, *Translating the Untranslatable*, 78.

[76] Its journal *Kārwān i-Adab* (Urdu) is intended to align literature within an Islamic ethos.

[77] See Abul Hasan Ali Nadwi, *Western Civilisation Islam and Muslims* (Lucknow, 1974), 202-15.

field.[78] For the purpose of giving tangible forms to his decades-long study, Shihābuddin Nadwi established the Furqania Academy in 1970 which has been responsible for the publication of his prolific writings. Among his celebrated works are his research findings about the amazing marvels of the Qur'ān in the light of modern science.[79] These are the guiding principles to his formulation of Islamic renewal in modern reformist thought. Shaykh Nadwi has lauded Shihābuddin Nadwi's scientific contributions in these words: "The work which is done by a full academy in Europe is being done by a single person here (India)."[80] This laudatory comment also holds true for other illustrious Nadwi scholars[81] who had dedicated their lives to the production of literary works that remain unrivalled in terms of their exacting, rigorous standards.

Before we attempt to map out Shihābuddin Nadwi's Qur'ānic contributions, his rationale and methodology are assessed to the period under study. Scientific exegesis of the Qur'ān largely caught the imagination of the Muslim world in the twentieth century. In this regard, *The Qur'ān and Modern Science* by Maurice Buccaille developed out of a lecture at the French Academy of Medicine. The learned author pointed out statements of a scientific nature contained in the Qur'ān.[82] It was a reaffirmation of the divine origin of the Qur'ān. It includes encyclopaedic information about the perfect conformity between faith and science. Across the spectrum of the Qur'ān and science discourse, is the translation by Rashad Khalifa. According to Kidwai, *The Qur'ān: The Final Scripture* is a bizarre interpretation of the so-called 'numerical theory', asserting that the computer establishes the miraculous nature of the Qur'ān.[83] In a similar vein, the phenomenon of nature and Qur'ān occupies a pivotal place in the scientific

---

[78] Shihābuddin Nadwi's memoir, *Exemplary Moments in my Literary Life* is a poignant description of his quest for a broader understanding of the *iqrā* paradigm. Cf *Ta'meer i-Hayāt* (April, 2002), 24-6 for his obituary.

[79] Shihābuddin Nadwi has written over fifty books in the Qur'ān and science domain.

[80] Ayubi, *Nadwi Fuzalā*, 76.

[81] Mention may be made of Sayyid Sulayman Nadwi who produced the monumental *Sirat al-Nabi*.

[82] Maurice Bucaille, *The Qur'ān and Modern Science* (Jeddah, 1977).

[83] Kidwai, *Translating the Untranslatable*, 286.

writings of Sayed Abdul Wadud.[84] His *hadithophobic* tendencies, representative of the Ahl i-Qur'ān movement are self-evident. Against these contesting strains of scientific studies related to the Qur'ān the contributions of Shaykh Shihābuddin are markedly different. His works are not swayed by scientific predilections; instead, they are informed by an authentic/accurate representation of Qur'ānic worldview. For Shaykh Shihābuddin, the Qur'ānic philosophy in a contemporary setting is aimed at countering the misguided thought and philosophies of atheists and materialist-leaning intellectuals.[85] In the light of the shari'ah, for example, there appears no contradiction between man's quest for an ideal life that is Qur'ānic-inspired.

Another reason for Shaykh Shihābuddin's animated engagement with the Qur'ān and science discourse is the distorted interpretation of selected verses by liberal scholars to bolster in exaggerated ways the scientific spirit of the sacred text. The works of Ghulam Jilani Burq, for example, are emblematic of the wayward mindset of pseudo-Qur'ānic scholars about the scientific contents in the Qur'ān.[86] To this end, the sterling contributions of Shaykh Shihābuddin to restore the balance are indeed laudable.

Two writings reflect the brilliant exposition of science, eschatology and Islamic renaissance. Belonging to the surah-science theme is Surah Al-Takwir: 81. According to Sayyid Qutb, the surah sketches a scene of great upheaval which will envelop the whole universe. The principle of Resurrection affects the sun and the stars, the mountains and the seas, heaven and earth, wild and domestic animals as well as man.[87] According to Shaykh Shihābuddin, the Day of Resurrection (*Qiyāmah*) is supported by Qur'ānic facts, which reaffirms the perpetual miracle (*'ijāz*) of the sacred text. The textual evidence is culled from authoritative commentaries as well. In Shaykh Shihābuddin's view, the process

---

[84] See Syed Abdul Wadud, *The Heaven and the Earth and the Qur'ān* (Lahore, 1982). It must be pointed out that scientific discoveries are not always definitive conclusions. In contrast, the Qur'ān is the only infallible guide to interpret the natural phenomena.

[85] Ayubi, *Nadwi Fuzalā*, 77.

[86] Ibid., 78.

[87] Sayyid Qutb, *In the Shade of the Qur'ān*, vol. xviii (Leicester, 2004), 76-7.

of reconciling two worldviews does not suggest two mutually exclusive research approaches. Rather, these are complementary in the spirit of objectivity and impartiality. At the heart of his rigorous analysis of *Qiyāmah*[88] is man's submission to Allah's supreme power and majesty. The concept of *Qiyāmah* is a palpable reality that provides life- turning lessons for mankind.

What are the implications of Shaykh Shihābuddin's scholarly works of a scientific nature for Muslims? His exploration of the Qur'ān's eternal message is a purview   of the Islamic renewal project. Several key points are highlighted to exhort the *ummah* not to deviate from the authoritative sources of Islam. First, the Qur'ān promotes a progression of ideals which are abiding. Second, the *ummah* should not be overwhelmed by the pervasive influence of modern science even though it has expanded its footprints in the collective Muslim psyche. In other words, the equilibrium between Islam and science has the potential to grow the *ummah* as worthy representatives of *khilāfah* (vicegerency).

In sum, the sterling contributions of this exceptionally gifted scholar has not been faithfully carried out by Nadwah. Fortunately, Anis al-Rahman Nadwi (b. 1974), son of Shaykh Shihābuddin has preserved this legacy by producing works of the same scholarly spirit. A positive development of the Furqan Academy (Bengaluru) under his directorship is the publication of *i'jāz* works derived from Qur'ān and hadith literature. Anis al-Rahman is also a software engineer by profession, which has also enhanced the technical production of his works.[89] In the hadith perspective, the solar eclipse with specific reference to the death of the Holy Prophet's son, Ibrahim, is critically examined by him in the light of astronomical evidence. Similarly, Anis al-Rahman examines the phenomenon of volcanic eruptions based on geological studies.[90] Overall, his writings reflect his thorough familiarity with scientific disciplines.

The confluence of faith (*Islam*) and science, according to Anis al-Rahman encapsulates the Qur'ānic view of knowledge. It is a totality,

---

[88] Ayubi, *Nadwi Fuzalā*, 81-2.

[89] Ibid., 150.

[90] Ibid., 151.

an integrated approach that sees no conflict in the natural phenomenon operating within the divine system (*rububiyat*). However, man is responsible for tampering with this balance on account of his inordinate obsession to fulfil his physical needs. Climate change and global warming, Anis al-Rahman argues in his article[91] present a major challenge for mankind. Furthermore, this imbalance in nature which is marred by man's rapacious needs, is tersely expressed in the Qur'ān and hadith literature. Anis al-Rahmān has the uncanny ability to contextualise these global concerns by citing Qur'ānic words and phrases. To this end, his analysis of hadith literature is an excellent example of his mastery over Arabic linguistics. Broadly speaking, climate change and global warming have been described as a prelude to the big event: Doomsday. Even scientists seem to accept the fact that the events of climate change may end up with the extinction of all living species on earth.[92]

In the last two decades of the twenty-first century there have been positive developments by Nadwi contributions to the tafsir genre. These are independent and refreshing pieces of work covering principles of tafsir (*usul al-tafsir*). In our study, the comprehensive work of reference for more than two centuries is *Al-Fawz al-Kabir*. Commentaries on this work tend to be super glosses or uncritical adoption of classical works relating to *usul al-tafsir*. However, a marked departure from this established tradition reflects the growing interest of expanding the domain of tafsir, particularly in the Arab world.

Muhammad Sarwar Fāruqi (b. 1968) ranks prominently among the new generation of Nadwi scholars who have enriched the tafsir tradition. His *Ma'āni al-Qur'ān al-Karim*[93] as the title suggests is a contemporary translation. It is an easy-read work for common people. Fāruqi deftly inserts explanatory notes within brackets for

---

[91] Anis al-Rahman Nadwi, "Climate Change in the light of Qur'ān and Hadith", in Muhammad Mubeen Saleem Azhari (ed.), *National Seminar on Peaceful Coexistence in Multicultural Societies: The Qur'ānic Perspective* (Aligarh, 2014), 201-20.
[92] Ibid., 201.
[93] Ayubi, *Nadwi Fuzalā*, 133-4.

the purpose of greater clarity throughout the text. Also other translations are consulted to supplement his explanatory notes.

A classical language like Sanskrit is akin to Latin which influenced several European languages. Sanskrit enjoys an unrivalled position for its linguistic, cultural, philosophical and scientific spirit. Its strong influence on regional languages is a manifestation of its enduring link to the Indian soil. Urdu, for example has its fair share of etymological connections with this classical language. Likewise, Hindi has an indissoluble link with Sanskrit's classical heritage. As the official language of India, Hindi has made great strides supported by state funding.

Without delving into the rise of Hindi and the diminishing influence of Urdu among the Muslim constituencies[94] the need for Hindi translations was acutely felt in the nineteenth and twentieth centuries. Apart from its shared connection with Urdu, the 'ulama and Islamic organisations realised the potential growth of *da'wah* by employing Hindi as a vehicle of communication. Perhaps it reflected the growing realisation for Muslims that the message of the Qur'ān was the best form of *da'wah* to be disseminated to other faith groups who were mainly from the Hindu community in the Hindi-speaking regions.[95] Against the rising tide of Islamophobia and the alienation of both religious communities, the Hindi translation was a first serious attempt to reconnect the dots of peace and harmony. In this historical perspective, the contribution of Fāruqi to the Hindi translation enterprise is indeed laudable. His thorough familiarity with Sanskrit under the tutelage of Sanskrit sages is a testament to his scholarly credentials.

A number of concise works in Hindi authored by Fāruqi is a preparatory course to understand the meaning and message of the sacred text. A seven-volume Hindi translation *Tafsir Fāruqi* is expressive of his groundbreaking commentary. Another concise

---

[94] See Nadwi, *Muslims in India*, 131-40.
[95] In the face of hostilities from Hindutva, the Jama'at i-Islami has made appreciable gains to reach out to the Hindu community through its forceful, enlightened production of Hindi literature.

work *Qur'ān kā Paighām* encapsulates the essential teachings of the Qur'ān. The endorsements (*taqriz*) underscore the intrinsic merits of the work.

Fāruqi's translation of selected Qur'ānic passages bear the following characteristics:

- o Several Urdu translations are consulted with particular focus on Jullundhri and Thānawi's tafsirs.
- o It is, however, a direct translation from Arabic to Hindi.
- o Words and phrases used are compatible with everyday Hindi.
- o Paraphrasing is employed to clarify meanings.
- o Arabic words like *Rahmān* are retained and Hindi equivalents are inserted in brackets.[96]

Gifted with intellectual insight (keeping in mind his specialisation in fatwa writing (*iftā*), training courses in Madinah University, Fāruqi's contributions to the tafsir genre in Urdu and Hindi are his singular accomplishments.

In line with new approaches to Qur'ānic studies is an excellent tafsir by Muhammad Hassān Nu'mani (b. 1952). Belonging to the distinguished Nu'mani/Sambhali family of scholars, Muhammad Hassān has earned accolades for his Qur'ānic contributions. His father, Mawlana Manzur Nu'mani (d. 1997)[97] enjoyed international fame for his motivational books on the Qur'ān and hadith. His *Qur'ān and You*[98] is a popular work among English-speaking readers.

Muhammad Hassān has carved out new pathways pathways by presenting a meaningful study of the sacred text. While not departing from the traditional translations, he adopts a selective style to reach out to a modern readership. For him the message should be concise and accessible for the target audience. His choice of Daryabadi's *Tafsir i-Mājidi* is illuminating. By way of

---

[96] Ayubi, *Nadwi Fuzalā*, 131-3.

[97] For Nu'mani's biographical details, see Nadwi, *Kārwān i-Zindagi*, vol. 7, 25-36.

[98] Nomani, *The Qur'ān and You* (Lucknow, 1971).

explanatory notes which are inserted in brackets, the fluency of the text is retained. In the same vein, the mainstream translation is preferred to sectarian readings that tend to mar the essential teachings of the Qur'ān. By the same token, translation should not reflect an eclectic disposition and in the process dilute the eternal message of the sacred text.[99]

Tawdihi Tarjuma is a collaborative effort: Muhammad Hassān's revered wife played an important role in the translation project. For historical reasons and the trajectory of Islamic reformist thought in the subcontinent, the feminist interpretation of the Qur'ān has made negligible progress. In fact, a translation in the early twentieth century by Mahmud al-Nisa Begum (d. 1965) is an authentic representation of the sacred text.[100] Interestingly, she has provided a reader-friendly translation with concise explanatory notes. This translation also enjoys the distinction of advancing the *Mudih al-Qur'ān* legacy. An updated version by Siraj al-Huda (b. 1980) has enhanced the merits of this important work.[101]

As mentioned elsewhere in the volume, albeit briefly, Nadwah had established a strong network with the Arabic intellectual tradition. Shaykh Nadwi's major works were recognised for their brilliant exposition of the Islamic legacy (*turāth*). His association with the Ikhwan movement drew Nadwah to the Islamic renaissance in the Arab world. In more than one way, his *Rise and Fall of Muslims*[102] underpinned the transnational character of Islamic reformist thought. Therefore, it was not surprising that the plethora of writings by Nadwi scholars over the decades have been appreciated in Arab academia. This tacit endorsement represents the critical engagement of intellectual thought between Nadwah and the Arab world.

To return to the Ikhwan movement. Zainab al-Ghazāli (d. 2005) was one of Ikhwan's leading activists[103] and exegete whose two-

---

[99] Muhammad Hassān Nu'mani's *Tawdihi Tarjuma i-Qur'ān* is referenced as a widely acclaimed Hindi translation.

[100] Ayubi, *Nadwi Fuzalā*, 161.

[101] Ibid.

[102] See Abul Hasan Ali Nadwi, *Rise and Fall of Muslims: Its Impact on the World.* Edited by Abdul Kader Choughley (Aligarh, 2020), xxxiii-xxxv.

[103] Zainab Ghazali's *Return of the Pharaoh* (Leicester, 1996) is a poignant account of

volume tafsir *Nazarāt* was written in the shadows of her prolonged years in prison. Her deep reflections are impressed in her exposition of Qur'ānic themes. The intra-Qur'ānic methodology articulates a *da'wah*-focused interpretation. Among the interesting points raised in the tafsir are the status of women, their rights and other pertinent issues.[104] Overall, it is a comprehensive tafsir that in some way is reminiscent of the activist thirty- volume *Fi Zilāl al-Qur'ān* (Arabic) of Sayyid Qutb. The Urdu translation by 'Abdul Hamid Athar (b. 1977) was completed in three volumes. For the Urdu translation *Tafhim al-Qur'ān* of Mawdudi was a preferred option on two counts: elegance of style and precise expression. Another plausible reason is Mawdudi's Islamic activism which had considerable influence in terms of his interpretive reading of the sacred text.

According to Athar, *Nazarāt* has contemporary relevance.[105] By and large, it is a priceless gift for female readers seeking to understand the message of the Qur'ān as elaborated by Zainab al-Ghazāli. Interestingly, another translation of the Qur'ān has been produced in English by three American female converts. It uses 'modern and easy English words' and 'adding only footnotes where it is necessary' to draw readers to the spirit and message of the Qur'ān[106].

Athar is an accomplished scholar in tafsir. This is borne out by his translation of the Qur'ān into *Nawā'iti*. A Muslim language in the Karnataka state, *Nawā'iti* has its roots in Marathi and Kokani languages. Descendants of the Quraysh tribes and Hadhramis in Yemen, the *Nawā'its* possess a distinct Arab culture which they have retained over the centuries. Both oral and written traditions are meticulously maintained. The *Nawā'iti* tradition is thinly spread in particular regions like Kerala, for example. Other distinguished Islamic scholars like Professor Muhammad

---

her *da'wah* activities during Jamal Nasser's despotic regime.

[104] See "Zainab Al-Ghazali's Vindication of the Qur'ānic Verse on Women (4: 34)", in *Aligarh Journal of Qur'ānic Studies*, 3:2, October 2020, 53-55.

[105] Ayubi, *Nadwi Fuzalā*, 159.

[106] Jibreel Delgado, "Muhammad Hamidullah: Bringing a Heritage to Light", in *The Maydan*, December 2017.

Hamidullah (d. 2002) are of *Nawā'iti* descent.

Athar has produced a brilliant translation of the Qur'ān in the *Nawā'iti* language. It is a direct translation from Arabic. Additionally, the translator has consulted important tafsir sources like *Tafhim al-Qur'ān* and others.[107]

Contemporary Qur'ānic contributions: A Nadwian Appraisal

In the last two decades Nadwi scholars have set new trends to broaden the scope of tafsir studies. Their depth of knowledge and range of study are admirable attributes. The common thread that weaves their contributions is the contemporary study of the sacred text.

Sayyid Ahmad Mahidh (b. 1970) is a brilliant scholar who has contributed substantially to journals dedicated to Islamic revivalism. His works focus largely on the Islamic intellectual thought pertaining to contemporary challenges. To this end, Mahidh has approached the study of the Qur'ān in a broader perspective. As the title suggests, it deals with multiple aspects that are connected to the *i'jāz* theme. Mahidh takes the reader to a journey of discovering the gems of the Qur'ān. It reconnects a timeline of Qur'ānic history in the background of its universal message. Key themes of science and technology, numerical computation, etc. also bring out the *i'jāz* of the Qur'ān. His brief survey of Qur'ānic translations by Orientalists/non-Muslims and Hindu scholars makes interesting reading.[108] A new publication, *Qur'āni Safar* ventures to explore specific topics in the light of the thirty-part (*ajzā*) of the Qur'ān.[109] According to Ayubi, this work contains principal themes that are suited for the *madāris.*

Faisal Ahmad Bhatkali's (b. 1975) works represent a critical engagement with the sacred text. His competence in Arabic may be gleaned from his postgraduate dissertation: a critical evaluation of the virtues of surahs/*āyāt* it notable exegetes. It will not be out of

---

[107] Ayubi, *Nadwi Fuzalā*, 158-9.
[108] Ibid., 147-9.
[109] Sayyid Ahmad Anis Nadwi, *Qur'āni Safar* (Firozabad, 2020).

place to state that the *fadhā'il* genre percolates many tafsirs; in fact, the calculator reward mindset tends to diminish the lessons and message of the Qur'ān.

The principles of tafsir is a sub-genre of Qur'ānic studies. In the subcontinent *Al-Fawz al-Kabir* continues to enjoy an eminent status in the madrasah curriculum. However, the *usul* is an evolving science and no work may be considered a definitive contribution. Faisal Bhatkali has ventured to add new dimensions to the sub-genre by his incisive analysis of modern tafsirs and his thoughtful insights into their varied aspects. He is a discerning scholar who undertakes comparative studies of contemporary translations in the spirit of impartiality. Likewise, the science and *i'jāz* aspect receives greater clarity in his discussion. Finally, Faisal Bhatkali offers readers positive messages to interact with the Qur'ān soulfully and meaningfully.[110]

Muhammad Sam'an Khalifa is a promising, accredited scholar. He has made his foray into Qur'ānic studies by undertaking a comparative study of Urdu translations. According to Ayubi, this comprehensive work is encyclopedic in its scope. It avoids the trodden path of polemics and mediocrity by focusing meticulously on the sources of reference of each translation. In the field of translation, Sam'an Khalifa brings to the fore his consummate Arabic skills. His translation of an important work from Arabic, *Scientific Miracles of the Qur'ān*[111] is telling example of his familiarity with Islam and the science discourse.

A word about Tariq Ayubi. A prolific scholar and translator of contemporary Arabic works, Ayubi's multidimensional and activist personality cuts across the domains of traditional learning. His Qur'ānic contributions are contained in many of his writings. His *Nadwi Fuzalā* is a major contribution to the tafsir series co-ordinated by the K. A. Nizami Centre.

Owing to length constraints, Ayubi makes brief references to scholars who have written substantively on the Qur'ān themes. Notwithstanding this limitation, *Nadwi Fuzalā* forms an important link to the general survey of Qur'ānic contributions in the

---

[110] Ibid., 155-6.
[111] The book was authored by the noted Yemeni scholar, 'Abdul Majid Zindani.

subcontinent.

In retrospect, a pertinent question may be posed: has Nadwah, committed to the reformist policy/vision, prioritised tafsir as an evolving discipline rather than a subject incorporated into its curriculum? Perhaps the Qur'ānic workshops may partially answer this vexing question. Abrar Ahmad Nadwi has sketched out the teaching of the Qur'ānic text in Nadwah's curriculum.[112] The direct translation method is only feasible after a intensive study of Arabic and its allied sciences. Hence, competence implies a thorough, holistic approach as opposed to the traditional teaching style prevalent in other *madāris*.

Another significant aspect of Nadwah's teaching approach is the segmentation of the surahs. First, surahs of Makkan revelation are taught for the purpose of instilling a correct understanding of *'āqā'id* and other related matters. *Stories of the Prophets* (*qasas*) by Shaykh Nadwi are integrated into the teaching programme to enable students to have a full grasp of *da'wah*.[113] At the advanced level of the alim course, certain tafsirs are taught according to a graded format. Among contemporary tafsirs, *'Ulum al-Qur'ān* by Mannah al-Qattān is a preferred choice. A theme-based methodology is employed to develop skills in Qur'ānic studies. In this way students at the post-graduate level are expected to write a thesis on aspects of tafsirs.[114] Overall, the Nadwi Qur'ānic programme is a self-conscious commitment to update existing approaches to the sacred text.

---

[112] Muhammad Mubeen Saleem Nadwi Azhari, *Model Syllabus for Teaching of the Qur'ān in the Madrasahs* (Aligarh, 2019), 15-27.
[113] Shaykh Nadwi's *Qasas al-Nabiyyin* is included in the Nadwah curriculum.
[114] Azhari, *Model Syllabus for Teaching of the Qur'ān*, 20-1.

Chapter 5

Ahl i-Hadith Contributions to Qur'ānic Studies

The phenomenon of sectarian orientation spanning over two hundred years has defined the trajectory of the tafsir tradition. The Ahl i-Hadith movement[1] emerged from the transnational Islamic scholarship networks. Two early *muhaddiths*, 'Ali Muttaqi and 'Abdul Haq Dehlawi[2] preceded Shah Waliyullah to the dissemination of hadith studies in the subcontinent. Their respective studies in the Hijaz under notable scholars brought a cosmopolitan outlook on the foundational sources of Islam.

Migration patterns determined the tenor of and focus on Islamic disciplines. As stated elsewhere in the volume, state patronage by various Muslim rulers also strengthened the presence of the Hanafi school of thought (*maslak*). The formation of the Ahl i-Hadith movement essentially was a reaction to *taqlid*[3] represented by the four schools of thought which were prevalent in the Muslim world. Non-conformist in outlook, it stridently advocated an unmediated access to the Qur'ān and sunnah. Their visible marker of divergence was in their approach to postures and *qirā'at* in *salāh*. In effect, the nineteenth century was marked by periodic spells of polemics against Hanafis on marginal issues.[4] The sectarian nature of *munāzarah* assumed alarming proportions and gave rise to misperceptions about the movement's scholarly profile. It is assumed that the Ahl-i-Hadith were pacifist, which belied their immense contribution to the *jihād* movement of Sayyid Ahmad Shahid and the First War of Independence in 1857.[5]

---

[1] For a historical account of the movement, see Metcalf, *Islamic Revival in British India*, 264-96.

[2] See Nizami, *Hayāt i-Shaykh 'Abdul Haq Dehlawi*, 118-33.

[3] Metcalf, *Islamic Revival in British India*, 265.

[4] Ibid., 275.

[5] The *mujāhids* belonging to different schools of thought rallied around the *jihād* call by Sayyid Ahmad Shahid. Likewise, their participation in the 1857 freedom struggle was emblematic of their selfless sacrifice. See Ghazi, *Islamic Renaissance in South Asia*, 201-4.

Historical accounts and scholarly treatment provide an alternative picture of their selfless sacrifice to these causes.

In the field of tafsir the Ahl i-Hadith scholars gave fresh impetus to the Qur'ānic hermeneutics embodied in the *salaf* literature. However, it must be pointed out that the term *salaf* was a later accretion to connect the movement to a broader ideological framework. Interestingly, the term *Wahhābi* had a pejorative connotation and was misapplied to the *jihād* movement of Sayyid Ahmad by Orientalists.[6] Equally pernicious was the accusation levelled against Nawāb Siddiq Hasan Khan of Bhopal[7] for his supposed *Wahhābi* leanings. Obviously, this term served British colonial interests in the subcontinent.

Our focus on the Qur'ānic contributions by Ahl i-Hadith scholars rests with the assessment by Rafiq Ahmad Raees Salafi. As one of the contributors to the Qur'ānic studies series,[8] *salaf's* survey of the literature under discussion is instructive. While citing recent works that detail the immense translation and tafsir works of Ahl i-Hadith scholars in Arabic, Urdu and regional languages, their salience is marked by their strict adherence to the foundational sources of Islam.[9] By the same token, their referential point is to the Waliyullah *tajdidi* tradition. Furthermore, Salafi consults eight important tafsirs that are used for comparative analysis among the non-Salafi scholars. Two notable features stand out in these tafsirs: first, a conspectus of works related to Qur'ānic studies are given. This approach facilitates a clearer understanding of the exegete's broader scholarly treatment of the Qur'ānic message and teachings. Second, the readers are exposed to the methodology adopted by the exegete with regards to his presentation of *nazm*, literary style and other aspects of the Qur'ān. A merit worthy point is the objective analysis and forceful presentation of views from the Ahl i-Hadith perspectives to these tafsir reviews.[10] Abdur Raheem

---

[6] Nadwi, *A Misunderstood Reformer* (Lucknow, 1979), 42-3.

[7] Rafiq Ahmad Raees Salafi, *Ahl i-Hadith Fuzalā ki Qur'āni Khidmāt* (Aligarh, 2019), 20.

[8] This volume is listed as no. 5 in the series.

[9] Ibid., 11.

[10] Ibid., 14-5.

Kidwai has succinctly outlined the purpose of these different strands of tafsirs against the background of conflicting sectarian orientations in the subcontinent.[11] This approach, therefore, is sectarian-free and brings to the fore the rich repository of the tafsir genre that continues to influence contemporary Islamic thought in the subcontinent.

Nawāb Sayyid Siddiq Hasan Khan

A towering figure and among the founding fathers of the Ahl i-Hadith movement, Nawāb Sayyid Siddiq Khan (hereafter Nawāb Siddiq) rose to prominence in the state of Bhopal that was ruled by Begums for over a hundred years.

Nawāb Siddiq (d. 1890) belonged to a distinguished family who maintained close ties with Shah Waliyullah's thought and the *jihād* movement of Sayyid Ahmad Shahid. The reconstruction of Muslim society articulated by Sayyid Ahmad had resonance for Nawāb Siddiq to his conceptual framework of *tajdid*. His perceptive comments are revealing:

> A sign of God was his guiding the people on the right path and making their hearts incline to God. A large number of people became pure-hearted saints through the potent influence exerted by him, while his spiritual successors swept the country clean of all innovations and polytheistic thoughts and practices. These measures made the masses follow the path of the Book and the sunnah. The blessing of his noble efforts are still visible.[12]

The consolidation of the Ahl i-Hadith movement can be traced back to the tireless efforts of Nawāb Siddiq. His years in Bhopal as an erudite scholar and consort of Shah Jahan Begum (d. 1901)[13]

---

[11] Ibid., 9.

[12] Cited in Nadwi, *A Misunderstood Reformer*, 47.

[13] For the scholarly contribution of Shah Jahan Begum, see Claudia Preckel, *Begums*

strengthened his mission to disseminate the pristine teachings of Islam. Among his teachers who had settled in Bhopal was Shaykh Husayn ibn Muhsin Yemeni[14] who was considered the last word on hadith studies. His charismatic personality drew distinguished 'ulama from the subcontinent to Bhopal, which in more than one way was symbolically associated with Al-Azhar on account of its singular contributions to hadith. These positive developments were supported by Nawāb Siddiq.

In the domain of Qur'ānic studies, Nawāb Siddiq wrote prolifically in Arabic, Persian and Urdu. The point of convergence in these works was Islamic authenticity as elucidated by the *salaf*. Implicit in his elaboration of the *asāla* (authentic sources) of tafsir was his critique of *taqlid*.

However, Nawāb Siddiq presented a scholarly treatment on *ikhtilāf* issues, which in his estimation, was the Prophetic practice.[15] His articulation stands in line with Qur'ānic literature of the outstanding *salai* tradition which Nawāb Siddiq vigorously espoused. Sadly, the spectre of *salai* thought today is conflated with *takfir*[16] - intolerance that discredits the decorum of *ikhtilāf* (difference of opinion).

The popularity of Nawāb Siddiq's works extended to the Middle East and left indelible imprints on the emergence of Salafi thought within the framework of *islāh*.

Works related to the tafsir genre are a conspectus of Nawāb Siddiq's wide-ranging contributions. A comprehensive account of two of his tafsirs, Arabic and Urdu,[17] is a locus of the intersecting points of his reformist thought.

---

of Bhopal (New Delhi, 2000), 125-36.

[14] The Yemeni influence, particularly in hadith studies is examined in (Karachi, 1984), 209-12. Abul Hasan Ali Nadwi, *Purān i-Charāgh*, vol. 1.

[15] Nawab Siddiq launched a unrelenting campaign to curb the prevalence of *bid'āt* in the princely state of Bhopal. Cf. Salafi, *Ahl i-Hadith Fuzalā*, 22-7.

[16] The proliferation of anti-*madhab* literature supported by state patronage has diluted the robust scholarly tradition of *ikhtilāf* in the Arab world. Instead, *kufr*-bashing *fatwās* are issued by keyboard warriors - a reference to non-traditional Muslim scholars.

[17] 'Abdur Razzaq Gondal, *Nawāb Siddiq Hasan Khan ka Tafsiri Minhāj awr Tafsir Tarjumān al-Qur'ān bi Latā'if al-Bayān ka Tafsiri Adab me Maqiim* (Lahore, 2019), 94-344.

Fath al-Bayān

According to Nawāb Siddiq, his Arabic tafsir is considered among his renowned works devoted to the genre.[18] Salim Kidwai sums up the approach of the tafsir:

> This tafsir follows in the style of Suyuti's *Durr al-Manthur* by combining related information from other tafsirs. While citing weak *ahādith*, (Nawāb Siddiq) by virtue of his specialised knowledge in hadith literature, deftly sifted out the flaws in these types of hadith narrations. In this way he substantiates his preference on sound scholarly basis. A characteristic feature of his tafsir is the combination of narration (*riwāyah*) and tradition (*dirāyah*) which gives it a scholarly edge.[19]

A structural analysis of *Fath al-Bayān* reveals the following points. First, knowledge of tafsir points out to the "flawless order of the sacred text which accentuates its practical manifestation." Simply put, the Qur'ān embodies legal prescriptions (*ahkām*). Second, *wahy* (revelation) has an inherent miraculous content and has challenged mankind to produce short surahs in terms of its unmatched literary beauty and majesty. Therefore, the Qur'ānic Arabic can only be interpreted by adhering to its standard rules. Hence, the risk of misrepresentation is even greater in this regard for those who lack the knowledge of Qur'ānic sciences. Third, interpretation is not an arbitrary exercise or has an uncharted exploratory course. By contrast, it must conform to the unwavering conviction (*yaqin*) that the text is of divine origin. Therefore, textual evidence or deduction is best understood by the interpretation of the Sahabah and the next generation (*Tābi'un*).[20]
Nawāb Siddiq theorises the Salafi sources to broaden the scope

---

[18] Nawab Siddiq Khan, *Fath al-Bayān i Maqāsid al-Qur'ān* (Beirut, 1992).
[19] Salim Kidwai, *Hindustāni Mufassirin*, 102 (Adapted).
[20] Salafi, *Ahl i-Hadith Fuzalā*, 23-4.

of *ta'wil*. He contends that the consensus (*ijmā*) on certain verses was diluted over time. As a result, the divergent opinions that have appeared after the *Tābi'un* period are emblematic of the steady departure from the unambiguous or precise explanations as transmitted by the Sahabah. This point is reinforced in Surah Al-Fatihah (1:7). For Nawāb Siddiq, the terms *maghdub* (incurred wrath) and *dāllin* (gone astray) refer specifically to the Jews and Christians.[21]

In the domain of tafsir literature Nawāb Siddiq makes a pertinent remark about the changing composition of commentaries. The term genealogical tradition has much relevance in this regard. For example, *Kashshāf* approaches the Qur'ānic text largely from a linguist angle whereas *Tafsir al-Kabir* has a philosophical thrust. Across the spectrum of the tafsir output, hadith analysis is relegated to the margins. This approach, in Nawāb Siddiq's view, accounts for the indiscriminate citation of *ahādith*. Again, the *Kashshāf* is illustrative of this trend. However, it must be borne in mind that Nawāb Siddiq's hadith acumen shaped by Shawkani's tafsir[22] was among the contributing factors to his critical examination of the classical *tafsirs*. Thus his slant or bias in this respect is understandable.

Elsewhere in the chapter, reference was made to the influence of the Waliyullah tradition on Nawāb Siddiq's Qur'ānic writings. In this regard he expresses his indebtedness to the important writings of Ibn Taimiyyah and Shah Waliyullah who elucidated the principles of tafsir in their respective exegetical works. The *Aksir i Usul al-Tafsir*[23] explains Nawāb Siddiq's methodology to his tafsirs in Arabic and Urdu, respectively.

---

[21] Ibid., 24.
[22] Ibid., 25-6.
[23] Ibid., 37.

Tarjumān al-Qur'ān[24]

Almost a century after Shah 'Abdul Qādir's tafsir was published, the *Tarjumān al-Qur'ān* appeared as an invaluable contribution to this genre. A collaborative work completed in 1898, the multivolume work had a significant impact on scholars with *salafi* leanings.

In his Introduction,[25] Nawāb Siddiq provides a detailed account for writing this outstanding tafsir. In his assessment, this work was an extension of the tafsirs produced by Waliyullah and Shah 'Abdul Qādir. Its aim was clear: to be a reference guide for those who are not conversant with the specialised knowledge and disciplines relating to the Qur'ān. Technical details are kept to a minimum to allow the Qur'ān to speak for itself. However, the focus on hadith literature and the opinions of Sahabah are given prominence. Nawāb Siddiq deplored the trend of tafsir anchored on independent reasoning/deduction.

The framework of *Tarjumān al-Qur'ān* makes reference to two important historical events in the text that require a contextual reading according to the *salafi* worldview. Furthermore, metaphysical and eschatological realities, mentioned in the Qur'ān are elaborated in the classical commentaries with well-developed explanations. However, speculative theology, according to Nawāb Siddiq, borders on *kufr*.

Theological disputation about the nature of the Qur'ān infiltrated into the Qur'ānic domain in the early years of Islamic history. For instance, the Mu'tazilite argument[26] about the created nature of the Qur'ān raised a storm of controversy by sparking off counter responses to this disputed doctrine. Nawāb Siddiq approached this issue in a different perspective. He argued

---

[24] The complete title is *Tarjumān al-Qur'ān bi Latā'if al-Bayān*. Two words contained in the title are a pointed reference to the *mufassir's* overall interpretation of the sacred text.

[25] See Gondal, *Nawāb Siddiq Hasan Khan*. Our summative assessment of the author's Introduction has bearing on the themes elaborated in Nawab Siddiq's multivolume commentary.

[26] For a critical examination of the Mu'tazilite creed, see M.M. Sharif, *A History of Muslim Philosophy*, vol. 1 (Karachi, 1983), 199-213.

that disbelief in the divine origin of the Qur'ān was '*aqidah*-based and, therefore, a fine line existed between *imān* and *kufr*. Similarly, *kufr* was extended to those people who rejected the prohibition of interest (*ribā*) and the Qur'ānic guidelines on inheritance (*farā'idh*).[27]

As a founding figure of the Ahl i-Hadith movement, Nawāb Siddiq critically examines the notion of *taqlid* framed from the lens of the Qur'ān and sunnah. Therefore, he critiques the authoritative role of the four Imams of their explication of *Fiqh*-related issues as derived from the Qur'ānic text.[28]

The Isra'ilite tradition had over the centuries elicited conflicting opinions among the exegetes. Nawāb Siddiq adopted a cautious approach to the unscrupulous adoption of these non-Qur'ānic sources. He avoided extrapolating narratives that he deemed inconsistent with the ethos of the sacred text. In the same way, he avoided the extreme positions by carefully accepting Isra'ilite narrations that were not censured or to which Islam was non-committal.[29] In sum, Nawāb Siddiq was an exceptional scholar with profound Qur'ānic knowledge. Ideological perspectives aside, he was definitely not a dyed-in-the-wool non-conformist (*ghair muqallid*) as portrayed by his critics.

In terms of methodology, Nawāb Siddiq followed a particular pattern. The title of the surah, the number of verses, brief comments of the surah being Makki or Madani are given; these details prepare readers for an overall description on the surah under discussion. Furthermore, the *ikhtilāf* factor is generally highlighted for the purpose of robust exchange of views. One point, however, deserves mention: virtues of the surah. The fault line of the *fadhā'il* (virtues)[30] narrative has reflected a poor grasp of 'ulum al- hadith by many exegetes. As a result, exaggerated accounts of *fadhā'il* with exponential rewards (*thawāb*) crept into creditable tafsirs. Nawāb Siddiq deplored this

---

[27] Salafi, *Ahl i-Hadith Fuzalā*, 42.

[28] Ibid.

[29] Ibid., 43.

[30] Zamakhshari's inclusion of weak (*da'if*) *ahādith* is a case in point.

trend   and instead offered a sober analysis of particular *fadhā'il* generally considered acceptable and consistent with the ethos of the Prophetic practice (*sunnah*).

Tarjumān al-Qur'ān is not necessarily a verse-by-verse annotation. By contrast, the exegete groups several verses for translation purposes. By and large, he reproduces comments from Shah Abdul Qādir's work and then provides his own tafsir. In a similar vein, if the Qur'ānic text opens up *Fiqh*-related discussion, Nawāb Siddiq focuses primarily on the *salaf* sources to support his interpretation. Also important points are incorporated from his Arabic tafsir. A noteworthy feature of the tafsir is the insertion of the letter "fa" to discuss particular verses in context. Likewise, the letter "ma" denotes an exhaustive examination of textual sources pertaining to the issues of *Fiqh*. By way of example, the following discussion about the *i'jāz* of the Qur'ān demonstrates Nawāb Siddiq's mastery over the tafsir tradition:

> *"If you are in any doubt whether it is We Who have revealed this Book to Our Servant, then produce just a surah like it, and call on all your supporters and seek in it the support of all others save Allah. Accomplish this if you are truthful. But if you fail to do this and you will most certainly fail - then have the fear of the ire whose fuel is men and stones and which has been prepared for those who deny the truth."*

> (2:23-4)

After the exposition of *tawhid*, the declaration of Prophethood (*nabuwwat*) is expounded. The disbelievers are addressed to produce a similar surah by enlisting the support of people they choose. If they express their inability then they have no right to make audacious claims about the divine origin of the Qur'ān. The challenge to match, equal or reproduce surahs of flawless elegance and majesty had silenced its critics. There are several verses that repeatedly remind the disbelievers to accept the Qur'ānic challenge. These verses have a circumstantial setting and have a direct bearing on the Qur'ān's eternal truth and wisdom.[31] Like many tafsirs, the effect of time impinged on their fluency, relevance and relatability. Nawāb Siddiq adapted *Mudih al- Qur'ān* in view of the evolving nature of Urdu. Thus idioms and expressions become cliched and incomprehensible to common readers. His tafsir, too, required a reader-friendly version. In 2003 two volumes[32] were brought out keeping the new readership in mind. Other important works linked to tafsir studies have also been simplified. The *Mudih al- Qur'ān* served as a template for subsequent translations in Urdu. It was adapted, and in some places revised. The rationale or justification for these textual changes has been proffered by these translators.

In the field of English translations, the tafsir of 'Abdullāh Yusuf Ali (d. 1953) *The Meaning of the Glorious Qur'ān: Translation and Commentary* has undergone dramatic changes. According to Abdur Raheem Kidwai, two new revised editions of Yusuf Ali's work appeared in 1989 and 1990, respectively. However, the debate about the 'propriety of the exercise' and intellectual rights have evoked sharp responses from scholars. Unlike *Mudih al- Qur'ān* which is a mainstream tafsir contribution, Yusuf Ali's work contained pseudo-rational and apologetic explanations to eschatological beliefs and contentious views on *ribā* (interest), etc. The expurgated version was intended to realign this important work to the authentic expression of the sacred text.[33] Fortunately, *Mudih al-Qur'ān* has not been morphed into a new work. The *tashil* (simplified) version project is a recent phenomenon in the publishing market of Urdu books. This version is intended to make scholarly works widely accessible in view of their growing popularity among Muslim readers who are not inclined to read voluminous tafsirs. The recently simplified editions of *Bayān al-Qur'ān* demonstrate the enduring legacy of Thānawi's singular contributions to this field.

A cursory survey of the life and thought of Thanā'Allah Amritsari

---

[31] Cf. Gondal, *Nawāb Siddiq Hasan Khan*, 273-84.

[32] Salafi, *Ahl i-Hadith Fuzalā*, 52.

[33] For a detailed discussion of Yusuf Ali's tafsir, see Kidwai, *Translating the Untranslatable*, 24-31.

(d.1948) shows the steady rise of tafsirs framed around socio-economic issues. Amritsari is described as a 'Qur'ānic exegete, traditionist (*muhaddith*), jurist, researcher and successful Muslim polemicist.'[34] of the nineteenth century. His varied contributions were recognised in the Ahl i-Hadith circles and beyond. Likewise, his studies at Madrasah Faidh i-'Am (Kanpur) and Deoband[35] broadened the scope of his intellectual acumen. As a first-rate *muhaddith*, Amritsari acquired *ijāzah* to transmit *ahādith* from the eminent 'ālim, Sayyid Nadhir Husayn who established an independent madrasah in Delhi. Initially, Amritsari taught hadith and tafsir, which were based on *Mudih al-Qur'ān*. His long and illustrious career as a *muhaddith* resulted in the unprecedented interest in this discipline. Additionally, his students made great strides in the popularisation of hadith studies through their original commentaries of the hadith literature.[36] Also dictionaries were compiled to encourage a direct study of the tafsir and hadith genres.

Exegetical Contributions

Amritsari's exceptional command over Arabic is evident from his Qur'ānic writings. By all accounts, his *Tafsir al-Qur'ān*[37] is written in chaste Arabic, expressing the sublimity of Amritsari's unique style, which was lauded by illustrious scholars like Sayyid Sulayman Nadwi.[38] A defining characteristic of his tafsir is the intra-Qur'ānic methodology: a particular verse or a cluster of verses are interpreted in the light of its related verses.[39] In many instances, it has rivalled Suyuti's *Jalālayn* for its precise and lucid expressions. Taught verbatim in many *madāris*, the *Tafsir al-Qur'ān*

---

[34] Majeed, *Qur'ān Interpretation in Urdu*, 89.

[35] Amritsari studied hadith under the famous scholar-activist, Shaykh al-Hind of Deoband. The cross-currents of hadith studies in particular reveal the impact of the Waliyullah tradition on different schools of thought.

[36] Ghazi, *Islamic Renaissance in South Asia*, 245-7.

[37] Thanā'Allah Amritsari, *Tafsir al-Qur'ān bi Kalām al-Rahmān* (Lahore, n.d.).

[38] Sulayman Nadwi, *Yād Raftagān* (Azamgarh, 2012), 367-70.

[39] Majeed, *Qur'ān Interpretation in Urdu*, 91.

also drew harsh criticism from the Ghaznawi 'ulama[40] who also belonged to the Ahl i-Hadith movement for its conciliatory approach to other *maslaks*. Nevertheless, Amritsari opened new pathways to unravel the inner beauty of the Qur'ān.

According to *Nuzhat al-Khawātir*, Amritsari engaged vigorously in debates with the Christian and Arya Samaj movements, and the Qadianis who were rooted in Punjab.[41] His polemical style also extended to sectarian groups like the Barelwis[42] whose tafsirs he critiqued. All in all, his trenchant evaluation of the Qur'ānic translations like the Qadianis and Bahais are contained in his *Tafsir bi al-Ra'iy*.[43]

It must be noted that Amritsari possessed consummate skills in the *munāzarah* genre which he skillfully applied to silence his critics. Even so, he did not hold extremist positions in his tafsir that would otherwise characterise its sectarian character. By way of example, he was an executive member of the Nadwah Shura Council. His recommendations were generally adopted judging by the resolutions passed in the meetings regarding the institution's vision and mission statement.[44] In the biographical dictionary penned by Sayyid 'Abdul Hayy Hasani, his comments about Amritsari's intellectual acumen are illuminating.[45]

According to Dietrich Reetz, Amritsari was a pivotal figure of the Ahl i-Hadith who "exerted a rather strong influence on the affairs and debuts of the Nadwah pushing forward reformist educational concerns and at several junctures supporting the reformism of Shibli."[46] This statement, however, does not suggest Nadwah was

---

[40] For a synoptic overview of the Ghaznawi 'ulama and their reformist contributions, see Nadwi, *Purāni i-Charāgh*, vol.2 (Karachi, 1981), 275-84.

[41] 'Abdul Hayy Hasani, *Nuzhat al-Khawātir*, vol. 8 (Rae Bareli, 1993), 105. Mirza Ghulam Ahmad Qadiani's vitriol against the 'ulama who opposed his claims to Prophethood was well known. His vituperative remarks against Amritsari ironically evoked an irrepressible fear for this illustrious 'alim. See Nadwi, *Qadianism: A Critical Study* (Lucknow,1974), 97-8.

[42] Reference to Ahmad Riza Khan's Urdu translation, *Kanz al-Imān*.

[43] Amritsari singled out this type of tafsir as akin to arbitrary interpretation. Cited in Salafi, *Ahl i-Hadith Fuzalā*, 110.

[44] Shams Tabriz Khan, *Tārikh Nadwat al-'Ulama*, vol.2 (Lucknow, 1984), 383, 388.

[45] See Abul Hasan Ali Nadwi, *Kārwān i-Zindagi*, vol. 2 (Lucknow, 1982), 22.

[46] Diedrich Reetz, *Islam in Public Space: Religious Groups in India, 1900-1947* (New

completely amenable to the reformist impulse of Amritsari. Rather, its policy sought to integrate reformist strands of which Ahl i-Hadith was one such strand.

Tafsir Thanā'i

Written in Urdu, the eight-volume tafsir was completed in 1931 over a period of 36 years. In keeping with Amritsari's intellectual framework, the scholastic and polemical elements are very much evident in the work. Amritsari has given the background to this important tafsir. First, the growing gap between readers and the sacred text was an increasing concern largely on account of their detached interest in its message. Second, the steady erosion of the Qur'ān's essential teaching by critics and controversial translations impelled Amritsari to counter these toxic responses.[47] To this end, his well-developed rebuttal of movements like the Arya Samaj which vehemently attempted to undermine the eternal message of Islam was incorporated in his tafsir. Constructive criticism,[48] in the main, feature prominently in his approach to sects of all hues.

For Amritsari, the disconnected letters (*muqatta'āt*) had an encoded message as supported by the explanation of 'Abdullāh ibn 'Abbās. These letters specifically have a pointed reference to Allah and His attributes. There are, however, exceptions as in many instances they have a direct reference to the Holy Prophet (SAW). Two examples are cited to understand Amritsari's interpretation:

Surah Al-Shura (42:1)

I am Allah the Most Beneficent, the Most Merciful. I have full knowledge, cover all faults and shortcomings (of man) and

---

Delhi, 2006), 190.
[47] Salafi, *Ahl i-Hadith Fuzalā*, 112-3.
[48] Ibid.

have absolute power and authority.[49]

Surah Yasin (36:1)

O Perfect person, Muhammad the Messenger of Allah.

The above interpretations are suggestive clues based on the separate Arabic letters to the related surahs. Therefore, these are not authoritative and definitive meanings.

Comparative religious studies appeared on the tafsir domain following the spate of debates (*munāzarāt*) with other faith groups. Amritsari's incisive comments reveal his familiarity with the Gospels which he cites to counter Christian polemics. In a historical context he amplifies the distortion of the original Gospels based on the following Qur'ānic verse:

Those who believe in what has been revealed to you
and what was revealed before you. (2:2)

In the light of the above comments, the interpolation of the Torah (The Old Testament) and Gospels, which originally were of divine scriptures does not suggest that Muslims are expected to believe unconditionally in their veracity.

Interest in the Old and New Testament Scriptures on a scholarly level is credited to Sayyid Ahmad Khan (d. 1898). His *Tabyin al-Kalām* is an incomplete 'Mahomedan Commentary of the Holy Bible'. Sayyid Ahmad's critical examination of the authenticity of Old and New Testament Scriptures and the theological place of pre-Islamic scriptures are illustrative of his extensive study of these original sources. His assessment is not based on superficial study as is generally assumed but a systematic, structured analysis of the word *tahrif* (tampering) in a Qur'ānic context.[50] Furthermore, Sayyid Ahmad studied Hebrew under distinguished scholars[51] to

---

[49] Ibid., 114.

[50] Abdur Raheem Kidwai, *Sir Syed Ahmad Khan: Muslim Renaissance, Man of India* (New Delhi, 2017), 322-38.

[51] The influence of Mawlana Ināyat Khan Chiryākot on Sayyid Ahmad's learning of

access directly the original text of these Scriptures.

Rational interpretation marked Sayyid Ahmad's tafsir about historical accounts and eschatological issues on which there is *ijmā* (consensus) among the *Ahl al-Sunnah*. Amritsari's critique, therefore, is not a lone voice among exegetes in the 19th and 20th century. We will cite one example of Sayyid Ahmad's rationalisation which evoked a hostile reception from the 'ulama belonging to various schools of thought.[52] (A detailed examination of his tafsir appears in Chapter 9). For him the only miracle (*mu'jizā*) attributable to the Holy Prophet (SAW) is his Prophetic role, which is revelational but thoroughly consonant with nature. Essentially, it implies that the Word of God must reflect the Work of God- a synthesis that contradicted the manifestation of miracles.[53] Keeping in mind Amritsari's theological background, it is hardly surprising of him to adopt a harsh tone on this cardinal belief in his tafsir.

At the heart of *Tafsir Thanā'i* is the unity in diversity theme. Amritsari draws the readers' attention to the core message of the Qur'ān: guidance for mankind. For Muslims who are embroiled in sectarian disputations, Amritsari warns them of the dire consequences as tersely expressed in the following verse:

> *Surely you have nothing to do with those who have made divisions in their religion and have split into two factions. Their matter is with Allah and He will indeed tell them (in time) what they have been doing.*

(6:159)

It is clear that Amritsari deplored intra-sectarian conflict and urged the *ummah* to reconcile their differences (*ikhtilāf*) in the spirit of the *salaf*.[54]

Hebrew receives brief mention in Firoz Ahmad, *Ihsānullah 'Abbāsi: Hayāt awr Kārnāme* (Aligarh, 2019),19.

[52] Ahmad, *Islamic Modernism in India and Pakistan*, 47.

[53] Salafi, *Ahl i-Hadith Fuzalā*, 116-7.

[54] Ibid., 119-21.

Overall, *Tafsir Thanā'i* is a work of exceptional merit and must be contextualised in the backdrop of religious intolerance in the subcontinent.

Muhammad Haneef Nadwi

The life and times of Muhamad Haneef Nadwi (d. 1987) offers interesting insights into the scholarly networks between the Ahl i-Hadith and Nadwah. At its very outset Nadwah had a two-pronged strategy:

- To reform the curriculum in the light of changing circumstances.
- To create an ambience of unity regardless of *ikhtilāf* which it believed was a source of mercy for the *ummah.*

By the late nineteenth century Nadwah's objectives crystallised into positive outcomes. Notwithstanding the challenges the Nadwah administration faced, their tireless efforts, in more ways than one, bridged the precarious gaps between sectarian-oriented institutions. In fact, the Ahl i-Hadith saw a semblance of striking similarities between themselves and Shaykh Nadwi's account of their flexible and progressive approach.[55]

Muhammad Haneef Nadwi was born in Gujranwala (Punjab) and studied under the famous Salafi teacher, Muhammad Isma'il. Thereafter he proceeded to Nadwah and completed his postgraduate course in Arabic literature and Qur'ānic studies.[56] Interestingly, it was at this institution that he developed his aptitude for tafsir and hadith studies. By dint of his profound study and brilliant academic calibre Muhammad Haneef produced works of outstanding merit during his tenure as research scholar at the Institute of Islamic Culture (Lahore). A semi-state sponsored institute, it drew intellectuals from the Pakistan cadre

---

[55] For an overview of Nadwah's conciliatory initiatives, see Sultan Nadwi, *Nadwat al-'Ulama ka Fiqhi Mizāj awr Abnā i-Nadwah ki Fiqhi Khidmāt* (Hyderabad, 2004), 82-9.
[56] Salafi, *Ahl i-Hadith Fuzalā*, 127-8.

who contributed significantly to the research and publication of works relating to the progressive aspects of Islamic culture and thought.

The broad sweep of Muhammad Haneef's works is an indication of his impressive grasp of the Islamic intellectual tradition. His critical study of the life and thought of Ghazali, Ibn Khaldun and Ibn Taimiyyah[57] weaves a storyline of his creative mind. Our focus of study, however, is his Qur'ānic contributions. Muhammad Tariq Ayubi has raised a pertinent point about Muhammad Haneef's preoccupation with the study of the Qur'ān. His works *Mutāla'a Qur'ān* and *Lisān al-Qur'ān* give a holistic picture about his tafsir. Broadly speaking *Mutāla'a* merit-worthy reviews the widely held opinions about particular issues related to the Qur'ānic composition, literary approaches, interpretations, etc. Muhammad Haneef's works have unmistakable traces of independent study and divergent viewpoints.[58] However, the tenor of the work bears the hallmark of scholarly excellence.

Two volumes of his *Lisān al-Qur'ān* are a rigorous analysis of Qur'ānic vocabulary encapsulating its literary charm. This aspect is explained in *Sirāj al-Bayān*. The tafsir is a remarkable work by Muhammad Haneef who had completed it in 1934 when he was 25 years old. Like many other scholars, he held Qur'ānic lessons (*dars*) which attracted professionals and prominent 'ulama among whom included famous editors of prestigious Islamic journals. His lessons were subsequently serialised in *Al-I'tisām* and later produced in book format. His teaching methodology combined both traditional and modern approaches. The vast corpus of intellectual tradition he acquired was discernible in his critique of Orientalists' misrepresentation of the Qur'ān.[59]

Key concepts are marked on each page to give a proper understanding of the text. In view of his decades-long academic study, Muhammad Haneef cites modern sources to show the continuity of the Qur'ānic worldview. Likewise, he shares his

---

[57] Ibid., 129.

[58] Muhammad Tariq Ayubi Nadwi, *Nadwi Fuzalā ki Qur'āni Khidmāt* (Aligarh, 2019), 40-2. Cf. Azami, *The History of the Qur'ānic Text*, 43-82.

[59] Ibid., 40.

insightful comments on contemporary issues that are anchored on his deep understanding of the primary sources of Islam. To this end, he seeks to make the Qur'ānic text reader-friendly for ordinary readers who wish to understand its message and teachings.[60] This, however, does not imply that the text may be read arbitrarily without specialised knowledge which has been developed over the centuries by classical exegetes. In terms of the literary excellence of the Qur'ān, the exegete by virtue of his deep study of *adab* (literary criticism) elucidates its vocabulary from a different angle. The discussion centres around grammatical connotation and inter-textual relationship. These features are inherently linked to *i'jāz*.[61] In this strain, *Lisān al-Qur'ān* serves as a reference work to the tafsir. For example these aspects are comprehensively covered in Surah Al-Fatihah.[62]

Muhammad Haneef has the uncanny ability to engage constructively with sectarian groups promoting exaggerated views on *aqā'id* (beliefs). While upholding the *salaf* tradition (as an Ahl i-Hadith scholar), his rational argument is supported by his vast Qur'ānic learning. His critique on the Barelwi doctrine regarding the Holy Prophet's knowledge of the unseen (*'ilm al-ghayb*) is revealing. According to Muhammad Haneef, this doctrine runs counter to the clear text of the Qur'ān.

> *(O Muhammad)! Say: I do not say to you that I have the treasures of Allah; nor do I have knowledge of what is beyond the reach of perception; nor do I say to you that I am an angel. I only follow what is revealed to me.*
>
> (6:50)

In Muhammad Haneef's view, this explicit declaration hinges on two important aspects:

- Prophethood is a divine dispensation that is

---

[60] Salafi, *Ahl i-Hadith Fuzalā*, 132-3.
[61] Ibid., 134.
[62] Muhammad Haneef Nadwi, *Tafsir Sirāj al-Bayān*, vol. 1 (Lahore, 1983), 2-3.

dependent on sources of knowledge granted to the Prophets by Allah for specific functions. The varying degree of 'extraordinary' knowledge is not innate to their personality nor is it uniquely associated with the Prophets.

- On rational grounds, imagine if we suppose that the Holy Prophet (SAW) possessed *'ilm al ghayb*, how did he not anticipate the injury that was inflicted on his noble personality at Ta'if or a tragic event like Karbala during which his beloved grandson was brutally killed? Muhammad Haneef provides a number of historical events from the Qur'ān to highlight the inconsistency of holding such a belief.[63]

In sum, *Sirāj al-Bayān* is a notable contribution to the rational exposition of the Qur'ān's abiding message for mankind.

Taysir al-Rahmān[64]

It will be worthwhile to make an introductory comment on tafsirs that have sectarian readings. To clarify a point: the term sectarian is distinguished from deviant translations which include Shi'ite, Qadiani and other Muslims harbouring un-Islamic beliefs. However, in the study this definition is narrowed down to translators of the *Ahl al- Sunnah* affiliation with differing positions on issues like *tawassul* (intercession), etc. The line of demarcation is rather thin and precarious, to say the least. In several instances, the sectarian-deviant formation is a self-contradiction.[65] A positive development is that tafsirs particularly of the twenty-first century have moved away from sectarian orientation to sectarian alignment. In the context of Dr. Muhammad Luqmān Salafi's tafsir this trend is more pronounced.

A brief biographical sketch of Luqmān Salafi's academic career

---

[63] Salafi, *Ahl i-Hadith Fuzalā*, 143-4.
[64] Muhammad Luqman *Salafi, Taysir al-Rahmān li Bayān al-Qur'ān* (Chandpura, 2001).
[65] Choughley, *The Contributions of Abdur Raheem Kidwai*, 173-4.

will help us in examining his contribution to the tafsir tradition. Born in 1943 he completed his 'alim course at Dar al-'Ulum Ahmadia Salafiyah. Like other Dar al-'Ulums which affix a title to indicate their academic link or association, Salafi has a similar connotation. It must not be conflated with the current extremist and ideological positions adopted by certain groups or political outfits.

Luqmān Salafi completed his doctorate in Saudi Arabia. At the same time he was employed in the Dār al-Iftā (Riyadh) and worked in the office of the noted 'alim, Shaykh 'Abdullāh bin Baz. His close association with Shaykh Baz enhanced his own academic profile and gave him leverage to interact with Muslim communities around the world on Islamic matters. In his memoir, *Kārwān i-Hayāt* Luqmān Salafi details the influence of world renowned 'ulama[66] who had a decisive influence on his intellectual career. For our study purpose, two influential figures and their Qur'ānic contributions are highlighted.

Taqi al-Din Hilāli (d. 1987)

A pre-eminent scholar in Arabic literature, Taqi al-Din Hilāli's influence in the subcontinent was significant. An embodiment of the transnation *salafi* scholarship, Hilāli played a leading role with the Egyptian *salafi* reformist, Muhammad Rashid Rida (d. 1935) in promoting "a conscious return to the ethical ideals of the early Islamic period without ignoring the general conditions of the prevailing time."

In 1930 Hilāli was employed for a short period of three years to teach the Arabic language and literature at Nadwah. During this period Hilāli served as an important link to consolidate the network of transnational scholarship between Nadwah and the Arab world. The cultural exchange of publications and journals was a corollary to the intensive exchange of ideas between the reformist scholars of the Arabic-speaking world and South Asia. The expansion of these transnational relations had a personal

---

[66] Salafi, *Ahl i-Hadith Fuzalā*, 173-4.

impact on Shaykh Nadwi (d. 1999). Hilāli was responsible for the publication of the Arabic monograph *Tarjamat al-Imām Sayyid Ahmad bin Irfān Shahid* by Shaykh Nadwi in Rashid Rida's journal *al-Manār*. This work marked the beginning of Shaykh Nadwi's publishing activities and was a forerunner to his promotion of Islamic resurgence in the Arab world. The influence of Hilāli is described in these words:

> An international scholar who was peerless in Arabic, Hilāli drew capable students from across the country and developed their skills- his *sanad* (certificate) was a testimony of his students' competence in Arabic. In the company of Hilāli, two realities unfolded before us for the first time: the difference between language and literature. Language is the foundation of *adab* (literature) which is the gallery of the former and adorns its words and portraits. *Adab* represents the highest form of literary expressions through which progressive thoughts are a vehicle.[67]

Hilāli's *salafi* leanings in India had far-reaching implications. He was successful in preparing a team of scholars for publishing Arabic works which had a niche market in the Arab world. Several decades later Hilāli was involved in a collaborative initiative: the translation of the Qur'ān into English. The *salafi* influence stands out clearly in the translation with Saudi patronage making the work easily available worldwide. The proliferation of *salafi* works created contestations of Islamic authenticity, and at the same time gave rise to polemical literature dealing with the function and scope of Islamic resurgence.

The network of scholarship is clear in the Ahl i-Hadith collaborative project with Salafi scholars in the Saudi kingdom. In this respect, the translation of *The Holy Qur'ān* into Urdu[68] is

---

[67] Cited in Choughley, *Islamic Resurgence: Sayyid Abul Hasan Ali Nadwi and his Contemporaries* (New Delhi, 2011), 164-7.
[68] Salafi, *Ahl i-Hadith Fuzalā*, 199.

illustrative of the close ties contemporary scholars of the movement have established over time. Additionally, the Saudi patronage of their publications has reached out to a wider readership particularly in South Asia and the Arab world.

Manna al-Qattan (d. 1999) was a brilliant Saudi scholar whose contributions to Qur'ānic studies are widely acknowledged in Islamic institutes of higher learning. His celebrated work *Mabāhit i'ulum al-Qur'ān*[69] is a contemporary study of aspects and rules of the sciences of the Qur'ān. Its impact on Dar al-'Ulums in India having a progressive outlook to Qur'ānic studies is considerable. Nadwah, for example, has incorporated *Mabāhith* in its curriculum alongside Waliyullah's *Fawz Al-Kabir*. This approach augurs well for broadening the horizon of Qur'ānic studies in a contemporary setting. A cursory survey of *Fuyudh al-'Alām* reveals Luqmān's *Salai's* clear inclination to Shawkani's methodology of tafsir. He classifies the legal aspects (*ahkām*) of verses and its commentary on the basis of *Fath al-Qādir*. Thereafter, he elucidates their importance in relation to the shari'ah prescriptions. Of course, this work is framed in a *Salai* perspective and has been incorporated into the syllabus of shari'ah faculties in the Arab world.

Taysir al-Qur'ān is an important tafsir that is widely read and studied in mosques and study circles in Europe, Middle East and South Asia. Under Saudi patronage it has been translated into Hindi and English. A contributing factor to its popularity is the projection of the *salafi* literature within an Islamic authenticity conceptual framework. defining characteristics include *tawdihi* (self-explanatory) interpretation as opposed to the religious fusion practices (*bid'āt*) of the subcontinent. A critique of shrine-based Islam, innovation and pseudo-*tasawwuf* features prominently in this work. As a corollary, the exegete restates the shari'ah position on *Fiqh* issues as elucidated by the *salaf*.

Luqmān Salafi has selected two levels of tafsir sources for his work. Ibn Taimiyyah's Qur'ānic writings is widely consulted and supplemented by *Tafsir Thanā'i*. Also, the illustrious work in

---

[69] Manna al-Qattān, *Mabāhith i 'ulum al-Qur'ān* (Beirut, 2008).

the Urdu tafsir tradition, *Mudih al-Qur'ān*[70] is an indispensable source for the Luqmān Salafi. Essentially, *Taysir al-Rahmān* surpasses many Urdu translations on two counts: it is idiomatic, reader-friendly and closer in meaning/explanation to the Qur'ānic text.[71] Our evaluation of the tafsir genre takes into account the differing positions on *ahkām* which are unavoidably connected to *ikhtilāf*. However, we have focused on key elements that have enriched the genealogical tradition over the centuries. An important work like *Taysir al-Rahmān* brings into sharp focus divergent responses to *sirah*-related issues and important historical events within the Qur'ānic framework.

The *Ahl al-Bayt* (family of the Prophet (SAW) issue is a dividing line between the *Ahl al-Sunnah* and Shi'ahs. A related development among sectarian groups of the *Ahl al- Sunnah* is their almost identical view like the Shi'ahs on this matter. It implies that the 'Ali, Fatima, Hasan and Husayn are exclusive members of the Holy Prophet's family mentioned in the Qur'ān. In many Friday *khutbās* (sermons), eulogies are read out that bear semblance to the Shi'ite mindset. This exclusionary practice may be linked to hyper-religiosity. Luqmān *Salai* cites the following Qur'ānic verse to support his contention that the wives of the Prophet (*Ummahāt al-Mu'minin*) are included in the *Ahl al-Bayt* description:

> *Allah only wishes to remove uncleanliness from your members of the (Prophet's) household, and to purify you completely.*

(33:33)

The hadith narrated by A'isha is a clear indication that the wives belong to the *Ahl al-Bayt*. The famous exegete Ibn Kathir makes explicit reference to the above verse as the textual veracity (*nass*) to a correct interpretation of this Qur'ān term.[72]

---

[70] Luqman Salafi, *Fuyudh al-'Alam 'alii Tafsir al-Ayāt al-Ahkām* (Riyadh, 2002).
[71] Salafi, *Ahl i-Hadith Fuzalā*, 177-8.
[72] Ibid., 178.

Mi'rāj Conundrum

Based on the solitary hadith reports, *mi'rāj* (heavenly ascension of the Holy Prophet) has elicited divergent responses. For some scholars the spiritual dimension of the *isrā* is emphasised while the majority of scholars (*jumhur*) emphatically describe the Prophetic ascent as both a physical and spiritual experience. The modernist interpretation of the *mi'rāj* abounds in apologia. In fact, exegetes like Sayyid Ahmad Khan were overwhelmed by the divine law of nature schema that they repudiated miracles. At best, these exegetes treated *mi'rāj* in pure symbolic, allegorical terms and ventured into *tasawwuf* phraseology to describe it as a mystical experience.[73] By contrast, Luqmān *Salai* makes a reappraisal of these opposing opinions, classical and contemporary, and draws upon the scholarly elucidation of Qadi 'Iyad in his *Al-Shifā*. It is clear from Qadi Iyad's irrefutable proof that the *mi'rāj* was a physical and spiritual ascent that transcended spatial dimensions. In Qur'ānic parlance the word 'His servant' is used rather than a metaphorical allusion[74] to the Holy Prophet's soul. Other stronger arguments by Qadi 'Iyad bring out clearly the significance of the night journey.

Zia-ur-Rahmān Azami

A renowned scholar, Professor Zia-ur-Rahmān Azami (d.2020) was a Brahmin convert from Azamgarh whose pursuit of Islamic *'ulum* in Madinah earned him the honorific title of *muhaddith*.[75] His fame rests with his collation of the *sahih* hadith literature culled from an array of authentic collections. The twenty-volume work is a groundbreaking initiative that underscores his thorough familiarity with this field of study.[76] In recognition of his sterling

---

[73] Ibid., 187-9. Cf. Ahmad, *Islamic Modernism*, 46-7.
[74] Qadi Iyad, *Muhammad Messenger of Allah: Al-Shifii* (Granada, 1991), 96-108.
[75] For an autobiographical account, see Zia-ur-Rahman Azami, *From Ganga to Zamzam* (2017).
[76] *Jāmi' al-Kāmil i al-Hadith al-Sahih al-Shāmil*.

services he was appointed professor of hadith studies in Madinah University.

Another notable contribution of Zia-ur-Rahman is the *Encyclopaedia of the Glorious Qur'ān* in Hindi. More than 300 topics are listed alphabetically which includes maps to locate the sites of the Prophets, landmarks and historical places. In this original work Azami has countered the misguided beliefs of Qadianis, Bahais, etc. in order to apprise readers about their dubious claims to Prophethood. More importantly, he presents a concise introduction about the pristine purity of Islam which is very much in the strain of *Salafi* thought. All in all, the *Encyclopedia* contains invaluable information for readers who are not acquainted with the original sources in Arabic and Urdu.

Chapter 6

Madrasat al-Islāh Contributions to Qur'ānic Studies

Madrasat al-Islāh occupies a pre-eminent place in Qur'ānic studies. According to the noted scholar, Abu Sufyān Islāhi (hereafter Islāhi) the institution was committed to promoting a structured, analytical study of the sacred scripture. Among its objectives was the realignment of the Qur'ān as a lived experience, an exposition of its universal message as outlined by the Prophetic practice. Therefore, a contextualised reading of the text was essential to fathom the depth of meaning, subtlety of thought and precision of expression. It also implied a critical analysis of the sacred text and to bring to the fore its eternal guidance for mankind.

The founding father of Qur'ānic hermeneutics was the notable exegete, Hamid al-Din Farāhi (d. 1930). A maternal cousin and student of Shibli Nu'mani, Farāhi's teaching years at Aligarh Muslim University (AMU) exposed him to the progressive trends of academia. He studied Hebrew under an Orientalist lecturer which honed his skills to have direct access to previous Scriptural sources. In fact, Sayyid Ahmad Khan was among the forerunners who established new trends in comparative religious studies. Of particular interest was Qur'ānic studies which was viewed from the prism of hermeneutics that placed emphasis on reflection (*tafakkur*) and contemplation (*tadabbur*). These key concepts were seminal areas of study to which Farāhi assiduously applied his mind. It was his two notable students, Akhtar Ahsan and Amin Ahsan who developed these concepts as indispensable tools to an unfettered understanding of the message of the Qur'ān. To this end, literary theories were further developed to open up critical engagement and serious discourse with the divine text.

Semantics embodied new approaches to grammatical construction that impacted the nuanced interpretation of *i'jāz*. In more than one way, the Farāhian model assumed greater importance in relating the Qur'ān as the divine text, possessing inner logic, syntactic structure, symmetrical design and flawless patterns of connectivity and coherence. These interlinking connectors (*munsibāt*) and structured flow (*nazm*) were irrefutable proof of the Qur'ān's divine origin. In the same way, verses (*āyāt*) and surahs were unmissable indicators of the internal order that defied rational explanation. More intriguing was the twenty-three year period of revelation (*wahy*) that made no explicit reference to the text's chronological order.

Farāhi's singular efforts were Qur'ān centric in comparison and reflections on other tafsirs or classical Qur'ānic works, his writings reflect a deep study of the text embedded in specific frameworks. Islāhi has correctly observed that the incremental interest in Farāhi's Qur'ānic contributions are avidly studied and researched in Arab countries. This in itself is a tacit endorsement of Farāhi's thematic approach to the Qur'ān.

A survey of the literature related to Farāhi's prodigious writings brings new insights into, reflections on critical explorations about the traditional understanding of theme-based interpretation which are religiously elucidated in classical and pre-modern tafsirs.

Islāhi Contributions

Before we attempt to survey the Qur'ānic contributions by Islāhi scholars, a few points need to be considered to develop a clearer understanding of their tafsir production in the subcontinent. The overlapping features of Qur'ānic works are positioned within the broader framework of ideological underpinnings. These scholars represent a spectrum of scholarly tradition that is inextricably linked to three reformist movements: Nadwah, Jama'at Islami and AMU.[1]

Abu Sufyān Islāhi, an internationally acclaimed figure of Arabic

---

[1] Abu Sufyān Islāhi, *Idārah Sir Sayyid Muslim University ke Mashā'hir i- Qur'āniyāt* (Aligarh, 2017). Cf. Ayubi, *Nadwi Fuzalā* (Aligarh, 2019). Cf. Muhammad Raziul Islam Nadwi, *Naqd i-Farāhi* (Aligarh, 2010).

and Qur'ānic studies, has brought out the rich scholarly tradition of Qur'ānic works.[2] A graduate from Madrasat al-Islāh (Azamgarh), Islāhi has undertaken important research studies to examine the diversity of the Islāhi tradition. The focal point is Hamid al-Din Farāhi (1930) who is considered a pioneer in the *nazm* theory[3] (discussed elsewhere in the chapter). While Mawlana Muhammad Shafi' is credited for the establishment of the institution, Farāhi and his maternal cousin Shibli Nu'mani were instrumental in providing the madrasah an ideological base. This point becomes clearer if Farāhi and Nu'mani's erstwhile association with AMU is taken into account. Both of these influential figures nurtured the intellectual tradition on the AMU campus which by then had established a growing reputation in the domain of Islamic studies.[4] A nascent institution, AMU brought to its fold a number of Orientalists who opened up new conversation between Islamic and Western learning. We are not concerned about the presence of Muslim modernism which emerged from AMU. Notable intellectuals like Nu'mani and Farāhi were beneficiaries from these emerging patterns of scholarship.[5] They enhanced their scholarly profile through their association with Dar al-Musannifin (Azamgarh) and Madrasat al-Islāhi, respectively. In retrospect, they shaped the Islamic tradition which was on the cusp of intellectual resurgence.

In the domain of Qur'ānic thought Farāhi stands out as a brilliant 'alim who developed the principles of tafsir in a *nazm* perspective. Gifted with a thorough knowledge of Qur'ānic sciences, competence in literary Arabic, and historical acumen combined with his grounding in Hebrew language, Farāhi was eminently qualified to make a foray into the uncharted terrain of Qur'ānic studies.[6] Critical studies of the Farāhi school of thought,[7]

---

[2] Ibid., 174-8.

[3] Abu Sufyān Islāhi, *Mawlana Hamiduddin Farāhi, Muhaqqiq-o- Mufassir* (Aligarh, 2007).

[4] See Hamiduddin Farāhi, *Majmu'ah Tafāsir i-Farāhi* (Lahore, 1973), 9-10.

[5] Ibid., 11-3.

[6] Amin Ahsan Islāhi, *Tadabbur e-Qur'ān: Pondering over the Qur'ān*, vol. 1 (Kuala Lumpur, 2007), 667-71.

[7] For example, Farhad Salti, *A Comparative Analysis of the Farāhi School of Thought: A Case Study Approach* (Edinburgh, 2016).

with particular reference to his original contributions to the *nazm* theory have created platforms for a critical, robust approach to the sacred text. In all fairness, these works are substantive contributions; however, they are not definitive feats of accomplishment. Farāhi's works should therefore be examined in this light. Likewise, traditional interpretation, if rigidly applied, blurs out possibilities of critical engagement with the sacred text.

According to Islāhi, the Farāhi thought (*ikr i-Farāhi*) was conceived in the 1930s after the establishment of the Hamidia Academy. Thereafter, a plethora of institutions and journals appeared with the specific purpose of disseminating the Qur'ānic legacy of Farāhi. Their contributions have been wide and varied; in fact, they have expanded the horizons of Qur'ānic analysis.[8] To this end, the commentorial tradition has been filtered with new exegetical approaches and have significantly enriched the patterns of Urdu tafsirs.

In Islāhi's estimation, Qur'ānic methodologies patterned along Farāhi lines have developed multidisciplinary sub- genres of tafsirs. The vast corpus of Qur'ānic studies are informed reviews of traditional sources, intra-Qur'ānic interpretation and contextualised reading of the sacred text for the modern mind.[9] All in all, the Islāhi output of Qur'ānic literature is impressive within the established scholarly tradition. Islāhi, himself, has written over 5 000 pages on Qur'ānic studies.[10] He also holds the enviable distinction of bringing out the Qur'ānic contributions by AMU scholars. Through his writings, the confluence of divergent intellectual traditions is highlighted.

In the following pages the Qur'ānic contributions of selected Islāhi 'ulama are examined. A survey of the Qur'ānic literature contained in Islāhi's volume illustrates the range and depth of knowledge possessed by these distinguished scholars. Additionally, their creative engagement with the sacred text reaffirms the essence and power of the Qur'ān's limitless possibilities of interpretation.

---

[8] Islāhi, *Madrasat al-Islah*, 16.
[9] See Amin Ahsan Islāhi, *Tadabbur e-Qur'ān*, 21-2.
[10] Islāhi, *Madrasat al-Islah*, 12.

At the heart of the Qur'ān's message lies its divine source:

> *Say, even if the ocean were ink for (writing) the words of my Lord, The ocean would be exhausted before the words of my Lord were exhausted, even if we were to add another ocean to it.*

(18: 109)[11]

Akhtar Ahsan Islāhi

Akhtar Ahsan Islāhi (d. 1958) was a high-ranking Qur'ānic scholar whose fame rests on his intellectual affinity with his teacher, Farāhi. The consolidation of Madrasat al-Islāh and the publication of early journals devoted to the life and thought of Farāhi are his praiseworthy achievements.

By nature, Akhtar Islāhi was an unassuming figure whose preoccupation was centred on the study of the Qur'ān. His close relationship with Farāhi developed a common goal: to unravel the intrinsic structural design contained in the surahs. Hence, the analytical tools devised by Farāhi were adeptly employed by Akhtar Islāhi for a fuller, in-depth study of the Qur'ān.[12]

Islāhi has made a noteworthy point about Akhtar Islāhi's reticent personality. *Taqwā* was the hallmark of this towering figure of Qur'ānic studies. For him, *taqwā* opened up new pathways of discovering the inner dimensions of the Qur'ānic teachings and message. Akhtar Islāhi led an exemplary life that reflected his sense of independence. Three core activities defined his career: dissemination of Farāhi's Qur'ānic contributions, promotion of the madrasah's intellectual ambience and advancement of the Hamidia Academy.[13] He worked unfailingly to bring these plans to fruition. Akhtar Islāhi did not leave behind

---

[11] For a compelling read about the Qur'ān's enduring legacy, see Carla Power, *If the Oceans were Ink: An Unlikely Friendship and a Journey to the Heart of the Qur'ān* (New York, 2015).

[12] Islāhi, *Madrasat al-Islah*, 17-9.

[13] Ibid., 21-2.

any voluminous work to his scholarly career. There are, however, slim volumes[14] that contain gems of his vast Qur'ānic knowledge. Needless to add, he embodied Farāhi's deep reflections (*tadabbur*) on the *nazm* formulation and *rabt* (structural linkage) contained in the sacred text. He was quintessentially the Farāhi legacy.

Islāhi outlines two important aspects of Akhtar Islāhi's vast Qur'ānic learning. In line with Farāhi's Qur'ānic approach, the erudite alim employed a structural design methodology ('*umud*) to demonstrate the concept of the surah as a unity.[15] The following example underscores Akhtar Islāhi's brilliant exposition of *nazm*:

> *Be watchful over the Prayers, and over praying with utmost excellence.*

> (2: 238)

Mawdudi elaborates:

> The expression used here is *al salāt al-wustā.* The adjective *wustā,* in addition to signifying the middle position of the subject that it qualifies, also its excellence. Hence the expression could legitimately be interpreted both in the sense of the middle prayer as well as in the sense of the Prayer which is performed at the right time and with full devotion and attention to God, a Prayer which contains all the attributes of excellence.[16]

Akhtar Islāhi derives his understanding of the above verse from Farāhi's Introduction (*muqaddimah*) to the surah in general. For him, the context of this verse is based on preceding and succeeding verses. The subject matter relates to the veracity of Prophethood and an elaboration of his divine mission. Therefore,

---

[14] Mention may be made of his articles which appeared in the *Islāh* journal.

[15] For an elaboration of the surah-in-unity theme, see Amin Ahsan Islāhi, *Tadabbur e-Qur'ān*, vol. 1, 21-2.

[16] Abul A'la Mawdudi, *Towards Understanding the Qur'ān*, 75.

the focus of these verses (in his holistic sense) is *tazkiyah* (purification of the soul).[17] Implicit in Akhtar Islāhi's discussion is the ethical dimension of the Qur'ānic teachings. Likewise, he ably counters the notion that the Qur'ānic verses lack coherence and significance.

Another outstanding attribute of Akhtar Islāhi in his critical examination of contemporary Qur'ānic studies. A case in point are the writings of Ghulam Ahmad Parwez. Being the ideologue of the Ahl i-Qur'ān movement, his controversial Qur'ānic views have elicited a spate of rebuttals among the 'ulama fraternity. Akthar Islāhi has forcefully countered Parwez's misrepresentation of the Qur'ānic concept of salvation by pointing out the latter's ignorance of the primary sources of Islam. Hence his bizarre elucidation. Moreover, Parwez has displayed a patently lack of familiarity with Qur'ānic literary features like *nazm,* resulting in his distortion of credal interpretation.[18]

A remarkable trait of Akhtar Islāhi's literary output is his meticulous attention to Qur'ānic details. Take the binary of virtue and vice as eloquently expressed in the sacred text. Framed in the Qur'ānic perspective, pride (*kibr*) and humility (*khashyat)* are contrasted by Akhtar Islāhi to emphasise the innate predisposition of man. Tracing the Qur'ānic description of Prophet Ibrahim's community (*ummah*) as upright, the learned scholar brings into broad relief the constituents of an ideal society. Essentially, an unblemished character is the embodiment of *taqwā*, faith, truth and discernment. In this regard, historical accounts from the surahs are referenced to add greater weight to his articulation of the Qur'ānic moral code.[19]

Islāhi's thoughtful comments about Akhtar Islāhi's contributions are illuminating. A teacher and mentor, he critiqued differing views based on his excellent grasp of Qur'ānic sciences. In the main, he shunned the path of *tafsir bi-al rā'i* (independent interpretation) which according to him compromised scholarly credentials. For Akhtar Islāhi, a thorough

---

[17] Islāhi, *Madrasat al-Islah*, 26.
[18] Ibid., 34-6.
[19] Ibid., 39.

familiarity with classical Arabic (including pre- Islamic poetry)[20] was pivotal to a clearer of the Qur'ānic worldview.

Amin Ahsan Islāhi

The vast corpus of literature dealing with the *nazm* of the Qur'ān by Islāhi scholars has a direct bearing on the robust engagement with the immeasurable contents of the sacred text. It also epitomises the quest for decoding its universal message in keeping with the rapid changes of modern life. While our focus is on the twentieth century, technological advances have to a large extent impacted on our understanding of the Glorious Qur'ān. Amin Ahsan Islāhi's (d. 1997) serious efforts to explore the divine status of the sacred text illustrate its principal role as a guidance for mankind.

It is a truism that the layers of Qur'ānic meaning and structure are not time-specific. In other words, the study of the text is not limited to earlier tafsirs and, therefore, their interpretations do not always carry the final word. Amin Ahsan, by virtue of his vast learning, ably shows the trajectory of *nazm* through the various writings of Farāhi. In this regard Islāhi's *Madrasat al-Islāh* and *Essays on Qur'ānic Interpretation* in Urdu will guide our discussion on Amin Ahsan's remarkable Qur'ānic contributions.[21] For the purpose of sketching his biographical account the *Tadabbur e-Qur'ān* (vol. 1) in English is extensively used. These works are complementary and represent fresh perspectives on approaching the Qur'ān.

There are three distinct academic phases in Amin Ahsan's brilliant career. First, under the tutelage of Farāhi, the learned scholar gave the madrasah a 'distinct personality and a special academic environment conducive to realising its educational

---

[20] Ibid., 40.

[21] For an overview of Amin Islāhi's Qur'ānic contributions, see Islāhi, *Idārah Sir Sayyid*, 174-9. The convergence of Aligarh University and Madrasat al-Islāh is competently discussed in Islāhi's excellent research works on the scholars who were associated with both these institutions.

goals.' Second, his active association with Jama'at i-Islami was a productive phase in terms of his intellectual growth which included works of *da'wah* content. Third, after 1958 Amin Ahsan embarked on his multivolume *Taddabbur e-Qur'ān*, which was completed in 1980. At the same time he established academic centres (*halqahs*) as sites of higher learning for university students and professionals. The core study areas were Qur'ān and hadith.[22] These three phases brought out the distinct intellectual strands in Amin Ahsan's Qur'ānic worldview.

Madrasat al-Islāh was a referential framework for developing Farāhi's Qur'ānic methodology, which in many traditional circles was deemed 'too progressive'. Therefore, it was understandable when the chorus of dissenting voices attempted to stifle the Farāhi-Islāhi approaches to the sacred text. Nonetheless, Amin Ahsan devoted his years at the institution to edit, prepare and publish Farāhi's unpublished works which were mostly in Arabic. The establishment of Da'ira Hamidia as an academic institution successfully carried out Farāhi's ambitious goals to reframe a clearer, well-structured understanding of the Qur'ān. To this end, the *nazm* theory was thoroughly researched, refined and presented for academic discussion.

From 1925 to 1930, Amin Islāhi remained with his mentor and assimilated his methodology of the Qur'ān. A distinctive element of the madrasah was its Socratic approach: to formulate questions for a critical engagement with the sacred text. This required an open mind for enquiry and analysis and most importantly, *tadabbur* - deep reflection.[23]

Amin Ahsan's common revivalist vision with the founder of Jama'at i-Islami, Abul A'la Mawdudi was of great significance. Perhaps it was a continuity of his intellectual expertise which he developed at his *alma mater*. His writings on ethical issues are reflective of the Jama'at's vision of reformist thought. At a later stage these views would be encapsulated in his multivolume tafsir. In the realm of *tazkiyah* (purification of the soul) Amin

---

[22] Majeed, *Qur'ān Interpretation in Urdu*, 167-216.
[23] Amin Islāhi, *Tadabbur e-Qur'ān*, vol. 1, 672-3. These biographical notes are collated by Mohammad Saleem Kayani, translator of the tafsir in English.

Ahsan explores its diverse elements from the Qur'ānic angle.[24] His conclusions are couched in a reformist mould. There is no link, however, to the *tasawwuf* interpretation that is largely rooted in a spiritual-ethical culture. Implicit in his dilation of Islamic morality is the imperative to realign *tazkiyah* as understood, interpreted by the Prophetic practice. Again, Amin Ahsan competently advanced the Jama'at's *da'wah* programme for the modern mind. In 1958 because of some differences over policy issues and strategies he resigned from the Jama'at and returned to his work on the Qur'ān.

The rationale for authoring an eight-volume commentary is located in a contextual setting. Amin Ahsan had earned immense fame for editing works relating to the principles and methodologies of the Qur'ān. Central to these important works is the theme of *nazm*.[25] It was a formidable challenge to offer refreshing insights into *nazm* as a sub-genre of the tafsir tradition. Farāhi's works did indeed cause a stir among the 'ulama on account of his unconventional approaches to Qur'ānic study. Additionally, it cast a new mould for reshaping Qur'ānic hermeneutics. As a leading proponent of Farāhi intellectual thought, Amin Ahsan provided indisputable evidence in his commentary about the intrinsic value of *nazm*.[26] Contrary to presuppositions, *nazm* structure is intrinsically connected to the composition of the sacred text and reflects a 'divine work at hand' to its production. According to the consensus among the exegetes, '*ijāz* has multiple layers of meaning and *nazm* is one of its constituents.

In his tafsir, Amin Ahsan pays tribute to Farāhi by making copious reference to the latter's writings. "My thought is an extension of my teacher's thought; it has no separate or independent existence."[27] This comment is illustrative of Amin Ahsan's reverence for his mentor and his own sense of humility.

---

[24] Ibid., 673.

[25] Amin Ahsan Islāhi, *Self-Purification and Development* (Delhi, 2000). Cf. Abdur Rashid Siddiqui, *Tazkiyah: The Islamic Path of Self- Development* (Leicester, 2004), 133-214.

[26] Amin Islāhi, *Majmu'ah Tafsir i-Farāhi*, 29-36.

[27] Ibid., 37-66. The *Muqaddimah* (Introduction), consisting of sixteen chapters are systematically developed in this commentary.

Polemical literature feeds into the narrative of mediocrity. Hence, Farāhi's works and the *Tadabbur e-Qur'ān* were exposed to tirades of anti-hadith accusations. There was no plausible reason to accuse these revered 'ulama of heresy charges. A counter response or a pointed reference to Amin Ahsan's scholarly credentials on hadith studies may be gleaned from the lectures which were published by his illustrious student, Khalid Mas'ud.[28] In fact, the *halqahs* or study circles introduced the students to the principles of hadith. Amin Ahsan taught the *Mu'attā of Imām Mālik* and portions of *Bukhāri.* On account of his consummate skills in the Qur'ānic and hadith disciplines, Amin Ahsan held independent views without contradicting *aqā'id.* Rather he wanted his students and readers to develop a living contact with the eternal message of the Qur'ān through the process of *tadabbur* in its widest sense. Hence the title of several of his publications bearing the term *tadabbur.*[29]

Salient features of *Tadabbur e-Qur'ān*

Rationality is a dominant theme in Amin Ahsan's commentary.[30] In this respect there exists consistency and harmony in the Qur'ānic text. Farāhi makes an insightful argument about the function of reason in these words:

> Intrinsically, human beings derive guidance and contentment through reason, and argue against something through reason, gain knowledge whether it is absolute knowledge or knowledge derived through deliberation and reflection. Revelation comes only to motivate and activate the ability to use reason, to be rational, to orient it rightly, to uplift its level and corroborate it. Therefore, revelation has promoted reason

---

[28] Amin Islāhi, *Tadabbur e-Qur'ān*, vol. 1, 674.

[29] Islāhi, *Madrasat al-Islah*, 46-7.

[30] For example, *Principles of Pondering over Hadith*, edited by Khalid Mas'ud.

reasoning and appreciates these who use their reason.[31]

The synergy of reason and revelation is emphasised here. Amin Ahsan draws upon Farāhi's method of rationality to develop his critical analysis framework. Rationality is a euphemism for independent thinking which crosses barriers of traditional interpretation. This is subtly discussed by Amin Ahsan.

> About this commentary, I have made it clear in its introduction that in order to grasp the meaning of the Qur'ān and tackle the difficulties in its comprehension, I have employed the direct approach. It means that I have placed the Qur'ān at the centre of my research; the coherence of its verses and the facts that its records have been given prime importance while extracting the meaning of its verses. I have shunned in totality the conventional approach of relying upon the quotes from previous commentaries. To solve the problems pertaining to multiple meanings of a word, I have keenly gone through the original Arabic sources. Mere collecting the quotes of previous commentators have never been my way of doing things. Moreover, while explaining the verses, the language of the Qur'ān, theme of chapters and facts and incidents that are discussed in the book have been given prime importance. I have never borrowed any opinion just because it has been adopted by some conventional scholars. I have keenly observed all the sources and arguments and then presented my version of the things. The Qur'ānic logic and the foundations of its wisdom have also been highlighted in *Tadabbur e-Qur'ān* in order to bring

---

[31] Majeed, *Qur'ān Interpretation in Urdu*, 175.

to fore, convincingly, its method of argumentation as natural (*fitri*) and different from the futile reasoning of the scholastic theologians.[32]

The Farāhi approach is very much evident in the journey to discovering the structural design of the Qur'ān. Mention may be made of *nizām al-Qur'ān* (symmetrical design), very is discernible in his tafsir. This, however, does not suggest a replication of Farāhi's views as is mistakenly believed by various Qur'ānic scholars.

The central importance of Arabic literature is a tendentious issue among several commentators. In certain instances, pre-Islamic poetry is marginalised on account of its *jāhili* character. However, Islāhi contends that the primary sources are reflected in the social and tribal life in Arabia; hence, its importance. There are numerous examples where Amin Ahsan has accessed Arabic literature to examine different literary technicalities.[33] Islāhi, an Arabic linguist, has discussed in detail the literary genres straddling the Umayyad and Abbasid periods to delineate the connotation of Qur'ānic words. For this reason the concept of *tadabbur* is accentuated in order to derive an authoritative interpretation of certain Arabic words.[34] The linguistic and culture equivalence (as discussed in Chapter 2) underpins the unique characteristics of the Qur'ānic terms.

The multifaceted Qur'ānic approach adopted by Amin Ahsan is based on a hierarchical structure. Intra-Qur'ānic interpretation is an expanded notion in his writings.[35] The bond of association, to coin a term, strongly reflects the sacred text's interlinking relationship. In Islāhi's view, the nuanced interpretation of Qur'ānic words broadens the scope of its functionality.

He cites the following example to describe Amin Ahsan's proficiency in communicating the import of Arabic words in the

---

[32] Cited in Muhiuddin Ghazi, "Imām Farāhi's Views on Rationality: A Framework for Modernity Discourse", in *Al-Burhān*, 3:1 (2018), 6.

[33] Majeed. *Qur'ān Interpretation*, 175.

[34] Ibid., 178-9.

[35] Islāhi, *Madrasat al-Islah*, 57-9.

Urdu translation. Consider the word *din* and its shades of meaning. In shari'ah terminology it is religion-specific. It can also cover a legal value as discussed in Surah Yusuf (12:76). Likewise, it has a direct bearing on the law of submission in a cosmic sense (16:53). Additionally, it covers the concept of reward/ punishment (divine recompense) in relation to man's conduct and outcomes in the Afterlife (51:6).[36]

Amin Ahsan has offered a holistic presentation of the word *din* in context.[37] For example, Surah Al-Fatihah contains textual coherence and thematic continuity based on his categorisation of surahs.

> Looking at the end of Surah Al-Fatihah and the opening of Surah Al-Baqarah, we find that the relationship between the two surahs is very much similar to a supplication and the response it evokes, or the acceptance it receives. Surah Al-Fatihah ends with the words "Guide us the straight way - the way of those whom You have favoured, those who have not incurred Your displeasure and those who have not gone astray." Immediately thereafter follows Surah Al- Baqarah with the opening words: "*Alif, Lām Mim.* This is the book (of Allah); there is no doubt that it is from Allah and a guidance for those who fear Him." It is as if the Divine guidance sought by the servant in Surah Al-Fatihah is given to him right away, to abide and to follow. When a perceptive person witnesses such an instantaneous response to his supplication, he is naturally overwhelmed with a deep sense of gratitude and praise for Allah.
>
> We must also keep in view another aspect of this supplication. It not only seeks guidance to the path of the blessed but also protection against the ways of the misguided and the condemned who

---

[36] Ibid., 50.
[37] Ibid., 50-2.

incurred Divine wrath. Surah Al-Baqarah is thus not only the surah of the revival of the Ibrahimic community, but it is also an indictment of errant Jews. The brief allusion found in Surah Al-Fatihah to be blessed on the one hand and those who incurred Divine wrath on the other, is fully elaborated in Surah Al-Baqarah. Surah Al i-Imran can be seen in a similar light. It refutes and rejects the innovations introduced in true religion in the name of Christianity, especially Prophet Jesus. The fact that in the arrangement of the Qur'ān, these two lengthy surahs are placed immediately after Surah Al-Fatihah clearly shows that they both have a direct link to the acceptance of the supplication made in Al-Fatihah and further elaborate on what is succinctly alluded to in its last portion.[38]

In terms of the Qur'ānic coherence approach adopted by Amin Ahsan, the following comments raised by Mustansir Mir are a summative assessment of *Tadabbur e-Qur'ān*:

The Qur'ān, according to Amin Islāhi, is holistic and a well-integrated book. The chronological sequence of the Qur'ān was suited for a particular period: the times of the Holy Prophet (SAW) and his Companions. By the same token, the compilatory order was based on the principle of *nazm* and it is the commentator's task to discover the *nazm*. Amin Ahsan borrows the surah-in-unity theme from the writings of Farāhi. At the same time he develops his own methodology after careful scrutiny which in certain instances is at odds with Farāhi's conclusions. The 'umuds (hierarchical structures) in the Qur'ān is a case in point. Likewise, Amin Ahsan is credited for his concept of surah pairs/groups which enlarged the scope of Farāhi's *nazm* theory.

Another distinctive trait of the commentary is

---

[38] Amin Ahsan, *Tadabbur e-Qur'ān*, vol. 1, 87.

the complementarity of surahs. In other words, the thematic and structural aspects of *nazm* are discernible in the relationship between the surah groups and the larger sets of surahs. Overall, both Farāhi and Amin Ahsan have greatly enriched the concept of *nazm* and reformulated its relevance 'in a definitive context in order to arrive at cogent Qur'ān interpretation.[39]

Without delving into the semantics of the commentary, Amin Ahsan's meticulous study of *Fiqhi* issues has raised objections from the traditional viewpoint. Gifted with literary eloquence and mastery of the subject matter under discussion, Amin Islāhi does in several instances deviate from mainstream Qur'ānic interpretations. For example, his reflections on the (*huruf al-muqatta'āt*) suggest that these have specific meanings. If the Qur'ān possesses a timeless message, then assigning specific connotations with no conclusive evidence is a hazardous undertaking.[40] Moreover, to decode specific meanings belongs to the realm of speculative theology.

Another differing position adopted by Amin Ahsan is his explanation of oaths (*aqsām*) in the Qur'ān. There are recognisable signs about his dependence on Farāhi's celebrated work *Im'ān i Aqsām al-Qur'ān*.[41] This work was also translated into Urdu by him. For Amin Ahsan, the oath has multifunctional purposes and is context-based. Unlike other commentators, oaths may not only signify a pledge but a reaffirmation of the key themes in the particular surah.

Islāhi has raised a pertinent point about the merits and blemishes in the commentary. A human endeavour like a tafsir does often elicit contradictory and conflicting viewpoints based on

---

[39] Muntasir Mir, *Coherence in the Qur'ān: A Study of Islāhi's Concept of Nazm in Tadabbur i-Qur'ān* (Indianapolis, 1986), 102.

[40] Majeed, *Qur'ān Interpretation in Urdu*, 203-4.

[41] An annotated edition has been brought out by Tariq Mahmood Hashmi, *A Study of the Qur'ānic Oaths* (Lahore, n.d.).

the translator's intellectual temperament.[42] By dint of his painstaking research and well-articulated methodology, Amin Ahsan opens up new horizons of Qur'ānic hermeneutics. On a cautious note, these approaches are tentative conclusions and subject to critical scrutiny. In the final analysis, Amin Ahsan has made a candid assessment about the tafsir enterprise:

> Even though I have invested my entire life, including its last years when I was weak, in compiling this book but I do not present it before you with the claim that I have extracted from the Qur'ān all that was worth to be extracted. Neither do I claim that I have included all the topics dealing with the Qur'ān in this book. The Qur'ān, undoubtedly, is a treasure of knowledge and can be encompassed only by the one who has revealed it. But yes, I have tried hard to unlock the ways which lead one to the wisdom hidden in the Qur'ān and I am sure if you follow these ways, you will definitely find the pearls that are hidden in it. I do not claim anything more than this and I believe this is not a trivial thing to do. I am confident enough that if you will read the Qur'ān the way I have outlined, it will become such a criterion for you, upon which you can weigh every form of knowledge and idea. It will become easy for you to judge every concept of *Fiqh* and *tasawwuf* and filter it through the principles of the Qur'ān. This method of understanding the Qur'ān may be useful to eradicate the hurdle of sectarianism that has engulfed the Muslim world and pave the way for transforming this community into a decisive force on the globe from a disintegrated mob. To conclude with, I have highlighted the way out for understanding the Qur'ān better; there is still a lot to be done

---

[42] Majeed, *Qur'ān Interpretation in Urdu*, 204-5.

which is the responsibility of those who come after
me.[43]

Abu Lais Islāhi Nadwi

Continuity (*tasalsul*) of the Qur'ānic perspective is a central
aspect of the Farāhi-Islāhi methodology. Scholars of
international fame continued to explore themes within the ambit
of the *nazm* theory. Amin Ahsan, too, developed critical tools in
respect of reorienting the tafsir tradition. By the same token, the
critical evaluation of his tafsir work has indirectly broadened the
scope of the tafsir corpus in a modern setting.

Abu Lais Islāhi Nadwi (d. 1990) drew upon his Qur'ānic knowledge
from Madrasat al-Islāh and Nadwah. According to Shaykh Nadwi,
Abu Lais was a brilliant student of 'Allamah Taqi al-Din Hilali and
rose in rank and prominence on account of his excellent command
over Arabic. Among his peers was Mas'ud Alam, also an erudite
Arabic scholar. Like Shaykh Nadwi, he was appointed as lecturer at
Nadwah in 1934. A brilliant scholar, Abu Lais was an adept editor
of several Urdu magazines and his columns and articles were
widely read for their distinctive literary style.[44]

In the 1940s the clarion call for an Islamic state was taking
concrete forms. The Jama'at i-Islami embodied this ideal and the
inspirational force and leading figurehead was Mawdudi. This was
a crucial phase in the Jama'at's history which drew reputed
'ulama like Shaykh Nadwi, Manzur Nu'mani to its fold. Abu Lais
served in key positions which included Amir of the movement in
India. According to Shaykh Nadwi, he maintained cordial
relations with the 'ulama who otherwise were vocal in their
criticism, in fact condemnatory of the Jama'at's religious policies.
This was very much evident in Pakistan where intellectuals held

---

[43] Mir, *Coherence in the Qur'ān*, 101-2. Mir raises a pertinent issue that has a direct
bearing on the traditional exegetical corpus. If *nazm* becomes an integral part to the
Qur'ānic approach, then it diminishes the dependence on *asbāb al-nuzul* as an
exegetical tool.

[44] For brief biographical notes on Abu Lais Nadwi, see Nadwi, *Kārwān i-Zindagi*,
vol.4, 389.

positions of authority. The divide between 'ulama and Islamists posed a challenge about the future of Islam in a changing geopolitical landscape.[45]

Ideological and political affiliation apart, Abu Lais was a remarkable scholar of Qur'ānic studies. His works may be analysed at two levels: literary and historical aspects of the Qur'ānic text. He did not write prolifically on account of his responsibilities as Amir of the movement; however, these slim volumes contain in-depth discussions on key themes of the sacred text.

Poetic devices like the rhyming patterns (*Qāfiyah*) are replete in the Qur'ān.[46] They have a polyvalent significance for rhetorical purposes. In Abu Lais's view, these poetical features embellish and enhance the Qur'ānic terms and reaffirm their significance. Intellect is adorned with majestic words and thus the Qur'ānic mode of expression is articulate and precise. Moreover, the Qur'ān is not a prosaic text that is devoid of inner rhythm and beauty. In many verses, the poetical aspects are clearly defined. A rhetorical question is posed by Abu Lais. Why does the Qur'ān employ aesthetic appeals to present its abiding message?[47] This point is critically examined by Islāhi to demonstrate the complementarity between prose and poetry.

As a universal religion, the Qur'ān encompasses the history of notable Prophets, who have left a lasting legacy to human civilisation of which Judaism and Christianity form the trialogue of Abrahamic religions alongside Islam. In respect of the Scriptures, the true contents are discussed in the Qur'ān. However, it is an indisputable fact that these texts have been distorted and subjected to critical scrutiny.[48] At the same time, apologetic literature prodigiously produced by the Orientalists, Jewish and Christian scholars, have relentlessly waged a campaign to impugn the veracity of the Qur'ānic accounts of the Prophets. For example, Abraham Geiger (d. 1874), a German rabbi and

---

[45] Ibid., 392-3.

[46] The terms *Saj'ah* and *Qāiyah* are elaborated by Islāhi in *Madrasat al-Islāh*, 91-5.

[47] Ibid., 93-4.

[48] For a critical assessment of these Scriptures, see Azami, *The History of the Qur'ānic Text*, 249-331.

scholar who is considered to be the founding father of Reform Judaism wrote *Judaism and Islam* (Madras, 1898). His contentions in this essay deal with the Qur'ān's supposed inconsistency regarding the order of the Prophets' names. Abu Lais countered these controversial claims in his thought- provoking series of articles. His intellectual acumen and profound study of the sacred text are a testament to his vast learning.

Essentially, the Qur'ān does not follow a timeline approach to emphasise important facets of the Prophets under discussion. In keeping with its integrated approach, historical information or accounts are concise and lucidly described. Unlike the Old Testament or the Bible which abounds in laborious accounts of the Prophets,[49] the Qur'ān makes accurate, insightful comments so that readers may derive life-enriching lessons from the Prophets' lives. For the Qur'ān, sequence is secondary in respect of Prophetic accounts. It is, however, unequivocal in declaring the infallibility of the Prophets' message, their unblemished moral character and commitment to societal reform.

The Qur'ān adopts a hierarchical approach to highlight certain events in the Prophets' divine career. For example, Prophet Musa (peace be upon him) and his encounter with Pharaoh are discussed from different angles. *Tawhid* is integral to his *da'wah* and in the same vein Prophethood as a divine dispensation is reaffirmed. Mention is also made of Harun (peace be upon him) as a recipient of divine revelation. The choice of words in these verses (21:48-50) is an eloquent testimony to their two-pronged mission: guidance and reminder for those who are Allah-conscious. Likewise, it is a reflection about the purpose of their life which has a direct bearing on the Afterlife.[50]

A point worth considering is contextual relevance. The immediate environment of the Qur'ān is the Holy Prophet's mission to propagate *tawhid* among the disbelievers. His suffering, hardship and humiliation are reminiscent of the experiences of the previous Prophets. These Qur'ānic accounts are intended to provide renewed hope and moral support for the Holy Prophet

---

[49] Ibid., 297-88.
[50] Islāhi, *Madrasat al-Islāh*,100.

(SAW) under those trying circumstances. In a specific sense, the Qur'ānic accounts of the leading Prophets like Ibrahim (peace be upon him) epitomise the core values of patience, perseverance and submission (21: 68-70).[51] Likewise, the Qur'ānic repetition of accounts (with slight variation) serve as 'high alerts' for man who is inclined to be lured into moral vices. The Adam/Satan account repeated seven times in the sacred text, according to Abu Lais, is context based. In fact, the Qur'ānic style may best be appreciated in the light of the *nazm* methodology.[52] One example will suffice. Misguidance is the ingrained trait of Satan. And so is arrogance. A parallel is drawn between the disbelievers and Satan about their vicious designs. The consequences of their insolent conduct are grave. Hence, the purpose of *tadhkir* (warning) (38:88).

Overall, the writings of Abu Lais are characterised by the extensive study of the Qur'ānic sources and comparative religion. The tenor of his writing is scholarly and inspirational. The complementarity of Farāhi thought is borne out by two distinguished Islāhi scholars. Badruddin Islāhi (d. 1996) is considered to be the repository of Farāhi's major writings. His annotated editing of these Qur'ānic works is illustrative of the depth of his Islamic learning.[53] According to Islāhi, Badruddin's preoccupation with his studies revealed his exceptional standards of scholarship. His own writings, albeit monographs, are characterised by his grounding in Arabic literature, detailed exploration of intra-Qur'ānic verses and comparative religious studies.

The prophecy regarding the advent of the Holy Prophet (SAW) is clearly mentioned in the Qur'ān and the earlier revealed Scriptures, particularly the Torah. The common interpretation mentions the Qur'ānic affirmation of these Scriptures.[54] However, Badruddin adds a new dimension to the Qur'ānic affirmation (*tasdiq*) by arguing that it establishes the *nabuwwat* (Prophethood) of the Holy Prophet (SAW). In the backdrop of the denial theory by

---

[51] Ibid., 101.
[52] Ibid., 108.
[53] Ibid., 121-3.
[54] See Azami, *The History of the Qur'ānic Text*, 300-31.

the Jewish community, including their rabbis, the Qur'ānic term emerges as a clear contradiction of the widely-held beliefs about the Holy Prophet (SAW)'s advent. In the Biblical sources the term 'Paraclete' is used to describe this prophecy.[55] Even Sayyid Ahmad Khan had undertaken a comprehensive study to demonstrate its veracity. Of course, historical accounts authenticate these prophecies.[56]

Badruddin examines the Torah in the perspective of corruption (*tahrif*). Essentially, it challenges the notion about the purity of its text. He develops this position to highlight the factual inaccuracies that have obfuscated the unambiguous revealed message of the Qur'ān. His critical analysis based on concise Qur'ānic argumentation brings home the cleavage that exists between Islam and the People of the Book (*Ahl al-Kitāb*). Their penchant for allegorical interpretation has blocked out an unbiased acceptance and acknowledgement about the prophecy of the Holy Prophet's advent as the Final Messenger.[57] Badruddin opens up a discussion on the nature of *mutāshābihāt* in these words: "The status and wisdom of the Qur'ān is so exalted that it requires us to deepen our faith and submission (to its universal message).[58]"

In sum, Islāhi makes a relevant remark that Muslim disconnect or alienation from the Qur'ān has resulted in the crises Muslims are currently facing in their daily lives.

It is a misnomer to suggest that scholars belonging to the Farāhi school of thought developed their unconventional Qur'ānic interpretation within a certain framework. This view contradicts the different positions held by several Islāhi scholars in their understanding of the *nazm* methodology. By contrast, Farāhi's thought developed into a robust critical engagement with the sacred text, yielding varied interpretations.

---

[55] See Qur'ān, 2: 101 for an Islamic perspective of the Prophet's prophecy in the Torah.

[56] Kidwai, *Sir Syed Ahmad Khan: Muslim Renaissance Man of India*, 322-38.

[57] Islāhi, *Madrasat al-Islāh*, 131.

[58] For an examination of the unambiguous verses, see Mawdudi, *Towards Understanding the Qur'ān*, vol. 1, 236.

It also brought out a critique of their writings among the 'ulama establishment by challenging the primacy of *nazm* as a referential point in the tafsir tradition.

Sadruddin Islāhi (d. 1998) is a leading exponent of the Farāhi-Islāhi tafsir approach. However, his writings as Islāhi notes are not an articulation of the *nazm* theory. His important work *Tafsir al-Qur'ān* illustrates the expanding boundaries of tafsir from a Farāhi framework. The nexus between *da'wah* and political Islamic activism (read as *tehrik i-Islam)* is derived from Mawdudi's influential works.[59] Islāhi delineates the prominent features of the work under the following rubrics:

First, the order of the text is a revealed dispensation that reinforces the *'umud* (key content) of the respective surahs. The initial textual order is reflected in Surah Al- Fatihah. Second, the tafsir adopts a scientific approach that is free from minutiae and sets it apart from the general exegetical works. Rather, his choice of words is a broad-based illustration of linguistic and literary embodying that has a particular appeal to the readers. Third, his explanatory notes have a contemporary relevance; these meet the temperament of modern readers. For example, Sadruddin makes an important distinction about the universal character of the Qur'ān. Unlike previous Scriptures, the Qur'ān uses appropriate addresses (the vocative *Yā*) to deliver its message accordingly. The syntactical structure informs the tempo of its universal vision.[60]

A distinctive characteristic of *Tafsir al-Qur'ān* is its specific reach to the significant 'other' - the Hindu majority. *Da'wah* and *tabligh* are interchangeable terms and reconfigured for the purpose of inviting Hindus to the Qur'ānic message of *tawhid*. According to Sadruddin, the mission of the Prophets is categorical: to invite mankind to the Oneness of Allah. However, the followers zealously deviated from the clear-cut message by either deifying the Prophets or creating a phalanx of deities that were *shirk*-laden in concept

---

[59] *See* Abdul Kader Choughley, *Islamic Resurgence: Sayyid Abul Hasan Ali Nadwi and his Contemporaries* (New Delhi, 2011).
[60] Islāhi, *Madrasat al-Islāh*, 142-7.

and practice.[61] This point debunks the mythology surrounding Hinduism and presents the pristine purity of *tawhid* (Islam) as the only alternative. However, the missionary fervour contained in the tafsir has not somewhat successfully impacted on the Hindu mind. Overall, it appears to be more beneficial for the Muslim readership.

Islāhi points out an additional aspect of the tafsir: lexical explanation. Far from providing a sketchy definition of key Qur'ānic concepts, Sadruddin by virtue of his expertise in Arabic draws the readers' attention to the various shades of meaning. We focus on two primary words: *din* and *jihād*. By way of example, Mawdudi, in his major writings, expands the traditional understanding of *din*.[62] In a similar way, Sadruddin broadens its definition by bringing the gamut of human activity under its ambit. *Din* transcends ritual performance and racial affiliation. Therefore, Islam in its entirety is synonymous with *din*.

According to Sadruddin, the term *jihād*[63] is conflated with killing (*qitāl*) which has caused a great degree of misperception. In its lexical connotation it covers an array of tasks including exertion, perseverance and resilience. For example, to access technology for the purpose of *tabligh* is an expression of *jihād*. The primary aspect of this term is the execution of duty in a focused way.

In sum, Sadruddin has made serious attempts to explore new terrains of the tafsir tradition. In Islāhi's assessment, the tafsir is *da'wah*-oriented and does not reflect the domain of Farāhi thought. This comment does not, however, detract from the tafsir's eloquent presentation of the Qur'ānic worldview.

Dā'ud Akbar Isāhi

An erudite representative of the Farāhi school, Dā'ud Akbar (d. 1983)[64] was an amalgam of scholarship and *taqwā*. His unassuming lifestyle pointed out to his detachment from worldly comforts. In

---

[61] Ibid., 148. Cf. Nadwi, *Islamic Concept of Prophethood* (Lucknow, 1976), 7-38.

[62] See Mawdudi, *Towards Understanding Islam* (New Delhi, 1982).

[63] Abul A'la Mawdudi, *Jihād in Islam* (Lahore, 2017).

[64] There has been no serious study of Da'ud Akbar's contributions to tafsir. However, articles and essays have been assembled to present an overview of his life and times.

fact, his scholarly profile brings to the fore his profound study of the sacred text.

An interesting point raised by Islāhi is the decorum of *ikhtilāf*. It is common knowledge that cultic status is a barrier to the critical evaluation of the founder's contributions. In this case the Farāhi scholars offer a useful guide about the norms of *ikhtilāf*. In more ways than one way, Da'ud Akbar, by virtue of his versatility, offers alternative interpretations to Farāhi's seminal works, among which *aqsām* (oaths)[65] stand out as an original contribution. Da'ud Akbar's penetrative analysis of the Qur'ānic oaths has a contextual relevance. For him these oaths are a reaffirmation (*istishād*) of the subject matter contained in the surahs under discussion. They are meaning-specific. Therefore, it would be stretching the meaning of *ta'zim* (veneration) with which it is associated. For Da'ud Akbar, these are mutually exclusive terms with no overlapping significance to the surahs containing *aqsām*. One example supports his contention. In Surah Qaf (50)[66] the letter Qaf is intended to counter the misguided thoughts harboured by the disbelievers about the revealed scriptures. In a similar vein, the sanctity of Makkah is emphasised for Muslims of all eras and time.

According to Da'ud Akbar, there are two levels to understand the Qur'ānic vocabulary. First, context is pivotal to unravel its meaning. This also refers to syntactical structure in the text. A Qur'ānic term like *sajdah* (prostration) invariably yields different meanings in relation to the verses under discussion. It may refer to postures in *salāh* or a prostration of veneration in the celestial world. Second, the vast corpus of Arabic literature (*diwān*)[67] is an indispensable guide to a proper appreciation of the Qur'ānic terms. All in all, the Qur'ān projects extensive meanings to these terms which disallow restrictive interpretations in general.

A literary contribution like this work that carefully examines the structural order (*nazm*) of the Qur'ān bears close affinity to the tafsir genre in general. The Introduction (*muqaddimah*) to this tafsir elucidates the *tartib* (sequential arrangement) of Surah Al-

---

[65] Reference to Farāhi's *Aqsām al-Qur'ān*.
[66] Islāhi, *Madrasat al-Islāh*, 186-8.
[67] Ibid., 190.

Fatihah and the last sections of the Qur'ān.[68] According to Islāhi, this incomplete tafsir would have been a groundbreaking contribution to the tafsir tradition.

Apart from contributing substantially to Farāhi thought, Da'ud Akbar's articles to the *Al-Islāh* journal augments key Qur'ānic concepts that by and large have not been comprehensively examined. *Taqwā* is an instance in point. "It is our conviction that the spirit of the divine shari'ah is rooted in *taqwā*. The overall prescriptions are underpinned by the shari'ah. Without *taqwā* the whole gamut of beliefs (*aqā'id*), moral conduct (*akhlāq*) and righteous deeds (*a'māl*) cannot be strengthened."[69]

There exists a general perception that the Farāhi school attempted to deconstruct the tafsir tradition. Their overly preoccupation with the *nazm* theory has overshadowed other important aspects of the Qur'ān. Da'ud Akbar's systematic formulation of the Qur'ān challenge (*tahaddi'*) counters this misrepresentation. In line with contemporary Arabic scholars who delved into the *i'jāz* of the Qur'ān, Da'ud Akbar presents a refreshing engagement with this aspect of the sacred text. The Qur'ānic message is not exclusionary to Arabs, it extends to all mankind including the jinn species. As a guide to mankind it remains unrivalled to this day.[70]

Two contemporary exegetes, Mawdudi and Daryabadi,[71] have expressed similar views about the Qur'ānic challenge. However, their views do not essentially detract from the literary genius and inner logic of the Qur'ānic Arabic.[72] We may refer to Mawdudi's analysis of this aspect:

> (38) Do they say that the Messenger has himself composed the Qur'ān? Say: 'In that case bring forth just one *surah* like it and call on all whom

---

[68] Ibid., 195.

[69] Ibid., 198.

[70] Ibid., 200.

[71] Abdul Majid Daryabadi, *Tafsir i-Mājidi*, vol 1 (Lucknow, 2003), 79.

[72] For a critical examination of the Qur'ān's subtle beauty and literary charms, see 'Abdullāh Draz, *The Qur'ān: An Eternal Challenge* (Leicester, 2001).

you can, except Allah, to help you if you are truthful.' It is generally believed that the challenge embodied in this verse has a reference merely to the eloquence, rhetoric and other literary qualities of the Qur'ān. Were one to read the writings of Muslim scholars in connection with the explanation of this verse, it is not surprising that people should entertain such a misunderstanding. However, the Qur'ān is far above claiming its uniqueness and inimitability merely on the grounds of its literary merits. Although there can be no doubt about the literary excellence of the Qur'ān, the main ground on it is claimed that no human being could produce a book like it has to do with its contents and teaching. The Qur'ān alludes, in many places, to those characteristics of its inimitability which could not have been conferred upon it by man, thus hinting that those characteristics could have no other source but God himself.[73]

Ziauddin Islāhi

A renowned scholar, Ziauddin Islāhi (d. 2008)[74] held key positions at various Islamic institutions. His association with Dār al-Musannifin saw his administrative skills as a director; likewise, his position in the shura council of Nadwah repositioned him as an international scholar of Islamic higher learning.

Two aspects of his vast Islamic learning complemented his profile: his writings and his awards. The Indian Presidential award, for example, was a reaffirmation of his scholarly pursuits which were duly recognised. Several biographical accounts point out to his academic credentials in tafsir, hadith and comparative

---

[73] Mawdudi, *Towards Understanding the Qur'ān*, vol. 4, 36-7.
[74] For his life and works, see Abu Sufyān Islāhi, Aftab 'Ilm wa Adab: Mawlana Ziauddin Islāhi (Delhi, 2011).

religion. Our focus is on his *Aidāh al-Qur'ān*[75] - a treasure trove of rigorous Qur'ānic approaches. Unlike some other *maslaks* (schools of thought) which have to their credit complete tafsirs, Ziauddin Islāhi's work represents an amalgam of essays and articles that have augmented new insights into the historical accounts, linguistic variance and comparative tafsir issues.

The stories in the Qur'ān are embedded in a unique style to highlight two interesting aspects: interlinking themes and counsel. For Ziauddin Islāhi, ellipsis in the Qur'ānic construction reveals the rich brevity and precise expressions that were recognised by the *Jāhiliyyah* Arabs.

Ellipsis, therefore, was a salience that added aesthetic value to the *i'jāz* discourse. Another stylistic feature of the Qur'ānic expression is the complementarity of a single idea. In this regard, the appropriate choice of words to describe similitudes (*tamthil*) encapsulates the inimitable style of the Qur'ān. Two parallel styles play out the meaning and teachings of the sacred text. First, words like *tafakkur* (reflection) underpin the correlation between historical accounts and its essential teachings. Second, verses preceding historical accounts define the thematic significance of verses under discussion.[76]

We may refer to the sacrifice of the Prophet Isma'il (peace be upon him) from a Qur'ānic viewpoint. Islāhi contends that the description of the Prophet Ishaq by Jewish chronicles has no Qur'ānic basis. By the same token, the centrality of Ibrahim's sacrifice and devotion debunks the myth of the Orientalists' distorted representation of authentic Islamic history.[77]

There is no doubt that Ziauddin Islāhi gives a correct perspective on the terms relating to Allah's attributes.[78] In keeping with *sirah* sources and pre-Islamic literature it is wrongly assumed that these attributes or descriptive phrases were unfamiliar to the Arabs. The Divine Attribute (*Rahmān*) is an illustration in point. By contrast, the term *Rahim* is applicable to

---

[75] Ziauddin Islāhi, *Aidāh al-Qur'ān* (Karachi, n.d.).
[76] Islāhi, *Madrasat al-Islāh*, 210-2.
[77] Ibid., 214.
[78] Ibid., 215.

man as the following verses reveal:

> *There has come to you a Messenger of Allah from among yourselves, who is distressed by the losses you sustain, who is ardently desirous of your welfare and is tender and merciful to those that believe.*

(9: 128)

However, linguistically speaking, Ziauddin Islāhi's discourse of semantic valence, near-synonyms does not adequately convey the essence of Qur'ānic meanings. *Hamd* (praise) and *madah* (eulogy) do not have corresponding relationships. In fact, the latter term does not have Qur'ānic support in relation to Surah Al-Fatihah's conception of the all-embracing praise of Allah (*al-hamd*).

In our previous discussion of *'umud*[79] Farāhi and Amin Ahsan postulated their respective theories of the clusters in the Qur'ān. This opinion is in reference to the following verse:

We have indeed bestowed on you the seven-oft- repeated verses on the Great Qur'ān. (15: 87)

According to Ziauddin Islāhi, the above term has a direct bearing on the seven verses of Surah Al-Fatihah.[80] The divergence of opinion, in the man, illustrates the evolution of Qur'ānic thought on critical issues and reviews of the Farāhi approach.

The scholarly input of Ziauddin Islāhi's Qur'ānic scholarship is vividly expressed in his critical review of Imam Razi's tafsir. According to him, Razi's student Shamsuddin Al-Khali was the ghost writer of the remaining volumes of this outstanding tafsir.[81] Interestingly, Ziauddin Islāhi has contributed considerably to an objective assessment of the classical tafsir works.

In sum, Ziauddin Islāhi has left behind a Qur'ānic legacy in respect of his articles and essays that shed informative guidelines about the trends in Islamic studies. His incisive analysis of Qur'ānic themes has evoked critical response from scholars aligned to

---

[79] This aspect has been discussed in Mir's *Coherence in the Qur'ān*.

[80] Islāhi, *Madrasat al-Islāh*, 217.

[81] Ibid., 223.

Farāhi thought. One point deserves particular mention. Ziauddin Islāhi has drawn independent conclusions about aspects related to the Qur'ān which are at variance with mainstream Farāhi interpretation.[82] Nevertheless, his contributions have created new pathways in Qur'ānic studies.

As the director of Dār al-Musannifin, Ziauddin Islāhi established a professional rapport with Ishtiaq Ahmad Zilli who currently serves as secretary and director of the prestigious institution. An accomplished historian and eminent scholar of Qur'ānic studies, Zilli penned a biography of Amin Ahsan Islāhi. As a founder of Idārah Dār al-'ulum (AMU) he has earned worldwide recognition for his scholarly works. Zilli also edited Ziauddin Islāhi's *The Jews and the Qur'ān* (Urdu) in 2015.

Altāf Ahmad 'Azmi

Versatility on a range of subjects illustrates the depth and breadth of Altaf Ahmad 'Azmi's encyclopaedic knowledge. *Tibb, Iqbāliāt* and Qur'ānic studies are interwoven in his intellectual makeup. A graduate of Madrasat al-Islāh, 'Azmi's primary focus is on the layers of knowledge and wisdom embedded in the sacred text. Additionally, his exposure at AMU sharpened his critical skills to evaluate contemporary tafsirs. Of particular interest is his review of Sayyid Ahmad Khan's tafsir, which by all accounts has generated a barrage of criticism for its perceived modernist and rationalist interpretation. By contrast, 'Azmi provides a context-based defense to the storm of controversy raised against his 'heretical' beliefs.

Sayyid Ahmad Khan was a visionary and his Qur'ānic world was steeped in a colonial milieu which had shaped patterns of emergent intellectual thought. This factor had a substantive influence on his intellectual outlook, giving rise to the production of a tafsir which contradicted mainstream interpretation. In contrast, *Mudih al-Qur'ān* offered a traditional interpretation that

---

[82] Ibid., 231.

was not disconnected from the classical heritage of tafsir.[83]

'Azmi's foray into Qur'ānic studies is well-structured and offers new insights into themes or key subjects that are assumed as definitive interpretations. We may refer to his three-volume *Mizān al-Qur'ān*[84] to support our opinion that it departs in many ways from the normative interpretation. For example, 'Azmi provides a detailed counter response to the concept of intercession (*shafā'ah*) as is commonly understood by Muslims.

Islāhi's close study of 'Azmi's tafsir reveals three interesting strands. First, 'Azmi is an independent *mufassir* who by virtue of his academic background explores key Qur'ānic concepts along intra-Qu'ranic lines. For 'Azmi, this self-explanatory position adopted by the Qur'ān mitigates extrapolation of textual sources. In other words, context is strengthened within the text without taking recourse to sources that are untenable.

Surah 93 is illustrative of 'Azmi's articulation of the Prophetic message. For him, verse 93:3 (*Indeed, what is to come will be better for you than what has gone by*) identifies the early and latter part of the Prophethood which has a historical connotation.[85] The ebb and flow of Muslim fortunes is emphasised in respect of his Prophethood. Likewise, 'Azmi proffers a schematic understanding of the *iqrā* paradigm. Generally, the word is emphasised while ignoring the divine imperative contained in the sublime verse. Guidance is the buzz word that has contemporary relevance for Muslims under every circumstance.

Second, 'Azmi successfully offers a balanced scientific account of explanations of verses that are generally glossed over by exegetes. His scientific expertise is to the fore in his explanation of the embryonic stages of development[86] for the purpose of reaffirming Allah's universal laws. Quantum physics is also explored in relation to the folding of the sun and when it will

---

[83] For a critical examination of Sayyid Ahmad's tafsir, see Altaf Ahmad Khan's articles in the *Ma'arif* magazine (Azamgarh). April- May 2000 issues.

[84] According to 'Azmi, the first volume (Surah Al-Fatihah) is a comprehensive discussion of central concepts contained in the surah. See Islāhi, *Idārah Sir Sayyid*, 142.

[85] Islāhi, *Madrasat al-Islāh*, 253.

[86] Ibid., 255-6.

cease to radiate light.[87] His trenchant response is terse to the fallacious claims by scientists that the depletion of hydrogen is not feasible in view of the 'billions of years' theory for the sun's survival. In 'Azmi's estimation these claims are also illusory in comparison to the Qur'ānic declaration of the prelude to *Qiyāmat*.[88] Third, *Mizān al-Qur'ān* enjoys an important distinction in terms of its resource output. From classical tafsirs to lexical composition, the range of works consulted is marked by 'Azmi's comprehensive study of textual and non-textual sources. His profundity of thought is reminiscent of Daryabadi's *The Glorious Qur'ān* which abounds in multi- disciplinary information.[89]

Two points emerge from 'Azmi's tafsir. It is not in a conventional sense a literal translation religiously conforming to earlier exegetical tradition. In contrast, 'Azmi places in parenthesis his own translation that is in accord with the intended meaning of the text. More importantly, his independent views in particular instances illustrate his ability to navigate contentious discussions that tend to exacerbate the message of the Qur'ān. His guiding motto is the divine guidance that the sacred text offers to mankind. Given 'Azmi's predisposition to contextualise Qur'ānic verses, the phrase 'solid wall' (*bunyān al-marsus*) in surah 61:4 is illustrative. 'Azmi elaborates:

> What are the reasons for Muslim decline and their failure to maintain a dignified position as represented by the first generation of Muslims? Is it not a reality that our foundational structure is weakened by our obsession with *shirk*-laden practices like grave worship which is hidden shirk (polytheism).
>
> Muslims observe the pillars of Islam but the element of purification of the soul (*tazkiyah al- nafs*) is glaringly absent. Likewise, their lives are not

---

[87] Ibid., 257.
[88] Ibid., 265-7.
[89] Ibid., 263-4.

constructively built around the personality of the Holy Prophet's *sirah*. Conflict and disharmony are now the prominent traits of the fractious Muslim community. They are now descending into moral anarchy - this decline has grave consequences for their collective Muslim identity.[90]

Muhammad Ajmal Ayub Islāhi

In the selection of Islāhi scholars for the volume, Islāhi has attempted to provide their varied contributions to Qur'ānic studies and the Farāhi school of thought. Perhaps the expanding intellectual domain in contemporary Islamic thought is a strong indication about the changing patterns in Qur'ānic studies.

Muhammad Ajmal Ayub Islāhi represents a cadre of Islamic scholars who have added new facets to the field of tafsir. The network of scholarly tradition - madrasah and university education - has strengthened his proficiency in Arabic and Qur'ānic literature.[91] His membership of the prestigious Majlis al-'Ilmi (Damascus) and other notable awards are reflective of his international stature in the world of academia. Furthermore, his recognition in the Arab world in terms of his publishing output is indicative of his thorough familiarity with the corpus of classical Arabic/Islamic literature. Notwithstanding these accolades, Muhammad Ajmal has made significant contributions by editing classical works and most importantly Farāhi's works.[92] These are critical editions that encompass a variety of subjects from different eras and social milieu.

The *Mufradāt al-Qur'ān* genre is an essential component of Qur'ānic studies. Muhammad Ajmal has adeptly deployed this genre to examine Farāhi's conceptual framework of Qur'ānic terms. The pre-Islamic and classical poetry feature prominently to support his interpretation. In the same strain, Muhammad Ajmal provides explanatory notes -an annotated version- for this

---

[90] Ibid., 294.
[91] Ibid., 295-6.
[92] Ibid., 308.

purpose.[93] In general, his literary works are original contributions to Qur'ānic studies.

Islāhi scholars have not made substantial contributions to the critical analysis of the translation project. Although a few books have been published by the Islāhi-aligned organisations like Al-Mawrid,[94] these fall short of producing well-structured research in this rich field of Qur'ānic studies for English speaking readers. In this instance it has a limiting impact for a critical evaluation of the Farāhi/Islāhi contributions. Viewed from a different angle, there is a misperception that hadith studies is marginalised in preference to Arabic literature by Islāhi scholars.[95] Against the backdrop of polemical writings which are wrongly attributed to these remarkable scholars, I suggest a point of departure to their well-established credentials. Recent trends in Qur'ānic studies have focused on the textual relevance theories[96] as well as *nazm* formulation in the Qur'ān. Islāhi scholars will do well to examine in detail these Qur'ānic trends as an extension of their contributions. Likewise, collaborative efforts with other Islamic institutions sharing similar goals may augment the scope of this important genre.

---

[93] Ibid., 298-300. The examples raised by Muhammad Ajmal attests to his thorough familiarity with the epoch-making eras of Arabic poetry.

[94] The polarising influence of the controversial Islāhi scholar, Javed Ghamidi has met with trenchant criticism from the 'ulama establishment.

[95] Majeed, *Qur'ān Interpretation in Urdu*, 190-1.

[96] For example, Salwa El-Awa, *Textual Relations in the Qur'ān: Relevance, Coherence and Structure* (London, 2006).

Chapter 7

Jamā'at i-Islami Contributions to Qur'ānic Studies

In our series of Qur'ānic contributions by different schools of thought, the name Abul A'la Mawdudi features prominently. There are several factors that have contributed to his global fame among which is his monumental tafsir *Tafhim al-Qur'ān*.

Ziauddin Falahi is a brilliant Qur'ānic scholar whose writings have set new trends to this genre. It is my honour to state that his Urdu translation of my work on Abdur Raheem Kidwai is marked by impressive academic standards of excellence.[1] Falahi's introductory comments[2] about the translation project of *Tafhim* is a summative assessment of the continued interest to this learned work. Moreover, *Tafhim's* global impact (also translated in regional languages and English) is illustrative of Mawdudi's charismatic and visionary leadership in the Islamic resurgence discourse.

Our study of Mawdudi's tafsir is based on two guidelines: the Jama'at al-Islam (hereafter JI) as a mirror image of *Tafhim's* message and the centrality of *da'wah* as a catalyst of change for the *ummah*.[3] A brief background of Mawdudi's career illustrates his brilliant exposition of Islam as a *din*. Born in 1903 in Aurangabad, Mawdudi was a precocious child whose acquisition of knowledge underscored his versatile personality. Following the death of his father his studies were interrupted. However, the period 1921-8 in Delhi was a formative phase in his intellectual journey as an editor and scholar of eminence. His private lessons with leading 'ulama of the day enabled him to complete his 'alim course (*Dars i-Nizāmi*), Interestingly, this period also saw his impressive work, *Jihād in Islam* drawing the attention of intellectuals sharing common goals about the Islamic renewal in

---

[1] See Ziauddin Falahi, *Abdur Raheem Kidwai ke Qur'āni Mutāla'āt* (Aligarh, 2019).
[2] Ziauddin Falahi, *Jamā'at i-Islami ke Fuzalā ki Qur'āni Khidmāt* (Aligarh, 2019), 7-11.
[3] Ibid., 15-6.

the twentieth century. Likewise, his *Towards Understanding Islam* written for the princely state of Mir Osman Ali Khan (Hyderabad) in 1930 reiterated the status of Islam as a *din* (perfect way of life) and its relation to *'ibādah* (worship) and other fundamentals of faith.[4]

An independent mind and committed to Islamic resurgence (*tajdid*), Mawdudi used his journal *Tarjumān al- Qur'ān*[5] to advocate his views about the Islamic sovereignty (*hākimiyyah*). His association with Iqbal was intended to draw up a blueprint for the sovereign state in which Islam was its guiding principles. Alongside his revivalist initiative, Mawdudi undertook a translation of the Glorious Qur'ān from 1942. In 1972 the monumental work was completed. It would be correct to claim that his tafsir is an activist interpretation of the Qur'ānic message for the modern mind. In fact, his magazine *Tarjuman al-Qur'ān* was a prelude to the tafsir judging by its critique of Western civilisation and the universal role of the Qur'ān in the backdrop of emerging ideological systems.[6]

Keeping in mind his active political involvement as Amir of the JI, his tafsir was written under different circumstances. For example, he was imprisoned for writing on the Qadiani problem[7] and had to face a relentless campaign to silence his call for upholding the Finality of Prophethood. Worse was his deteriorating health with underlying medical problems which exacerbated his ability to write with ease and comfort. These debilitating conditions, however, did not deter him from completing this celebrated work in 1972.

Salient features of *Tafhim al-Qur'ān*

Unlike other contemporary tafsirs, Mawdudi's choice of the title *Tafhim* is intended to create an ambience for understanding the

---

[4] Masudul Hasan, *Sayyid Abul A'la Mawdudi and his Thought*, vol.1 (Lahore, 1986), 77-88.

[5] Ibid., 90-120.

[6] Majeed, *Qur'ān Interpretation in Urdu*, 144-55.

[7] See Sarwar Saulat, *Maulana Maududi* (Karachi, 1984), 42, 64.

sacred text. It requires an open mind, critical thinking and reverence. These pre-requisites do not suggest any arbitrary interpretation in the least. Rather, it invites readers to ponder, reflect and assimilate the Qur'ān's timeless message.

Khurshid Ahmad, a prominent Ideologue, has summed up the rationale and distinctive elements of *Tafhim*. First, it is a unique contribution to contemporary tafsir literature. *Tafhim* primarily focuses on the Qur'ān as the Book of divine guidance and a complete way of life (*din*). Second, *Tafhim* seeks to create a universal ideological (Islamic) movement by reflecting on the key themes of moral reconstruction. Framed from the lens of an activist perspective, Mawdudi approaches the Qur'ān in its historical totality to articulate his vision of *da'wah*. Third, its style and methodology are interlinked to *hidāyah*. This implies a meaningful dialogue between man and Allah. For Mawdudi, the study of *nazm* has a 'purposive unity' weaving together the surahs with overall objectives.[8] Falahi has undertaken a detailed study of Mawdudi's presentation of his tafsir. In this regard we reproduce the gist of Mawdudi's motivation for his tafsir:

> Literal translations of the Qur'ān tend inevitably to lack force, fluency, eloquence and stylistic charm. Such lifelessness is incapable of either arousing the reader to ecstasy, stirring his being, making eyes flow with tears, or raising a storm of emotion within his soul. Literal translations often leave one doubting whether the original book could indeed have been that which challenged the whole world to produce another like it. What filters though is merely the dry dusk of its contents, stripped of all literary enchantment. The violent, soul- shaking spirit which permeates the original text is thus evaporated into thin air. This is a serious drawback, for the literary force of the Qur'ān

---

[8] Abul A'la Mawdudi, *Towards Understanding the Qur'ān*, vol.1 (Leicester, 1988), xv.

> plays possibly as important a role in conveying its message as the teachings themselves. It was the literary quality of the Qur'ān - a quality acknowledged even by its opponents - which first melted the hearts of its opponents and shook the length and breadth of Arabia like a thunderbolt.[9]

Methodology and style make up *Tafhim*. Keeping in mind Mawdudi's extraordinary command over Urdu, fluency of thought, coherent presentation and logical representation - these are couched in his tafsir by his inimitable style. It is a unique contribution to exegetical literature. Likewise, Mawdudi employs precise words or phrases to explicate Arabic terms. As an inclusive language, Arabic is rich in linguistic expression and a translator requires a dexterous approach to retain the essence of the verses under discussion. In *Tafhim*, the format by way of paragraph clusters and explanatory notes has enriched the readers' perspective on Mawdudi's overall presentation of the Qur'ānic message.

Another aspect that lends considerable knowledge to Qur'ānic methodology is the occasion of revelation (*asbāb al-nuzul*). Mawdudi's approach is two-fold: a critical assessment of hadith literature relating to this discipline and reconciling conflicting narratives through the process of examining the internal evidence in the text.[10]

In *Tafhim*, a rich corpus of historical accounts is utilised to give context and relevance to Qur'ānic narrations. Additionally, Mawdudi had used scientific and geographical details to buttress his explanations of verses pertaining to historical figures or events. As an executive member of the *Rābita 'Ālam al-Islami* (Muslim World League), his interaction with leading scholars enabled him to broaden his knowledge of the sacred text.[11]

There is a misperception largely fuelled by sectarian interest that *Tafhim* does not conform to the traditional interpretation

---

[9] Ibid., 1-2.

[10] Falahi, *Jamā'at i- Islami Fuzalā*, 20-1.

[11] Majeed, *Qur'ān Interpretation in Urdu*, 145.

under which *tafsir al-ma'thur* is an essential element. Mawdudi counters these allegations by positioning the centrality of the Qur'ān's life-enriching lessons. It is evident that hadith literature has been carefully consulted without engaging into polemical discussions. Likewise, the intra-Qur'ānic interpretation seeks to authenticate the subject, purpose and principal themes of the sacred text. For Mawdudi, the Qur'ānic text remains incomparable to human interpretation and thus is the final arbiter of accuracy and authenticity.[12] This point is important to understand Mawdudi's overarching approach to make the Qur'ān accessible to readers who seek to gain close proximity to the spirit of Allah's revelation. His vigorous and invested engagement with the divine text is intended to make it relevant to the challenges of the day.

The scourge of errant interpretations is a defensive tool employed by Mawdudi's critics. A human production like *Tafhim* contains differing opinions, scholarly disagreements and to a lesser degree independent judgement. Against the chorus of dissenting and strident voices, Mawdudi's methodology steers away from polemical literature. Nevertheless, his critique of misguided movements like Qadianism, shrine-based Islam and Ahl al-Qur'ān are the hallmarks of his rational and constructive approach. By the same token, *takfir* language is an anathema to Mawdudi just as a counter response against his personality by a segment of traditional 'ulama is eschewed. All in all, Mawdudi strongly argues against the rigid interpretation of the Qur'ān along *Fiqhi* lines. His approach is markedly different from the *maslak* mindset. Mawdudi elaborates:

> Schism occurs when the very fundamentals are made a matter of dispute and controversy. It may also happen that some scholar, mystic, mufti, or leader pronounces on a question to which Allah and His Messenger have not attached fundamental importance, exaggerating the significance of the question to such an extent that

---

[12] Falahi, *Jamā'at i-Islami Fuzalā*, 25-6.

it is transformed into a basic issue of faith. Such people usually go one step further, declaring all who disagree with their opinion to have forsaken the true faith and set themselves outside the community of true believers. They may even go so far as to organise those who agree with them into a sect, claiming that sect to be identical with the Islamic community and declaring that everyone who does not belong to it is destined to hellfire.[13]

In sum, Falahi provides a succinct description of Mawdudi's Qur'ānic contributions. It is a master key that unlocked the potential for Arab and non-Arab exegetical works.[14] This explains the intrinsic merit of *Tafhim*: a clarion call for mankind to explore and assimilate the timeless message of the final revealed scripture. In its broadest sense, it reaches out to intellectuals, 'ulama, literary critics, students, institutions and other sectors seeking to rediscover the true essence of *da'wah*.

Falahi has rightly pointed out the creative approach adopted by Mawdudi of formatting the clusters of *āyāt* (verses) in paragraph forms. Readers are able to distil its holistic teachings, lessons and wisdom through an effortless reading of the cluster-based presentation.[15] In the words of Mawdudi:

> I have prefaced every surah with careful notes on the period of a particular revelation, the circumstances obtained at the time, the stage through which the Islamic movement was then passing and its chief needs and problems. Moreover, wherever specific background information is relevant to the understanding of a particular verse or group of verses, such information is supplied in the explanatory notes. In the

---

[13] Mawdudi, *Towards Understanding the Qur'ān*, vol.1, 30.
[14] Falahi, *Jamā'at i-Islami Fuzalā*, 31.
[15] Ibid.

explanatory notes, every effort has been made to avoid distracting the reader's attention from the Qur'ān itself. These notes have a two-fold purpose: first, to elucidate and clarify and second, to highlight the spirit and aim of the Qur'ānic passages. The reader is advised to go through the introductory sections of each surah before beginning a study of the surah itself and to refer back to them during his study.[16]

Tafhim is written in a unique style with the aim of developing man's understanding of the Qur'ān as the source of guidance. It is an interpretive translation that attempts to capture the original meaning and impact of the Qur'ān on Muslim culture and civilisation.

The initial translation of the Qur'ān during Mawdudi's lifetime was a mediocre production, hardly compatible with its scholarly acumen and literary excellence. Mawdudi realised these limitations and expressed the need for a forceful translation in modern English, bearing in mind the Western-educated readership. Zafar Ishaq Ansari (d. 2016) agreed to undertake this mammoth project. His command over Arabic, Urdu and English combined with his competence in Islamic studies qualified him to undertake this major task.

The first volume was published by the Islamic Foundation in 1988. Mention may be made of Abdur Raheem Kidwai who was associated with the institute and was a member of the editorial team of the translation project. The second volume appeared in 1989. In subsequent volumes the scope of Kidwai's collaborative effort was expanded. This aspect is clearly brought out by Zafar Ishaq Ansari:

The notes, which form the bulk of the work, were first translated into English by Dr. Kidwai of the Islamic Foundation. The draft served as a base out of which the present manuscript developed after a long process of editing and re-editing.

---

[16] Mawdudi, *Towards Understanding the Qur'ān*, vol. 1, 4-5.

Although no attempt is made to give the chronological sequence to Kidwai's contribution to the translation project, the following point merits attention: Kidwai's critical comments on the entire draft of the volumes reaffirm his credential as a renowned scholar of Qur'ānic studies. Likewise, the multivolume work of *Tafhim* represents a serious study seeking to address global concerns for a broad-based Muslim constituency.[17]

Jalil Ahsan Nadwi

A multifaceted scholar who represented an amalgam of the intellectual strands in the subcontinent, Jalil Ahsan Nadwi (d. 1981) contributed exceptionally to Qur'ānic studies. In Nadwah the reformist thrust was articulated by its emphasis on Arabic. Likewise, the focused competence in hadith studies was offered in Deoband. For the exemplary tradition of Qur'ānic hermeneutics Madrasat al-Islāh occupied a distinguished place.[18]

Under the influence of Mawdudi, Jalil Ahsan and Mas'ud 'Alam Nadwi[19] worked indefatigably to promote the JI vision of *da'wah*. To this end, the translation of Mawdudi's important writings in Arabic reflected their thorough grounding in Arabic. In several ways Jalil Ahsan advanced the cause of Qur'ānic studies by way of his close association with institutions of higher Islamic learning. Among his translation of Mawdudi's Qur'ānic writings, the *Four Qur'ānic Concepts* is an important contribution.

There are two complementary aspects of Jalil Ahsan's promotion of Qur'ānic studies. First, his writings contain a broad range of topics that enhance readers' understanding of the growth and development of Qur'ānic sciences (*'ulum*). Second, his lessons (*durus*) are indispensable to appreciate his deep reflection on the sacred text.

We may now refer to Jalil Ahsan's critique of *Taddabbur e-Qur'ān*

---

[17] Choughley, *The Contributions of Abdur Raheem Kidwai*, 19.

[18] Falahi, *Jamā'at i- Islami Fuzalā*, 35.

[19] Mas'ud 'Alam's name figures prominently regarding translations of Mawdudi's writings in Arabic. See Nadwi, *Purān i-Charāgh*, vol.1, 344-5.

authored by Amin Ahsan Islāhi. His incomplete work is a summative assessment of selected surahs which are critically analysed under the rubric of coherence, historical relevance and contemporary Qur'ānic studies. Common to his exposition of Qur'ānic themes is the Farāhi articulation of *nazm*. Like Amin Ahsan, Jalil Ahsan gives a reappraisal of Farāhi's conceptual framework of key Qur'ānic themes.

However, his line of argument and well-formulated explanation about Amin Ahsan's tafsir serve as a referential point for a clearer understanding of the Qur'ānic message, wisdom and teachings.[20]

Points of convergence or divergence are critical tools in explicating the timeless message of the Qur'ān. In contrast, the tendency to censure independent views in deference to a *taqlid* mindset vitiates a constructive approach to the sacred text. Jalil Ahsan's balanced approach is clearly expressed in his presentation of his impressions (*nadharāt*) of *Tadabbur-e-Qur'ān*. In view of the comparative analysis advanced by Farāhi, selected examples are intended to acquaint English readers on the emergent patterns of critical engagement with the Qur'ānic discourse.

Several exegetes have attempted to provide an allegorical interpretation of the transformation of the Jewish transgressors into apes (2: 65-66). This explanation has consensus in mainstream tafsirs and does not conform to Amin Ahsan's viewpoint that the Qur'ānic term *'qiradah* has a spiritual connotation.[21] In fact, Mawdudi strongly advocates its literal meaning without compromising the historical antecedents pertaining to the Isra'ilite nation. For Jalil Ahsan, this verse alludes to the observance of the collective acts of worship designated as Saturday - a sacrosanct day for Judaism. The translation by Mawdudi reinforces the authoritative view:

---

[20] Falahi, *Jamā'at i-Islami Fuzalā*, 40-2.
[21] Ibid., 46.

> *And you know the case of those of you who broke the*
> *Sabbath, how We said to them: "Become apes, despised*
> *and hated."*
>
> (2: 65)[22]

Interestingly, Jalil Ahsan references two tafsirs of the twentieth century, *Tafsir al-Qur'ān* and *Bayān al-Qur'ān*[23] to support his interpretation. This approach enables the readers to discover the gems of Qur'ānic wisdom and linguistic charms unfettered by sectarian readings.

It is a truism that tafsir possesses an inner logic and dynamic that cuts across time-specific meanings. This explains the overlapping features of Qur'ānic research and methodology by Islamic institutions. In this instance, Jami'at al-Falāh (Azamgarh)[24] has made important strides in Qur'ānic studies. Needless to add, Jalil Ahsan's intellectual acumen and linguistic prowess have strengthened the Qur'ānic scholarship over the years.

The subcontinent has enjoyed an unrivalled status of forging a structured approach to the tafsir tradition. An intellectual milieu which nurtured the Qur'ānic narrative in the early nineteenth century produced scholars of unmatched calibre like Shaykh Faiz al-Hasan Sahāranpuri (d. 1886). His academic pedigree includes Qur'ānic and hadith scholars like Farāhi, Shibli Nu'mani, Sayyid Ahmad Khan and Khalil Ahmad Sahāranpuri. Essentially, his literary contributions influenced strands of reformist thought across the sectarian lines. Qur'ānic studies and classical Arabic literature were his forte and these intellectual beneficiaries carried his vast learning to their respective institutions. In sum, Jalil Ahsan was an embodiment of Faiz al-Hasan's multidimensional personality.[25]

---

[22] Mawdudi, *Towards Understanding the Qur'ān*, vol. 1, 78.

[23] Falahi, *Jamā'at i-Islami Fuzalā*, 45

[24] Ibid., 47.

[25] For a detailed account of Sahāranpuri's illuminating contribution to Arabic literature, see Muhammad Yusuf Khan, *Mawlana Faizul Hasan Sahāranpuri: His Contributions to Arabic Language and Literature* (Aligarh Muslim University, 2008). Cf. Jalilur Rahmān Shaikh, *An Analytical Study on the Contribution of Al-Allamah Faizul Hasan Sahāranpuri to the Arabic Language and Literature* (Aligarh Muslim University,

The *durus* (lessons) are central to Jalil Ahsan's presentation of the range and depth of Qur'ānic knowledge. According to Falahi, the erudite scholar followed a consistent pattern to his exploration of Qur'ānic themes. These included a detailed analysis of grammatical rules in the background of classical Arabic literature and comparative tafsir studies. Additionally, students were encouraged to master Qur'ānic vocabulary, a prerequisite to grasp the essence of the sacred text.

In the tradition of approaching the Qur'ān as a revealed text with distinct structural patterns, Jalil Ahsan draws upon a variety of exegetical sources. Farāhi's cluster of surahs (*'umud*) formulation is accentuated in view of his deep reflection on the *nazm* theory. For Jalil Ahsan, these groupings are interwoven into the cosmos of the surahs under discussion. The thematic significance is generally emphasised. Overall, Jalil Ahsan maintained a positive balance between discussion and teaching. Students were urged to develop an inclusive approach to understand and assimilate the spirit and message of the Qur'ān. Not un-often Jalil Ahsan would open up vistas of engagement to demonstrate the limitless possibilities of interpretation. If he was predisposed to particular views or upheld Farāhi's Qur'ānic positions, these did not prevent him from offering alternative explanations. In this sense nurturing an intellectual mind implied knowledge based on textual sources. This is evident from his endorsement of tafsirs like Thanawi's *Bayān al-Qur'ān* which falls outside the Farāhi Qur'ānic line of thought[26]

Two important aspects emerge from Jalil Ahsan's merit-worthy work *Ifādāt* (guidance):[27] *da'wah* and *tawhid*. These are representative of the JI's vision for the modern mind. *Ifādāt* complements his major work on tafsir as discussed elsewhere in the chapter. Another point is the transitioning of classical sources to a modern interpretation that is expressive of the sacred text's

---

2017). Both these works were submitted as doctoral theses at the university.

[26] Falahi, *Jamā'at i-Islami Fuzalā*, 50-2.

[27] Cf. Nadwi, *Ifādāt i-Qur'ān*, a two-volume work which contextualises the varied aspects of the Qur'ān in modern idiom.

timeless message. In other words, the holistic approach adopted by Jalil Ahsan does not deviate from the normative understanding of the authoritative sources. Additionally, his views or interpretations are grounded in exemplary scholarship and do not betray streaks of a conformist mindset. His writings are an invaluable contribution to the rich tafsir genre.

It is generally believed that scholars associated with Farāhi reformist thought merely replicated his viewpoints. In contrast, the writings of Jalil Ahsan counter these misrepresentations. His interpretations are framed from the lens of originality and deep reflection on the Qur'ānic themes.[28]

Sayyid Hāmid 'Ali

An extraordinary figure, Sayyid Hāmid Ali (d. 1993) represented the core leadership of the JI whose primary aim was to articulate Islam as a way of life (*din*). Central to its overall objectives is the pivotal role of *da'wah* in a Hindu- dominated society.[29] Hāmid 'Ali by dint of his brilliance and dedication carried out the mission of Mawdudi through his writings and discourses. His debates with Hindu organisations pressed home the primacy of *da'wah* as envisioned by JI.

Anecdotal accounts mention his personal struggle and commitment to the JI cause. Despite the odds stacked against his religious conviction (his association with the JI), Hāmid 'Ali displayed exemplary scholarship and produced works of unequalled merit. It must be remembered that he accessed the influential writings of Mawdudi and Farāhi in his initial years to develop a systematic understanding of *da'wah* and Qur'ānic hermeneutics. Divergent strands of the Islamic reformist thought - Deoband, Nadwah, Ahl al-Hadith[30] moulded his interpretive reading of the

---

28 Falahi, *Jamā'at i-Islami Fuzalā*, 52.

29 See Choughley, *Islamic Resurgence*, 269-72.

30 The confluence of Islamic reformist thought is notable among the core leadership of JI. In pre-Partition India, Pathankot was the hub of Mawdudi's seminal ideas of Islamic reformist thought. Other leading 'ulama like Nu'mani and Shaykh Nadwi were founder members of the JI.

Qur'ānic text. Hāmid 'Ali has to his credit three principal translations of the Qur'ān. From a simple volume to a comprehensive tafsir, these works reaffirm the productive phase of the genre in the subcontinent.[31] Likewise, his interest in particular surahs has seen a shift away from the traditional analysis of their respective themes. The dominant theme, however, is the interrelationship and relatability of key aspects as outlined in these surahs. For example, Surah Al-Kahf is representative of this trend. Monographs written by Mawdudi, Manāzir Ahsan Gilani, Shaykh Nadwi[32] and Hāmid 'Ali are an analytical study of this important surah. In Hāmid 'Ali's perspective the surah has a structural link with the preceding surah (Bani Isra'il).

It would be worthwhile to assess the perceptive comments of Falahi about Hāmid 'Ali's Qur'ānic contributions. Apart from his consistent approach that is a marked feature of the esteemed scholar's erudition, the layers of Qur'ānic meanings and truths are systematically uncovered. His methodology is informed by a thorough mastery over Arabic literature and the tafsir genre.

Consider the translation of Sayyid Qutb's *Fi Zilāl al-Qur'ān*. An ambitious translation enterprise like this widely- acclaimed work is no mean feat. It is a formidable challenge on two counts: authenticity and versatility. Written in expressive Arabic, the masterpiece enjoys the unrivalled status of projecting an ethos that is distinctly *da'wah*-centred. By the same token, it is not a conventional tafsir that engages in theological and *Fiqhi* issues. At the same time, Qutb sets out new pathways to rediscover the sacred text's essential teachings. A litterateur par excellence, Qutb authored the tafsir famed for its reformist slant. Overall, it embodies the finest specimen of linguistic charm without compromising the fervour of an Islamic activist. *Fi Zilāl* was conceived and produced in the hostile environment of Egyptian jails notorious for subjecting prisoners to inhuman treatment. For the Ikhwan movement the Nasserist regime came to symbolise the

---

[31] Falahi, *Jamā'at i-Islami Fuzalā*, 76.
[32] See Nadwi, *Faith versus Materialism* (Kuala Lumpur, 2005).

anti-Islam narrative to its promotion of socialism. In the backdrop of the prevailing political events in Egypt, Hāmid 'Ali's translation of this celebrated multivolume work is revealing. Although incomplete due to his ill health, Hāmid 'Ali presented an authentic translation of the commentary. An Urdu translation required his own rendering of the sacred text. Hāmid 'Ali executed this task admirably by producing a new translation that is faithful to the essence and spirit of traditional and contemporary exegesis. He had to wade through seminal translations like *Mudih al-Qur'ān, Tafhim al-Qur'ān*, etc. for his own work so that it captured, in principle, Qutb's tafsir. A synthesis of two Qur'ānic worldviews, Hāmid 'Ali represented an emerging cohort of exegetes committed to making the message of the Qur'ān relatable to the modern mind. This undertaking has ignited renewed interest among Qur'ānic scholars to consider future projects along these lines.

The confluence of the tafsir tradition in the subcontinent has not always followed an even course. Invariably, there have been tafsirs that are a deviation from its established lineage. As a beneficiary of traditional learning, Sayyid Ahmad Khan produced a controversial tafsir that lent in no small measure to the culture of polemics. A product of colonialism, he was greatly influenced by the ebb and flow of Muslim fortunes. This explains his response through his tafsir about the Islamic renewal project. Hāmid 'Ali by his association with JI supported Mawdudi's elaboration of core Qur'ānic concepts. In this instance the latter's *Four Basic Qur'ānic Concepts* was critiqued by his contemporary, Shaykh Nadwi. It was Hāmid 'Ali who defended Mawdudi's conceptual framework of these concepts on which doctrinal beliefs (*'aqā'id*) hinge.

Essentially, Hāmid Ali is a pre-eminent figure in the field of *da' wah*. His writings are expressions of Islam as a way of life that allow for constructive engagement with other faith-based communities. His books are illustrative of *da'wah* concerns detailing the role of Messengers in different areas.

Shams Pirzāda

In line with Jama'at al-Islami Hind's (hereafter JIH) vision of expanding *da'wah* through the Qur'ān, Shams Pirzāda's (d. 1999) contributions are substantial.

Pirzāda has an interesting history pertaining to his scholarly life: his self-study[33] and interaction with reputed 'ulama enabled him to augment his familiarity with a wide array of Islamic disciplines. In this way he developed his competence in Qur'ānic sciences and Arabic, an expertise which he successfully employed to present a holistic interpretation of the sacred text. His formal association with JIH, inspired by Mawdudi's influential writings had a major impact on his conceptualisation of *da'wah*. Also his rapport with the great scholar and Amir of JIH, Abu Lais Nadwi[34] drew him to the wider terrain of Islamic thought. His Urdu translations of 'Allamah Yusuf Qardawi's widely-acclaimed books won him much esteem in the scholarly circles. By the same token, Pirzāda was not a diehard member of JIH and maintained his independent views which at times were at odds with Mawdudi's radical approach. The JIH's endorsement of Fatima Jinnah as a presidential election in Pakistan is a case in point.

Pirzāda was of *salafi* leanings and held strong views about the nature of *talāq and isāl i-thawāb*, which were implicitly endorsed by the *a'immah* (four Imams)[35] He provided irrefutable textual proof in his explication of these intricate issues. In fact, he drew his inspiration from the writings of Ibn Taimiyyah, considered an ideologue of the *salafi* movement. His views, therefore, underscored his ideological affiliation.

---

[33] Curiously enough, Mawdudi's self-study and private lessons with Deobandi 'ulama was downplayed in order to launch a tirade against his non- traditional Islamic training.

[34] For a contextual reading of the JIH, see Irfan Ahmad, *Islamism and Democracy in India: The Transformation of the Jamaat e-Islami* (Princeton, 2009). The term Islamism is a controversial definition of JIH in view of its global *da'wah* reach, dissemination of forceful Islamic literature and social activism.

[35] Falahi, *Jamā'at i-Islami Fuzalā*, 107. Many enlightened 'ulama were avid readers of Ibn Taimiyyah's works, which during this crucial period were gaining importance in the subcontinent.

Pirzāda produced his *Da'wah al-Qur'ān*, a two-volume tafsir that is a creative intersection of authenticity and *da'wah*. Translated into four regional languages, *Da'wah al-Qur'ān* holds the distinction of reaching out to non-Muslim readers for its depth of knowledge and relatability. In Pirzāda's estimation, the appropriate choice of translation combined with explanatory notes lends value to the message of the Qur'ān. To this end, his formulation of his tafsir contains ten distinguishing features as outlined by Falahi.[36] Pirzāda maintains strict adherence to the text without compromising to speculative meanings. The cornerstone of his interpretation is anchored on the sunnah for which a critical examination of the hadith literature is essential. Conversely, his critique of aberrant interpretations especially in the *bid'ah* strain underpins the Prophetic approach in which the essential teachings, spirit and guidance are discussed.[37] Likewise, Pirzāda is unsparing in his criticism of the cultic status of personalities or scholars whose words are taken as definitive and above reproach. For him, it is the unalloyed sunnah that is the final arbiter of Qur'ānic interpretation for which there is a latitude of flexibility (*rukhsah*). What is important for him is the *tazkiyah/nasihah* elements that represent the Qur'ān's timeless message.[38] According to Pirzāda, guidance is intrinsic to the overall form, structure and cohesion of the Qur'ān. In Pirzāda's perspective there are distinctive traits that mark out the inimitable style of the Qur'ān. This aspect is particularly important to reach out to non-Muslim readers. We may consider the following aspects as these have an interlocking significance to a critical appraisal of the Qur'ān:

The titles of the surahs are derived from specific events/incidents and have a covalent bonding to the text. This is not to suggest that a decoding of the text is required to unravel its overall design, structure and flow of ideas. Essentially, the key concepts of thematic significance play an important role in discovering the rationale and import of surahs. For example,

---

[36] Ibid., 96-9.
[37] Ibid., 107.
[38] Ibid., 102.

Surah Al-Baqarah contains historical narratives and legislative pronouncements on the evolution of the shari'ah. Judaism and Christianity, for example, are singled out for their transgression and interpolation, respectively. In contrast, the Qur'ān explores in its unique style the universality of its teachings in the backdrop of the previously revealed Scriptures. Far from the inchoate forms that supposedly mark out this surah, Pirzāda provides irrefutable evidence to show the inner dimensions of *nazm*. His articulation of Farāhi's Qur'ānic contributions are aligned to the Qur'ānic concepts and themes.[39]

Da'wah al-Qur'ān contains useful information about the history of religions, minerals in the Qur'ān, etc. from reputed reference works like the *Encyclopedia of Religion and Ethics*.[40] Likewise, Pirzāda consults a number of classical and modern tafsirs, which provide him a vantage point to present the Qur'ān's eternal guidance. His familiarity with English is evident from his extensive study of Abdullah Yusuf Ali's translation of the Qur'ān. A notable observation of Pirzāda's work is the variety of sources which he consults: *Tafhim al-Qur'ān, Tafsir i-Mājidi* and *Bayān al-Qur'ān* represent three divergent Qur'ānic explorations. These works reflect his proficiency in the tafsir tradition which is generally marred by sectarian prejudice in the subcontinent. Therefore, *Da'wah al-Qur'ān* is a welcome addition to the growing interest among different constituencies to a better understanding of the Revealed Book.

Muhammad Sulayman Qāsimi

It is a truism that the JIH has drawn its core leadership from various Islamic backgrounds. A graduate of Deoband, Muhammad Sulayman Qāsimi was an exceptionally gifted teacher who taught at the JIH institute in Rampur (1952-88). His writings are *da'wah-*

---

[39] Ibid., 102-3, 106.

[40] It may not be out of place to mention the magisterial writings in Urdu by Daryabadi on Western disciplines like Western philosophy, psychology, sociology and comparative religions, which have been sourced by many 'ulama for their research works.

focused, among which is his seven- volume *Durus al-Qur'ān.*[41]

The reach of JIH is through its widely disseminated literature that emphasises the centrality of the sacred text. In other words, the Qur'ān serves as the essential tool to foster the culture of *da'wah* among ordinary Muslims, intellectuals and well-wishers. The path and positive attachment (*ruju'*) to the Qur'ān may be gleaned from the lesson-based methodology espoused by JIH. To this end, the *durus* loosely translated as lessons have played a pivotal role in reconstructing *da'wah* and the establishment of *din* (*iqāmat*) in the Islamic renewal (*tajdid*) project.[42] In a particular sense, the *durus* evolved in response to the new generation's disenchantment with traditional tafsirs that did not offer an inclusive understanding of the Qur'ān's perennial source of guidance. As a result, the gulf widened and created a crisis of confidence among them. Qāsimi's *Durus* embraces the movement's projection of Qur'ānic ideals and his decades- long reflection on teaching in study circles (*halqāhs*) that have become markers of self-identity. This point may be rephrased in a circumstantial context. The emerging patterns of the *durus* are clustered around a central theme: the lived experience of the Qur'ānic teachings and message. In the public domain this experience becomes more pronounced for male and female participants. They share a common goal: how to translate the timeless teachings of the sacred text as a way of life (*din*).[43]

Falahi has offered perceptive comments about the structure of the multivolume tafsir. It envisions a universal Islamic movement guided by noble ideals rooted in a truly Islamic milieu. Interestingly, each volume contains a distinct subject matter with no replication. Each lesson transitions easily into another subject matter. The translation of these segments is direct and forceful. In keeping with its motivational style, Qāsimi

---

[41] The *durus* genre invariably points out to the growing interest among the youth and educated class to assimilate the timeless message, wisdom and guidance of the Qur'ān.

[42] In this instance, Khurram Murad's, *The Way to the Qur'ān* (Leicester, 1985) encapsulates this theme.

[43] Falahi, *Jamā'at i-Islami Fuzalā,* 137.

interrogates the text under discussion to elicit multiple responses. In sum, it is not a regurgitation of views which may be found in the corpus of tafsir literature but an interactive approach by guiding readers to the path of self-discovery. A work of this calibre embodies genuine scholarship. It negotiates the terrains of critical appraisal of the text while steadfastly upholding mainstream interpretation. Let us consider at random the relation between surahs and the subject matter delineated as key themes. Surah Al-Nas (114) is a pointed reference to the challenges of satanic forces while Surah Al-Quraysh (106) has relevance for Indian Muslims threatened by the Hindutva ideology.[44] These volumes are value-oriented prompting readers to broaden their understanding of the sacred text. For example, these lessons contain the following themes: *da'wah* and its prerequisites, the healing properties of the Qur'ān, divine law or man-made law, the Prophetic mission, etc.

The *Durus* has a brilliant feature: the *Iftāhiyah* genre. The English equivalent Introduction has a generic connotation and does not adequately convey its depth of meaning. Needless to add, Arabic and its diluted forms in Urdu are part of the Qur'ānic lexicon; therefore, a target language like English which does not share cultural or linguistic traits with Urdu does not reflect the nuanced interpretation and intricacies of Urdu's dynamic character. Falahi shows how selected *Iftāhiyah* are interlinked to the clusters of verses under discussion. Take volume 3 as an example. Two verses (75:19) and (49:9) are irrefutable evidence about the divine dispensation pertaining to the Qur'ān. This is the miracle of the sacred text in comparison to other Scriptures which were time-specific and had a relative effect on the communities concerned. In contrast, the Qur'ān has an infallible divine source which is in accord with innate logical norms.[45] It supersedes man-made laws, philosophies and ideologies. As a divine book it makes a bold claim about its divine status in the following verses:

---

[44] Ibid., 138.
[45] Ibid., 140-1.

Had it been from any other than Allah, they surely would have found it in much inconsistencies.

(3: 82)

Qāsimi makes a pointed reference to the Qur'ānic presentation of the universe, the huge tapestry of astronomy and the creation of man whose functions are comprehensively explained under the rubric of knowledge (*'ilm*). This is indeed the miraculous aspect of the sacred text. Mawdudi's comments on the above verse are revealing:

> The Qur'ān itself is a strong, persuasive testimony to its Divine origin. It is inconceivable that any human being should compose discourses on different circumstances and on different occasions and the collection of those discourses should then grow into a coherent, homogenous and integrated work, no component of which is discordant with the rest. It is also inconceivable that such a work would be permeated throughout with a uniform outlook and attitude, a work manifesting remarkable consistency in the mood and spirit of its Author, a work so perfect that it would never require any change or revision.[46]

We have made this Qur'ān easy as a reminder. Is there then any who will take heed?

(54:17)

For Qāsimi, possessing a logical sense and understanding of the Qur'ān entails these traits: reverence for the text and deriving maximum guidance without relying on extraneous sources that tend to mar its essential spirit. Most importantly, a strong bond with the text is sustained by a commitment for change in one's life and outlook (*hidāyah*). A seeker-after-truth or an aspirant

---

[46] Mawdudi, *Towards Understanding the Qur'ān* (Abridged), 177.

reader need not look beyond the intent of the Qur'ānic words as this tendency has the potential to misguide rather than offer guidance. This explains the repetitive reference to the above-quoted verse as the reaffirmation of its life-turning mission.

The *durus* tradition has in more ways than one developed into a sub-genre of tafsir in the subcontinent. It is highly organised with clear-cut objectives and is enjoyed among different classes of readership. Zafar al-Islam Islāhi of AMU has enriched this tradition by his *Qur'āni Durus*. A notable contribution, Manzur Nu'mani, a prolific writer, has encapsulated his decades-long expertise in the Qur'ānic field through his *Durus*. These works are recent developments and may be regarded as a baseline to new ways of approaching the Qur'ān. Additionally, the boundaries between academia and lay readership are gradually blurred out on account of social media's overwhelming accessibility.

Da'wah outreach programmes through regional languages have been one of the primary objectives of JIH. In particular, the Hindi translation of the Qur'ān has seen an incremental presence in view of its official status in the country. The importance of Mawdudi's tafsir reinforces the movements' *da'wah* trajectory: to reach out to the large constituency of faith-based readers. In other words, providing an easy-to-read, accessible Hindi translation for non-Muslims. This is a qualified statement because there is a significant percentage of Muslim readers also who are not familiar with the linguistic charm and stylistic usage of Urdu. Hence, their recourse to a simplified version in Hindi.

Muhammad Farouq Khan enjoys the distinction of translating the Qur'ān into Urdu and Hindi.[47] Likewise, he has also translated Mawdudi's abridged *Tafhim al- Qur'ān* into Hindi. His translation is couched in chaste Hindi, focusing largely on the Qur'ānic guidance for the uninitiated readers. Notes are concise and precise to enable an interactive engagement with the sacred text. Khan facilitates an easy approach for particular Qur'ānic terms by inserting equivalent words within brackets. For example, the word 'revelation' is placed in brackets to give a sense

---

[47] Falahi, *Jamā'at i-Islami Fuzalā*, 191-2.

of meaning for the Arabic term *wahy*. Khan has in mind the readers' range of Islamic knowledge and as such attempts to make the text purposive.[48] Without delving into the semantic field of polysemy Khan broadens the definitions that are otherwise restricted to commentaries. Take the word, *tazkiyah* which is generally associated with self-purification or self-development. However, Khan introduces the concept of maturation, a process of completion which adds new meaning to its spiritual content. According to Falahi, a comparative analysis of particular verses between Khan and Mawdudi's translation reveal their respective linguistic mastery. For Khan sentence construction, syntactic structure are essential tools for accuracy in the translation projects.[49] This explains his technical expertise - a distinguishing feature in his Urdu translation. In sum, Khan's contributions to tafsir studies are a testament to the contours of *da'wah* taking on greater importance in the subcontinent.

Khurram Murad

Da'wah in its institutional form is generally associated with Khurram Murad (d. 1996), a key figure in JI broad - based vision of taking the Qur'ān to the masses. Born in the princely state of Bhopal, Murad was a brilliant Qur'ānic scholar and activist who mobilised his intellectual resources to serve selflessly the cause of Islam.[50]

There are three distinct phases of his activist life which encompassed his articulation of the Qur'ānic message. His early years and association with JI saw the emergence of Murad as a capable administrator who harnessed the energies of students and the youth to study the sacred text through the formation of study circles (*halqahs*). Direct access to the text in a changing social milieu did, however, meet with resistance from certain segments

---

[48] Ibid., 194.

[49] Ibid., 192-4.

[50] On the life and times of Khurram Murad, see Muslim Sajjad (ed.), *Khurram Murad: Hayāt wa Khidmāt* (Lahore, 1997).

of the 'ulama fraternity who argued about the risk of arbitrary interpretation. Nevertheless, the success rate of the *halqahs* was an index of the rootage of Qur'ānic interest among the rising generation of disaffected youth. It was the tireless efforts of Murad that changed the course of their engagement with the sacred text at an activist level.[51]

A civil engineer by profession, Murad was instrumental in the expansion project of the *haram*. In the main, Islamic activities were close to his heart which he carried to the heartland of the West. This represented the second phase of his aligning *da'wah* to a changing landscape. As director general of Islamic Foundation (Leicester), he oversaw the forceful production of Islamic literature that was compatible with the growing needs of the diasporic Muslim communities in Europe and United States.[52] Among his writings are *The Way to the Qur'ān* and *Surah Al-Baqarah*. These works are reflective of a new methodology to approach the sacred text in the light of *tarbiyah* (self-development) and *sirah*. Likewise, Murad co-authored *Surah Kahf* which had a two- fold aim: to critique materialism and meet the intellectual needs of Muslims living in the West.[53]

Murad had a penetrative mind and synergised Islamic learning to the best interest of Islam. The publication of works by distinguished scholars embodies Murad's sectarian-free outlook. Of interest is the internationally recognised *The Muslim World Book Review* which has earned a reputation for promoting critical reviews of Qur'ān translations as well as books related to Qur'ānic studies. The contributions of Abdur Raheem Kidwai[54] have indeed broadened the scope of Qur'ān reviews as a sub-genre of the tafsir tradition.

Murad was an outstanding motivational speaker who sought to communicate in modern idiom the eternal guidance of the

---

[51] Ibid., 37-59.

[52] Ziauddin Falahi, *Hind-wa-Pāk ke Mashāhir ki Qur'āni Khidmāt* (Aligarh, 2020), 108-9.

[53] These works are characterised by Murad's vision of making the Qur'ānic message accessible to modern man.

[54] See Abdur Raheem Kidwai, *Translating the Untranslatable* and *God's Word Man's Interpretations*.

Qur'ān. These study sessions contain nuggets of wisdom minted over the years and are a mine of his rich experience in the field of Qur'ānic studies. Murad deftly navigates the challenges of materialism by presenting a holistic understanding of Qur'ānic themes. For him extensive study, fathoming the oceans of knowledge and discovering layers of meaning are possible through the meaningful bonding with the sacred text. In contrast, an academic study does not yield productive results; rather, it inhibits personal growth and alienates the reader from gaining insight into the demands of faith. The spiritual dimensions of his writings are lucidly encapsulated in *The Early Hours*.[55] Meditation and contemplation are seamlessly woven into the tapestry of *dhikr*. It is a powerful reminder about a believer's intimate relationship with his Creator, the transitory nature of life and most importantly the requisites of self-development. In a similar vein, *The Islamic Movement*[56] is enriched by Murad's brilliant exposition of *da'wah* framed around the challenges of modernity. His writings are evocative of a sublime soul who has devoted his whole life to the cause of Islam. An institution builder with a corporate vision Murad has reconfigured the enduring presence of the Qur'ān as the civilisational tool for mankind.

The third phase of Murad's exemplary *da'wah* profile is his *Dars i-Qur'ān*. The audio recordings/cassettes served as an effective tool of communicating the Qur'ānic message. Written in two volumes, the commentary covers 24 surahs (*Shams-Nās*). Noteworthy points are Murad's motivational approach that takes into account target audience, relevance and self-development. His well-researched discourses encompass classical and contemporary Qur'ānic sources that are meant for practical implementation. For Murad, terms like *tabligh* and *tadhkir* are not time-specific concepts; rather, they reflect life-enriching experiences for a believer to reach goals of

---

[55] Khurram Murad, *In the Early Hours: Reflections on Spiritual Self Development* (Leicester, 2013).

[56] Abul A'ala Mawdudi, *The Islamic Movement: Dynamics of Values, Power and Change* is an edited version of *Tehrik i-Islami ki Akhlāqi Bunyādein*. The copious notes covering 100 pages attests to Murad's depth of knowledge and incisive analysis of issues raised by Mawdudi in this monograph.

spiritual excellence (*ihsān*). Therefore, the Qur'ān has a voice that amplifies its inner meanings in all times and circumstances. Murad reiterates the timeless message of the Qur'ān in circumstantial settings that are not restricted by ideological bias or preferences. His academic credentials do not betray blind conformity to Mawdudi's establishment of Islam as a way of life (*iqāmat al-din*) as is wrongly assumed.[57] During his Bhopal years (148-9) Murad benefited greatly from the Qur'ānic sessions of Sayyid Sulayman Nadwi. These phases were preparatory grounds for his *dars* classes conducted in Lahore. Apart from the executive position he held in the JI hierarchy, Murad's primary focus was related to the Qur'ān-in-action blueprint.

Murad's deep reflections on the Qur'ānic themes concerning life, faith, guidance, etc. are illuminating. Modern man has been grappling with these serious issues in their respective societies and invariably have a direct bearing on their relationship with their Creator. Here Murad offers the Qur'ānic directives as an infallible guide to man's pursuit of real happiness. Again, self-development is fostered as an important tool of spiritual culture. Consider the following verse:

Sure it is for Us to show the Right Way

(92:12)

According to Murad, the famous philologist Raghib Isfahani (d. 1108) outlines four characteristics of guidance (*hidāyah*). Essentially, guidance flows from *wahy* (revelation) which sanctions a divinely- mandated life. The rewards of obedience also falls in this category. At the end of the spectrum, guidance refers to that pathway that leads to *jannah*. In Murad's view, the comprehensive definition of guidance attests to the miraculous nature (*i'jāz*) of the Qur'ān.[58]

And did We not exalt your fame?

(94:4)

---

[57] Falahi, *Hind-wa-Pāk ke Mashāhir*, 111-2.
[58] Ibid.,113.

This verse has been interpreted in several ways to reaffirm the exalted status of the Holy Prophet (SAW). Murad makes a thoughtful statement: The Prophetic message built a civilisation and culture that continues to dominate world events. In the past, kingdom and regimes appeared and disappeared over a period of time. However, the Prophetic call and guidance have not been affected by the unpredictable nature of time. According to Murad, the Islamic civilisation poses an existential threat to competing/rival ideologies which have failed dismally to fight off its global influence. In the context of this verse, the exalted position, call and message of the Holy Prophet (SAW) are perpetuated.

Surah Al-Kawthar is succinctly explained by Murad within the *da'wah* framework. It refers not only to the fountain of abundance but includes all the special favours bestowed on the Holy Prophet (SAW). His translation is largely derived from the commentary of *Bayān al-Qur'ān*.[59]

The credit goes to Murad for disseminating the *durus*, albeit in different forms, in the West. The heart of his *da'wah* mission is encapsulated in *The Way to the Qur'ān*:

> Reading the Qur'ān will be of little benefit to
> you, it may even bring misery and harm, unless
> you, from the first moment, begin to change and
> reconstruct your life in total surrender to God
> who has given you the Qur'ān.[60]

It will be worthwhile to consider the trends of the progressive tafsir understanding in a JI perspective. In its mission statement, the dynamics of global *da'wah* are articulated. Murad has forcefully outlined this vision within the orbit of power and

---

[59] Ibid.,111-25. Falahi given a concise overview of the key themes contained in Murad's *Durus*. His perceptive comments on Surah Al- Kawthar are illuminating.
[60] Murad, *Way to the Qur'ān*, 111. Cf. Sajjad, *Khurram Murad*, 115-9. These impressions are a summary of Murad's brilliant Qur'ānic contributions.

change. A God-centred life is a Qur'ānic imperative from which flows the civilisational role of Islam. Essentially, *da'wah* may assume different forms and will have to be adapted for the modern mind.[61]

In a particular sense, Murad's noteworthy initiatives in the West have spurred scholars like Irfan Ahmad Khan to provide a broader definition to the Qur'ānic message in different sociopolitical settings.

Irfan Ahmad Khan

A veteran Qur'ānic scholar, Irfan Ahmad Khan (d. 2018) was an amalgam of multidisciplinary learning. A graduate of physical science at AMU, Khan proceeded to Chicago to complete his doctorate in Western philosophy. An active member of the JI he organised several seminars in India for the youth and worked actively in interfaith training sessions. It was in the US that these activities took tangible forms: president of the Association for Qur'ānic Understanding, founder of the revived Parliament of World Religions and initiator of interfaith dialogue across the world.[62]

For Khan the Qur'ān sharpened his understanding of the cosmos in relation to man's relationship with Allah, the concept of *khilāfah* and Islam's universal role in history. He offered his life as an example of the Qur'ānic ideals which he steadfastly upheld and promoted throughout his life. His academic background in Western and Islamic philosophy contributed substantially to his thematic presentation of the Qur'ān from various angles. His *An Exercise in Understanding the Qur'ān* developed his thesis about the thematic structure of the sacred text. Khan's interpretive approach supported by his explanation of the inner harmony of

---

[61] Cf. Mawdudi, *The Islamic Movement*, 30.

[62] See Tanveer Azmat, An Introduction to the Qur'ānic Hermeneutics of Irfan A. Khan, in *Islamic Studies*. Vol. 56, No. 1-2, 2017, 77-82. Cf. Tanveer *Azmat, Understanding the Qur'ānic Revelation: The Dynamic Hermeneutics of Irfan A. Khan* (2016), 4-18.

the Qur'ān (*nazm*) is a singular contribution.[63] On a broader level, his passionate devotion to Qur'ānic truth (bearing in mind his philosophy background) led him to an exploratory journey, which cut across textual analysis. He, in turn, inspired readers to align their lives in total surrender to the Will of God.

We now focus on *Reflections on the Qur'ān: Understanding Surah al-Fātihah and al-Baqarah*. Falahi has neatly summarised a ten-point guideline[64] to a reflective reading of the Qur'ān offered by Khan. The following reflection reveals the overarching theme in Khan's comprehensive tafsir:

> The *tawhidic* movement embodies the life and time of the Prophets of Allah who were sent throughout the human world. This mission aimed at giving mankind their true freedom and dignity. It liberated their minds and spirits from all slavery - including their blind following of so-called religious leaders. The Prophets emphasised the use of reason. According to them, our intellectual faculties are divine blessings which must be properly used.[65]

The above statement delineates Khan's Qur'ānic hermeneutics: an open, inclusive approach to reflect on the divine text. Likewise, guidance and revelation may be interpreted at a different level: the Qur'ān is the text and the text is divine. Thus the Qur'ān as the final revealed Book opens up immense possibilities of being understood by human beings. Humankind will be in a position to understand it better and better as they keep on reading it with their growing abilities to understand and in the perspective of their changing human situations.[66] In other

---

[63] Irfan Khan, *An Exercise in Understanding the Qur'ān: An Outline Study of the Last Thirty Divine Discourses - Surahs 85-114* (Chicago, 2015).

[64] Falahi, *Jamā'at i-Islami Fuzalā*, 74-5.

[65] Irfan Khan, *Reflections on the Qur'ān: Understanding Surahs Al- Fātihah and Al-Baqarah* (Leicester, 2005), 3.

[66] Ibid., 9.

words, Allah has full knowledge of the possible social, cultural and technological developments in the future history of mankind. Khan makes a perceptive comment about the readers' relationship with the Divine text. In the case of Surah Al-Baqarah, the overall structure helps to understand the internal structure and organisation in the divine discourse. The fundamental principles in understanding the Qur'ān are based on the following:

- One part of the Qur'ān explains another part
- Repetition in the Qur'ān of *āyāt* or words/phrases which deal with the unity theme enhances the readers' grasp of its essential message.
- There is greater continuity in the Qur'ānic text which creates a sense of sequence and order.[67]

The Qur'ān being a well-integrated Book aims to guide mankind of situations which they will face till the Last Day. This explains its timeless message under every circumstance. A key factor in understanding the Qur'ān is the sincerity of the reader. Guidance is preceded by faith (*yaqin*). The end result of such an attitude is promising:

> When, for a reader and the Qur'ān itself is not the ultimate source of guidance and find authority, he/she manipulates the Qur'ān in the light of his/her opinions when he/she has been forced under the impact of various factors which influence his/her thoughts. The person does not receive guidance from the Qur'ān. He/she tries his/her best to guide his/her understanding from the Qur'ān from his/her viewpoint. And it is

---

[67] Ibid., 17-23.

a very dangerous practice.[68]

Falahi, by way of example, has offered useful insights into Khan's approach to the study of the Qur'ān. Consider the following verse:

It is not virtue that you turn your faces are the God- fearing

(2:177)

Irfan gives a detailed reflection on the contents of this verse under the heading *Truly Virtuous People.* A systematic study of the verses can be briefly discussed under the following topics:

- o The point of faith - (a) the meaning of *imān* in general, (b) and the meaning of five specific items of *imān*: i.e. belief in God, the Hereafter, angels, the Book and the Prophets.
- o The point of spending or giving - (a) the meaning of spending general, (b) the meaning of six specific items of spending: "for those who are closely related, orphans, the poor, the wayfarer, and those who ask for help, and to free those in bondage," (c) the meanings of "in spite of its love" and consideration "of the point of spending" in the surah, while having a cursory look at what was said in its earlier part.
- o The point of establishing *salāh* and paying *zakāh* - (a) its meaning and significance and (b) its occurrence in the surah.
- o The point that only those are virtuous who fulfil their covenant.
- o The point that people's perseverance and steadfastness is the test of their being truly virtuous.

---

[68] Ibid., 33.

- o How are truthfulness and virtue related? There are other explanatory notes dealing with 'truthfulness' as the highest value – its significance and its development in some Qur'ānic surahs which will be discussed in the same sequence.
- o How are *taqwā* and virtue related?[69]

The rational underpinnings of Irfan's Qur'ānic works bring out his deep reflections on the sacred text. What is remarkable about his critical engagement with the text is that it is free from layers of the tafsir overload. Direct access guided by the foundational sources of Islam unlocks divine guidance for the readers wishing to realign their lives in the Qur'ānic mould.[70] Irfan's Qur'ānic approach is representative of new trends, particularly in the West attempting to contextualise its essential teachings in their daily lives. There are no linguistic barriers or particular tafsirs to which the readers have to depend on for understanding and reflecting on the divine discourse. Unsurprisingly, English as a dominant language among the Muslim diaspora communities, is now the preferred language of communication. To this end, the production of a contemporary tafsir like *Towards Understanding the Qur'ān* has resonance in the Islamic renewal (*tajdid*) tradition.

Zafar Ishaq Ansari

A prolific writer and intellectual, Zafar Ishaq Ansari (d. 2016) possessed impeccable credentials in the field of Islamic studies. His early works on classical *Fiqh*, and on Islam and the modernity theme highlighted his global reach to Muslims who sought to translate Islam as a way of life (*din*). His close association with internationally reputed universities in the West (McGill University, for example) provided him with deeper perspectives on the Islam and West encounter.[71] Likewise, he contributed a

---

[69] Ibid., 362.

[70] Falahi, *Jamā'at i-Islami Fuzalā*, 187-8.

[71] See Zafar Ishaq Ansari and John Esposito (editors), *Muslims in the West: Encounter and*

number of articles to reputed journals, *Encyclopedia Britannica* and *Encyclopedia of Religion.*

Ansari's academic career spans across several continents which enabled him to contribute significantly to the Islamic resurgence discourse. As a close associate of Mawdudi, he co-edited *Islamic Perspectives: Studies in Honour of Sayyid Abul A'la Mawdudi.* Likewise, Ansari's academic expertise as the Director of Islamic Research Institute (*Islamic Studies*) had given the institution a global presence. The number of peer- reviewed journals in English, Urdu and Arabic attests to his remarkably impressive contributions. In the field of Qur'ānic studies his collaborative efforts opened up a robust study of the sacred text. For example, he played an important role in Muzaffar Iqbal's *The Integrated Encyclopaedia of the Qur'ān.*

Falahi has detailed Ansari's outstanding English translation of *Tafhim al-Qur'ān,* widely acclaimed for its contemporary relevance and readability. The background of the English translation is also succinctly expressed by Khurshid Ahmad:

> The need to produce a complete translation of the *Tafhim* in the English language has been felt ever since its publication in Urdu. To fulfil this need, Islamic Publications, Lahore has published an English translation of the *Tafhim.* Although this rendered a useful service, it was commonly realised that the translation could not capture the real force and elegance of the *Tafhim al-Qur'ān,* which is not only a masterpiece of scholarship, but also a rare piece of literary excellence. The text of the Qur'ān as translated in Urdu by Sayyid Mawdudi, could not be effectively reproduced in the English translation. Explanatory notes were abridged in a number of places. Editorial language standards and the physical production of the book left much to be desired. Sayyid Mawdudi

---

Dialogue (Islamabad, 2001).

realised these limitations and wanted a new and more forceful translation of the *Tafhim al-Qur'ān* in modern English and was eager that the same be printed to professional and international standards. It was with this ambition that the late Chaudhri Ghulam Muhammad and the present writer discussed with Sayyid Mawdudi the plan for a new translation of the *Tafhim*. We all agreed that Dr. Zafar Ishaq Ansari would be the most competent person to undertake this onerous task. His command over Arabic, Urdu and English and his deep understanding and insight into the thought and style of Sayyid Mawdudi qualified him for the job. It was in deference to the wish of Sayyid Mawdudi that Chaudhri Ghulam Muhammad and I persuaded Dr. Zafar Ishaq Ansari to commit himself to this assignment, a responsibility that he shouldered with some reluctance. It is unfortunate that both Sayyid Mawdudi and Chaudhri Ghulam Muhammad are no longer with us to see the fruit of Dr. Ansari's heroic effort to recreate the *Tafhim* in English. Their souls would, however, be happy to see that their dream is now coming true.[72]

The motivation to undertake this monumental translation *Tafhim al-Qur'ān* is expressed by Ansari in these words:

In order to help the lay English reader – who needs more information on certain basic features of Islam and its history than an average Urdu reader – a few more additions were considered necessary. A Glossary of Terms has been included to explain some of the major terms that have been used. Likewise, Biographical Notes

---

[72] Mawdudi, *Towards Understanding the Qur'ān*, vol. 1, xvii-xviii.

have been added to give at least some basic information regarding the persons whose names occur in the text. Also, in addition to the Subject Index (which is a translation of the Index prepared by the author of *Tafhim*), a General Index has been added. A Bibliography of the books referred to in the work has also been provided. Finally, a few-very few-notes have been added at places where elucidation seemed necessary.

Additions made by the editor have been kept to a minimum and wherever they appear it has been indicated that they are from the editor.

It took me quite a long time to prepare the manuscript of the present work, and then a number of reasons caused considerable delay in bringing it to the light of day. During the course of these years, I have received assistance and encouragement from a large number of people. To all of them I owe a debt of gratitude and here at least a few, if not all, must be mentioned.

The greatest encouragement, of course, came from the late Sayyid Abul A'la Mawdudi who honoured me immensely by reposing his trust in me as one suited for the task of rendering *Tafhim* into English. It is a matter of great sorrow for me that when the first volume of this work is appearing in print, he is no longer in our midst. May Allah reward him with eternal peace.

Likewise, I receive much encouragement from the late Chaudhri Ghulam Muhammad and my life-long friend, Professor Khurshid Ahmad, both of whom urged me to apply myself to a task whose stupendousness made me shrink.[73]

A critical editing of the manuscript (14 volumes) containing

---

[73] Ibid., xxii.

additional features required specialist scrutiny. For example, the editorial expertise of Abdur Raheem Kidwai is acknowledged by Ansari. The following extracts reveal the scholarly contribution of Kidwai in terms of his Qur'ānic output:

> The first volume was published by the Islamic Foundation in 1988. Mention may be made of Abdur Raheem Kidwai who was associated with the institute and was a member of the editorial team of the translation project. The second volume appeared in 1989. In subsequent volumes the scope of Kidwai's collaborative effort was expanded.

Although no attempt is made to give a chronological sequence to Kidwai's contributions to the translation project, the following point merits attention: Kidwai's critical comments on the entire draft of the volumes reaffirm his credential as a renowned scholar of Qur'ānic studies. The multivolume work of *Towards Understanding the Qur'ān* represents a serious study seeking to address global concerns for a broad-based Muslim constituency.[74]

A multivolume like *Towards Understanding the Qur'ān* is a laborious undertaking that attests to the prodigious efforts of Ansari. In a similar vein, his translation of Mawdudi's abridged Urdu version is no mean feat. Ansari elaborates:

> I felt greatly honoured when I was asked to render Sayyid Mawdudi's monumental work *Tafhim al-Qur'ān* into English. Over the years seven volumes of this work have been published by The Islamic Foundation, Leicester, UK under the title *Towards Understanding the Qur'ān*. Some time ago I was asked by my friends at the Foundation to suspend this major work for a while and devote my time and energy instead to complete the

---

[74] Choughley, *The Contributions of Abdur Raheem Kidwai*, 19.

translation of the Qur'ān and the short explanatory notes that Sayyid Mawdudi had written for his abridged, one-volume work on the Qur'ān *Tarjuma-'i Qur'ān-i Majid ma' Mukhtasar Hawāshi* published in 1976. The idea was to make available an English translation of the Qur'ān with short explanatory notes that would meet the needs of the readers of the Qur'ān who are concerned with knowing its essential teachings.[75]

Elsewhere in the volume mention is made about the convergence of Islamic reformist thought. Ansari is among the foremost scholars who have translated the writings of Mawdudi and Shaykh Nadwi. This is important in view of the different scholarly temperaments of these influential figures. *Towards Understanding the Qur'ān,* an abridged version is a singular accomplishment of Ansari. Likewise, he translated. Shaykh Nadwi's *Qadianism* which is a critical study of and a masterpiece on the study of this deviant movement. In the same strain Kidwai has also translated a number of Shaykh Nadwi's major works which have been widely acclaimed among English-speaking readership. This cosmopolitan outlook is in stark contrast to English translators following a rigidly sectarian approach to their narrowly defined Islamic worldview. Thus the proliferation of Islamic writings are now accessible online allowing readers to make an informed choice about scholarly, well- balanced works.

---

[75] This refers to the abridged version of the multivolume *Towards Understanding the Qur'ān.*

Chapter 8

Aligarh Muslim University's Contributions to Qur'ānic Studies

A cursory view of the tafsir tradition may create the impression that barring Sayyid Ahmad Khan's incomplete tafsir, Qur'ānic studies was not given much importance at Aligarh Muslim University (hereafter AMU). However, two factors account for this misperception. First, the entrenched prejudice about the founder's controversial views expressed in his tafsir downplayed the institution's noteworthy contributions to Qur'ānic studies. Second, the overlapping presence of scholars associated with different schools of thought has not given it a distinctive identity. Notwithstanding these issues, AMU continues to enrich Qur'ānic studies by its scholars whose works have made a mark in Urdu and English.

Sayyid Ahmad Khan

Our focus is on Sayyid Ahmad's *Tafsir al-Qur'ān*, an incomplete commentary that has drawn critical responses for a number of reasons. Two earlier works, *Essays on the Life of Muhammad*[1] and *Tabyin al-Bayān*[2] have a historical context and partly reveal his liberal interpretation of the sacred text.

The rise of Orientalism was synonymous with the entrenchment of British rule which effectively supported the missionary efforts in the subcontinent. As a counter response, Sayyid Ahmed produced this work (*Essays on the Life of Muhammad*), which may be considered a pioneering contribution to the *sirah* genre. Likewise, his competence in Hebrew[3] enabled him to access directly the

---

[1] Sayyid Ahmad Khan, *Essays on the Life of Muhammad* (Delhi, 1976).

[2] Khan, *Tabyin al-Kalām i Tafsir al-Tawrāt wa'l Injil* (Aligarh, 2004).

[3] Inayat Rasul Chiryākoti played a pivotal role in Sayyid Ahmad's familiarity with Hebrew and other Islamic disciplines (*'ulum*). See Firoz Ahmad, *Ihsānullah 'Abbāsit: Hayāt awr Kārnāme* (Aligarh, 2019), 19.

scriptural sources of Judaism and Christianity. The comparative study of religions rooted in a colonial milieu reflected the formidable challenges the subcontinental Muslims were faced with. In many ways, Sayyid Ahmad's literary output embodied the gradual emergence of Muslim modernism that was inextricably tied with the future destiny of AMU. The Qur'ān as a divine scripture was subjected to scrutiny which was based on inchoate hermeneutics - a trend that set dangerous precedents for Qur'ānic studies.

The limitation of our study does not allow for an exhaustive critical examination of Sayyid Ahmad's *Tafsir al-Qur'ān.* However, a brief overview of his methodology will acquaint readers about his motivation to offer a rationalist interpretation of eschatology and social reforms. His fifteen principles are a trajectory of his Qur'ānic worldview. These include Sayyid Ahmad's articulation of the God's Word and God's Work discourse. There exists a consonance between revelation and Nature without which the sacred text may be exposed to distortion. In other words, there cannot be a contradiction in or violation of the natural laws. For Sayyid Ahmad, the verses in every surah follow a chronological order; therefore the theory of *naskh* (abrogation of verses), a textual and exegetical reality in classical Islam must be rejected in the study of the Qur'ān. By the same token, linguistic analysis encompasses pre-Islamic literature which is essential to interpret Qur'ānic verses in context.

Conversely, historical narratives derived from Hebrew sources (Isra'ilite tradition) have vitiated the rationale and wisdom of the Qur'ān and are, therefore, an accretion that has no relevance for exegetes.[4]

In his reformulation of the tafsir principles, Sayyid Ahmad shows traces of apologia. Rationality and the overwhelming influence of science are his sources of authority to reinterpret the Qur'ānic eschatology in particular. According to Sayyid Ahmad, the existence of angels has been embellished with supernatural descriptions that defy logical scrutiny. His appraisal is based on

---

[4] See Abdur Raheem Kidwai (editor), *Sir Syed Ahmad Khan, Muslim Renaissance Man of India: A Bicentenary Commemorative Volume* (New Delhi, 2017), 1-24.

classical schools of thought like the Mu'tazilite, linguistic analysis and Hebrew sources. The angels are, in his view, the "potentialities and powers operative in the universe at the bidding of God."[5]

An unconventional interpretation by Sayyid Ahmad is the existence of the jinn species. According to him, the term has been figuratively employed in the Qur'ān for Satan who tempts man or savage people with devious intents.[6] Or it could be 'rhetorical counter arguments' for imaginary beings which the polytheists believed in. This position resonates with Muhammad Asad's analysis of the jinn species.[7]

About the phenomenon of miracles,[8] Sayyid Ahmad dismisses its physical reality as it runs counter to the Qur'ānic rational approach. For example, Moses's rod turning into a snake is essentially a manifestation of his psychic powers. In the same strain, miracles performed by the Prophets (peace be upon them) have an allegorical meaning. It is only the Qur'ān that can justifiably be labelled as a miracle in its literary and rational perspectives.

Overall, the *Tafsir al-Qur'ān* has not really enjoyed any measure of success and has remained out of print for more than a century. Apart from its citation in polemical literature, its terminology and concepts have been a hurdle in assessing its merits.

Blending Tradition with Modernity[9], an apt title by Tauseef Ahmad Parray, who in his analysis of Sayyid Ahmad's multifaceted contributions reveals the latter's rationalism overload. This is exemplified in his Preface to his tafsir in which he develops a cluster of fifteen principles[10] that seemingly belong to the tafsir

---

[5] Ibid., 11-6.

[6] Ibid.,18-20.

[7] *Muhammad Asad, The Message of the Qur'ān (Gibraltar, 1980), 994-5.*

[8] Aziz Ahmad, *Islamic Modernism in India and Pakistan 1857-1964* (Karachi, 1967), 43-5. *Cf.* Hadi Husain, *Syed Ahmed Khan: Pioneer of Muslim Resurgence* (Lahore, 1967), 175-96.

[9] Tauseef Ahmad Parray, "Blending Tradition with Modernity: Sir Sayyid's Stance on Legal and Scientific Issues at the Aligarh Muslim University", in Juhi Gupta and Abdur Raheem Kidwai (editors), *Oxford of the East: Aligarh Muslim University 1920-2020, Centenary Commemorative Volume* (New Delhi, 2020), 226-57.

[10] For the gist of Sayyid Ahmad's fifteen principles, see "Muhammad Daud Rahbar, Sir Sayyid Ahmad Khan's Principles of Exegesis. Translated from his Tafsir Usul al-

genre. However, Kidwai has countered this assumption by pointing out to Sayyid Ahmad's flawed interpretation which "carry a refrain-like reference to his 'personal belief', 'reason', 'laws of nature' and his belaboured attempt at reconciliation between the Word of God and Work of God."[11]

Sayyid Ahmad had a restive personality that breached the boundaries of the traditional interpretation of the sacred text. Therefore, it was not surprising when he superimposed 'his own dogmatic presuppositions on the Qur'ānic text'[12] in clear disregard to its unambiguous message of being a Book of guidance. A binary term, tradition and modernity was a veneer to conceal his disdain for the mainstream understanding of the Qur'ānic text. Likewise, his unconventional views were fundamentally a garbled version of undermining the authenticity of hadith literature, and presenting his Mu'tazilite mindset in the light of scientific advancement. Clearly this approach set him on a collision course with the 'ulama who firmly rejected his conjectural tafsir. In contrast, his tafsir was warmly received by the Muslim modernists, a fringe outfit who have not made any substantive contribution to the tafsir tradition.[13]

The *tahrif* (interpolation) element was accentuated in the latter part of the nineteenth century. Colonialism and its counterpart Orientalism, in the main, were contributing factors to undermine the divine origin of the Qur'ān. Muslim modernists were frontline activists who attempted to divest the unambiguous meanings of particular verses for their liberal-leaning interests. The twenty-first century, too, has witnessed a rebranded form of *tahrif.* The universal symbolism of key themes in the Qur'ān is explored in the backdrop of mystical teachings. Jalaluddin Rumi (d. 1273)[14] represents the archetype of the Perfect Man (*Insān i-Kāmil*) whose *Mathnawi* is regarded as the Qur'ān in Persian. For many avid

---

Tafsir: The Thirteenth Principle", in *The Muslim World*, October 1956.

[11] Kidwai, *Oxford of the East*, 132.

[12] Ibid., 133.

[13] Among the notable Muslim modernists was Charāgh Ali, whose apologetic views on eschatology resonates in his writings. See Aziz Ahmad, *Islamic Modernism*, 48, 57-64.

[14] See Afzal Iqbal, *Life and Work of Rumi* (Lahore, 1976).

readers of Rumi's inspirational works, this multivolume is believed to be quintessentially Qur'ānic with a distinct worldview.[15] Therefore, its appeal is global and cuts across faith communities as is evident in the translation projects by Western translators. Curiously enough, inherent in this particular approach is the jettisoning of the corpus of the tafsir tradition. Key Qur'ānic terms are now under the anvil of arbitrary interpretation. Worse is the dubious attribution of the 'enlightened' Qur'ānic meanings and wisdom to Rumi. Needless to add, the plethora of works produced largely by Western writers are the distorted versions or Rumi's *Ahl al-Sunnah* presentation. This alarming trend is also discernible among segments of Muslim readers whose penchant for Rumi's works is, in reality, a veneer to be detached from the Qur'ānic authenticity paradigm.[16]

'Abdul Haqq Haqqāni

Two contemporaneous tafsirs with different ideological temperaments have brought into sharp light the trends of Islamic reformist thought during the nineteenth century. *Tafsir i-Haqqāni* by Muhammad 'Abdul Haqq (d. 1917) stood out for its firm adherence to the *Ahl al-Sunnah* creedal beliefs against the background of the rising modernism represented by Sayyid Ahmad Khan. Colonialism contributed to the steady growth of Islamic reformist thought that firmly challenged the entrenched beliefs of Islamic eschatology. *Tafsir i-Haqqāni* was a pioneering work that critiqued the emerging patterns of modernism spearheaded by Sayyid Ahmad and other rationalists who advocated a non-traditional interpretation of the sacred text. His *Tafsir i-*

---

[15] *Ma'ārif-e-Mathnawi* by Hakim Muhammad Akhtar (d. 2013), is a spiritually rejuvenating commentary of this immortal piece of work. The spiritual lineage of this illustrious Pakistani *sufi* can be traced back to Hāji Muhajir Makki (d. 1899), who, too, wrote a celebrated commentary on the *Mathnawi* in Persian.

[16] See Rozina Ali, "The Erasure of Islam from the Poetry of Rumi", in *The New Yorker*. January 05, 2017. Oddly enough, the works of Rumi have been morphed into American verse by interpreters, not translators. Thus the spiritual colonialism in the West is glaringly evident.

Ahmadi is representative of this mindset.

For our study purpose, three distinguishing aspects of Haqqāni's Introduction (*muqaddimah*) inform our understanding of issues that he considered to be challenges of his social milieu in the beginning of the nineteenth century. The rise of rationalist thought had important ramifications on the Qur'ān's timeless message. For Haqqāni, the symbiosis of 'aql (reason) and *naql* (tradition) is embedded in the Qur'ānic text. Therefore, it would be a travesty of justice to insinuate that there exists no balance between these two concepts. A more telling example is the Qur'ānic worldview about the creation of the universe and its life-enriching lessons for mankind. Likewise, Haqqāni draws the readers' attention to the everyday phenomena that are indisputable indicators of the 'aql-naql discourse. No doubt, the Qur'ānic framework reinforces the trajectory of harmony – material and spiritual virtues – that enables man to view life in a qualitative sense rather than a hedonistic perspective. Therefore, any attempts to disconnect the 'aql-naql framework will yield grave consequences. Haqqāni's trenchant criticism of Sayyid Ahmad's views rests on two foundational principles: supernatural occurrence *(khāriq i-'ādat)* is the prerogative of Divine Providence. His wisdom is immeasurable and is not fixed in tempo-spatial dimensions. Similarly, Sayyid Ahmad's presentation of miracles is illogical from a Qur'ānic viewpoint. A rational interpretation invariably brings out layers of skepticism, which is a corollary of Hellenistic thought.

Belonging to narratives of the Prophets, Haqqāni highlights previous nations like the Thamud who asked for a miracle from the Prophet Salih as proof of his noble mission. In this connection, he makes copious references to the mystical works of Muhiyuddin Ibn 'Arabi (d. 1240) in response to Sayyid Ahmad's fallacious views about the reality of miracles. Moreover, Haqqāni's philosophical approach is a counter response to the rising tide of rationalism among the Muslim intellectuals of his time.

The phenomenon of revelation (*wahy*) is critically examined by Haqqāni. His presentation of (*wahy*) and *ilhām* (inspiration) sets the tone for his response to critics like the Christian missionaries in the subcontinent whose avowed aim was to undermine the authenticity of the Qur'ān. Haqqāni successfully marshals an armory of well-developed arguments to repudiate the distorted claims advanced by the Christian priests. In a similar vein, he rejects the theory of the distorted Qur'ān (*tahrif*) which forms part of Shi'ite beliefs and doctrines. By quoting authoritative sources on Shi'ah scholars, he disproves the spurious claims made by Christian missionaries in their sinister campaign to discredit the divine nature of the sacred text. More importantly, Haqqāni brings out the discrepancies of Biblical texts from a historical angle to press home the point that the Qur'ān is the only revealed text free from corruption and manipulation.[17]

Haqqāni is among the foremost scholars who have made an analytical study of the Old and New Testaments. His conclusions are revealing. These previous Scriptures were tampered, thus making it more problematic to verify their respective authenticity. His timeless approach bears out his remarkable scholarship in comparative religions. The ambiguities of faith pertaining to Christianity are hollowed out in the backdrop of the distorted interpretation by the clergy.

In contrast, the Qur'ān in its imitable and unique style provides an authentic and original account of doctrines, historical events, etc. as a corrective to the perceived beliefs around the Scriptures. Another noteworthy point in his analysis of the Biblical sources is the hadith tradition. His standpoint is succinctly summed up in the Holy Prophet's cautionary approach to these Scriptures in general.[18]

Tafsir i-Haqqāni has become a standard reference work for subcontinental exegetes. The reliance on issues originating from the nineteenth century reflects its established popularity. Keeping in mind that the tafsir was written more than a century

---

[17] This is a summative assessment of Haqqāni's comprehensive Introduction (*muqaddimah*) of *Tafsir i- Haqqāni*.

[18] Muhammad Shebaz Hasan, "Mawlana 'Abdul Haq Haqqāni and the Distorted Torah: An Analytical Study", in *The Scholar* (July- September 2015), 54-69.

ago, it continues to enjoy a reputable status among exegetical works.

Nazir Ahmad Dehlawi

The multifaceted career of Deputy Nazir Ahmad Dehlawi (d. 1912) offers interesting insights about the changing socioeconomic realities facing class and gender relations, particularly among the elite Muslim communities in the nineteenth century.

Dehlawi's literary contributions, a trilogy of novels[19] have a reformist fervour set in a milieu of colonial modernism. These novels created public space for Muslim women who were screened off from education that was male-oriented. Furthermore, the decadent Nawabi culture,[20] in the throes of moral decline after the 1857 struggle offered no respite for Muslim women belonging to the *Ashrāf* culture to embrace changes that reflected the emerging progressive trends affecting communities and other faiths. Viewed from the prism of colonial modernity, the didactic content of Dehlawi's literary works was a bold attempt to reconfigure education[21] for Muslim women within an *islāhi* framework.

Interestingly, Dehlawi's academic credentials encompass a binary: orthodoxy in critical conversation with modernity. His Arabic studies in Delhi College under Mawlana Mamluk 'Ali[22] pointed out to the various strands of reformist activities that would play out in the form of Dar al-'Ulum Deoband under Mawlana Muhammad Qāsim Nanautwi (d. 1880) and the Aligarh Muslim University headed by Sayyid Ahmad.

Dehlawi held key posts in British colonial India that enhanced

---

[19] For a critical analysis of Dehlawi's literary works, see Gull i-Hina and Tahir Mahmood, "Muslim Identity in late Nineteenth Century India: The Constructs of Class and Gender in Nazir Ahmed's Novels", in *Pakistan Historical Society* (July-December 2018), vol. lxvi, 120-38.

[20] Ibid. 125.

[21] Ibid.

[22] On Mamluk Ali's Arabic contributions, see Muhammad Anwar al-Hasan Sherkoti, *Anwār i-Qāsimi* (Karachi, 2014), 133-47.

his career as a literary critic, educationist and administrator. His proficiency in English advanced his popularity in the British establishment in respect of the penal law works, which he translated into Urdu.[23]

Dehlawi's literary writings broadened the scope of Islamic morality as a didactic construct. In other words, his trilogy was not embedded in Western theories of literature; however it had identifiable traits of progressive trends that were partly influenced by Sayyid Ahmad's modernisation project.[24]

In the field of Qur'ānic studies Dehlawi's translation provides a brief autobiographical account about his journey to explore the contours of the sacred text. Alongside his literary writings, his deep interest in the Qur'ān which he memorised at the age of fifty guided his worldview of Islamic reform. It was, therefore, no fortuitous circumstances that his leap of faith was a unifying factor that prompted him to undertake the mammoth task of translating the Qur'ān into Urdu.[25] *Tarjuma i-Qur'ān* was a collaborative effort by Dehlawi and 'Abdur Rahman Muhammad that attempted an almost idiomatic translation accompanied by a glossary and index.[26] The review process of translation was an arduous task that involved verification by prominent exegetes like Fateh Muhammad Jāllandhari.[27] In any case, the final product of the translation project according to Dehlawi was an authoritative representation of the sacred text.

Like many of the translations produced in the nineteenth century, *Mudih al-Qur'ān* served as a template for a mainstream interpretation of the Qur'ān. Its iconic status has survived the vagaries of dramatic changes taking place in the subcontinent. However, its idiomatic expression couched in literary style

---

[23] Nazeer Ahmad Ab. Majeed, *Qur'ān Interpretation in Urdu: A Critical Study* (New Delhi, 2019), 28-30.

[24] Hina and Mahmood, *Muslim Identity in Late Nineteenth Century India*, 124.

[25] Majeed, *Qur'ān Interpretation in Urdu*, 32-3.

[26] Metcalf, *Islamic Revival in British India: Deoband, 1860-1900* (Karachi, 1982), 203.

[27] *Qur'ān Kareem: Urdu Tarjuma* (Lahore, 2000). In recent years the phenomenon of combining Urdu/English translations is motivated by monetary considerations. See Fateh Muhammad Jāllandhari (Urdu) and Muhammad Marmaduke Pickthall (English).

became cliched, in fact, archaic. Dehlawi's response to this shortcoming was essentially a collective voice by nineteenth century exegetes to embark on a new translation. After a lapse of a century the *Tarjuma i-Qur'ān* appeared centre stage for its stylistic approach that reflected a strong cosmopolitan literary outlook. However, its colloquial language was deemed by many critics as irreverent to the spirit of the sacred text.[28] Nevertheless, its popularity grew out of print capitalism that saw multiple editions of this important translation. By 1892 its first edition was hailed as the 'perfect example of Urdu literary writings, coherent sentence construction and clarity of expression.' Subsequent editions, however, did not leverage its important place amid other comprehensive tafsirs that continue to have an influential presence among mainstream constituencies.[29] The *Bayān al-Qur'ān* (Thānawi) and *Kanz al-Imān* (Ahmad Raza Khan) are illustrative of the fundamental shift to sectarian-oriented tafsirs.

Viewed from a different angle, the reformist thought of Dehlawi countered the intrusive presence of Westernisation fervently advocated by Sayyid Ahmad. Regardless of their shared vision of Muslim reform, ideological differences converged on a central point: fidelity to Islamic faith and practice. Dehlawi "propagated conservative social practices, most notably in his novel *Ibn al-Waqt* (The Opportunist), where he mocked those who aped British dress and manners. Ironically, his notion of progress hinged on societal reform that was frowned upon by his critic like Thānawi whose *Bihisti Zewar* (Heavenly Ornaments) was an attempt to bring the shari'ah, its doctrines and laws within reach of common man's intelligence."[30] His incisive critique of Dehlawi's translation is based largely on semantic issues which do not detract from the merit of this important translation.

A critical reappraisal of *Tarjuma i-Qur'ān* brings out a few blemishes about the brief notes in this important tafsir. *Fiqh* discussion does not feature at all particularly for verses that require elaboration or clarification. A balanced approach, in the

---

[28] Metcalf, *Islamic Revival in British India*, 333.
[29] Majeed, *Qur'ān Interpretation in Urdu*, 34.
[30] Metcalf, *Islamic Revival in British India*, 332.

least, should provide an overview of the exegete's understanding of the *ahkām* (legal injunctions). Juristic rulings need to be separated from the legal significance of relevant verses in the Qur'ān.

Another blemish is the embellished and historical accounts that militate against the spirit of the Qur'ānic message. Dehlawi incorporates unauthentic material in respect of Prophet Yusuf's royal position that compromises his integrity.[31] Ambiguity and the uncritical evaluation of source material definitely impugns the universal message of the historical accounts in the Qur'ān. Nevertheless, the work is an important contribution to Qur'ānic studies.

Ihsānullah 'Abbāsi

The network of Islamic tradition and modernity assumed important dimensions at AMU in the early twentieth century. The prestigious institution attracted a cadre of scholars and intellectuals who made singular contributions to the reformist thought of Sayyid Ahmad Khan. Among them was Ihsānullah 'Abbāsi (d. 1928) who rose to prominence for his literary works, including his Urdu translation of the Qur'ān.

'Abbāsi's academic career straddled three places and personalities who moulded his reformist orientation. At Chiryākot his association with Mawlana Fāruq inducted him to the study of Qur'ān and Arabic. It was Mawlana Ināyat Rasul, the famous polymath who developed 'Abbās's competence in the *Dars i-Nizāmi* at Ghazipur where Sayyid Ahmad held the position of sub judge for the British government. There is no doubt that Sayyid Ahmad owed a large measure of debt to Ināyat Rasul for his proficiency in Hebrew and other secular sciences. His *Khutbāt* bears distinctive traces of Ināyat Rasul's vast knowledge of the Islamic sciences (*'ulum*).[32] It was at AMU, however, that 'Abbāsi nurtured his academic potential. Also through Ināyat Rasul's

---

[31] Majeed, *Qur'ān Interpretation in Urdu*, 36.
[32] Firoz Ahmad, *Ihsānullah 'Abbāsi*, 18-9.

recommendation he was admitted to Madrasat al-'Ulum,[33] a nascent institution established by Sayyid Ahmad that was to grow into a fully-fledged university in 1920. For 'Abbāsi, the congenial environment opened up vistas of both Islamic and secular knowledge, a synthesis that had been relegated to the margins in other Islamic institutions due to a number of political factors. It was at AMU that brought 'Abbāsi into close contact with Sayyid Ahmad's reformist vision at educational and social levels. Not surprisingly, therefore, he became an ardent advocate of the latter's reformist policies that evoked admiration as well as condemnation from the Muslim community.

'Abbāsi pursued law, a family profession and settled in Gorakhpur. His cosmopolitan outlook is discernible in his array of writings during this period. As a novelist his writings resonated with social themes that were considered taboo among Muslim aristocracy. According to Sayyid Ahmad social vices were largely responsible for Muslim backwardness and their antipathy to embrace modern education. Nazir Ahmad Dehlawi, a social reformer and exegete, too, made trenchant criticism against the deteriorating Muslim society in Northern India on account of their entrenched social habits. For example, 'Abbasi took the bold step to marry his widowed cousin as his second wife that effectively challenged the social norms of his aristocratic (ashrāf) community.[34]

There are three works related to his religious contributions. Essentially, the *Dars i-Nizami* did not sufficiently prepare graduates like him to grow into an intellectual environment. In effect, it impacted negatively on the creative ability of aspirant scholars. For a better appreciation of 'Abbāsi 's literary acumen, two Urdu books have complementary importance. The *History of Islam* has a broad sweep and covers historical events beginning from the Prophet's biography to Muslim sultanates and Muslim heroes. It is a comprehensive account of the rise and fall of the Muslim world. 'Abbāsi's copious references in this work reaffirm his credentials

---

[33] See Khaliq Ahmad Nizami, *History of the Aligarh Muslim University* (Delhi, 1995), 1-12.

[34] Ahmad, *Ihsānullah 'Abbāsi*, 19.

as a brilliant scholar and a historian. In fact, it received critical acclaim from scholars like Syed Amir Ali who is well known for his widely acclaimed book *The Spirit of Islam.* During his lifetime, *The History of Islam* was prescribed as a textbook in schools and universities.[35]

Another important work Islam has a reformist strain. Like Sayyid Ahmad Khan's reconstruction of society discourse, 'Abbāsi highlighted the ebb and flow of Muslim collective life. The motivation for this work, *Islam* is reflected in his Introduction to his Qur'ān translation. Two issues come to the fore. First, the Muslim decline is based on their inferiority complex. On account of their indifference to Islam as a way of life they have failed to project the universality of the Qur'ānic teachings.[36] For' Abbasi, Islamic teachings are value-added and wisdom-oriented. To this end, he elucidates the Qur'ānic presentation of *ahkām* (legal injunctions) and critiques social vices that are commonplace in Western society. Second, 'Abbāsi makes a pertinent remark about modern philosophy. Like Greek sciences that were refuted during the 'Abbasid era, this period (early 20th century) was exposed to the pervasive influence of modern philosophy in all its manifestations. Therefore, a counter challenge was essential to prove the uniqueness of Islam against the rising tide of materialism. According to 'Abbāsi, Islam possesses its own philosophical system encoded in moral ethics that is justifiably suited to mankind's temperament and needs.[37]

In the light of the above comments, the relevance of his Qur'ān translation in Urdu becomes clearer. In 'Abbāsi's view, the translation should steer away from a literal interpretation so that readers may actively participate in its glorious message.[38] His translation has a target audience and therefore offers a simple, direct and graceful style. Notwithstanding 'Abbāsi's unassuming approach, the translation contains linguistic charm and presses

---

[35] Ibid., xiv.

[36] Ibid., 52-3.

[37] Ibid., 61.

[38] Ibid., 45.

home the point that the Qur'ān is a marvel whose layers of meaning have unfolded over the centuries.

Distinctive features of *Tarjuma Qur'ān i-Majid.*

Falahi has delineated the distinctive features of the translation which establishes its importance in the early twentieth century. Unlike other existing Urdu translations, this work aims to offer a holistic interpretation of the sacred text. Keeping in mind the 'maturing of Urdu', the need for a reader-friendly text cannot be over-emphasised. By way of comparison, 'Abbāsi's translation enjoys distinction over Nazir Ahmad's on the following counts: the sentences are fluent without using brackets. Furthermore, the origins of surahs - Makkah or Madinah - are clearly marked out in brackets and key themes are briefly mentioned in the *ruku's* (units employed to facilitate the reading of the text).

In respect of the notes (*hawāshi*) 'Abbāsi offers a broader definition of the *nuzul* so that readers may grasp its essential teachings. It is a truism that these notes have an operative value: historical and legal issues are dispassionately discussed in order to avoid giving them a sectarian character. For this purpose 'Abbāsi's makes copious reference to his *History of Islam* to support his viewpoints.

A merit-worthy aspect of the translation is 'Abbāsi's attitude to other translations. In the spirit of scholarly camaraderie, 'Abbāsi acknowledges the merits of differing interpretations to illustrate the ethics of disagreement (*ikhtilāf*). Likewise, he avoids the trodden path of the Isra'ilite narratives by citing authoritative works. He offers a range of insights into issues relating to social relations, interpersonal communication, etc. An independent researcher and exegete, 'Abbāsi does not represent the controversial views of Sayyid Ahmad in his tafsir. By contrast, he steadfastly upholds the *Ahl al-Sunnah* viewpoint - a positive trait about his scholarly profile.

In sum, 'Abbāsi 's multifaceted contributions to Qur'ānic studies are pioneering efforts to make accessible the timeless message of the sacred text for Muslims seeking to develop a meaningful relationship with God's Word.[39]

After a lapse of a hundred years, interest in 'Abbāsi's tafsir has brought together a collection of articles for the purpose of evaluating his meticulous study of the sacred text.[40] The varied aspects of his translation brings to the fore the strands of his reformist thought. A leading alumnus of AMU, 'Abbāsi was not overawed by Sayyid Ahmad's radical interpretation of core issues in the Qur'ān on which *ijmā'* (consensus) exists.

A noteworthy point to consider are the cross-cultural currents of modernity that swept across the subcontinent. 'Abbāsi too was not immune to these overwhelming influences. The deepening challenges of fidelity to the divine text, however, are not evident in his tafsir. Ayub Akram has attempted to provide a synoptic account of the tafsir based on the Preface of the translation. While acknowledging the positive traits or merits of the work, Akram highlights the problematic areas of semantic relevance. 'Abbāsi 's presentation about the phenomenon of *wahy* in certain instances poses a conundrum on account of his diction. Keeping in mind 'Abbāsi s legal and literary background, the fluency of expression might have not adequately conveyed the intent contained in the verses under discussion.[41] At the same time the blemishes that Akram identifies in the text should in no way be construed as arbitrary interpretations. In fact, 'Abbāsi has consistently projected the mainstream line of thought in the backdrop of the intellectual ferment that shaped the contours of the emergent tafsirs. By the same token, the beginning of the twentieth century was on the cusp of reformist thought in many parts of the Muslim world. Therefore, 'Abbāsi 's lapses (*nuqā'is*) are not to be conflated with a rupture of Islamic authenticity. In the subcontinental context, it is a euphemism for Sayyid Ahmad's errant readings of eschatology.[42] 'Abbasi's praiseworthy work did not receive wide

---

[39] Adapted from Falahi, *Hind-wa-Pāk Fuzalā ki Qur'āni Khidmāt* (Aligarh, 2020), 33-42.

[40] Gowhar Quadir Wani and Faiza 'Abbāsi (editors), *'Allāmah Ihsānullah 'Abbāsi ki Qur'āni Fehmi* (Aligarh, 2020).

[41] Ibid., 84-6.

[42] Ibid.

publicity on account of its perceived rationalist tendency which he supposedly inherited from his association with Sayyid Ahmad. Sadly, sectarian prejudice, an ingrained trait of a coterie of 'ulama did not allow a scholarly analysis of his tafsir, thus relegating it to the margins.[43] In recent years this unfortunate trend has been reversed owing to Farhat Ali and Faiza 'Abbāsi's sterling efforts to restore the prestige of this important tafsir.

Muhammad Aslam Jayrajpuri

In the field of Qur'ānic studies Muhammad Aslam Jayrajpuri (d. 1955) has produced a credit-worthy work. His association with AMU also saw the productive phase of his Qur'ānic acumen. A celebrated work like *Tārikh al-Qur'ān* is a historical account of the varied facets of the sacred text. In this work, Jayrajpuri gives preference to the intra- Qur'ānic approach in support of his arguments rather than the traditional extra- Qur'ānic evidence.

Gowhar Wani has provided a synoptic overview of Jayrajpuri's *Nikāt-e-Qur'ān* in these words:

> *Nikāt-e-Qur'ān*, another book by Jayrajpuri, comprises an account of different key- points (*nikāt*) related to the 114 chapters of the Qur'ān. These Qur'ānic points have been formulated into 379 questions and with their answers which bring to the fore different aspects of the Qur'ānic. Instead of borrowing from the early commentaries of the Qur'ān, Jayrajpuri has attempted to draw on the Qur'ānic text as much as possible. The Qur'ānic verses included in this book have been translated into Urdu by Jayrajpuri himself. However, he has acknowledged that in the translation of some Qur'ānic words, he has relied on Shah Abdul Qadir's translation of the Qur'ān (*Mudih al-Qur'ān*).[44]

---

[43] Ibid., 183.

[44] Gowhar Quadir Wani, "Contributions of Jayrajpuri, Akbarabadi and Amini to the

Fazlur Rahmān Gannori

An eminent scholar, Fazlur Rahman Gannori (d. 2013) carved out a niche for himself in Qur'ānic studies. His scholarly expertise encompassed classical and contemporary writings both of which received critical acclaim. In the domain of the critical examination of established classical tafsirs, his review of *Kashshāf* by Zamakhshari is an appreciable contribution. His analysis of the social milieu in which the tafsir was written is a snapshot of the upsurge of Islamic intellectual thought. Mu'tazilite discourse was on the ascendency and created a climate for polemical writings. Additionally, *Kashshāf's* approach to the phenomenon of miracles (*mu'jizāt*) on rational grounds was later taken up by liberal thinkers like Sayyid Ahmad. These issues gave shape to the intellectual trends in the tafsir tradition.[45]

Muhammad Abdul Haq Ansari

Not an 'alim in the formal sense but a Qur'ānic scholar who exemplified academic excellence through his several writings, Abdul Haq Ansari (d. 2012) embodied the knowledge-in-action (*'ilm*) ideal. His pursuit of Islamic authenticity spurred him to study a course in Arabic under Amin Akhtar Islāhi. Ansari mastered the language which enabled him to write works of exemplary standards. His *Learning the Language of the Holy Qur'ān* (1997) is an original, creative approach to connect with the Qur'ān at linguistic and literary levels. For Ansari, familiarity, consolidation and application are core themes that build a living relationship with the sacred text.[46]

Ansari developed deep reverence for the overarching message of the Qur'ān which he sought to disseminate for modern readership. To this end, his annotated translation of Ibn

---

Qur'ānic and Islamic Studies: An Overview", in *Aligarh Journal of Qur'ānic Studies.* Vol. 3, Issue 2 (October 2020), 112.

[45] Abu Sufyan Islāhi, *Idārah Sir Sayyid Muslim University Aligarh ke Mashāhir Qur'āniyāt* (Aligarh, 2017), 103.

[46] Ibid., 108.

Taimiyyah's *Principles of Qur'ānic Tafsir*[47] is couched in chaste, simple English that cuts through technicalities. It is a forceful presentation of the varied aspects that inform a proper, meaningful understanding of the sacred text.

As Amir of the Jama'at i-Islami, Ansari worked tirelessly to articulate the synthesis between the outer and inner dimensions of Islam. His *Sufism and Shari'ah*[48] is a groundbreaking work that examines the authentic relationship between the shari'ah and *tasawwuf* dimensions of Islam. Interestingly, his choice of Shaykh Ahmad Sirhindi (also known as Mujaddid) reveals his deep insight into the evolution of the Naqshabandi order in the subcontinent. Moreover, his objective analysis of the Mujaddid's letters (*Maktubāt*) positions this work in a sociopolitical context.

Muhammad Nejatullah Siddiqi

A world authority on Islamic economics, Nejatullah Siddiqui (b. 1931) has developed structured models of interest-free banking systems. His writings in this field reflect his mastery over Western and Islamic disciplines, making him the 'Muslim voice' against an economy dominated by capitalism.

Siddiqui was closely associated with Madrasat al-Islāh which prided itself in the exemplary study of Arabic and Qur'ānic methodology. In this respect, Farahi, Amin Ahsan Islāhi and Akhtar Ahmad Islāhi are considered to be the forerunners of the progressive trends in Qur'ānic thought. At the heart of Siddiqi's presentation of his Qur'ān work is relevance and reverence. These two attributes reconnect the serious readers to the timeless truth and wisdom of the Qur'ān. A starting point, according to Siddiqi, is an emotional and spiritual dialogue - a reverential posture that elevates readers to fathom the Qur'ānic themes for a clearer understanding of Allah's revelation. More importantly, a recommitment to its teachings should be a personal testament

---

[47] Abdul Haq Ansari, *An Introduction to the Exegesis of the Qur'ān* (Riyadh, 1989).

[48] Abdul Haq Ansari, *Sufism and Shari'ah: A Study of Shaykh Ahmad Sirhindi's Effort to Reform Sufism* (Leicester, 1985).

of one's faith to lead a purposeful life.[49]

Zafar al-Islam Islāhi

A distinguished historian of medieval Islamic history, Zafar al-Islam (b. 1950) is a graduate of Madrasat al-Islāh. His doctoral dissertation is a reappraisal of Muslim contribution in the subcontinent. His collaborative efforts in the compilation of articles gleaned from the journal *'Ulum al-Qur'ān* is a treasure trove of information for researchers in Qur'ānic studies.[50] In a similar vein, his multifaceted writings on Qur'ānic topics have broadened the scope of the tafsir tradition.

Zafar al-Islam has been committed to disseminating the teachings of the Qur'ān and, therefore, offered home-based lessons (*durus*) on the sacred text. He avoids an academic approach and instead focuses on the Qur'ān in the perspective of *da'wah*.[51] The following extract from his slim volume *Qur'ān and Service to Mankind* is illustrative of his deep attachment to the spirit of the Qur'ān.

> The evidence of the Qur'ān being the greatest and most precious gift of Allah is that its revelation is reflective of the phenomenon of Allah's attributes of kindness and graciousness, as it is evident from these verses: "[This is] a revelation from the Entirely Merciful, the Especially Merciful" (Haa. Mim al-Sajdah: 41/2). "[This is] a revelation of the Exalted in Might, the Merciful" (Ya Sin: 36/5) "The Most Merciful taught the Qur'ān" (Al-Rahmān: 55/1-2). The mention of Allah's attributes of 'graciousness'

---

[49] Siddiqi's major works on the Islamic banking system have been written in English. For example, *Dialogue in Islamic Economics* brings to the fore his vast knowledge and expertise to this sector of economics.

[50] Islāhi, *Idārah Sir Syed*, 123.

[51] Ibid., 154-6.

and 'kindness' in these verses in the context of the revelation of this Holy Book is very significant. The purpose of it is to instill into the minds of human beings that the sender of this book is Most Merciful and Most Gracious to humanity and that the revelation of this book is a result of His limitless kindness. So, humanity can benefit from His special benevolence. And it is apparent that man will deserve this kindness only when he believes in Allah honestly and sincerely, accepts His message of kindness and follows His Commands in everyday life.[52]

Masood Ahmad

Holistic knowledge based on the *iqrā* model is a distinctive characteristic of the Aligarh school of thought. Masood Ahmad is a biochemist by profession whose attachment to Qur'ānic studies has seen the publication of his thought-provoking works in Urdu and English. In the description of his profound inspiration from the Qur'ān the following comments appear:

> It is beyond the comprehension of the common people as to how this Divine Book is so powerful in its appeal. It is in this context that the author realised the need for the crucial task of elaborating the ways and means of Qur'ānic understanding. Moreover, the author's endeavour herein was to emphasise that Al-Qur'ān's unique style, contents, meanings, messages and guidance have made it the most appealing and revolutionary book of all time. Amazingly, it not only provides a soothing effect on the human mind, soul and spirit, but also makes its followers very dynamic and ambitious

---

[52] Zafarul Islam Islāhi, *Qur'ān and Service to Mankind* (Aligarh, 2019), 14.

to carry out the humanistic tasks of diverse nature. Various ways of enhancing the ability of understanding the noble Qur'ān and approaching it correctly have been dealt with by the author in detail for the reader to appreciate the underlying beauties of this living miracle.[53]

Ahmad's books are an epitome of the universal guidance offered by the Qur'ān. He draws upon his scientific background to elucidate the Qur'ānic account of the ants in relation to the Prophet Sulayman's military organisation. Additionally, his forceful presentation of the Finality of Prophethood is a rejoinder to the misguided doctrines of Qadianism. In the true spirit of reverence Ahmad has explored the Qur'ānic themes that are relatable to contemporary society.

Ubaidullah Fahad Falahi

An amalgam of three strands of reformist thought Farahi, Ikhwan al-Muslimin and Jama'at i-Islami, Ubaidullah Fahad Falahi (b.1960) has made his mark in Qur'ānic studies. His critical examination of the *nazm* theory as well as the aesthetic representations in the Qur'ān text has introduced new insights to the field of tafsir. The range of his literary output is impressive, judging by his translation of works of contemporary Arab scholars who have advocated an interpretive reading of the sacred text.[54] Amid the plethora of writings dealing with the science discourse, Falahi's collection of articles and essays in *Culture, Science and Violence* explores the Qur'ān's presentation of the relationship between science and the sacred text.[55] In the same vein, the phenomenon of terrorism is critically examined in the light of

---

[53] Masood Ahmad, *Inspirations from the Qur'ān* (Bellsville, 2012).

[54] Islāhi, *Idārah Sir Syed*, 182-3. Taha Jabir Alwani wrote prolifically on *fiqhi* issues in the backdrop of Muslims living as minorities in the West. He was associated with the International Institute of Islamic Thought (IIIT) in US.

[55] Cf. Ubaidullah Fahad, *Diversity, Dissent and Dialogue: Some Selected Readings* (New Delhi, 2012).

the Qur'ānic formulation of *jihād*. Islāhi has made a perceptive comment about the intrinsic merits of this book for English-speaking readership that faces formidable challenges to access sources directly from the Qur'ān and hadith literature.[56]

Two contributors to the multivolume tafsir series deserve honourable mention in this article.

Abu Sufyan Islāhi (b. 1960) is an outstanding scholar of Qur'ānic studies. His academic career from Madrasat al- Islah to AMU bears out his remarkable scholarship. Arabic literature is his area of specialisation and his versatility in this field is exemplified by his impressive contributions to the tafsir genre. Reflections and research are rigorously undertaken by him to delineate the terrain of Qur'ānic thought.[57]

Muhammad Tariq Ayubi (b.1981) is a distinguished writer, literary critic and social activist. His contributions to the life and legacy of Abul Hasan Ali Nadwi are framed from the reformist discourse, particularly the future prospects of the Indian Muslims amid the hostile policies of the Indian government. In a spirit of promoting meaningful ideologue among the various faiths, Ayubi examines the theme of tolerance and peaceful co-existence in the Qur'ānic perspective. Kidwai's insightful foreword brings out Ayubi's competence in Qur'ānic studies.

> It is common knowledge that *Al-Rahmān* (Most Compassionate) and *Al-Raheem* (Most Merciful) are the most recurrent names of Allah in the Holy Qur'ān. Both of these underscore His boundless love, affection and kindness for mankind. Muslims are expected to emulate the same divine attributes. The learned author has done a laudable job in pressing home the tolerant policy and practice of the Muslim rulers in the context of the medieval Indian history. While reading his account, readers will realise how maliciously the

---

[56] Islāhi, *Idārah Sir Syed*, 183.
[57] Ibid., 177-8.

history of the Muslim rule over India has been distorted in order to demonise the Muslim rulers. Equally important is Dr Ayubi's profoundly insightful exhortation to Indian Muslims to act with restraint and tact in today's emotionally surcharged atmosphere. His advice for developing and deepening human communication with adherents of other faiths is highly welcome.

One of the main objectives of the Centre for Qur'ānic Studies, Aligarh Muslim University is to produce such books which relate the life- giving message of the Qur'ān to our times. The book under study admirably serves this noble aim.[58]

Abdur Raheem Kidwai

A brilliant scholar of Qur'ānic studies, Abdur Raheem Kidwai's (b. 1956) prolific writings spanning over thirty years have covered fields as diverse as Literary Orientalism, education and Qur'ānic studies. His academic credentials and familial tradition have immensely enriched the current trends of Islamic scholarship.

In relation to Qur'ānic studies Kidwai holds the distinction of writing reviews as early as 1985 for prestigious journals dedicated to advancing the cause of Islamic scholarship. His association with the Islamic Foundation (Leicester) may be better appreciated with reference to his contributions to Qur'ānic studies on three levels: (i) a cluster of books dealing with Qur'ānic teachings and wisdom (ii) translation of notes for Mawlana Mawdudi's *Tafhim al-Qur'ān* (*Towards Understanding the Qur'ān*), and (iii) reviews on English translations/commentaries of the Qur'ān dating as early as 1649.

The number of publications devoted to Islamic studies extends the scope of Kidwai's scholarly profile. In fact, the range of articles, reviews and chapters underscores his versatility in the rich field of Islam and the Qur'ān. Kidwai has added new

---

[58] Muhammad Tariq Ayubi Nadwi, *The Qur'ānic Guidance on Tolerance and Peaceful Co-Existence* (Aligarh, 2019), 6.

dimensions by his rigorous scholarship, creative output and original contribution. Through the pages of *The Muslim World Book Review*, a robust exchange of critical reviews on varied aspects of Islamic culture and civilisation are examined.[59] Kidwai's extensive contributions have crystallised into books that set new pathways to an objective study of the Qur'ānic translations. His incisive analysis of contemporary Islamic trends with special reference to Qur'ānic studies has elicited positive response from Muslim organisations. In 2017 Kidwai was commissioned by Peter Lang Publishing Inc. (US) to present his study of the Prophet (SAW) against the backdrop of Islamophobia which paradoxically has evoked a genuine interest in Islam. *Images of the Prophet Muhammad in English Literature* examines literary texts from the twelfth to nineteenth centuries. Kidwai's expertise in Literary Orientalism is encapsulated in this meticulously researched study.

A translator of the Qur'ān, Muhammad Marmaduke Pikhtall carved out a niche for his literary contributions on Islamic culture. However, his translation published in the 1930s has attracted greater interest in his approach to the study of the Qur'ān. Kidwai's assessment of Pickthall's translation is included in Geoffrey Nash, *Marmaduke Pickhtall: Islam and the Modern World* (Leiden, 2017).

It is a truism that Qur'ānic studies dominate Kidwai's multidimensional career. As Director of K.A. Nizami Centre for Qur'ānic Studies (Aligarh Muslim University, India) he has introduced additional courses for students pursuing careers in fields other than Islamic studies. The *Qur'ān Nāzira* classes are offered to students wishing to improve their skills in the recitation of the Qur'ān (*tilāwat*). The rapid rise in student attendance is a testimony to the visionary leadership of Kidwai. Needless to add, the *Qur'ān-in-Action* programme is a commendable initiative to draw students closer to the meaning and message of the Holy Book. Likewise, the Centre's partnership with the Department of Islamic studies and Arabic at AMU has resulted in several students pursuing their doctoral theses in Qur'ānic studies. The nurturing

---

[59] See Kidwai, *Translating the Untranslatable* and *God's Word, Man's Interpretations*.

influence of Kidwai and his indelible imprints may be gleaned from the several outstanding graduates of Islamic studies.

Ziauddin Falahi

Ziauddin Falahi is a renowned scholar of Qur'ānic studies. Among his pioneering works is the Qur'ānic contributions by Hindu scholars. The ingrained Orientalist prejudice in recent decades has indirectly inspired Hindu scholars to make substantial contributions to the Qur'ān translation project. In contrast, the culture of co-existence and harmony between Muslims and Hindu majority has also nurtured a positive study of the sacred text.

Falahi has competently translated the author's Qur'ānic work *The Contributions of Abdur Raheem Kidwai to Qur'ānic Studies* (2019) into Urdu.[60] His detailed Introduction has enhanced the merit of this work on the renowned Qur'ānic scholar and researcher. Another significant translation in the Qur'ānic field *Qiyāmat al-Kubra* is an invaluable addition to the eschatological themes.

The aftermath of the Arab Spring (2011) has been devastating for a sizeable Muslim population who have taken refuge in Europe. The migration patterns have severely impacted on their Islamic identity amid Islamophobia and integration programmes imposed by the respective host counties. In retrospect, the Muslim diaspora communities are faced with the bleak prospects of the erosion of their Islamic values on foreign soil.

Yasin Mazhar Siddiqui makes incisive analysis about the Muslim diaspora in these words:

> Majority communities and dominant civilisations are liable to accept the identity of minorities only up to an extent. For demonstrating their political strength or social and cultural supremacy, for assessing their numerical advantage, for introducing cultural

---

[60] Ziauddin Falahi, *Abdur Raheem Kidwai ke Qur'āni Mutāla'āt* (Aligarh, 2019), 12-20.

integration and for a variety of social and psychological complexes, they often seek to deprive minorities of their identity. The Muslim minority has been their prime target. For their distinct culture is inextricably interlinked with their faith. As a result, they are often persecuted at the hands of the majority. The Prophet's role model for them is that they should preserve their identity at any cost. This alone is the way to fight against evil forces.[61]

Three areas of Islamic specialisation mark out AMU as a site of scholarly tradition. We may refer to the oldest department (*Sunni Theology*) which attracted a number of renowned 'ulama in this field of study.

Among the eminent scholars mention may be made of Muhammad Taqi Amini (d. 1991) whose range of writings include Qur'ānic studies. His *Hikmat al-Qur'ān* as the title suggests, is an exploration of the concept of wisdom in its broadest sense. According to Amini, there are several levels of wisdom that are connected with mankind, society and the cosmos. His copious citation of particular verses brings into full the fusion between human endeavour and spirituality. Moreover, the term is an all-embracing description of the harmony that operates in the universe, which gives it a distinct form and meaning on the purpose of creation.

Tawqir Ahmad Falahi has come up with a brilliant exposition about the Qur'ān's multidimensional character. Among his Qur'ānic writings, his English works have been widely recognised for their eloquent style, rigorous scholarship and broad sweep of themes. Take for example *The Qur'ānic Directives for Islamic Society*. The concept of humanity as a universal ideal is an oft-repeated refrain for the reconstruction of society. In other words, this ideal is located within a moral code that is supported by the relevant

---

[61] Yasin Mazhar Siddiqi, *The Prophet Muhammad: A Role Model for Muslim Minorities* (Leicester, 2006), 192.

Qur'ānic verses.[62]

The history of the Department of Islamic Studies is indicative of Sayyid Ahmad's visionary leadership. As early as 1920 positive steps were taken to confer an academic status to the Department. According to Gowhar Wani, it transitioned from the Institute of Islamic Studies to a fully- fledged faculty. Qur'ānic studies was a thrust area which positioned the primacy of the foundational source in its programme of study. However, the publishing output of Qur'ānic works has not been wide and varied bearing in mind its decades-long existence.

Established in 2012, the K. A. Nizami Centre for Qur'ānic Studies has made significant strides to disseminate the timeless message and guidance of the Qur'ān. It has the enviable record of producing more than twenty titles over a relatively short period. An ambitious project, the tafsir series covers various strands of Qur'ānic scholarship in the subcontinent. This is indeed a major enterprise.

The Department of Arabic has an established record of bringing out exceptional works in the domain of Qur'ānic studies. Articles and books written in Arabic have found a niche in academic circles, which attests to the excellent trends of Qur'ānic scholarship taking shape in AMU.[63]

---

[62] Muhammad Mubeen Saleem Nadwi Azhari, *Hindustān me Mutāla'ah Qur'ān Majeed: Mu'āsir Manzar Nāma* (Aligarh, 2020), 186-7.

[63] Details have been gleaned from Saleem Nadwi, *Hindustān me Mutāla'ah Qur'ān Majeed: Mu'āsir Manzar Nāma.*

Chapter 9

Selected Twentieth Century Qur'ānic Contributions

This chapter explores the trends of Qur'ānic scholarship of the twentieth century, which have had a far-reaching impact on the sociopolitical milieu of Muslims in the subcontinent. These works are independent contributions and have significantly enriched the tafsir tradition.

Abdul Majid Daryabadi

Abdul Majid Daryabadi (d.1977) holds the distinction of having written two tafsirs in two languages, English and Urdu. These tafsirs are independent works that cater to different readership. While the English one is directed at Western educated Muslims, the Urdu tafsir is aimed at average, practising Muslims seeking to derive a better understanding of the Qur'ān's teachings and message. Written in forceful Urdu, *Tafsir i-Mājidi* continues to have a direct appeal to readers in this century.

After the completion of his English commentary, Daryabadi commenced his Urdu work which was extensive in its scope and coverage. There was no doubt that he benefitted immensely from Thānawi's *Bayān al-Qur'ān* which is a detailed exploration of the multidisciplinary Islamic 'ulum. Thānawi's scholarly erudition also had a distinct influence on *Tafsir i-Mājidi.*

In 1944 Daryabadi submitted his manuscript for publication to Taj Company (Lahore), the same publishing house that undertook to bring out the English tafsir. After several years the tafsir was published. However, the format (interlinear translation and commentary on the margin of the page) was a serious shortcoming for a remarkable work like *Tafsir i-Mājidi.* Like his English work, Daryabadi continued to revise his Urdu tafsir. In fact, it was considerably enlarged and updated by the late 1960s. It is ironic that his prolific writings were ardently read while no publisher came forward to bring out his revised tafsir. Under these challenging circumstances, Daryabadi used his meagre resources to publish only two parts of his exceptional work up to surah Yunus (10). Sadly, his wish to have it published by a reputable company remained unfulfilled until his death. It was at Shaykh Nadwi's recommendation that the Academy of Islamic Research and Publication (Lucknow) acquired its publishing rights. Unforeseen circumstances could only allow the Academy to bring out six volumes covering Surah Al-Hujurāt (1977-2013). The prolonged delay was reminiscent of the fate suffered by his English tafsir. Kidwai has made a pointed reference to sectarianism, group politics, personality cult and apathy that have been obstacles to the publication of excellent works like Daryabadi's tafsir. Nevertheless, the Academy produced a commendable version of *Tafsir i-Mājidi.*[1]

Daryabadi's sources of reference illustrate his brilliant grasp of classical tafsirs. Apart from *Bayān al-Qur'ān* his approach encompassed a wide range of studies in Western scholarship. According to Shaykh Nadwi, Daryabadi culled from numerous sources valuable material on the Qur'ānic allusions to persons, places, communities and sects. By the same token, Daryabadi never deviated from mainstream Islamic viewpoints.[2] Daryabadi's contemporaries lauded his pioneering work in terms of its literary charm and unapologetic elucidation of eschatology, comparative religion, modern knowledge, etc. Most importantly, the tafsir motivated Muslim readers to reconnect with the 'eternal, excellent message of Islam and the Qur'ān.' The relevance and uniqueness of *Tafsir i-Mājidi* created new pathways to exploring the Qur'ānic teachings in a contextual setting.[3]

For a detailed appraisal of the wisdom and truth of the sacred text, Daryabadi relied on the erudition of Thānawi on account of his vast experience in Qur'ānic studies. To a lesser extent he drew his knowledge from Hamiduddin Farāhi, who did an

---

[1] For a detailed study of Daryabadi's life and Qur'ānic contributions, see Akhtarul Wasey and Abdur Raheem Kidwai (editors), *Journey of Faith: Maulana Abdul Majid Daryabadi* (Delhi, 2016).

[2] Ibid., 126.

[3] Ibid., 132.

extensive study of the *nazm* theory of the Qur'ān which continues to influence hermeneutic approaches in this field. For Daryabadi, a living guide like Thānawi is essential to access the authoritative authentic understanding of the Qur'ān. By the same token, Daryabadi raises an important point: there is no definitive interpretation that can be ascribed to any particular tafsir. Layers of meanings may be unearthed, interpretations may be formulated but these are 'labours of love and human effort.' This pragmatic approach is a recurrent theme in Daryabadi's Qur'ānic works.[4]

In his critique, Yasin Mazhar Siddiqi has identified the following distinctive features of *Tafsir i-Mājidi.*

- o Daryabadi's Urdu rendering is remarkable for being in consonance with the Qur'ānic syntax and idiom. He has done well in listing in his "Preface" some of the problems in translating the Arabic Qur'ān into Urdu. Moreover, he has spelled out certain norms and principles, of which the observance helps resolve these problems.
- o In this translation he has been faithful to the Qur'ānic syntax and word order. It is quite a task to accomplish this.
- o He is the first among the Urdu *mufassirun* to have drawn upon such a variety and large number of sources on the Qur'ān.
- o His tafsir notes provide the quintessence of his deep and wide study of important sources.
- o His taking recourse to modern academic studies, including the Western ones, is breathtaking. Both the classical Muslim and modern Western sources are represented well in his tafsir.
- o While dealing with the Orientalists' writings, he does not reject these out of hand. Rather, he

---

[4] Falāhi, *Hind-wa-Pāk ki Qur'āni,* 55.

> acknowledges the valid points made by them.
> - Likewise, he both endorses and refutes the Biblical statements in the Qur'ānic terms of reference.
> - His interpretation is both academic and Islamic, as it happens to be in accordance with the Qur'ān and sunnah.
> - He does not betray blind conformity to his predecessors. Rather, he cites them as long as their stance fits in with the tenor of the Qur'ān.
> - Daryabadi was a stylist of Urdu prose. No Urdu *mufassir* matches him on this count. His translation and tafsir are characterised by distinct literary charms.[5]

In *Journey of Faith* Kidwai has provided a detailed account regarding Daryabadi's contributions to Qur'ānic studies. Of particular interest are the latter's scholarly views on the prerequisites and challenges of tafsir in the modern age. The points raised are incorporated in his work and are reflective of his profound scholarship. For Daryabadi, a *mufassir* today owes a far greater responsibility in explaining more logically the meaning and message of the Qur'ān by taking recourse to modern knowledge. Daryabadi's extensive grounding in Islamic eschatology and comparative religion and modern disciplines deepened his understanding of Qur'ānic references which were distorted by other translators. Kidwai's comments are revealing:

> Far from so ruthlessly ruling out the palpable, physical forms of the Qur'ānic eschatology, Daryabadi explains these in accordance with the authentic Islamic doctrines. Never does he shy away from presenting the message of the Qur'ān as it is. Rather, on the basis of evidence and arguments culled from the Western sources he brings out the truth of the Qur'ānic statements.

---

[5] Wasey and Kidwai, *Journey of Faith*, 126-7.

He cites passages after passages illustrating how and why the Qur'ān excels it, which, in turn, proves that the Qur'ān is the final Word of Allah for all time and place and that the Bible has been altered and corrupted. He quotes also the latest Western scholarship in order to assert that all the Qur'ānic commands, be these on *jihād*, women, or the Hereafter are perfectly compatible with human nature. His tafsir helps Muslims realise that they should profess and practise Islam which alone would ensure the best for them in both the worlds. Moreover, throughout he presents the Qur'ān as the book of guidance, which should govern both individual and collective life. His frequent references to *ahādith* and classical *mufassirun* (*tafsir* writers) assure readers of the authenticity and reliability of his assertions. At the same time, he draws judiciously upon the latest, modern studies in order to vindicate the Qur'ānic statements on almost every issue. As a result, his *tafāsir* displays a remarkable and highly welcome blending of tradition and modernity, and of classical tafsir corpus and modern learning. This constitutes a valuable addition to the tradition of *tafsir*, and a testament to Daryabadi's mission of serving the cause of the Islam/the Qur'ān in today's context.[6]

Abul Kalam Azad

A multifaceted personality, Abul Kalam Azad (d.1958) symbolised the changing religious landscape in the subcontinent. His early years embodied a traditional Islamic education under the supervision of his father, Mawlana Khayruddin. Azad's prodigious memory and precocious soul balked at the religious accretions

---

[6] Cited in Choughley, *The Contributions of Abdur Raheem Kidwai*, 51-2.

that were upheld by his father in the name of *tasawwuf*. His surreptitious reading of writings beyond the *Dars i-Nizāmi* was a turning point to his non-conformist mindset. Thus his epithet 'Azad' fittingly portrayed his future career as an independent scholar.[7]

Azad's foray into journalism at a comparatively young age produced brilliant magazines, *al-Hilāl* and *al-Balāgh*, known for their fiery articles and anti-British sentiments. These remarkable pieces of writings brought Muslims closer to his pan-Islamic vision.[8] Through these columns the Muslim identity was articulated. At a broader level, Azad's intellectually maturing process brought out his revolutionary fervour as well as scholarly erudition. This phase also marked his Islamic activism which was juxtaposed with his patriotic aspirations. His association with leading organisations and institutions further bolstered his image as a trailblazer in the backdrop of the emerging patterns of modernity. There is no doubt that his involvement in national politics and proactive role in the Indian National Congress shaped the contours of his religious thinking. Amid the dominant presence of the Hindu ideology it was therefore not surprising that identity politics would resurface as a strong contender in the power dynamics taking place in the foreseeable future. After the Partition of India, Azad served as Minister of India until his death in 1958.[9] His outstanding contributions to the establishment of educational institutions are his abiding legacy.

A fervent admirer of Ibn Taimiyyah, forerunner of the *salai* movement, Azad's writings bear the imprints of creative originality. Likewise, his celebrated tafsir, *Tarjumān al-Qur'ān* (an incomplete work) is a marked departure from the traditional Urdu tafsirs which were generally aligned *to Mudih al-Qur'ān*. *Tarjumān* was written during the heyday of Azad's political activities

---

[7] See 'Abdul Hayy Nadwi, *Nuzhat al-Khawātir*, vol. 7 (Rae Bareli, 1993), 24-30.

[8] Syeda Saiyidain Hameed, *Islamic Seal on Indian Independence: Abul Kalam Azad- A Fresh Look* (Karachi, 1998), 55-80.

[9] Like other frontline Congress leaders including Mawlana Husayn Ahmad Madani (d. 1957), Azad championed the cause of composite nationalism, which effectively rejected the creation of Pakistan carved out in the name of Islam.

against the background of the draconian laws enacted by British rule. His poignant recollections about his tafsir are illuminating:

> Notwithstanding my (Azad) preoccupations in politics, a further demand was made on my time, by calling upon me to publish *Tarjumān al-Qur'ān* also. Since its printing type was not considered suitable, an arrangement was made for its printing in lithograph. The Arabic text was first completed in November 1921. But hardly had this work begun when the decree of time was pronounced once again against my plan.
>
> This time my arrest should not have disturbed the work of printing. The manuscript was in a completed form, and I had made every arrangement to carry on the printing of it in my absence. But the event which followed my arrest was distressing. It not only blocked the publication of the *Tarjumān al-Qur'ān* and the commentary, but cooled down all my enthusiasm for literary work. When fifteen months after I was set free, I applied to the government for the restoration of my papers (manuscript). It took a long time to return them. The material reached my hands in a ruined state. It presented the spectacle of a jumbled mess of mere rags.[10]

According to Syed Abdul Latif, two volumes of *Tarjumān* were published in 1945. The remaining volumes appeared to have been lost during his jail period and to this date have not been retrieved.[11] Azad conceived a grand plan for the translation: a commentary (*al-Bayān*) and Introduction (*muqaddimah*) that would encompass his extensive study of the Qur'ān. These volumes, however, did not materialise as Azad was imprisoned for

---

[10] Abul Kalam Azad, *The Tarjumān al-Qur'ān*, vol.1 (Lahore, n.d.), xxviii-xxx.
[11] Ibid., xiv.

long periods due to his anti-British campaigns.[12]

A brief overview of *Tarjumān* is meant to give it a textual relevance. Otherwise, readers are generally inclined to make assumptions that are not befitting the calibre and intellectual integrity of this illustrious scholar. Azad outlines his particular approach to the study of the Qur'ān which is prompted by the 'low standard' evident in many tafsir works.[13] His resolve is based on the gradual decline of the Muslim mind. For Azad, *taqlid* was a contributing factor to this mindset. Therefore, the well-argued response required a commitment to "lift those veils to the spirit of the Qur'ān and then search for the reality about it in our pages."[14]

Azad draws the readers' attention to the obstacles that have hampered the true appreciation of the sacred text. These include the predominant influence of Greek literature that gave Muslims new literary tastes and initiated them into their art of dialectics (*kalām*). His critique of Imam Razi's tafsir is a case in point. Muslim scholars' penchant for artificial and embellished molds vitiated the simplicity and forceful presentation of the sacred text.

By the same token, the *salaf* tradition features conspicuously in his *Tarjumān*. As beneficiaries of the Qur'ānic revelation, their authoritative interpretations have timeless relevance. By contrast, Azad laments the abuse or the manipulation of the hadith corpus by exegetes for sectarian interests.

Speculative theology created a myriad of dialectical propositions of Qur'ānic terms that were divested of their original meanings. This trend is discernible in several tafsirs pursuing a philosophical approach. In a similar vein, scientific tafsirs were on the rise which had unintended consequences. It advocated the idea that the Qur'ān should support and endorse every new discovery of scientific knowledge. This mindset has in varying degrees been entrenched over the decades by Muslim modernists advocating a rational approach to the study of the

---

[12] For a detailed discussion on these proposed volumes, see Ian Henderson Douglas, *Abul Kalam Azad: An Intellectual Religious Biography* (New Delhi, 1993), 200.

[13] Azad, *The Tarjumān al-Qur'ān*, vol. 1, xxxii.

[14] Ibid., 2.

Qur'ān.[15]

Sources of Azad's Qur'ānic Interpretation

Azad's list of sources is a reflection of classical tafsirs which he consulted for *Tarjumān*. In line with his *salaf* orientation the profound influences of Ibn Taimiyyah, Shah Waliyullah and Sayyid Ahmad Khan are glaringly evident.[16] For Azad, Sayyid Ahmad's critique and somewhat rational interpretation of doctrinal matters are not endorsed; instead, he supports the latter's views on Jewish narratives (*Isrā'iliyyāt*) and Qur'ānic abrogation (*naskh*) in some instances. Overall, Azad establishes the middle path between tradition and modernity to present his detailed explanation of Qur'ānic issues.

Let us turn to Azad's commentary of Surah Al-Fatihah. In this pioneering commentary of the opening surah, Azad navigates the intellectual terrain that has hitherto not been explored by exegetes. Several key themes in the surah contain marked influences of his study of comparative religions as well as his political philosophy.

Divine Providence (*Rububiyat*)

Azad maintains that the universal law of life (*takhliq bi'l haq*) serves a specific purpose and moves towards a specific goal. Therefore, the emphasis on reason or reflection (*tadabbur*) is a corollary to *rububiyat*.[17] Majeed has correctly observed that the "evidence of *rububiyat* (serves) as an argument for divine unity, order of providence and as an argument of divine revelation, for the afterlife, the design of the universe as an outcome of divine benevolence."[18] From the concept of *rububiyat* Azad builds up his theory of universalism. Foremost among writers who have elaborated on this theme is J.M.S. Baljon. He argues that Azad

---

[15] Ibid., xxii-xxvii.
[16] Majeed, *Qur'ān Interpretation in Urdu*, 80-1.
[17] Azad, *The Tarjumān al-Qur'ān*, vol. 1, 32
[18] Majeed, *Quran Interpretation in Urdu*, 71.

promoted a commonality in religious traditions particularly in the subcontinent - a precursor to religious pluralism that is commonplace in national politics. Azad's position is somewhat ambivalent as he wades through religious literature of Hinduism to demonstrate its timeless message. Two constituents strengthen the base of tolerance, good deeds (*a'māl al-sālih*) and justice (*'adālah*). Any imbalance disturbs its equilibrium. At a philosophical level, divine justice represents a balance in life and produces unity. It is this principle which is responsible for beauty and proportion in every form of thought and life. It is really the basis on which the scheme of the universe rests.[19] Thus the overarching attributes of *rububiyat* is emphasised.

Azad's familiarity with historical scholarship is skillfully expressed in his identification of Dhu al-Qarnayn (Surah Al-Kahf). His thesis of Cyrus as a possible historical figure is supported by his contemporaries like Mawdudi and Mufti Shafi.[20] In recent decades, Azad's thesis has been the subject of debate over Cyrus's religious image. This anomaly presents a religious dilemma: was Zoroastrianism by extension a monotheistic faith? A counter response to this historical figure is presented by Shaykh Nadwi in his *Faith versus Materialism.* He contends that there is no need to seek historical evidence for the identification of events/figures in the Qur'ān. It should be sufficient that the Qur'ān had indicated the dominant characteristics of Dhu al-Qarnayn like military prowess, limitless resources and nobility of character.[21]

According to Majeed, many ideas of Azad's tafsir have been borrowed, improved and adapted by erudite scholars like Mawdudi and Islahi in their respective commentaries.[22] The labour of love -*Tarjumān* - is the outcome of twenty- seven years of rigorous study of the Qur'ān. Understanding the essence of each and every verse was like drawing blood. In this pursuit Azad cut himself away from family, society and traditional education, and

---

[19] Azad, *The Tarjumān al- Qur'ān*, vol. 1, 94.

[20] Majeed, *Quran Interpretation in Urdu*, 76.

[21] Abul Hasan Ali Nadwi, *Faith versus Materialism: The Message of Surah Kahf* (Kuala Lumpur, 2005), 104-5.

[22] Majeed, *Qur'ān Interpretation in Urdu*, 104-5.

ventured alone. He used *tahqiq* (research) in preference to *taqlid* (imitation). The explanatory notes combined with a simple, forceful translation are embedded in Azad's Qur'ānic worldview. A critical examination of the *Tarjumān* is a testament to his pioneering work.[23]

Israr Ahmad

Israr Ahmad (d. 2010), a medical doctor by profession, was actively involved in the propagation of *da'wah* activities. Among his impressive contributions is his multivolume *Bayān al-Qur'ān* which was initially drawn from his popular lessons (*dars*) taught at his institutions.

A brief background to his extraordinary career will help in understanding his devotion to the Qur'ān. Ahmad was a member of the JI and held several important positions. His continued interest in Qur'ānic studies motivated him to complete his M.A. (Islamic studies) in Karachi University. He also gave up his medical practice to serve selflessly the cause of Islam.[24] Ahmad was not an 'alim in the traditional sense on account of his academic orientation. However, this did not deter him from accessing his knowledge through the tafsirs of scholars like Shaykh al-Hind Mahmud al- Hasan, Shabbir Ahmad Usmani, Abul A'la Mawdudi and Amin Ahsan Islāhi. Although they represented different perspectives on the tafsir tradition, Ahmad maintained that these were referential sources of Qur'ānic authenticity.[25] By the same token, Ahmad made an independent study of the Qur'ān based on its rich repository of tafsirs, classical and contemporary. Therefore, his extensive study honed his skills to offer a holistic interpretation of the Qur'ān based on personal reflection and contemplation. Additionally, his *dars* sessions enhanced the merit of his work through the interactive consultation with attendees from diverse backgrounds.

---

[23] Hameed, *Islamic Seal in Independence*, 151.
[24] Muhammad Ramadān Arāi', "Contributions of Dr Israr Ahmad in the Interpretation of the Qur'ān", in *Islamic Culture*, 2019: 41, 119.
[25] Ibid., 120.

Asrar believed that the Qur'ān possesses the potential to have a revolutionary impact on the *ummah*. To this end, his Qur'ān Academy and the Markazi Anjuman Khuddām al-Qur'ān[26] sought to disseminate the knowledge and wisdom of the Qur'ān' on a higher intellectual level so as "to launch a popular movement for the revitalisation of faith. In essence, his organisations were committed to the Islamic renaissance and more importantly "ushering in for the second time in history, the blessed era in which the true Islamic way of life reigned supreme."[27]

According to Ahmad, practical measures were envisaged to implement his vision of the Qur'ān's revolutionary impact on the *ummah.* It was well-planned constructive steps relatable to contemporary needs, especially the intellectual elite. A number of booklets[28] were published as a start-up kit for the rational understanding of the Qur'ān's meaning and message.

One of Israr's popular works is his tafsir on Surah Al-'Asr.[29] For him, this concise surah is a poignant and forceful description relating to the path of salvation. It urges the readers to go beyond a superficial reading of the surah by focusing on the Qur'ānic worldview. Two terms are employed to reactivate its message: *tadhakkur* and *tadabbur.*

> The Glorious Qur'ān call is this *tadhakkur bi'l Qur'ān*, i.e. realising through the Qur'ān the fundamental truths implicit in human nature. From this point of view it is the easiest of books to understand. The highest stage of contemplation of Qur'ānic verses has been termed *tadabbur i-Qur'ān* which means reflection and pondering over every

---

[26] Israr Ahmad, *Ta'āruf Tanzim i-Islami* (Lahore, 1997), 66-80. The establishment of the Markazi Anjuman was envisioned by Israr Ahmad.

[27] For an outline of the Islamic slogans adopted by Israr Ahmad's organisation, see Israr Ahmad, *The Qur'ān and World Peace* (Lahore, 1982).

[28] Ahmad's prolific writings are Qur'ān-oriented. A useful introduction to this series is *The Obligations Muslims Owe to the Qur'ān* (Lahore, 1995).

[29] Israr Ahmad, *The Way to Salvation in the Light of Surah Al-Asr of the Holy Qur'ān* (Lahore, 1982).

word deeply, in order to deduce the philosophy and wisdom of the holy book.[30]

In this slim volume, there are definite traces of Farāhi's elucidation of the Qur'ānic elan. Ahmad, for example, cites Farāhi's discussion of *imān* in support of his viewpoint:

> Belief or *Imān* refers to a particular mental and spiritual state which rules over man's total creed and actions. It has two pillars: knowledge and action. If we pull down either one of the two, the entire edifice will collapse. A man who is well-versed in theological doctrines. but continues to indulge in sinful and forbidden activities, does not have an iota of that belief or *imān* which alone is creditable in the sight of Allah.[31]

Ahmad constructs a moral universe in which belief and action are integral to man's salvation. The surah pithily exemplifies the theme of belief and action. A noteworthy point in this slim volume is Ahmad's important comments on the *rabt* (interlinking) surahs.[32] The preceding surah (Al-Takāthur), according to Ahmad, exposes the hollowness of materialism. As a corollary, Surah Al-'Asr gives explicit exhortations to avoid the pitfalls of materialistic trappings. The succeeding surah Al-Humaza is a graphic account of the punishment that awaits those whose lives are 'replete with sins and vices.'[33]

Ahmad's major Qur'ānic writings are based on his *dars* sessions. The thematic significance is borne out by the following aspects:

- Circumstantial setting of verses that are

---

[30] Ibid., 30. Cf. Israr Ahmad, *The Obligations Muslims* (Lahore, 1984), 22-34. These terms have a transformative significance for a believer desiring to reflect on and relate his life to the sacred text.

[31] Ahmad, *The Way to Salvation*, 17.

[32] Ibid., 52.

[33] Ibid.

gleaned from his Qur'ānic methodological approach.

- Unifying themes of the Qur'ān are systematically articulated.
- Relevant *ahādith* are cited to clarify Qur'ānic meanings and terminology.
- Synthesis of the Sahabas' explanations to bring these closer to the spirit of Qur'ānic overarching message.
- Integrating Qur'ānic terminology for readers who are not familiar with its grammatical construction.
- Expanding meanings of specific verses in relation to changing socioeconomic circumstances.[34]

Salient Features of *Bayān al-Qur'ān*

In line with classical commentaries Ahmad examines in detail the clusters of surahs to determine their significance for ordinary readers. His analysis of Surah Al-Baqarah is illuminating.[35] The longest surah in the Qur'ān, Al-Baqarah forms a complete whole consisting of an introduction, four purposes and a conclusion. Briefly speaking, it covers the main Islamic beliefs (*aqā'id*), the Qur'ān's address to the Jews with special reference to the nascent Muslim community in Madinah, Muslims at the time of the Holy Prophet (SAW) and an index of the legislations (*ahkām*). Ahmad terms this surah as the climax in respect of its summative assessment of particular historical events and the evolution of

---

[34] Arāi', *Contributions of Dr Israr Ahmad*, 126-30.

[35] Ibid.,131-2. Cf. Drāz, *The Qur'ān: An Eternal Challenge*, 137-79. Drāz examines this longest surah in terms of its semantic design and makes a perceptive comment: "The Qur'ān is miraculous not only in its powerful style, method of elucidation and its true prophecies, but also in its legislation which is appropriate for all generations."

the *ummah* within a legislative framework.[36]

The hadith citation features prominently in his tafsir. Clarity of Qur'ānic meaning and supplementary explanation form the basis of Ahmad's approach to hadith literature. The following example is an instance in point: *"And hold firmly to the rope of Allah"* (2:37) is a point of reference to the Holy Qur'ān in several *ahādith*.

Counsel and admonition[37] are binaries that critically examine Qur'ānic verses in a contemporary context. Ahmad expresses his candour at the Pakistani nation for abandoning the cause of Islam. Their sloganeering has not advanced the Prophetic mission; instead, the vice of hypocrisy is ingrained in their hearts. In Ahmad's view, a breach of trust as elucidated in Surah Al-Tawbah (9:75-7) has dire consequences for believers:

> *Some of them made a covenant with Allah: "If Allah gives out of His bounty, we will give alms and act righteously. Then, when He gave them out of His bounty, they grew niggardly and turned their backs (upon their covenant). So He caused hypocrisy to take root in their hearts and to remain therein until the Day they meet Him because they broke their promise with Allah and because they lied.*
>
> (9:75-77)

Exegetes have attempted to decode the possible meanings of the *huruf muqatta'āt.*[38] Ahmad is clear on this issue: its meaning is known to Allah and His Prophet (SAW). Therefore, speculation does not yield positive results.

The philosophical persona of *Bayān al-Qur'ān* does not betray Ahmad's sensibilities to poetry in context. Indeed, he is guided by the Qur'ānic declaration about the mob mentality (Al-An'ām: 116) that has strayed from the path of Allah. In a similar vein, he critiques democracy for its dubious projection of values and rights

---

[36] Ibid., 132.

[37] Ahmad, *The Obligations Muslims*, 47-8.

[38] Arāi', *Contributions of Dr Israr Ahmad*, 134.

which contradict the unambiguous principles of Islam. Iqbal's terse verses are aptly used for his critique on Western civilisation as well.

Fiqh has over the centuries been the arena of sectarian battles fought in the name of pristine Islam.[39] Ahmad's primary focus is reaching out to intellectuals and the educated classes to imbibe the life-enriching lessons of the Qur'ān. His balanced approach to *ikhtilāf* conforms to his Qur'ānic vision of mutual tolerance. While generally adhering to Hanafi *Fiqh* Ahmad departs from its ruling that allows an alternative interpretation.[40] The vocalised recitation of Surah Al-Fatihah reveals his independent reasoning judgement.

Religious upheaval has largely characterised the sociopolitical milieu of Muslims in the subcontinent. The rise of homegrown deviant movements[41] posed an existential threat to Islam's universal character in this populous Muslim region. Claimants to Prophethood[42] were making their mark among vulnerable communities. Ahmad vociferously condemned these sects who were reminiscent of the apostates during the Prophet's time. Another *Fitnah*, according to Ahmad, was the Ahl al-Qur'ān movement.[43] Which sought to eradicate the hadith/sunnah from Muslim collective identity (*tashakkhus*). The modernists made gradual strides among the intellectuals who were disenchanted with traditional Islam. Moreover, their modernist proclivities which were bred in many Western institutions were emblematic of their covert rejection of hadith as the foundational source of Islam. Hence the term *Munkar i-hadith*. According to Ahmad, this misguided movement is more dangerous than the Finality of Prophethood issue on two counts: first, it has an insidious agenda

---

[39] Recent scholarly works have deplored the polemical writings that characterise a sectarian slant particularly on *Fiqh*-related issues. See Taha Jabir al-'Alwani, *The Ethics of Disagreement in Islam* (Herndon, 1993).

[40] Arāi', *Contributions of Dr Israr Ahmad*, 135.

[41] Syed Habibul Haq Nadvi, *Islamic Resurgent Movements in the IndoPak Subcontinent* (Durban, 1987), 131-51.

[42] Ibid., 153-85.

[43] See Aziz Ahmed, *Islamic Modernism*, 224-36.

that is not easily discernible; second, its proliferation has the potential to lure vulnerable Muslims to its fold. Ahmad's incisive analysis is echoed in the following verse:

> *There are those who disbelieve in Allah and His Messengers and seek to differentiate between Allah and His Messengers and say: "We believe in some and deny others," and they seek to strike a way between the two.*

> (4: 150)

In sum, Ahmad articulates a Qur'ānic line of though according to the *salaf* tradition and civilisational paradigm. For him, Muslims need to delve deeper into the sources of Islamic authenticity of which the Qur'ān serves as the infallible guide.

It is interesting to note that Ahmad has employed the twin concept of *tabligh* and *tabyin* to reinforce his Qur'ānic revolution vision. For him, *tabyin* in the Qur'ānic terminology refers to exposition: the meaning, interpretation and dissemination of the Qur'ānic message must be institutionalised. In his view, the universal proclamation of Allah's message has been marginalised by Muslims with the result that widespread ignorance and indifference are rampant in the *ummah*. Amid the doom and gloom syndrome it is the vision of *tabyin* which can extricate the *ummah* from its intellectual stagnation. Ahmad explains:

> *Tabyin* in its highest form is rather a job with a challenge. One who resolves upon fulfilling his duty of explaining the Qur'ān in this sense of the term will not merely translate its text but he will try to unfold the knowledge and wisdom contained in this great book. He will endeavour to establish the truth of the Qur'ān and its teachings, reasoning convincingly at the highest place of thought accessible to people according to its intellectual advancement. *Tabyin* can only be discharged unless we set up all over

the Muslim world a network of such universities and academies as may concentrate on the 'Qur'ānic study and research' assigning it the central place in the scheme of their disciplines. Through (this) we shall be able to explain the teachings of the Qur'ān to the people of the modern world.[44]

The choice of Ahmad's tafsir *Bayān al-Qur'ān* reflects his multifaceted approach to bring out its universal guidance and eternal message. Regardless of the outcomes of such a revolutionary project, Ahmad has opened up new pathways to interpreting the dynamics of the sociopolitical order as envisioned in the Qur'ān.

Wahiddudin Khan

The revival and reform concept has taken on new meanings in the twentieth and twenty first centuries. In the subcontinent it has also seen a surge of reformist thought from a spectrum of different ideological perspectives. Wahiddudin Khan (b. 1925) is an eminent religious figure belonging to the reformist tradition.

An influential 'alim, intellectual and thinker, Khan's Islamic training in Madrasat al-Islāh exposed him to the Farāhi-Islāhi Qur'ānic thought. Likewise, his association with other Islamic institutions and organisations broadened his framework of *da'wah*. His writings are reflective of his pragmatic approach to the challenges Muslims face, particularly in the Hindu-dominated India.

It is interesting to note that Khan did not restrict himself to studying Islamic *'ulum*. On the contrary, he pursued a rigorous study of the English language as well as other Western disciplines, which equipped him to promote his Islamic resurgence project. For this purpose he set up his Islamic Centre in New Delhi through which he disseminated his ideas about Islam's universal role as a

---

[44] Ahmad, *The Obligations Muslims*, 54.

peaceful religion amid the growing Islamophobic tensions in the West. His monthly magazine *Al-Risala,* initially published in Urdu was widely received for its refined version of Islamic teachings. Implicit in Khan's peace initiatives was the establishment of the Centre for Peace and Spirituality (CPS) which sought to foster interfaith dialogue without compromising the Islamic universal values. The international awards received by him are in recognition of his peace initiatives. Common to all the goals Khan has set out is the renaissance of Islam to the modern mind. Interestingly, Azad, too, worked tirelessly to promote the interfaith dialogue through the unity-in-diversity theme, which was translated as religious universalism.[45]

There are four distinct phases of Khan's intellectual career. His search for truth after graduation from a madrasah brought in the 'dark days' of rationalism (1945). Thereafter, his association with JI, Academy of Islamic Research and Publications (Nadwah) and Jami'at al-'Ulama (Hind) was a turning point in reassessing the trends of Islamic intellectual thought. By 1976, Khan established himself as a widely acclaimed scholar with several books of significance to his credit. In fact, from 2001 onwards his international presence was noticeable on account of his celebrated works, including a translation of the Qur'ān in Urdu.[46]

Before we attempt to examine Khan's Qur'ānic contributions, two books of his deserve mention regarding his *da'wah* formulation. His *God Arises* (English)[47] attempts to present the basic teachings of Islam in the light of modern knowledge and consistent with scientific advancement. In the chapter *The Challenge of the Qur'ān,* Khan provides irrefutable evidence about the Qur'ān's scientific spirit. Another chapter relates to man's quest for true happiness as outlined in the Qur'ān's ethico-spiritual framework.

---

[45] For a detailed analysis of Wahiddudin Khan's life and thought, see Anjum Awan, *Revisiting Islam: The Reformist Thought of Wahiddudin Khan* (Delhi, 2018), 89-136.

[46] Ibid, 111.

[47] Wahiddudin Khan, *God Arises: Evidence of God in Nature and in Science* (New Delhi, 1987).

Muhammad: The Prophet for All Mankind[48] is an important work, delineating the universal influence of the Holy Prophet (SAW). It is drawn largely from Khan's extensive reading of the *sirah* literature. His presentation is aligned to his *da'wah* mission and does not portray fully the unique character of the Holy Prophet (SAW). For Khan, relevance and readability are prioritised, which has the potential to blur out the Qur'ānic presentation of the Prophet's role as the 'Mercy unto mankind.'

Essentially, the thematic classification of Khan's published works include revivalism and reform (*tajdid*), Islam in the modern world, peace, dialogue and *da'wah*, philosophy of life and spirituality. There is a resemblance to Fethullah Gulen's interpretation of the Prophetic mission, Qur'ānic wisdom and teachings, ostensibly to reach out to the Western audience. Here we may refer to Khan's *Simple Wisdom: A Daybook of Spiritual Living* which is very much an inspirational work, selectively located in his reformist discourse.[49]

Al-Qur'ān Mission

It was established in 2010 with a pledge of dedication by a group of Muslims to spread the Word of God to the whole of humanity on an individual and collective level. The crux of this mission statement was Khan's English translation of the Qur'ān brought out in 2008 and subsequently translated into many languages as part of the 'The Good Word Books' and the CPS International projects. Its success is considerable in view of the available resources and the appropriation of the social media.

Falahi has made some important remarks about the method of in interpretation in *Tadhkir al-Qur'ān:*

- o A work of guidance, it serves as an admonition for the reader.
- o For the purpose of consistency, paragraphs have

---

[48] Wahiddudin Khan, *Muhammad: The Prophet for All Mankind* (New Delhi, 1988).

[49] Wahiddudin Khan, *Simple Wisdom: A Daybook of Spiritual Living* (New Delhi, 2008).

o   been used to convey the essential divine message.
o   The translation and commentary are separated by a continuous line to enable readers to grasp the meaning of the text.
o   Each paragraph represents a complete message to facilitate a holistic interpretation of the sacred text.
o   In view of Khan's *da'wah* approach, the literal and idiomatic/contextual translation is maintained.
o   The absence of technical terms is intended to retain its natural simplicity.[50]

Two aspects of the *Tadhkir al-Qur'ān* are representative of Khan's Qur'ānic line of thought. The inner spirit and God-realisation (*ma'rifah*) are inextricably linked to the 'intellectual revolution' within man. Essentially, the Qur'ān reiterates the importance of man's discovery of truth at all levels of *ma'rifah*. Hence, it has the potential to guide man to understand the Creation plan of God. As the title of the translation suggests, the Qur'ān is a Book of divine warning (*tadhkir*). Life-turning lessons are in fact admonitions and expressive remarks about the purpose of life. In his scheme of interpretation, Khan advocates alternative definitions to Qur'ānic concepts that are meant to reflect on its perennial message.[51]

Like any other tafsir, *Tadhkir al-Qur'ān* is embedded in Khan's conceptualisation of key themes of the Qur'ān. At the outset, he dismisses a political reading of the divine text as it militates against the Messengers' *da'wah* which according to him was premissed on personal reformation and salvation. Therefore, societal reform is of secondary importance. In line with this mindset, Khan explores new terrains of *da'wah* and peace to justify the Qur'ānic mission of individual reform. It is, therefore, not surprising for Khan to downplay the importance of semantics and other Islamic *'ulum* as these are essential tools to understanding the comprehensive guidance of the Qur'ān. Rather, he dilates on

---

[50] Falāhi, *Hind-wa-Pāk ki Qur'āni*, 118-9.
[51] Ibid., 225. The element of wisdom and rationale (*hikmat*) forms the crux of several surahs in the tafsir.

his two-pronged approach which he believes is indispensable for unlocking the gems of Qur'ānic wisdom. In essence, the meaning of life and spiritual ethos blended with ethical teachings are marked features of his tafsir. The following example is a gist of his Qur'ānic methodology:

> No work may commence without his Lord whose treasures of mercy are boundless. Man needs to pray for these favours for the fulfilment of his deeds. It reinforces his servitude to his Lord. Words like *Bismillah* create a heartfelt communication with the Divine and eventually becomes his natural traits. This God-given gift is innate to the Divine system and in consonance with the way of life planned by Allah for man.[52]

A brief analysis of the explanatory notes reveals Khan's approach to the Qur'ānic text. At the heart of this discussion is the moral content of the verses which he amplifies according to his hierarchy of Qur'ānic values. According to Khan, a God-oriented life cannot always be equated with the rich hadith literature on this surah (Al-Fatihah). In other words, the classical sources should be sparingly used to allow the readers to assimilate the moral aspects of the Qur'ānic text. Khan has advanced unique explanations to Qur'ānic terms, which are tendentious, to say the least. These *tafarrudāt*[53] are illustrative of his non-conformist views and his overstrained interpretation. These differing positions are a rebranded version of Sayyid Ahmad's controversial tafsir. For example, the term *dābbah* is categorically described in the hadith literature. It is a beast that will emerge from the earth before the Last Day. However, Khan describes it as a well-designed web of the communication network system. The ecosystem like the green revolution also finds place in his unique interpretation of verses.

According to Khan, politics and peace are exclusionary;

---

[52] Ibid., 220-1 (Adapted).
[53] Majeed, *Qur'ān Interpretation in Urdu*, 224-5.

therefore, his interpretations are evident in his discussion of the Messengers' mission. Consider the following verse:

Who wants to drive you out of your land by his sorcery?
Now what do you advise?

(26: 35)

"Moses' mission was peaceful and had no direct bearing on politics and government."[54] In a similar vein, he disingenuously attempts to downplay the societal and political role which is divinely mandated, in order to vindicate his individual reform theorisation.

Two serious misinterpretations have raised a storm of controversy in *Tadhkir al-Qur'ān* among Islamic scholars prompting a tirade of polemical writings against Khan, which are very much reminiscent of the Mawdudi era. Apolitical Islam is clearly expressed in his definition of *jihād.* According to Khan, *jihād* is a peaceful ideological struggle that is in accord with the philosophy of non- violence. Curiously enough, his pacifist version of *jihād* is akin to the much-vaunted presentation of defensive wars in Islam portrayed by Muslim modernists.[55] Khan's vague remark about the physical ascension of Prophet 'Isa comes to the fore as well.[56]

Falāhi has analysed the *tadhkiri* themes from a random selection of Qur'ānic verses. We reproduce three examples which encapsulate Khan's motivational style.

Surah 103: Man is moving headlong to his death. It implies that if man does not use his allotted time meaningfully then whatever befalls him will be sheer destruction. Therefore, success entails personal effort.

---

[54] Ibid., 225.
[55] Wahiddudin Khan, *Tadhkir al- Qur'ān*, vol. 1 (New Delhi, 1990), 81.
[56] Ibid., 758.

Surah 114: To challenge the overall effects of trials and tribulations (*fitan*), man needs to awaken his consciousness.

Surah 17:84: The Arabic word *Shākilitih* denotes a particular way. Everyone acts in his own way. It is a mindset that is influenced by circumstances and predispositions. These traits develop into an attitude or a mindset.[57]

Abdul Karim Parekh

Self-study has become synonymous with modernist leanings in Islamic learning. In our study two *mufassirs* stand out for their respective Qur'ānic contributions if we were to consider them as self-made scholars, namely, Mawdudi and Daryabadi. However, this categorisation is an oversimplification as it tends to blur out their exceptional contributions to Islamic resurgence. In this instance, the term *islāh* has wide ranging connotations and may be reconfigured in different settings.

Abdul Karim Parekh (d. 2007) was a self-taught scholar who is best remembered for his social activism and communal harmony initiatives. A successful timber merchant in Nagpur (Maharashtra), his range of knowledge in Islamic sciences was remarkable. Likewise, he was competent in Arabic, English and Hindi with several of his writings translated into these languages. In recognition of his social activities, Parekh was conferred the highest civilian award, Padma Bhushan in 2001 by the Indian government.

Parekh was well known for his active participation in mainstream Islamic life. He was an executive member of the All India Muslim Personal Law Board and also of the Department of Sunni Theology (AMU). His broad-based outreach programmes were extended to non-Muslims particularly in the Maharashtra state.

Two Qur'ānic works of Parekh bear the imprint of exemplary

---

[57] Cited in Falāhi, *Hind-wa-Pāk ki Qur'āni*, 226-8. These notes are excerpted from *Tadhkir al-Qur'ān*.

scholarship. These are *An Easy Dictionary of the Qur'ān* and *Tashrih al-Qur'ān*. The latter is an Urdu translation written in an easy, comprehensible language for ordinary readers seeking to assimilate the Qur'ānic teachings in their lives. This work was also translated into English and Gujarati. Its Urdu translation has seen multiple editions, a testament to its widespread popularity.[58]

Parekh was largely inspired by Shaykh Nadwi, his spiritual mentor to bring out this translation by highlighting the Qur'ānic themes. Viewed from a different angle, *Tashrih al-Qur'ān* was intended to reach out to non-Muslims based on the *Payām i-Insāniyat* (message of Humanity) vision. Shaykh Nadwi wrote a Foreword to this work and lauded its distinctive facets. As an influential literary figure, Shaykh Nadwi examined the work in the light of its linguistic features and aesthetic appeal. Relevance and coherence are the hallmarks of this important tafsir.[59]

Parekh may be counted among the top-ranking exegetes who have attempted to present the sacred text to the modern mind.

Muhammad Rafiuddin

Not belonging to the tafsir tradition as such, the Qur'ānic writings of Muhammad Rafiuddin (d.1969) have, in no small measure, influenced the intellectual trends in the subcontinent.

Rafiuddin was a distinguished philosopher and educationist whose work *Ideology of the Future* received critical acclaim in the academic circles. The chapter entitled *Prophethood and Evolution* is a brilliant exposition of the phenomenon of *wahy*.[60] His elaboration of Islamic ideals finds full expression in another noteworthy work *First Principles of Education*.[61]

In the realm of Qur'ānic studies his *The Qur'ān and Modern Knowledge*[62] delineates Islam's universal influence on human

---

[58] *Mawlana Abdul Karim Parekh: A Brief Sketch*. www.edocr.com. Accessed on 19 July 2020.

[59] See Abdul Karim Parekh, *Tashrih al Qur'ān*, vol. 1 (Delhi, 1995), 13-5.

[60] Muhammad Rafiuddin, *Ideology of the Future* (Lahore, 1970), 473-6.

[61] Muhammad Rafiuddin, *First Principles of Education* (Lahore, 1983).

[62] Muhammad Rafiuddin, *Islam and Modern Knowledge* (Lahore, 2010).

civilisation. Equally enlightening is his critique of the ideological systems many of which are premised on the Darwinian theory of evolution. According to Rafiuddin, the Qur'ānic ideals are innate to human nature and are rationally explained in many verses dealing with the cosmos and morality. The scientific spirit of the sacred text is universal in its application provided it is correctly interpreted. His philosophical elucidation of modern knowledge in the light of the Qur'ān has important ramifications in the Islam and science discourse. The following points reinforce the intellectual character of the sacred text:

- It is not a contradiction to any scientific truth but remains completely harmonious and consistent with all the scientific truths during all ages and continues to absorb into itself every new truth as and when it may emerge.

- All its ideas are mutually related and organised rationally and support and confirm one another rationally. This is possible only when all its ideas have a rational relationship with the central and basic idea of the Qur'ān, the doctrine of *tawhid*.

- It is an effective refutation of all the erroneous philosophies.

- It is a complete philosophy of the universe and provides scientific guidance on important problems of the reality of man and the universe, and shows the path to truth and righteousness.

- It makes the whole sequence of the rationale and wisdom for religious injunctions (shari'ah) known to us and gives us an idea of it which has no internal contradiction.[63]

---

[63] Ibid., xxxi-xxxii.

Chapter 10

Shi'ah Contributions to Qur'ānic Studies

It is to the credit of the K. A. Nizami of Qur'ānic Studies that an impartial study by Ridā 'Abbās has cleared misperceptions about the Shi'ite beliefs regarding the Qur'ān. It is generally believed that the Shi'ahs reject the present form of the Qur'ān declaring it to be distorted. This stems from the alleged missing surah extolling the virtues of the fourth Caliph of Islam, 'Ali ibn Abi Tālib. Another motivation for this volume is the assumption that the subcontinent has not produced tafsir works of merit.[1]

'Abbās traces the genealogy of the Shi'ite tafsir genre in the light of several important Sunni works which include the widely acclaimed *Al-Itqān* by Suyuti. Likewise, he brings into broad relief the significant influence of the Ahl al-Bayt, particularly Imām Baqir and Imām Ja'far Sādiq through whose charismatic personalities and vast learning the Shi'ite tafsir construction received considerable impetus.[2] Political factors also contributed greatly to the growth of tafsir in Shi'ite dominated regions as in the case of Karbala and Najaf (Iraq). Arabic rather than Persian was used as a vehicle of giving tafsir a sectarian slant. For example, the celebrated tafsir of the illustrious scholar Muhammad Tabatabai (d. 1981), *Tafsir Al-Mizān*[3] written in 20 volumes is commended for its philosophical and metaphysical methodology of the sacred text. A number of volumes have been translated into English indicating its widespread popularity within a geopolitical spread.

The Shi'ite tafsir tradition in the subcontinent developed over the centuries largely on account of state patronage and aristocratic support. The Shi'ite dynasty in Awadh is illustrative of the power dynamics that expanded the footprint of religious

---

[1] Ridā 'Abbās, *Shi'ah Fuzalā ki Qur'āni Khidmat* (Aligarh, 2019). For a critique of the 'distorted' Qur'an, see Muhammad Manzur Nu'mani, *The Iranian Revolution* (Karachi, 2000).

[2] Ibid., 12-3.

[3] Muhammad Husayn Tabatabai, *Tafsir al-Mizān* (Qum, n.d.).

sectarianism. Migration patterns from Iran/Persia was also a contributing factor to its visible intellectual presence in this princely state.[4]

Sayyid `Ali

Historical sources suggest that *Tawdih al-Majid* by Sayyid Ali (d.1843) was largely patronised by the Awadh ruler, Amjad 'Ali Shah (d. 1847). He is described as a strictly religious king who scrupulously followed the dictates of the shari'ah.[5] He established a madrasah in Lucknow which was recognised for its excellent standards of teaching. A brilliant scholar and adept in several Islamic sciences, Sayyid 'Ali took an exceptional interest in Qur'ānic studies. His regular journeys to the hubs of learning in Najaf and Karbala are a testimony to his intellectual pursuits and scholarly achievements.

According to Ridā 'Abbās, *Tawdih al-Majid* was the first tafsir to be written in Urdu although *Mudih al-Qur'ān* is considered to be the seminal translation published in 1829. A work of this stature was completed during the sociopolitical developments in Awadh and reflected the evolution of the Urdu literary thought. Therefore, the emphasis of stylistic usage is to the fore in this tafsir.[6] Unlike Sunni works, *Tawdih al-Majid* is primarily based on narrations traced back the illustrious Shi'ite Imams. Following this line of sectarian thought the corpus of hadith literature has a Shi'ite slant – a common characteristic in all their tafsirs. Interpretations are invariably sourced out in this perspective, which significantly widens the Sunni/Shi'ite divide on Qur'ānic hermeneutics.[7]

A distinguished work in the Shi'ite tradition, Sayyid 'Ali has

---

[4] See Mirza Ali Azhar, *King Wajid Ali Shah of Awadh* (Islamabad, 1982), 78-191.

[5] Ibid., 188-9. A namesake, Sayyid 'Ali penned a tafsir in six volumes, which was published in 1982-7. His Introduction was brought out separately in 1359H. According to Shahid Ali, the tafsir is marked by the simplicity of style and literary elegance. Although Sayyid 'Ali consults mainstream commentaries, he has the tendency to distort clear meanings of the Qur'an to suit his Shi'ite predilections. See Syed Shahid Ali, *Urdu Tafaseer Beeswin Sadi Mein* (Delhi, 2001), 80-1.

[6] Majeed, *Qur'ān Interpretation in Urdu*, 19.

[7] Ibid., 24.

attempted to portray the esoteric dimension of his tafsir. In fact, it encapsulates the inner meanings of the sacred text that have been uninterruptedly transmitted from Caliph 'Ali to the holy Imams. In this respect, if a solitary hadith has been reported from the Sunni sources then it has a direct bearing on the status of the Ahl al-Bayt (Prophet's household). The tafsir has an unusual feature: *Zuhur-o-Bayyinah*.[8] By adding numerical values to the letters of the *abjad* system, hundreds of verses are interpreted in this light.

'Abbās makes a perceptive comment about Sayyid 'Ali's translation of Surah Al-Fatihah. The choice of words is precise and supplemented by explanatory notes that deal with Allah's attributes and His relationship with His slave *('abd)*.[9] This explanation is consistent with the thematic approach adopted by the Shi'ite exegetes. The popularity of *Tawdih al-Majid* can be gleaned from its multiple editions and commendations as far as Iraq and Iran.

Sayyid Muhammad Taqi Ma'āb

'Abbās has relied on the comprehensive work of Sālim Kidwai to present the contributions of Sayyid Muhammad Taqi Jannat. A teacher at Madrasah Sultāniyah (Lucknow), he was well known for his deep learning in the various Islamic 'ulum. His two-volume *Yanā bi'al Anwār* has common ground with the philosophical and metaphysical exposition of Fakhruddin Rāzi. According to Sālim Kidwai, the tafsir contains a detailed discussion of abstruse issues. Otherwise, there are no polemics against Sunni viewpoints with regards to differing historical accounts. In the spirit of tolerance and sectarian-free dialogue the learned translator has also consulted Sunni sources to interpret Surah Al-Fatihah. His focus is on the virtues of the surah which fall under the rubric of *Fadhā'il* in the hadith literature.[10]

---

[8] Ibid.
[9] Ibid.
[10] 'Abbās, *Shi'ah Fuzalā ki Qur'āni*, 61, 65.

Sayyid `Ali Muhammad

An illustrious scholar whose range of Islamic writings has received critical acclaim, Sayyid 'Ali Muhammad has brought out two important tafsirs that are a mark of his scholarly erudition. For example, Surah Yusuf is illustrative of his excellent command over Hebrew sources and comparative religions. Salim Kidwai has highlighted the distinctive aspects of Sayyid 'Ali's comprehensive tafsir on this surah. It recounts Prophet Yusuf's encounter with his siblings and his relationship with the Egyptian royalty. Furthermore, his test of personal integrity is mentioned in the light of the glaring discrepancies found in Hebrew sources, which are critically examined by Sayyid 'Ali. Again his citation of extensive Hebrew sources is a unique feature of his tafsir. Based on the Shi'ite line of thought the interpretation of dreams is given an esoteric edge.[11]

From the sketchy details available, Abul Qāsim Haeri's *Lawāmi 'al-Tanzil* has been fairly popular. Written for a Persian readership, it, nonetheless, gives a general translation of the verses followed by citations from other exegetical works. In a particular sense, it may be classified as a translation only.[12]

Hāji Farmān 'Ali

Pre-modernity in the subcontinent transcended sectarian barriers and created the impulse for renewed translations that were compatible with the growing needs of a new target audience. In this context, the steady growth of Shi'ite translations also demonstrated the reformist discourse in their academic circles. Although Farmān 'Ali's work predated the Partition of India (1947), his approach, however, suggested his sensibilities to the rising challenges facing the Shi'ah community.

Farmān 'Ali has provided a lucid account about his motivation to work on a contemporary translation. Urdu as an influential language was making positive changes in the different domains

---

[11] Sālim Kidwai, *Hindustāni Mufassirin*, 141.
[12] 'Abbās, *Shi'ah Fuzalā ki Qur'āni*, 68.

of Muslim society and its impact was acutely felt among the educated class. In response to the challenges facing the Shi'ah community, Farmān 'Ali undertook an idiomatic translation of the Qur'ān. For him the pressing demands by the media to render a reader- friendly version was an opportunity to make accessible the meaning, wisdom and thematic structure of the sacred text.[13] Needless to add, Farmān 'Ali was inspired by the long established tradition of presenting a Shi'ite perspective - a version representative of the Ahl al-Bayt's inseparable link with the revealed Book. This approach implied a strong reliance on their interpretation in the light of Shi'ite authorities. Accordingly, Farmān 'Ali by virtue of his accredited scholarship brought out an original translation with concise notes. He also adopted the interlinear format that was vogue in the subcontinent. The commendations from the *mujtahids* who belonged to the lower rank of the *marja*` hierarchy and regarded as the final source of religious and moral authority in the Shi'ite tradition reaffirmed Farmān 'Ali's Qur'ānic expertise.[14]

Interestingly, the translation contains detailed entries of topics that Farmān 'Ali culled from his decades-long study of the Qur'ān. The range and depth of the selected topics cover legal issues, narratives, specific historical events, referential points to the *Ahl al-Bayt*, etc. It is indeed an exhaustive subject index that gives a holistic overview of the sacred text. Farmān 'Ali sought to maintain a balance (*i'tidāl*) in his notes by citing authorities from classical tafsirs that are non-sectarian in content and approach. Likewise, mystical elements, not necessarily *tasawwuf*, are given prominence, which demonstrate the overwhelming influence of the Ahl al-Bayt on the tafsir tradition.[15]

Farmān 'Ali's translation has enjoyed wide popularity among Shi'ite scholarship; the multiple editions to date since its first publication are a strong indication of the continued interest this tafsir has generated in the Shi'ite world of Islamic learning.

It is a paradox that mystical teachings are conflated with

---

[13] See Farmān 'Ali, *Tarjuma wa Tafsir* (Lucknow, n.d.).
[14] 'Abbās, *Shi'ah Fuzalā ki Qur'āni*, 73-6.
[15] 'Ali, *Tarjuma wa Tafsir*, 14-20.

particular Qur'ānic verses for spiritual remedies. Zuraykh Husayn Amrohi has included in his tafsir a litany of *'amaliyāt* (liturgies) derived from classical works of *tasawwuf*. Amrohi believes that *basmala* and Surah Al-Fatihah possess potent medical properties for patients suffering from chronic ailments.[16]

Muhammad Harun Zangipuri, on the other hand, offers thoughtful comments in his Introduction[17] about the distinctive aspects of the Qur'ān. He examines the names and attributes of the Divine book to reaffirm the universal solutions offered to mankind. Similarly, the *i'jāz* component illustrates its inimitable style, corruption-free textual evidence and enduring influence on human civilisation. This work, although limited in scope, underscores the progressive thoughts embraced by Shi'ite scholars of the Qur'ān.

Mirza Mahdi Poya

A distinguished 'alim from Iran, Mirza Mahdi Poya (b.1900) studied at the reputed institutions of Najaf (Iraq). After the Partition of India, he was appointed Professor of Arabic and English. His Qur'ānic notes were utilised for his Urdu tafsir, which incorporated the translation done by Mir Ahmad 'Ali. Several editions of this work were brought out in Karachi.[18]

Sayyid ʿAli Naqi Naqvi

Sayyid 'Ali Naqi Naqvi (d. 1988) is ranked among the foremost Islamic thinkers of the twentieth century. His studies were completed in Lucknow and Najaf, sites of higher Islamic learning in the Shi'ite tradition. His intellectual brilliance established his credentials as a *mujtahid* on account of his mastery of *Fiqh*. He was also the Chairman of *Diniyāt* (Islamic Theology: Shi'ite Department) in AMU. A high profile researcher, Sayyid 'Ali had

---

[16] 'Abbās, *Shi'ah Fuzalā ki Qur'āni*, 78.

[17] Ibid., 79-80.

[18] Ibid., 82.

contributed significantly to Islamic studies.

According to Sayyid 'Ali, the Qur'ānic Arabic is unsurpassed in its beauty and charm, and was intrinsically appreciated by the Arabs who had an unmatched literary taste. Over the centuries the diluted form of Qur'ānic Arabic was a poor reflection of mediocre works. Qur'ānic Arabic is not restricted to specific milieus and its universal influence is also perpetuated in institutions of higher Islamic learning. As a graduate of a madrasah, Sayyid 'Ali's grounding in classical Arabic is a testament to his excellent grasp of Qur'ānic sources, particularly the tafsir genre.

Sayyid 'Ali's approach to tafsir is two-fold: first, his translation covers a detailed discussion of issues relevant to the *āyāt* or surahs. Second, he has developed new approaches to analysing the sacred text through different layers of interpretation. In his appraisal of the archetypal Adam, Sayyid 'Ali draws largely upon Shi'ite narrations, Sunni hadith literature, contemporary Egyptian tafsirs and extensive research by Islamic authorities to support his scientific claims. The same line of thought is adopted to his explanation on the origin of the universe.

An enlightened *mujtahid*, Sayyid 'Ali does not necessarily restrict his interpretation of the Qur'ān to Shi'ite sources. Rather, the element of reformist thought is forcefully articulated in his well-grounded writings. We may refer to the recent tafsirs which are formulated within the framework of progressive Shi'ite thought. The multivolume encyclopaedic tafsir in Arabic, *Al-Mizān* written by the internationally recognised philosopher and theologian, 'Allamah Tabatabai stands out for the exemplary standard of Arabic taught in Shi'ite institutions. Rational interpretation also informs Sayyid 'Ali's presentation of the Qur'ānic phenomenon. In this instance, the revealed order rather than the chronology of revelation as dictated by the Holy Prophet (SAW) is a manifestation of *i'jāz* in the Qur'ān. The consensus of opinions (*ijmā'*) reaffirms the divine origin of the sacred text.[19]

Modern Qur'ānic scholarship in Shi'ite academia follows a

---

[19] Ibid., 83-9 (Adapted).

similar trend like the contemporary tafsirs in a the Sunni perspective. Socioeconomic issues, for example, which affect the Shi'ah community are discussed at length in Qur'ānic works. The ambitious efforts by Mohsin 'Ali to produce a contemporary translation is indeed laudable.

Ali Muhammad Naqvi

An accomplished academician and scholar of international repute, Ali Muhammad Naqvi (b. 1953) pursued his post- graduate studies at AMU. Thereafter, he proceeded to Iran and studied *Ilāhiyāt* (Islamic scholastic theology) under the tutelage of the renowned 'alim, Murtadā Muttahiri Shahid (d. 1979) in Tehran University. In recognition of his brilliant contributions to Islamic 'ulum in Persian, Ali Muhammad received accolades from distinguished scholars. He also had the rare distinction of having his influential works prescribed as textbooks in several Shi'ite universities. His credit-worthy publications include tafsir, *sirah*, interfaith dialogue and comparative religions.

Our focus is on Ali Muhammad's two-volume English translation of the Qur'ān. Each volume contains his methodology and delineates the theme of divine guidance (*hidāyah*) couched in elegant literary style. Essentially, the poetic/prosaic style differs significantly from existing translations. According to Ali Muhammad, the translations from the twentieth century cover specific themes: literature, law, *Fiqh*, history, *kalām*, etc. which do not adequately convey the essential message of the Qur'ān as a book of guidance. From it flows the blueprint of character development. The Qur'ān envisions a complete code of life that cuts across the Arab region where it was revealed. In this perspective, it offers guidance for mankind for all eras.

A notable feature of Ali Muhammad's work is the transliteration system for readers who are not familiar with Arabic. Another point raised in the translation is the *nazm* theory. A cluster of verses definitely help readers to identify the central theme under discussion. This view underpins his independent position in direct contrast to the modalities developed by Farāhi and the Islāhi scholars. Interestingly, the second volume title *Islam, The Middle Way* works around the theme of *wasatiyyah*, which fleshes out the concept of balance and equilibrium (*i'tidāl*). For Ali Muhammad, *wasatiyyah* is the fulcrum of the ideal Islamic society and the catalyst for positive ideals that will benefit humanity at large.[20]

It must be noted that the selection of these tafsirs is based on the synoptic assessment by 'Abbās. It would be worthwhile to conclude the chapter with a review of Ali Quli Qarai's English translation of the Qur'ān by Kidwai:

> Qarai deserves credit for adopting a fresh approach in his presentation of the meaning of the Qur'ān. In this work the Qur'ānic verses in the original Arabic are divided and subdivided thematically, with their English translation in parallel column. Qarai calls it a new 'phrasal approach' as highlighted in the title of the work. Qarai is remarkably successful in applying this approach which is indeed "most useful for those who are eager to collate the Arabic text with the English translation." He displays his thorough familiarity with both the art and craft of translation in his Preface. His command over both the source and target languages -Arabic and English- are commendable. He has therefore acquitted himself well of the task of producing a faithful and lucid translation. To his credit, he has managed to achieve, in large measure, the objectives which he set for himself that the translation should i) be able to convey the meaning of the source text in an intelligible manner; ii) have a natural and easy form of expression; iii) convey the spirit and the manner of the original; and iv) produce a similar response in the reader.[21]

---

[20] Ibid., 97-101 (Adapted).
[21] Kidwai, *Translating the Untranslatable*, 179-80.

Conclusion

The distinct strands of tafsir in the subcontinent show a variation in terms of ideological orientation, methodology and approach. This is unavoidable given the nuanced interpretations from different primary sources and adaptation to circumstantial settings. As a genre it has evolved over two centuries without deviating from classical works which were assiduously studied and on which commentaries were written. To this end, Dār al 'Ulum Deoband has contributed appreciably to restate the unbroken link within the tafsir tradition.

Earlier commentaries were primarily written in Arabic for an academic readership. This meant that the sacred text with its timeless message and teachings were inaccessible to ordinary Muslims. Not surprising, therefore, was the codification of *Fiqh* literature supported by the various sultanates for political reasons. Again the trajectory of Islamic learning reached a limited audience and was reconfigured to create the culture of Islamic authenticity. However, not all Muslim rulers were amenable to the Islamic state which effectively would compromise their religious autonomy. Akbar and his *Dini Ilāhi* is a case in point. The forces of religious anarchy in the form of Mullah Nagpuri and his sons vindicated Akbar's dubious claim to divinity by advocating a bizarre interpretation of Islamic sources, thus opening the doors of religious apostasy (*irtidād*). Even their tafsirs were met with mixed response due to their tainted scholarly credentials.

Syncretism was an amalgam of Hindu practices and shrine-based Islamic rituals. This accretion was gradually accepted as an integral component of Islam. The emergence of Mujaddid's reform movement and the Waliyullah family's promotion of the sacred text through their translation project managed to stem the tide of irreligiousness among Muslims. It was a bold step to initiate the transformation process by restoring the primacy of the Qur'ān and sunnah on the Indian soil. Of real significance was the medium of Urdu, an evolving language, to reach out to the Muslim masses. In this context the far reaching impact of Shah 'Abdul

Qadir's *Mudih al-Qur'ān* may be assessed. The sacred text was now accessible to ordinary Muslims in simple, chaste Urdu supplemented by concise explanatory notes. This work has a remarkable record on account of its impact on successive tafsirs written over two centuries. Furthermore, its genealogical tradition network has extended to the West, particularly the United Kingdom which is now a confluence of diverse sectarian groups (*maslaks*) belonging to the Indian subcontinent.

In the late nineteenth century popular tafsirs like *Tafsir i-Ahmadi* were written with a reformist thrust. The controversial views contained in this incomplete tafsir were censured by a mainstream commentary, *Tafsir i-Haqqāni*. Over time, the contestation of ideas became a marked feature of future tafsirs. However, it was the emergence of Dār al-'Ulum Deoband which gave definite shape to mainstream interpretation of the Qur'ān. The pioneering work of Mahmud al-Hasan and the commentary of Shabbir Ahmad Usmani reaffirmed the indissoluble link with *Mudih al-Qur'ān*. Amendment and simplification of the original text became a viable option due to its wide popularity. A distinguished work like *Bayān al-Qur'ān* has paid rich credit to this work. The continuity of mainstream tafsirs may be gleaned from the multivolume *Ma'āriful Qur'ān*. Its exceptional merit is contained in the amalgam of various Islamic disciplines. At the same time it has elaborated the Qur'ānic standpoint according to the Deoband *maslak*.

Qur'ānic studies has also taken centre stage in Deoband reformist thought. Many of these books cover important aspects that may rightly be termed tafsir segments. There is a positive trend to contextualise the message of the Qur'ān in a contemporary setting. However, the tendency to overplay mainstream affiliation has hampered a progressive interpretation of the Qur'ānic worldview in relation to a changing multi-plural and multi-religious world. This lacuna is visible within the *da'wah* framework which has had a limited exposure. With the proliferation of technology new interpretive readings of the sacred text are now under the anvil of critical analysis. Without breaking from the rich traditional history of tafsir the discursive tradition is essential as it embraces multidisciplinary disciplines in order to foster a robust exchange of intellectual thought.

Nadwah's contribution to the tafsir genre may be assessed from its formulation of a progressive curriculum. Tafsirs representing classical and contemporary works are taught at the institution. However, its commentary output has not yielded positive outcomes keeping in mind its reformist initiatives. On the other hand, it has made a significant mark in presenting new approaches to the study of the Qur'ān. Nu'mani stimulated a substantial interest in the study of the sacred text in view of his vast learning. Sayyid Sulayman Nadwi, too, gave a new lease of life by undertaking a detailed study of its historical and geographical features. In a literary perspective, Shaykh Nadwi integrated the Qur'ānic teachings for a wider readership. His speeches and writings are infused with the Qur'ānic narrative, reflecting his mastery over Arabic and Urdu. The Qur'ānic contributions by contemporary Nadwi scholars have been significant. Apart from their critical appraisal of Arabic works, their writing are rooted in the Indian setting. In a particular sense the tafsir tradition has gradually shifted away from recycled topics. Instead, these works are original, creative and challenging which take into account the universality of the sacred text. For example, the Qur'ān and science discourse has assumed importance for a proper appreciation of the *iqrā* framework. Societal issues are a recurrent theme in the changing Indian landscape and therefore the Qur'ānic underpinnings require a repurposing without compromising its timeless guidance.

Nadwah has made serious attempts to offer *da'wah*-centred Qur'ānic translations in regional languages. It augurs well in terms of making the sacred text accessible in modern idiom. Essentially, the translations should meet the growing needs of a new generation who are nurtured on science and technology. Their mindset and intellectual quest for religious meaning and authenticity have increased manifold. Nadwi scholars have fallen short in this direction to provide inspirational works that are compatible with the rational temperament of readers. Progressive Islamic thought should be separated from Islamic modernism if we were to understand the dynamics of knowledge as presented in the Qur'ān. Too often there exists a vacuous relationship between knowledge and pragmatism with the result that the Islamisation vision is touted as the only alternative to address this widening gulf. In fact, a superficial reading of the clusters of verses dealing with the cosmos, flora and fauna, etc. presupposes a thorough familiarity with science and its theoretical formulations. Several exegetes have institutionalised this mindset by selectively referencing their Qur'ānic writings along this pattern. Only a tenuous link is established by this approach. Against this background, the limitation of Nadwah's production of tafsir/Qur'ānic studies needs serious reconsideration.

The emergence of the Ahl i-Hadith movement had mutated in the subcontinent. Its ideological founder, Sayyid Siddiq Khan was a prolific writer who established a network with Salafi scholars in the Arab world. His tafsir is a prodigious production relating to the primacy of the Qur'ān and hadith literature. Other exegetes belonging to this school of thought advanced its cause through its balanced commentaries. Early twentieth century witnessed the scholarly tradition of tafsirs written by graduates from Deoband and Nadwah. Their *salafi* leanings were inconsequential; likewise, their *ikhtilāf* (juristic disagreements) were no barrier for them to vigorously pursue their interpretation of Islamic authenticity. However, not all the Ahl i-Hadith scholars could tide over the entrenched *taqlid* dominance in the subcontinent. This historical phase witnessed the theatre of sectarian conflicts which were played out in their Qur'ānic writings. Polemical literature exacerbated the robust exchange of views and further caused an irreparable split within the *ummah* of the subcontinent. Nevertheless, the surge of tafsir works from the late twentieth century is a telling example of rapprochement that defines the movement's reformist vision. These graduates from the *madāris* and universities have forged ahead in the interpretation of the sacred text without prejudice. This accommodationist approach reflects the growing realisation about the Qur'ān's multivalent character. In retrospect, the Salafiyyah mindset in general persists in its rigid interpretation of Islamic doctrines and this has negatively impacted on an open-ended conversation with scholars belonging to other schools of thought.

The Barelwi exegesis has an interesting history. Its illustrious founder, Ahmad Raza Khan developed a tradition steeped in scholarship and customary practice (*'urf*). His formulation of Islamic authenticity was at variance with Deobandi thought. Reverence for the Holy Prophet (SAW) at higher planes of spirituality and the intercessory presence of the saints (*awliyā*) figure prominently in his reformist discourse. His translation is considered an iconic text of Barelwi tafsirs. In a historical context, polemics became a defining characteristic of the movement in the backdrop of Ismai'il Shahid's influential work *Taqwiyat al-Imān* and the Deobandi 'ulama's views of Allah's attributes and the Holy Prophet's divine status. The culture of polemics is evident in several tafsirs. In recent decades there has been a more tolerant approach to these controversial issues judging by works like *'Irfān al-Qur'ān*. It deals with current issues like the ecosystem, terrorism, multi - pluralism, etc. These trends are visible in Qur'ānic works by contemporary writers of Barelwi affiliation. Without entering into the arena of debates, the Barelwi exegetes have the potential to transform at grassroot level the religious landscape that we are witnessing in the subcontinent and beyond. By virtue of their charisma and religious persona they are able to reconnect their constituencies to a deeper understanding of the sacred text. Qur'ānic works with a reformist thrust should be produced to share a lived experience with the guidance, spiritual gems and wisdom that the Qur'ān offers.

The Islāhi production of tafsirs and Qur'ānic writings are deeply rooted in literary theories and are best represented by the distinguisted works of the pre- eminent scholar, Farahi. A structured analysis of the *nazm* theory and its overarching wisdom have been explicated in renowned tafsirs like *Tadabbur i-Qur'ān*. Contemplation, reflection are deftly woven into the Qur'ānic framework by allowing the readers to examine its contextual relevance. In a similar vein, Arabic literature is accorded an important place in the tafsir genre to underscore the organic and thematic peculiarities of the clusters of verses and surahs under discussion. Like other Qur'ānic writings Farahi's formulations have been critiqued by Islāhi scholars without diminishing his immense contributions in this field. Overall, the growing interest in the *nazm* theory has found fertile ground in the Arab world making it a transnational area of study. It must, however, be conceded that the literary theories employed to unlock the genius of the Qur'ān, if given primary importance, have the potential to devalue its universal guidance for mankind. A preoccupation with this approach is a hazardous undertaking as it mars the literary charm and forceful style that was understood by the Qur'ānic generation.

New modes of translation are encapsulated in Mawdudi's *Tafhim al-Qur'ān*. Written for the modern age the multivolume tafsir has influenced millions of readers in the subcontinent. The number of translations in regional languages reaffirms its pivotal role in the Islamic renewal project. *Da'wah* is embodied in the Jama'at i - Islami (Hind) manifesto and to this end the production of forceful literature within the Qur'ānic framework has enriched its mission of reaching out to members of other faiths. Interestingly, tafsirs as well as Qur'ānic works have been written for this purpose by scholars from different ideological backgrounds. The JI in the formal sense does not represent a madrasah with a distinct sectarian temperament. The study illustrates the shared vision of the movement rather than a formal affiliation. Several scholars have critiqued the writings of Mawdudi without renouncing their position within the structure. In more ways than one the mission statement of the movement has had far-reaching implications on the global scene. In the subcontinent *da'wah* is gaining ground amid the Islamophobic tendencies by the Hindutva and several media outfits. The prospect of realigning a tafsir to meet the growing needs of other faiths in the spirit of tolerance and co-existence is indeed a daunting task. With its decades-long experience in *da'wah* and productive literature, JI is ideally suited to perform this life-enriching undertaking.

A positive feature of the tafsir series is the production of exemplary works by Aligarh graduates. Interestingly, these contributions have a cosmopolitan outlook and are not restricted to a particular sectarian strand. Keeping in mind the prejudices built around Sayyid Ahmad Khan's reformist contributions, AMU has rightfully restored its prestigious place in Qur'ānic studies. The broad sweep of works by the internationally recognised scholars of AMU is a testament to their brilliant contributions in this field of study.

It is a misperception to assume that tafsirs in the main are ideologically oriented. While there may have been formative influences, their works stand out for their scholarly independence. In this respect *Tafsir i-Mājidi* is a magisterial work that remains unrivalled for its cogent presentation of the Qur'ānic teachings in the light of modern scholarship. Likewise, Israr Ahmad has enriched Qur'ānic scholarship by virtue of his academic and Islamic background. Across the spectrum of Qur'ānic studies are the impressive works like Azad's *Tarjumān al-Qur'ān* and Wahiduddin's *Tadhkir al-Qur'ān*. The core issues relate to the universality of Islam in a Hindu - dominated society. It has some streaks of religious syncretism with an overdose of apologia. For whatever inexplicable reasons both these erudite exegetes have attempted to reconfigure particular verses of the Qur'ān with their narrative of religious adaptability. Reviews of their respective tafsirs range from censure to guarded endorsement. Their differing positions, however, in general do not deflect from the mainstream interpretations. In our study Qur'ānic works of the Ahl i-Qur'ān have not been analysed because they do not fall under the rubric of the *Ahl al-sunnah* framework.

The survey of Shi'ite tafsirs is very brief on account of the paucity of details contained in the tafsir volume. A redeeming factor is the well - researched review of two contemporary tafsirs which bears the hallmark of outstanding scholarship. The tenor of these tafsirs reaffirms its inclusive approach: referencing classical commentaries and Sunni sources to adduce their respective viewpoints. It is gratifying to note how the Theology Department at Aligarh University has since its establishment provided the forum for sectarian tolerance and co-existence. This was the visionary leadership of Sayyid Ahmad Khan.

Feminist literature on Qur'ānic studies has taken an anti-patriarchy slant. The steady growth of Qur'ānic literature by advocates of gender equality illustrates the polarising element of rejection of particular verses. This trend may be attributed to the glaring absence of tafsirs produced by female scholars. This is one of the challenges that needs to be seriously addressed.

In sum, the future of the tafsir genre is likely to be guided by the changing sociopolitical landscape in the subcontinent.

Bibliography

'Ali, Farmān, *Tarjuma wa Tafsir* (Lucknow, n.d.).

'Arif, Mahmud al-Hasan, *Tadhkirah Qādi Muhammad Thanā'Allah Pānipati* (Lahore, 1995).

'Azami, Muhammad 'Arif, *Tadhkirah Mufassirin i-Hind* (Azamgarh, 2006).

'Azami, Muhammad Mustafa, *Studies in Early Hadith Literature* (Indianapolis, 1978).

Ahmad, Aziz, *Islamic Modernism in India and Pakistan 1857-1964* (Karachi, 1967).

Ahmad, Aziz, *Islamic Modernism in India and Pakistan, 1857-1964* (London, 1967).

Ahmad, Firoz, *Ihsānullah 'Abbāsi: Hayāt awr Kārnāme* (Aligarh, 2019).

Ahmad, Irfan, *Islamism and Democracy in India: The Transformation of the Jamaat e-Islami* (Princeton, 2009).

Ahmad, Israr, *Ta'āruf Tanzim i-Islami* (Lahore, 1997).

Ahmad, Israr, *The Obligations Muslims Owe to the Qur'ān* (Lahore, 1984).

Ahmad, Israr, *The Qur'ān and World Peace* (Lahore, 1982).

Ahmad, Israr, *The Way to Salvation in the Light of Surah al-Asr of the Holy Qur'ān* (Lahore, 1982).

Ahmad, Masood, *Inspirations from the Qur'ān* (Bellsville, 2012).

Akram, Mohamed Aiyyoob, *Barelwi Fuzalā ki Qur'āni Khidmāt* (Aligarh, 2020).

Al-'Alwāni, Tahā Jābir, *The Ethics of Disagreement in Islam* (Herndon, 1993).

Al-Ghazali, Muhammad, *The Sociopolitical Thought of Shah Wali Allah* (Islamabad, 2001).

Ali, Syed Rizwan, *Izzadin al-Sulami: His life and Works* (Islamabad, 1978).

Ali, Syed Rizwan, *Qur'ān ki Roshni me* (Karachi, 2005).

Ali, Syed Shahid, *Urdu Tafaseer Beeswin Sadi Mein* (Delhi, 2001).

Al-Qattan, Manna, *Mabāhith i 'ulum al-Qur'ān* (Beirut, 2008).

Amritsari, ThanāAllah, *Tafsir al-Qur'ān bi Kalām al-Rahmān* (Lahore, n.d.).

Anjum, Ghulam Yahya, *Qur'ān i-Karim ke Hindustani Tarājim wa Tafsir ka Ijmāli Jā'iza* (New Delhi, 2017).

Ansari, Abdul Haq, *An Introduction to the Exegesis of the Qur'ān* (Riyadh, 1989).

-*Sufism and Shari'ah: A Study of Shaykh Ahmad Sirhindi's Effort to Reform Sufism* (Leicester, 1985).

Ansari, Fazlur Rahman, *Communist Challenge to Islam* (Karachi, 2018).

Ansari, Zafar Ishaq and Esposito, John (editors), *Muslims in the West: Encounter and Dialogue* (Islamabad, 2001).

Asad, Muhammad, *The Message of the Qur'ān* (Gibraltar, 1980).

Awan, Anjum, *Revisiting Islam: The Reformist Thought of Wahiddudin Khan* (Delhi, 2018).

Ayubi, Muhammad Tariq Ayubi Nadwi, *Nadwat al-'Ulama ki Fikri wa Milli Shu'ur* (Aligarh, 2015).

Nadwi Fuzalā ki Qur'āni Khidmāt (Aligarh, 2019).

Azad, Abul Kalam, *The Tarjumān al-Qur'ān*, vol.1 (Lahore, n.d.).

Azami, Muhammad Mustafa, *The History of the Qur'ānic Text: From Revelation to Compilation* (Kuala Lumpur, 2011).

Azami, Zia-ur-Rahmān, *From Ganga to Zamzam* (2017).

Azhar, Mirza Ali, *King Wajid Ali Shah of Awadh* (Islamabad, 1982).

Azhari, Karam Shah, *Diyā al-Qur'ān*, vol.1 (Lahore, 1978).

Azhari, Mubeen Saleem Nadwi, *Model Syllabus for Teaching Qur'ān in the Madrasahs* (Aligarh, 2019).

-*Hindustān me Mutāla'a Qur'ān: Mu'āsir Manzar Nāma* (Aligarh, 2020).

-*Model Syllabus for Teaching of the Qur'ān in the Madrasahs* (Aligarh, 2019).

Azmat, Tanveer, *Understanding the Qur'ānic Revelation: The Dynamic Hermeneutics of Irfan A. Khan* (2016).

Bigelow, Anna, *Sharing the Sacred: Practicing Pluralism in Muslim North India* (Oxford, 2010).

Bilgrami, H. H. *Islamic System of Education: Search for a Solution* (Karachi, 1992).

Bucaille, Maurice, *The Qur'ān and Modern Science* (Jeddah, 1977).

Chagatai, Ikram, *Muhammad Asad: Islam's Gift to Europe* (Lahore, 2006).

Choughley Abdul Kader, *Fazlur Rahman Ansari: Life and Thought* (Springs, 2012).

-*How to Study the Qur'ān: Sayyid Abul Hasan Ali Nadwi's Approach* -(Rome, 2024).

-*Islamic Resurgence: Sayyid Abul Hasan Ali Nadwi and his Contemporaries* (New Delhi, 2011).

-*Islamic Resurgence: Sayyid Abul Hasan Ali Nadwi and his Contemporaries* (New Delhi, 2011).

-*Sayyid Abul Hasan Ali Nadwi: Life and Works* (Rome, 2023).

-*Towards Salvaging Humanity* (Rome, 2024).

Daryabadi, Abdul Majid, *Mu'āsirin* (Kolkata, 1979).

-*Tafsir i-Mājidi*, (Lucknow, 2003).

Doi, Abdur Rahmān, *'Ulum al-Qur'ān: A Study in Methodology and Approach* (Pretoria, 1997).

-*'Uthmān Dan Fodio, The Grand Mujaddid of Africa* (Pretoria, 1998).

Douglas, Ian Henderson, *Abul Kalam Azad: An Intellectual Religious Biography* (New Delhi, 1993).

Drāz, Muhammad ' Abdullāh, *The Qur'ān: An Eternal Challenge* (Leicester, 2001).

El-Awa, Salwa, *Textual Relations in the Qur'ān: Relevance, Coherence and Structure* (London, 2006).

Ernst Carl and Lawrence Bruce, *Sufi Martyrs of Love* (New York, 2002).

Fahad, Ubaidullah, *Diversity, Dissent and Dialogue: Some Selected Readings* (New Delhi, 2012).

Falahi, Ziauddin, *Abdur Raheem Kidwai ke Qur'āni Mutāla'āt* (Aligarh, 2019).

-*Hind-wa-Pak ke Mashā'ikh ki Qur'āni Khidmāt* (Aligarh, 2020).

-*Jamā'at i-Islami ke Fuzalā ki Qur'āni Khidmāt* (Aligarh, 2019).

Farāhi, Hamiduddin, *Majmu'ah Tafāsir i-Farāhi* (Lahore, 1973).

Faruqi, Ziya-al-Hasan, *The Deoband School and the Demand for Pakistan* (Lahore, 1976).

Ghazāli, Zainab, *Return of the Pharaoh* (Leicester, 1996).

Ghazi, Mahmood Ahmad, *Islamic Renaissance in South Asia, 1707- 1867: The Role of Shah Wali Allah and his Successors* (Islamabad, 2002).

Gilāni, Manāzir Ahsan, *Sawāni Qāsimi*, 2 vols. (Multan, 1427H).

Gondal, 'Abdur Razzāq, *Nawāb Siddiq Hasan Khan ka Tafsiri Minhāj awr Tafsir Tarjumān al-Qur'ān bi Latā'if al- Bayān ka Tafsiri Adab me Maqām* (Lahore, 2019).

Gorke, Andreas and Pink, Johanna, *Tafsir and Islamic Intellectual History: Exploring the Boundaries of a Genre* (London, 2014).

Gupta, Juhi and Kidwai, Abdur Raheem (editors), *Oxford of the East: Aligarh Muslim University 1920-2020, Centenary Commemorative Volume* (New Delhi, 2020).

Hallaq, Wael and Little, Donald (eds.), *Islamic Studies: Presented to Charles C. Adams* (Leiden, 1991).

Hameed, Syeda Saiyidain, *Islamic Seal on Indian Independence: Abul Kalam Azad- A Fresh Look* (Karachi, 1998).

Hasan, Masudul, *Sayyid Abul A'la Mawdudi and his Thought*, vol.1 (Lahore, 1986).

Hasani, Bilāl Abdul Hayy, *Āsān Ma'āni Qur'ān* (Rae Bareli, 2015).

Hasani, Muhammad Thāni, *Khānwade 'Alam al-lāhi* (Rae Bareli, 1992).

Hasani,'Abdul Hayy, *Yād i-Ayyām* (Aligarh, 1919).

Hashmi, Tariq Mahmood, *A Study of the Qur'ānic Oaths* (Lahore, n.d.).

Hermansen, Marcia, *The Conclusive Argument from God* (Islamabad, 2003).

Hoosen, Afzal, *Knowlegeable Discourses of 'Allāmah Mufti Sa'eed Ahmad Palanpuri* (Karachi, 2014).

Akhalq Husayn Qāsimi, *'Ulama Deoband ki Tafsiri Khidmāt* (Deoband, n.d.).

Husain Omar, *Gateway to the Qur'ānic Sciences* (London, 2017).

Ibrahim, Sayyid Muhammad, *Qāzi 'Ubaidullah: Life and Works* (Ajmer, n.d.).

Iqbal, Afzal, *Life and Work of Rumi* (Lahore, 1976).

Islāhi, Abu Sufyān, *Idārah Sir Sayyid Muslim University Aligarh ke Mashāhir Qur'āniyāt* (Aligarh, 2017).

-*Mawlana Hamiduddin Farāhi, Muhaqqiq-o-Mufassir* (Aligarh, 2007).

Islāhi, Amin Ahsan, *Self-Purification and Development* (Delhi, 2000).

-*Tadabbur e-Qur'ān: Pondering over the Qur'ān*, vol. 1 (Kuala Lumpur, 2007).

Islam, Zafarul, Islāhi, *Qur'ān and Service to Mankind* (Aligarh, 2019).

Jabi, Shagufta, *'Allāmah Ghulam Rasul Sa'eedi: Hayāt wa Khidmāt* (Lahore, 2012).

Jullundhry, Rashid Ahmad, *Qur'ānic Exegesis in Classical Literature* (Kuala Lumpur, n.d.).

Kaskas, Safi and Hungerford, David, *The Qur'ān with Reference to the Bible* (Fairfax, 2016).

Khan, Ahmad Raza, *Thesis of Imam Raza Khan* (Durban, 2012).

Khan, Ghulamullah, *Jawāhir al-Qur'ān* (Rawalpindi, 1984).

Khan, Irfan, *An Exercise in Understanding the Qur'ān: An Outline Study of the Last Thirty Divine Discourses - Surahs 85-114* (Chicago, 2015).

-*Reflections on the Qur'ān: Understanding Surahs Al-Fatihah and Al-Baqarah* (Leicester, 2005).

Khan, Muhammad Yusuf, *Mawlana Faizul Hasan Sahāranpuri: His Contributions to Arabic Language and Literature* (Aligarh Muslim University, 2008).

Khan, Nawāb Siddiq, *Fath al-Bayān i Maqāsid al-Qur'ān* (Beirut, 1992).

Khan, Sayyid Ahmad, *Essays on the Life of Muhammad* (Delhi, 1976).

-*Tabyin al-Kalām i Tafsir al-Tawrāt wa'l Injil* (Aligarh, 2004).

Khan, Shams Tabriz, *Tārikh Nadwat al-'Ulama*, vol.2 (Lucknow, 1984).

Khan, Wahiddudin, *God Arises: Evidence of God in Nature and in Science* (New Delhi, 1987).

-*Muhammad: The Prophet for All Mankind* (New Delhi, 1988).

-*Simple Wisdom: A Daybook of Spiritual Living* (New Delhi, 2008).

-*Tadhkir al- Qur'ān*, vol. 1 (New Delhi, 1990).
Kidwai, Abdur Raheem, *Sir Syed Ahmad Khan: Muslim Renaissance,*
-*Man of India* (New Delhi, 2016).
-*Translating the Untranslatable: A Critical Guide to 60 English Translations of the Qur'ān (New Delhi, 2017)*
-*God's Word Man's Interpretations* (New Delhi, 2017).
Kidwai, Muhammad Salim, *Hindustāni Mufassirin awr unki 'Arabi Tafsire* (Lahore, 1993).
Majeed, Nazeer Ahmad Ab., (ed.), *Qur'ān Interpretation: A Critical Study* (Aligarh, 2019).
Mas'udi, Shah, *Naqsh i-Dawām: Hayāt i-Muhaddith Anzar Kasmiri* (Multan, 2006).
Mawdudi, Abul A'la, *Jihād in Islam* (Lahore, 2017).
-*Towards Understanding the Qur'ān*, vol.1 (Leicester, 1988).
-*The Islamic Movement: Dynamics of Values, Power and Change* (Leicester, 1998).
Metcalf, Barbara, *Islamic Revival in British India: Deoband, 1860- 1900* (Karachi, 1982).
-*Perfecting Women: Mawlana Ashraf Ali Thānawi's Bihishti Zewar* (Oxford, 1992).
Mian, Syed Muhammad, *The Prisoners of Malta: Asirān i-Malta* (New Delhi, 2005).
Mir, Muntasir, *Coherence in the Qur'ān: A Study of Islāhi's Concept of Nazm in Tadabbur-i Qur'ān* (Indianapolis, 1986).
Misbāhi, Mubarak Husain, *Al-Jamiatul Ashraia* (Mubarakpur, n.d.).
Misbāhi, Yāsin Akhtar, *Ta'āruf i-Ahl i-Sunnat* (New Delhi, 2019).
-*Imām Ahmad Raza awr Jadid Afkār wa Tahrikāt* (New Delhi, n.d.).
Moosa, Ebrahim, *What is a Madrasa* (Chapel Hill, 2015).
Muhammad Taqi, Usmani, *An Approach to the Qur'ānic Sciences* (New Delhi, 2006).
Murad, Khurram, *In the Early Hours: Reflections on Spiritual Self Development* (Leicester, 2013).
-*The Way to the Qur'ān* (Leicester,1985).
Murādabādi Na'imuddin, *Khazā'in al-'Irfān* (Lahore, 2012).
Nadvi, Syed Muzaffar-ud-din, *A Geographical History of the Qur'ān* (Lahore, 1981).
Nadwi, 'Abdul Hannān, *Hadhrat Mawlana Sayyid Muhammad Rabey Hasani Nadwi: Shakhsiyyat awr Khidmāt* (Lucknow, 2012).
Nadwi, 'Abdullāh 'Abbās, *Qur'ān i-Karim: Tārikh i-Insāniyat ka sabse Barā Mo'jizah* (New Delhi, n.d.).
Nadwi, Abdul Hayy, *Nuzhat al-Khawātir*, vol. 7 (Rae Bareli, 1993).

Nadwi, Abul Hasan Ali, *Da'wah in the West: The Qur'ānic Paradigm* (Leicester, 1992).

-*Faith versus Materialism: The Message of Surah Al-Kahf* (Kuala Lumpur, 2005).

-*Kārwān i-Zindagi*, vol. 2 (Lucknow, 1982).

-*Muhammad Rasulullah* (Lucknow, 1979).

-*Muslims in India* (Lucknow, 1976).

-*Purān i-Charāgh*, vol. 1 (Karachi, 1984).

-*Rise and Fall of Muslims: Its Impact on the World*. Edited by Abdul Kader Choughley (Rome, 2024).

-*Saviours of Islamic Spirit*, vol. 3 (Lucknow, 1983).

-*Studying the Glorious Qur'ān: Principles and Methodology* (Leicester, 2003).

-*The Islamic Concept of Prophethood* (Lucknow, 1976).

-*Western Civilisation Islam and Muslims* (Lucknow, 1974)

Nadwi, Mu'inuddin Ahmad, *Maqālāt i-Sulaymāni*, vol.3 (Azamgarh, 1971).

Nadwi, Muhammad Haneef, *Tafsir Sirāj al-Bayān*, vol. 1 (Lahore, 1983).

Nadwi, Muhammad Rabey, *Qur'ān Majeed Insān i-Zindagi ka Rehbar i- Kāmil* (Lucknow, 2013).

Nadwi, Muhammad Raziul Islam, *Naqd i-Farāhi* (Aligarh, 2010).

Nadwi, Sulayman, *Hayāt i-Shibli* (Azamgarh, 2014).

-*Yād Raftagān* (Azamgarh, 2012).

Nadwi, Sultan, *Nadwat al-'Ulama ka Fiqhi Mizāj awr Abnā i-Nadwah ki Fiqhi Khidmāt* (Hyderabad, 2004).

Nadwi, Sayyid Ahmad Anis, *Qur'āni Safar* (Firozabad, 2020).

Naqhbandi, Muhammad, *Ahd i-Risālat ke Mufassirin i-Kirām* (Karachi, 2010).

Nasr, Seyyed Hosein, et.al, *The Study Qur'ān: A New Translation and Commentary* (New York, 2015).

Nizami, Khaliq Ahmad, *History of the Aligarh Muslim University* (Delhi, 1995).

-*Tārikh Mashā'ikh Chisht* (Allahabad, 1980).

-*Akbar and Religion* (Delhi, 1989).

-*Hayāt i-Shaykh 'Abdul Haq Muhaddith Dehlawi* (Aligarh, 2015).

Nu'mani, Manzur, *Qur'ān and You* (Lucknow, 1978).

-*The Iranian Revolution* (Karachi, 2000).

-*Tahdith i-Ni'mat* (Lahore, n.d.).

Osman, Yunoos, *Life and Works of 'Allāmah Anwar Shah Kashmiri* (Durban, 2002).

Palanpuri, Sa'eed, *Hidāyat al-Qur'ān*, vol.1 (Deoband, 2017).

Parekh, Abdul Karim, *Tashrih al Qur'ān*, vol. 1 (Delhi, 1995).

Parwez, Ghulam Ahmad, *What is Islam: The Qur'ānic Perspective* (Lahore, 2000).

Preckel, Claudia, *Begums of Bhopal* (New Delhi, 2000).

Qureshi, Ishtiaq Husain, *Ulema in Politics* (Karachi, 1972).

Qutb, Sayyid, *In the Shade of the Qur'ān*, vol. xviii (Leicester, 2004).

Rafiuddin, Shah, *Al-Qur'ān al-Karim* (Lahore, 2000).

Rafiuddin, Muhammad, *First Principles of Education* (Lahore, 1983).

-*Ideology of the Future* (Lahore, 1970).

-*Islam and Modern Knowledge* (Lahore, 2010).

Rahmani, Khalid Saifullah, *Āsān Usul i-Tafsir* (Hyderabad, 2014).

-*Modern Problems: Islamic Perspectives* (Hyderabad, 2010).

-*Muslim Personal Law awr Badh Ghalat Fehmiya* (Hyderabad, 2017).

Reetz, Diedrich, *Islam in the Public Sphere: Religious Groups in India: 1900-1947* (Oxford, 2006).

Rizwi, Sayyid Mahbub, *Tārikh Dār al-'Ulum Deoband*, 2 vols. (Deoband, 1992).

Robinson, Francis, *The 'Ulama of Farangi Mahal and Islamic Culture in South Asia* (Lucknow, 2001)

Sa'eedi, Ghulam Rasul, *Tibyān al-Qur'ān*, vol. 1 (Lahore, 2000).

Saeh, Bassam, *The Miraculous Language of the Qur'ān: Evidence of Divine Origin* (London, 2015).

Sajjad, Muslim (ed.), *Khurram Murad: Hayāt wa Khidmāt* (Lahore, 1997).

Salafi, Muhammad Luqman, *Fuyudh al-'Alam 'alā Tafsir al-Āyāt al-Ahkām* (Riyadh, 2002).

-*Taysir al-Rahmān li Bayān al-Qur'ān* (Chandpura, 2001).

Salafi, Rafiq Ahmad Raees, *Ahl i-Hadith Fuzalā ki Qur'āni Khidmāt* (Aligarh, 2019).

Salahi, Adil, *Muhammad: Man and Prophet* (Leicester, 2002).

Salti, Farhad, *A Comparative Analysis of the Farāhi School of Thought: A Case Study Approach* (Edinburgh, 2016).

Sanyal, Usha, *Devotional Islam and Politics in British India: Imam Ahmad Riza Khan Barelwi and his Movement, 1870-1920* (New York, 1996).

Saulat, Sarwar, *Maulana Maududi* (Karachi, 1984).

Schimmel, Annemarie, *Islam in the Indian Subcontinent* (Leiden, 1980).

Shafi, Mufti Muhammad, *Ma'āriful Qur'ān*, vol.1 (Karachi, 1996).

Shah, Muhammad Anzar, *Naqsh i-Dawām: Hayāt i-Muhaddith Kashmiri* (Multan, 2006).

Shah, Muhammad Sultan, *Diyā al-Qur'ān: A Unique Qur'ānic Commentary and the Commentator* (Lahore, n.d.).

Shahid, Muhammad Ismail, *Taqwiyat al-Imān* (Lahore, 1990).

Shaikh, Jalilur Rahmān, *An Analytical Study on the Contribution of Al-Allamah Faizul Hasan Sahāranpuri to the Arabic Language and Literature* (Aligarh Muslim University, 2017).

Shaikh, Muhammad Hajjan, *Mawlana Ubaid Allah Sindhi: A Revolutionary Scholar* (Islamabad, 1986).

Sherkoti, Muhammad Anwār al-Hasan, *Anwār i-Qāsimi* (Karachi, 2014).

Siddiqi, Yasin Mazhar, *The Prophet Muhammad: A Role Model for Muslim Minorities* (Leicester, 2006).

Siddiqui, Muhammad Mazheruddin, *Modern Reformist Thought in the Muslim World* (Islamabad, 1982).

Siddiqui, Muhammad Zubayr, *Hadith Literature: Its Origins, Development and Special Features* (Cambridge, 1993).

Tabassum, Farhat, *Deoband Ulema's Movement for the Freedom of India* (New Delhi, 2006).

Tabatabai, Muhammad Husayn, *Tafsir al-Mizān* (Qum, n.d.).

Tareen, SherAli, *Defending Muhammad in Modernity* (Notre Dame, 2020).

Tayyab, Muhammad, *Tafsir Surah Al-Mulk* (Karachi, n.d.).

Thānawi, Ashrāf 'Ali, *Tashil Tarbiyat al-Sālik,* 4 vols. (Karachi, 2009).

Thānawi, Jamil Ahmad, *Maqālat al-Qur'ān* (Lahore, 2001).

Tijarwi, Muhammad Mushtaq, *Fuzalā i-Deoband ki Qur'āni Khidmāt* (Aligarh, 2020).

Ushama, Thameem, *Methodologies of the Qur'ānic Exegesis* (Kuala Lumpur, 1995).

Usmani, Muhammad Taqi, *The Meanings of the Noble Qur'ān with Explanatory Notes* (Karachi, 2010).

Usmani, Shabbir Ahmad, *Tafsir i-'Uthmāni,* vol.1 (Azaadville, 1999).

Uthmāni, Abdul Qayyum Rajkoti, *Nuqush i-Buzurgān,* 2 vols. (Simlak, 2003).

Waliyullah, Shah, *Al-Fath al-Kabir* (Lucknow, 1314H).

Wani, Gowhar Quadir (ed.), *Waleed al-Amri's The Luminous Qur'ān: Critical Views* (Aligarh, 2019).

Wani, Gowhar Quadir and 'Abbāsi, Faiza (editors), *'Allāmah Ihsānullah 'Abbāsi ki Qur'āni Fehmi* (Aligarh, 2020).

Wani, Gowhar Quadir and Choughley, Abdul Kader (editors), *Abdul Majid Daryabadi's Tafsir-ul-Qur'ān: A Critical Study* (Aligarh, 2021).

Wasey, Akhtarul and Kidwai, Abdur Raheem (editors), *Journey of Faith: Maulana Abdul Majid Daryabadi* (Delhi, 2016).

Zarzour, Adnan, *The Qur'ān and its Study: An In-Depth Exploration of Islamic Sacred Scripture* (Leicester, 2018).